T0139083

# Social Media Analytics, Strategies and Governance

*Editors*

**Hamid Jahankhani**
Professor of Information Security and Cyber Criminology
Northumbria University London, UK

**Stefan Kendzierskyj**
Cyfortis
Surrey, UK

**Reza Montasari**
Senior Lecturer in Cyber Threats
Hillary Rodham Clinton School of Law
Swansea University, Swansea, Wales, UK

**Nishan Chelvachandran**
Iron Lakes
Kirkkonummi, Finland

CRC Press
Taylor & Francis Group
Boca Raton   London   New York

CRC Press is an imprint of the
Taylor & Francis Group, an **informa** business

A SCIENCE PUBLISHERS BOOK

First edition published 2022
by CRC Press
6000 Broken Sound Parkway NW, Suite 300, Boca Raton, FL 33487-2742

and by CRC Press
4 Park Square, Milton Park, Abingdon, Oxon, OX14 4RN

*Library of Congress Cataloging-in-Publication Data (applied for)*

ISBN: 978-1-032-15351-3 (hbk)
ISBN: 978-1-032-15360-5 (pbk)
ISBN: 978-1-003-24374-8 (ebk)

DOI: 10.1201/9781003243748

Typeset in Times New Roman
by Radiant Productions

# Preface

Social media has spread rapidly on the global stage, driving consumers' attention and influence, both consciously and subconsciously. Whilst this type of platform may have been initially designed as a tool for open communication and expression, it is also being utilised as a digital tool, with widescale use cases. This connectivity, the ubiquity of technology and the increase of information and the prevalence of Online Social Networks (OSN), have overcome traditional challenges and roadblocks such as physical borders and the constraints of time and distance. The dissemination, sharing and delivery of information to wider audiences, whilst providing beneficial impacts, can mean a higher risk of public perception to be more easily influenced and distorted by a small number of individuals through the dispersion of misinformation and disinformation. The growing use of social media to the point that it is considered normative and is ingrained in almost every sphere of modern life including social, business, personal, etc., means that the proliferation of any news, particularly fake news is increasingly highly likely. Social media analytics has therefore become critical to formulating strategies for a wide number of requirements and more increasingly push the debate for more governance due to the rapid increase in data volumes. The complex nature of this data explosion created an increasing demand and use of artificial intelligence (AI) and machine learning (ML), to help provide 'big insights' to 'big data'. AI and ML enable the analysis and dissemination of vast amounts of data, however the ungoverned pace at which AI and autonomous systems have been deployed, has created unforeseen problems. Hence the close interlinked topics of social media analytics and interpreting the data behind this with the support of AI and ML intelligence and how that may drive a clearer path forwards for governance.

This edited volume attempts to describe many of those benefits and importantly highlight critical strategies required to govern social media and overcome misinformation and fake news.

# Contents

*Preface*   iii

1. **Advancing Governance of News Provenance Posted on Social Media Platforms with the use of Blockchain Technology**   1
   *Michał Pawlicki and Hamid Jahankhani*

2. **The Forensic Investigation of Misinformation on Social Media**   31
   *Natasha Omezi, Stefan Kendzierskyj and Hamid Jahankhani*

3. **Data Protection and Privacy in the Ambient Assisted Living System for Patients with Mild Cognitive Impairment**   49
   *David Josef Herzog*

4. **Evaluating Countermeasures for Detecting Misinformation Attacks on Stock Exchange Market**   73
   *David Manford and Hamid Jahankhani*

5. **Profiling and Predicting Malware Threats during COVID-19 Pandemic**   102
   *Karishma Hiranna Raghupati and Sina Pournouri*

6. **Research into Modern-day Domestic Abuse and Digital Coercive Control: Focus on How a Framework could Assist Stakeholders with Technical Evidence Gathering in Order to Incriminate Abusers**   130
   *Megan Smith and Hamid Jahankhani*

7. **The Issues and the Misinformation that Social Media Creates and in Particular How This is Dealt with in Asia**   152
   *Kudrat-E-Khuda (Babu)*

8. **Are We in Trouble? An Exploration on Crime during Natural Disasters and Pandemics**   172
   *Bisola Ogunro, Amin Hosseinian-Far and Dilshad Sarwar*

9. **A Critical Analysis of the Dark Web Challenges to Digital Policing**   192
   *Olivia Bamsey and Reza Montasari*

10. **Multimedia Privacy and Security Landscape in the Wake of AI/ML**    **203**
    *Chaminda TER Hewage, Shadan K Khattak, Arslan Ahmad,*
    *Thanuja Mallikarachchi, Elochukwu Ukwandu* and
    *Vibhushinie Bentotahewa*

11. **An Explanation on Social Media**    **229**
    *Ramsha Ateeq* and *Umair B Chaudhry*

***Index***    **249**

# 1

# Advancing Governance of News Provenance Posted on Social Media Platforms with the use of Blockchain Technology

*Michał Pawlicki** and *Hamid Jahankhani*

## ABSTRACT

Fake news can spread on social media like a wildfire, changing people's opinions, causing chaos and may even result in influencing the election. This problem has been noticed by governors around the world as well as the researcher community and social media companies. There are methods used in preventing the spread of fake news, but it is either causing false positive results or does not work cross-platform. With that, the research focuses on the governance of social media platforms to provide tracking of news provenance, using blockchain technology. A framework draft is presented that can be applied to any social media platform. The research focuses on information governance and security aspects of the solution. The outcome is based on documents concerning Section 230 of the Communication Act, widely available journal papers, news articles and books that are discussing how information governance be constructed and what should be included. In addition to that, the research proposes a flowchart of the social media post cycle to better understand the mechanisms behind the social media platforms. The researchers recommend that the blockchain network is used to store the metadata and further recommendations for other researchers to analyze the ethics and legal aspect of the solution.

Northumbria University, London, UK.
Email: Hamid.jahankhani@northumbria.ac.uk
* Corresponding author: michalpawlicki@outlook.com

# 1. Introduction

Cybersecurity is a field of many different subfields that vary from strictly technical topics of engineering, through corporate governance, to understanding human behaviour when focusing on social engineering. This research emerged from the postgraduate studies carried out by the authors to understand why some people believe in certain false statements they find online. Though this is a broad topic, this research considers only the aspect of governance and the use of cyber technology to provide some direction to a possible solution to solving the misinformation online.

This research explores the work done on the issue of misinformation online, analyses the mechanism behind posting news on social media and presents the technical advancements that are used by the social media platforms together with proposed solutions by the researchers. As a result, the research presents the governance framework that considers these solutions, guidelines for creating governance policies and ethical considerations.

The main purpose of this project is to propose a governance policy that shall be used by the social media platforms for news provenance record keeping. The aim is to create a policy based on the research done so far in areas of policymaking and technology.

# 2. Literature Review

This chapter focuses on analyzing the available information on the research topic. It covers the work on the misinformation spread (2.1), and Section 230 of the Communication Decency Act in the United States (2.3), which is a crucial regulation to shape an online space. The chapter also includes the European response to Section 230 (2.4), while 2.5 concentrates on the state of self-regulation of a few social media platforms. Moreover, this literature review talks about various blockchain implementations to control the spread of fake news in social media (2.6).

## 2.1 Building Blocks of a Social Media Platform

The research problem tackles the spread of misinformation on social media platforms, setting the ground for understanding what a social media platform is and how a typical platform work can be proven to be useful for research clarity.

Firstly, social media is described as a 'computer-based technology that facilitates the sharing of ideas, thoughts and information through the building of virtual networks and communities' (Dollarhide, 2021). The same article differentiates the types of social media by various activities, such as photo sharing, blogging, social gaming, social networks, video sharing, business networks, virtual worlds and reviews. Though it is made mostly for individuals to stay in touch with others, it is also used by businesses as a communication and a marketing tool. Kietzmann et al. (2011) describe seven main building blocks of social media and its functionality. For instance, these platforms allow people to see who all are available, share news with them, create relationships, communicate and so on. Various social media groups may use these functionalities differently. A lot of popular apps use a contact list on the smartphone to fetch the data and available friends on the network. Some allow seeing who is active while others do not. Sharing content (whether it is text, video, or audio) is usually accompanied by some types of engagement—likes/dislikes that create a reputation for the user, comments or 're-posting' (sharing the content with further groups of people).

## 2.2 Misinformation Control by the Social Media Platforms

Social media networks see themselves as a powerful tool that brings people closer to each other.

The Facebook's statement, 'to give people the power to build community and bring the world closer together' (Facebook Inc., 2017) acts as a prior example of the way of thinking. They seem not to notice that bringing people together is causing a homophily bias (a phenomenon of social interaction where people tend to lean towards other people with the same interests, beliefs or political biases) and algorithmically enabling the echo chamber effect (an effect that supports homophily by presenting only relevant content). This was closely studied by Cinelli et al. (2021) who compare four major social media sites (Facebook, Twitter, Reddit, Gab) in terms of the echo chamber effect. Its results suggest that these networks are built to promote content according to users' biases and preferences, pushing them into their opinion bubble from which it is difficult to escape.

This itself would not be a problem if it were not for the appearance of posts that contain false information, made intentionally or unintentionally. This content is called fake news in a public conversation. In his research, Wardle (2017) describes this phenomenon and breaks it down into the umbrella of different types of misinformation, which is spread online.

When users encounter fake news which lies within their current system of beliefs, they are more likely to believe in it and potentially share it with other people—like, share, retweet, upvote, depending on the social media site (Vosoughi et al., 2018).

This is potentially dangerous for societies, as, according to Wylie (2019), it may, for example, change the outcomes of the political campaign, push people's opinions or even put people's lives at risk with false news information.

With the emergence of the Covid-19 virus at the end of 2019 and countries going under strict sanitary regimes and lockdowns, fake news started spreading on social media like wildfire. This situation proved to be particularly dangerous as some of the fake news suggested drinking methanol (which can be deadly) to cure Covid-19. Additionally, as the virus originated in China, there was a spread of hateful conspiracy theories targeted towards Asian people (Naeem et al., 2020), resulting in physical attacks on people with Asian backgrounds (Cabral, 2021).

The problem attracted the attention of governors, researchers and companies, with each of them having different ideas on solving the problem at the ethical, political and technological levels.

However, it is debatable if companies try to help out of their kindness and corporate ethical standpoint or are just incentivized by the 'goodwill' part of Section 230 of Communication Decency Act law, described in the next section.

Social media platforms are, after all, for-profit organizations and they generate a tremendous amount of money off the engagement on their platforms.

## 2.3 Social Media Regulations in the United States

Regulations differ geographically; however, some of them might influence other regions and their regulations. Section 230 of the Communication Decency Act is one of the oldest and well-known regulations that covers the liability of online content. It shapes how social media operate in the US and thus, all over the world. It was originally introduced in 1996 with the premise of protecting minors from online pornography (Murica, 2020). The law stated no 'interactive computer service' (currently that could be a social media platform, a blog, or an e-commerce store) shall be punished for the content generated by its user as long as the platform owners show the will to moderate the illegal content once they become aware of it. This law was later challenged by multiple court cases whose outcomes shaped the interpretation of the law and the Internet, as it is known now (Reidenberg et al., 2012)—where people can publish their thoughts under the free speech amendment on Facebook and Twitter, sell handmade crafts on Etsy, share thoughts, opinions, ideas on Medium and Tumblr. Section 230 is now described as 'the Twenty-six Words that Created the Internet' (Kosseff, 2018).

The regulation covers the 'illegal content', that is 'obscene, lewd, lascivious, filthy, excessively violent, harassing, or otherwise objectionable' (Cornell Law School, 2018) content. Would altering the news be objectionable? How should companies act upon such a content? Additionally, with almost 2 billion daily active users on Facebook (Tankovska, 2021), it is difficult to moderate every post uploaded and there are complaints that companies do little to protect their users and that many politicians try to change it. Section 230 by itself is not specific enough to cover how companies should behave in such situations.

In 2020 alone, there were many proposals to reform Section 230. Jeevanjee et al. (n.d.) compare proposals for the reforms that were published in 2020 and presented during the hearings in the House Committee on Energy and Commerce. They show the understanding and the general idea of the issue and indicate the possible directions of the reforms. The authors conclude three main trends in the proposals: (1) Repeal Section 230, (2) limit the scope, (3) impose new obligations, and (4) change Good Samaritan rule.

Four of the reforms propose to repeal the argument coverage of the law though the scope of it is limited and does not serve its purpose. It would be better for the freedom of speech not to have it. Nine of them suggest limiting the scope, with most of them actively promoting holding companies accountable for the content they host. Two of them talk about the use of algorithms as a way in which the content is spread and shown to the user. Imposing new obligations is presented by another nine proposals. These usually talk about the companies taking steps to prevent illegal content but do not specify anything further than that. Lastly, the rule of Good Samaritan (an exception from the liability if the platform acts in goodwill) is presented by eleven bills in combination with other categories.

None of the proposals was signed and enforced; all were dropped at the hearings. Nonetheless, neither of them focused directly on the fake news phenomenon described in this research.

## 2.4 European Countries on the Internet Law and Fake News

The European Union collaborated with leading social media providers—Facebook, Google, Twitter, Microsoft, and Mozilla (not a social media platform per se)—to publish a code of practice. It is a self-regulatory standard to prevent disinformation online. The companies which joined the collaboration post annual reports on the disinformation status on their respective platforms and the steps they take to prevent that from happening (European Commission, 2021a).

Since the outbreak of the pandemic, these companies also report on actions to fight the Covid-19 disinformation (European Commission, 2021b). These reports show that private companies are taking some action to fight back fake news; however, these actions are usually a slight nudge redirecting the official coronavirus resources. The code of practice does not include strict detection or prevention of fake news.

Focusing on the regulations, each country introduces small regulations that are previously described in Section 230. Germany introduced a Network Enforcement Act in 2017 which bounds large social media platforms (with at least two million German users) to remove illegal contact within 24 hours after receiving a complaint. In response, Facebook and Twitter added more human moderators to manage the content (Johnson and Castro, 2021). The whole regulation, similar to Section 230, talks only about the illegal content; not tackling the fake news problem. As of mid-2021, United Kingdom does not have any regulation targeting misinformation online. There is a proposal of the Online Safety Bill that is currently being worked on and which would force companies to prevent harmful posts, such as terrorist content and child abuse content (Barker, n.d.). However, aside from the legislation, Government Communications Headquarters (GCHQ) is openly working to protect its citizens from online harms, including disinformation campaigns as a part of a national strategy to protect the citizens. The tool proposed by GCHQ facilitates the power of Artificial Intelligence (AI) to combat the threat (GCHQ, 2021). As it is a matter of national security, there is no public information on how that tool is about to work. Nonetheless, it shows that it has become one of the priorities on the agenda of GCHQ.

## 2.5 Self-regulating Social Media Platforms

Aside from the bills that regulate illegal content or collaborations with the governments, social media platforms use their own rules and systems to moderate the content posted by the users. Facebook states, on their official press blog, a commitment to this issue. It says that Facebook tries to disincentivize profit-driven parties from spreading false posts and ads. That includes making it harder to purchase ads, using machine learning to target frauds and spam. Secondly, Facebook relies on users reporting posts that seem off beam. The company also hires contractors to decide on the report legitimacy and collaborates with third-party fact-checkers to manage the content on their website (Facebook Inc., n.d.). The post does not include any concrete information on the success rate of the system, such as the number of items removed. Some of the other information posted through their official channel includes tests of the global fake news fight (Kerr, 2017). Additionally, in late 2020, Facebook released a press note stating their use of AI in misinformation detection. The system checks not only text posts, but also images and memes. It flags the content 'wrong' if the fact-checkers have already debunked the information. The same tool is capable of detecting picture modifications and deep fakes[1] (Facebook Inc., 2020). Although the intentions are good, the execution is not quite visible in public statistics. Facebook publishes the Community Standards Enforcement Report every quarter, which specifies the current trends of hate speech, nudity, sexual content, and misinformation; however, it does not specify the efficiency of the AI tool used (Rosen, 2021).

Twitter is another popular platform that is in the centre of attention. It allows to share a short text content and attach media to it. The users can reply, give a star and 'retweet' – share on their profile. With that, tweets with false content can easily go viral. Twitter tries to keep an eye on the disinformation campaigns on their network. In the name of public interest, Twitter releases reports on the actions taken by the platform on its transparency webpage.[2] Additionally, due to the pandemic, Twitter released an official policy forbidding use of their platform to share misinformation regarding Covid-19, violating the results of their rule in tweet deletion, labelling tweets and accounts suspension (Twitter Inc., n.d.).

YouTube (owned by Google) is another interesting platform. It is based only on the video content with comments and likes. The website experiences a massive number of new videos each day, reaching 500 hours of videos uploaded every minute in May 2019 (YouTube and Tubefilter, 2019). With that number, the platform implemented an AI tool to monitor harmful content, hate speech, child abuse and nudity. This tool started flagging the content wrongfully and deleting videos that were complying with all the platform's policies. In response, the company hired additional contractors to add a human check to prevent misclassification (Vincent, 2020).

This case raises an ethical question on the use of automatic systems to classify the content and its efficiency in differentiating satire from the content that was designed to mislead.

## 2.6 Researchers Working to Tackle the Issue of Fake News

There are researchers who focus on a technical perspective of fake news prevention. A survey done by Bondielli and Marcelloni (2019) shows machine learning,

---

[1] Deepfake is a term that refers to a video content generated with the use of Artificial Intelligence to replace a face of an object.

[2] https://transparency.twitter.com/en/reports/information-operations.html.

deep learning, or computational fact-checking, among other things, as a way of detecting and preventing fake news. Most of them can work only on text-based online content. It is also prone to incorrect learning behavior which results in possible misclassification of the news as 'fake', possibly misclassifying the news as 'false'. This was already outlined in the situation with YouTube's algorithms above.

Other suggestions proposed tracking the origin of the published posts online so that the system can verify if anything has been modified or establish the reputation of the news. For that, the researchers use blockchain as a tool to-go.

Blockchain comes from the research on 'a purely peer-to-peer version of electronic cash would allow online payments to be sent directly from one party to another, without going through a financial institution' (Nakamoto, n.d.). That peer-to-peer vision was introduced in a form of Bitcoin cryptocurrency. Since its publication around 2018 (Lewis, 2018), many variations on the use of blockchain emerged, such as supply-chain management, insurance fraud detection, or detecting fake news.

### 2.6.1 Definition of Blockchain

Blockchain was introduced and popularized by the cryptocurrency Bitcoin in the whitepaper published by Nakamoto (n.d.). The goal of Bitcoin is to remove an intermediary broker (bank or banks) between transactions, enabling peer-to-peer connection by gathering participants who will take care of bookkeeping. The transactions are validated by using a special algorithm (that could be a Proof-of-Authority or Proof-of-Stake[3]) by so-called minors, who are usually competing to deliver the results first. Transactions are stored in blocks, each signed with the hash[4] that is later used to calculate another one for the next block. All transactions are visible for everyone, although there are variations in blockchains that enable privacy by making it visible only to the authorized parties (Lewis, 2018).

The main benefits of blockchain include the transparency of transactions—everyone can see and track them and integrity of the data—the data is immutable, cannot be altered and if that happens, the transaction will not be validated by the other nodes. The drawbacks, however, include the unstable cost of transactions for public blockchains and a great environmental toll for some of the algorithmic approaches.

---

[3] Proof-of-Authority is a low-energy consumption blockchain consensus method in which a few numbers of actors have the power to validate transactions on the network (Valente, 2019). Proof-of-Stake: 'A blockchain network in which access to ledger or network requires permission from an individual or group of individuals. Permissioned ledgers may have one or many owners. Consensus on a permissioned ledger is conducted by the trusted actors, such as government departments, banks, or other known entities.' (ConsenSys, n.d.). https://transparency.twitter.com/en/reports/information-operations.html.

[4] A hash function is a mathematical function that maps a data of a given size to a fixed-size value. The results are called hash values. Hash values should not be able to be reversed to its original form. The method is used in cryptography for securing and verifying content. Nonetheless, it is a technology that is still in its early stages of use development, and its benefits, as well as its drawbacks, are still being discovered. https://transparency.twitter.com/en/reports/information-operations.html.

### 2.6.2  Use of Blockchain in the News Provenance Management

The advantage of immutability is the reason for many other industries looking into blockchain uses other than finance. In the research of fake news detection and prevention, many authors use blockchain's feature of immutability in their proposals. Shang et al. (2018) provide a traceability framework in which media joins the network to run the blockchain, promoting the consensus and verification process of participating in it. Song et al. (2019) proposed a solution to detect fabricated screenshots of instant messaging apps (such as Facebook Messenger), ensuring the integrity of screenshots to prevent manipulations on social media by using a Public Key Infrastructure to hash each screenshot and post it on the network. Ochoa et al. (2019) go a step further and introduce a reputation-based system in which publications compete to deliver the most trustworthy content, but in a centralised system with news sources also being minors. This work focuses on combating fake news posted on social media by giving the users the power to decide whether they want to trust the source based on the reliability score. The work is based on the existing blockchain network – Ethereum, which shows that the current tools are already enough to run the system despite some drawbacks (described in the further chapters).

Chen et al. (2020) did extensive work to summarize the previous research on fake news classification, its identification in social media and the use of new technologies, such as Artificial Intelligence (AI) in the process of detection. With that, the authors propose a solution of a 'weighted-ranking system' which 'incentivize news organizations to produce authentic news and penalize those that produce and spread fake news'. The news goes to multiple users to validate or decline the content. Their decision changes the publisher's credibility score. However, only trusted users (those with high credibility scores) can take part in such judgements. The solution assumes that the system (the people in the system) should trust selected individuals as ones who can spot what is misinformation or not and will work to receive the highest credibility score. This approach visually seems to be similar to the upvoting and downvoting system that works in Reddit (an online news aggregation community with a discussion option), but with a more advanced engine behind it.

One other study worth mentioning is that done by Hasan and Salah (2019) which focuses on the video provenance to fight against the deep-fake videos by utilizing Ethereum blockchain to monitor video and audio published online and determine any modification and point out the original audio/video material. Unfortunately, the solution presented comes with associated costs per transaction. It is estimated to be around 0.095 US$ per transaction and although it is not a high price, it is unsure whether the cost should be covered by the user or the platform.

The most important research work on the topic of fake news was conducted by Chen et al. (2020); Ochoa et al. (2019) and Shang et al. (2018) to targeting fake news things. Most of them rely on news sources/publishers and social media platforms to join the network to provide its users with a trust system. However, as it is not presented as a mandatory system web-wide, it will not prevent the creation of other new fake websites (those who are made to spread false information or manipulate the truth) from existence and gaining an audience. Additionally, blockchain, as presented by these studies, does not consider the user and bot-generated content that is spread through sharing, forwarding, or reposting. This can significantly contribute to the spread of possible fake news (Shao et al., 2018).

Apart from the theoretical work, some less mainstream social media platforms (Steemit and Sapien) try to implement their system of fake news prevention. Guidi (2020) compares seven prominent social media platforms built on blockchain technology with the content being stored on the blockchain. It juxtaposes their ways of working as well as how they manage the spread of fake news. Although it is an insightful study, it shows that none of the complex methods described by the researchers above is seeing the real implementation. Most of them include the downvote or dislike function that can be used by a regular user. These functions rely, again, on the human emotion, the confirmation bias and will not prevent the real infectious spread.

The study also poses problems that could come up if the social media network is based purely on the blockchain. Some of these concerns include identity checking, scalability (as current social media solutions are not suitable for the speed of the content sharing that happens on Facebook) and censorship or lack thereof (immutability of the content). This suggests that the anti-fake news system may work well as a support for the regular centralized networks, not as a pure core for the social media platforms.

Moreover, there are projects initiated by for-profit companies that see the potential of blockchain in tracking the source origin. In 2019, the New York Times' Research & Development team, together with IBM Garage, worked on the initiative of tracking the imagery source, using blockchain. The idea was put into the proof-of-concept (Koren, 2019), but since then, it did not take off. Additionally, new projects emerge, such as the Project Origin, Content Authenticity Initiative (CAI) and C2PA, bringing tech companies, journalists and academics together to work on a solution (Rosenthol et al., 2020). CAI focuses on image-based content, especially on photojournalism, allowing the creators to add metadata signed cryptographically to the file. The role of blockchain comes as a decentralised identifier. The CAI's white paper is a great piece of work outlining one specific issue of modifying photos. It would allow owners to control their content but it does not tackle the practical issue of governing the all-type content on social media.

## 3. Research Methodology

This research aims to analyse the phenomenon of the spread of fake news posts on social media platforms and explore the role of governance and blockchain in managing the issue. This chapter provides an overview of the methodological choices that have been made so that the proposed solution could be proposed. Moreover, it aims at bringing transparency of the research methods, setting the baseline for the research. Two of the significant pieces that were used to provide the understanding of research methods and the contents for this chapter are the Saunders' Research Onion in which each layer helps a researcher to move the project further, understanding the crucial steps—such as the philosophy of the research, approach to theory development, strategies, time horizons, data collections and analysis methods (Saunders et al., 2007); second material is a chapter from An Introduction to Design Science on research strategies and methods that provide a comprehensive guide on well-established strategies for research for use in designing a study, investigating and evaluating artefacts of research (Johannesson and Perjons, 2014).

The first layer of onion defines the philosophy principle. The research philosophy is 'a reflection of your [researcher's] values, as is your choice of data collection techniques'. As shown in Fig. 1, there are many different philosophies. Three popular assumptions that are used by researchers are ontology, epistemology and axiology. Ontology is shaping how the researcher sees and studies objects, accepting the nature of reality. Epistemology, on the other hand, is an assumption about knowledge – what is acceptable, valid and legitimate knowledge and how that can be communicated to others. Lastly, axiology is an assumption of the role of values and ethics (Saunders et al., 2007).

Two recurring ontological positions are objectivism and subjectivism. Generally, the main positions used in studies are positivism—a position that assumes 'working with observable reality within society leading to the production of generalizations'. Alharahsheh and Pius (2020) show that interpretivism is a position that 'is more concerned with in-depth variables and factors related a context; it considers humans as different from physical phenomena as they create further depth in meanings with the assumption that human beings cannot be explored in a similar way to physical phenomena' (Alharahsheh and Pius, 2020). Furthermore, these stances go into an array of philosophies shown in the onion.

The next layer is the approach to theory development which is a base in which the results will be formulated. The deductive approach states that the results of the research are based on theory-driven premises. In contrast, the inductive approach states that results of research come from a gap in the logical argument

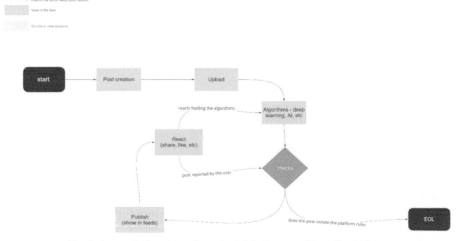

**Fig. 1:** A generic flowchart of a post published on a social media platform.

and are made by observation. Using one does not exclude the use of another one within research as this can be combined (Saunders et al., 2007). Selecting a proper approach can set a trajectory of research and help the researcher navigate and run the study research.

Research strategies tell the researcher how to collect and analyze the data. Choosing one that suits the need of research is the next layer in the research onion. To choose one that will suit the need of research, the researcher should answer a few questions beforehand – while comparing methodologies, a following set of questions pointed out by XYZ can help in setting up a methodology:

1. Is the method suitable with respect to the research question?
2. Is the method feasible, taking into account the resources of the research project?
3. Is the method ethical, taking into account its possible effects on people, animals and the environment?

The main strategies listed are an experiment, survey, case study, ethnography, grounded theory, action research and phenomenology. Each strategy serves a different purpose and facilitates different activities. For instance, an experiment investigates cause and effect relationship, survey dives into a certain aspect of a phenomenon, case study although like the survey, sets well-defined boundaries, etc. Before the data can be collected, a time frame shall be determined – whether the data will be sampled over multiple points of time (that is called longitudinal time horizon) or at a certain point in time (cross-sectional horizon). Data collection methods can also vary, depending on the need. The key methods include questionnaires, interviews, focus groups, observations and documents. The first four could be considered primary data in the case of researchers generating a unique set for the study. However, these could be also secondary data – data that has been generated for a different purpose but is reanalyzed with a new context (Johannesson and Perjons, 2014). This type of data could be considered more ethical as there is no risk of creating any harm on humans, animals, or the environment. However, it has its limitations as finding open-access resources can be limited and sometimes these sources might be lacking some ground-breaking information. On the other hand, collecting primary data is more time consuming and can incur additional costs for running questionnaires, interviews, etc.

After the strategy has been selected and the data collected, the method of analysis must be set. Depending on whether it is quantitative or qualitative data, the analysis will be carried out differently. Descriptive and Inferential statistics are used for quantitative analysis, whereas content analysis, grounded theory and discourse analysis are the three main options for qualitative data.

## 3.1 Methodological Choices

Based on the theory described earlier, a proper methodological approach must be selected for this research. This section summarizes the crucial decisions and elements taken for research.

This research is a part of computer science, hence it follows the philosophy of that field. Angius et al. (2021) talk about the role of ontology and epistemology of computational systems:

– Systems that focus on solving a particular problem, using either software or hardware. Although the research outcome does not aim to produce any software, it presents an intention and specification for the software that could be created, based on the research results. This is part of an ontological approach as defined by the chapter of a book by Angius et al. (2021). With emergence of new forms of niche social media platforms, such as Steemit[5] and Sapien[6], the researchers wanted to take a close look at them to perform a case study. However, this idea was discarded due to the time constraint, technical and ethical difficulties of collecting such data. Nonetheless, the research continued to focus on social media platforms to understand the cycle of social media post. This case study considered the few popular platforms – Facebook, TikTok, Twitter, YouTube and gathered data to create a cycle by observation of these platforms to get a general idea of how these systems work and what they have in common. Other data included in the research consist of documents conserving the Section 230 legislation, blockchain systems and information governance books that are used in the analysis of the issue and to suggest the solution. Concerning the points of the collection, Section 230 proposal focused on the data published in the year 2020 and observation of social media was done over a one-month in mid-2021. Other public documents – journal papers, online articles and press releases from social media platforms – used in supporting the work varied. However, it was important to base on relatively recent research to fully understand the current state of the problem. Since all of the data is in the form of a document, a text analysis approach was taken. In such an analysis 'a text is never only an objective representation of an existing world. Instead, the text contributes to creating and sustaining the world' (Johannesson and Perjons, 2014). This method allowed the researcher to write a framework proposal for tackling the misinformation issue and based the decisions on the documents gathered. A crucial element in developing a framework as a part of the research was a book written by Smallwood (2014), which talks about the best practices for writing an information governance policy. As a source, it is an important piece that understands the uniqueness of each organization and different needs for writing the policies; hence, it provides a great base for the work done. Additionally, the literature review takes a large space of the work as it forms the base for the proposal. The proposal for advancements in governance is drawn from the analysis of the existing Section 230 proposals, which are the blockchain-based technology solutions for news provenance.

---

[5] Steemti is a blockchain-based blogging and social media platform, launched in 2016. It is a competitor for Reddit. www.steemit.com.

[6] Sapien is a social media network with the aim to prioritize human interaction and privacy. www.sapien. network.

# 4. Data Analysis and Critical Discussion

This chapter presents the research results based on the data provided and attempts to discuss the results. The chapter is divided into six sections, with each discussing a different part of the research:

- (1) Designing a flow for online post publication and breaking down the current proposals in terms of controlling the content posted on social media and placing them within a graphical flowchart, (2) understanding the role of information governance and security in provenance management and explaining the main concepts with discussion on how that helps to build the proposed solution. Moreover, it adds the ethical aspect of providing the solution to governing the social media platforms and (3) introduces blockchain technology within the governance and presents a basic concept from the technological point of view and discusses the privacy complications of such a solution, giving the example of GDPR and the proposed walk around. Finally, Section (4) gives a proposal for the solution in a form of a framework proposal. The framework is embedded into a light blue frame to differentiate it from the rest of the document. The discussion is held in Section (5) of this chapter, which breaks down decisions taken upon writing a proposal. Lastly, (6) describes legal and ethical issues that might arise with the proposed solution.

## 4.1 Analyzing Cycle of Social Media Posts

Though the social media networks are defined above, it does not present a general idea of what is the lifespan, or a cycle of a post posted online. Therefore, this research presents a generalized flowchart of post creation and post cycle on the social media platform. The flow is based on the researchers' observations of the major social media platforms – Facebook, Twitter, TikTok, and YouTube. All the four platforms allow users to post some type of content. TikTok focuses on short-form videos allowing users to upload, create and manipulate those videos. Twitter's primary feature is to publish short text-based tweets, using hashtags to identify threads. YouTube is another video platform; however, users cannot 'repost' or 'reshare' content; they can interact, using the comment section below a video. Finally, Facebook is a combination of all that has been mentioned. The company is trying a variety of forms – text-based and video-based (both short and long). On each platform, users are defined as individuals or 'professional accounts', that being companies, public figures, and other influencers with a high number of people observing ('following' the account). The content could be a video, text, image, text, text with hyperlinks or all of them together. Once the user hits the 'publish' button, the media gets on the platform's server. Each of the main platforms uses sophisticated algorithms to assess the content and deliver it to the people that might be interested in it. Since 2017, Twitter uses a deep learning system to 'show the best Tweets [to a user] first' (Koumchatzky and Andryeyev, 2017). Facebook also uses deep learning algorithms that are open-sourced, to personalize recommended content (Naumov and Mudigere, 2019). Other platforms also use their system for content personalization, each trying to meet his or her business requirements. It is important to point out that these algorithms come under a backlash from the public, especially in the USA, where the people believe that the content chosen by the algorithm does not provide an accurate picture of the current affairs (Smith, 2018).

Figure 2 presents what happens to a post once it is published. As mentioned above, it usually goes through specific algorithms and then checks them as the platform might look for different things (i.e., copyright infringement on YouTube, child abuse on Facebook, etc.) and can decide whether the post will go to the public or end life. The post then appears on other users' timelines and the communication noise is created by them in reacting, commenting and sharing the posts. This information is fed to the algorithms that repeat the publication process to spread the content.

With that the content lifespan extends until it becomes redundant, losing engagement, becoming hidden underneath the other newer and more popular posts. Nonetheless, it does exist and it is ready to be rediscovered again if needed. This problem was noticed by The Guardian, which noticed its articles circulating on the social media platform as if they were new. Therefore, in mid-2019, The Guardian started marking articles older than a year with a clear message (Moran, 2019).

There is still a tremendous number of posts that go unnoticed under the radar of algorithms, fact-checkers and other tools, that spreading information which is either fully or partly false. The role of the fact-checking organization is crucial in flagging posts to remove, but it will be never as fast as the speed of the post that spreads.

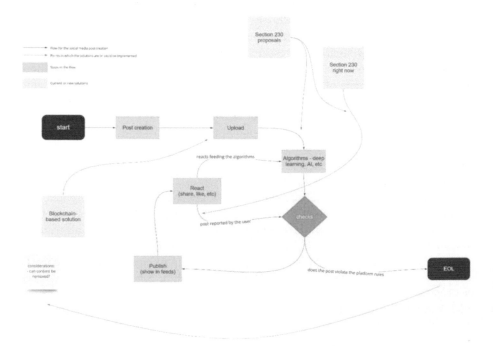

**Fig. 2:** Section 230 and blockchain-based solution within a flowchart of a post lifecycle.

Chapter 2 introduces Section 230 which is the main legislation to prevent illegal content on sites, such as social media platforms. The legislation is putting responsibilities on companies to act on the information that they are aware of. Therefore, a lot of that content is already on the platform. Considering the news that is spreading, for instance, misinformation about the vaccination, unless the algorithm is going to catch the post before it is posted, the message will keep on spreading. Some users would cross-check the source origin, but others would not as it is usually time-consuming and can be difficult. Therefore, allowing simple tracking of a news origin that could work cross-platform could result in slowing the spread of the fake posts by giving the user the power to quickly verify the source and to allow platforms to facilitate that tool to provide help for algorithms that are already trying to catch the misinformation and other illegal content. These tools are not perfect as discussed in the literature review—they can produce false positives which can threaten free speech by introducing censorship. Moreover, having a unified approach could help smaller players to implement this technique and not to spend a lot of resources on research and development of such technologies.

It is important to say that tracking the origin of news is unbiased—it does not tell whether the post is right or not. That is for a human to decide and the researcher believes, for instance, the news from a reputable source or a freshly created account with big claims.

## 4.2  The Role of Information Governance and Security

The previous section discussed the need for the news provenance approach and why it could be beneficial. Such a unified approach should be carefully crafted from a governance standpoint. This is discussed in the following section.

Information governance, commonly known as IG, is a wide field and a part of corporate governance, which is a broader term for procedures and policies which define how an organization works (Smallwood, 2014). IG is can be defined as 'the specification of decision rights and an accountability framework to ensure appropriate behavior in the valuation, creation, storage, use, archiving and deletion of information' as Gartner (n.d.) provides in its lexicon. It used to be that IG research focused mostly on governing physical IT infrastructure – hardware, software, networks as the 2013 paper by Tallon et al., presents. Nonetheless, there is much more covered by this topic as new technologies and communication methods emerge. The issue to address is an intriguing one as it concerns multiple different companies (social media platforms), all of which run differently and operate under different rules. A question of how the proposal could be unified in terms of governance is an important consideration of that work.

For the most part, a platform operates as a regular company, therefore following a general IG practice. Searching through various resources, it is difficult to find a document that studies the case of social media and how these should govern the flow of information posted on the platforms, as Section 230 already covers that.

The other aspect is a general cyber security aspect, which is explored in a publication of Eugen and Petru (2019) in which cyber security comes with a variety of other branches, such as operation security, information security, physical security and public/national security. All of these have importance in the project, especially information security is seen as a three-goal attribute – Confidentiality, Integrity, Availability (commonly known as CIA triad). Further study of the topic of information security is done by Veiga and Eloff (2007) by comparing most popular frameworks to comply with – the ISO 17799 (now revised as ISO/IEC 27002:2013), PROTECT, the Capability Maturity Model and the Information Security Architecture (ISA), with each requiring security policies and guidelines, user awareness, training and education, among other components. Although the frameworks work in a typical organization, it is difficult to assess how it would correspond to the initiative for a unified governance of social media platforms. It could be a significant influence on the proposed solution and even one of the frameworks can be included as a requirement to participate. With this, the platforms would have to provide a high standard of security of information, regardless of the system that is used. It would be difficult, however, to require a strict ISO certification for a small platform that is trying to come on the market with a new tool; therefore, a need for a simpler solution in that area could be beneficial. For that, a maturity model with outlined levels could be introduced. There are various CMMS from different organizations. Typically, models differentiate five levels of maturity (Carnegie Mellon University & The Johns Hopkins University Applied Physics Laboratory L.L.C., 2020; Proenca et al., 2016). One of the models available is one released by the Department for Homeland Security of the United States. Three main areas of that model are integrated governance, process and analytics and skilled practitioners and enabling technology that together achieve maturity (Department of Homeland Security, 2014). For unified solution across multiple platforms, this approach could ease out the implementation of security measures across all stakeholders. Therefore, levels provided by the CMM allow each organization to understand their maturity level and have a path to aim for a high security standard. The maturity model, however, does not solve the problem of this research. It is, however, a guideline that can be used in developing a framework.

### 4.2.1 *Information Security in Software Development of a Blockchain Solution*

Providing information security in such a project also involves a focus on software development. The development should prioritise the security of the data; therefore, as previously mentioned, CIA is a great overarching goal to follow. The triad is easy to understand but on its own might it can be difficult to understand in terms of development. Therefore, a clear development framework should be established. A work done by (Meland and Jensen, 2008) provides a Security-Oriented Software Development Frameworks – SODA, which works on the security principles that should be followed by the developers. These principles include, among other things, the principle of least privilege, fail-safe defaults, the economy of mechanism, complete mediation, open design, separation of privileges, least common mechanism and psychological acceptability. All these are basic design principles which allow software teams to develop a solution that prioritizes security. Moreover, SODA includes two other major factors that should be considered – threat modelling and security design review. Threat modelling is a process of understanding potential threats with hypothetical scenarios to design a system that is resilient to these threats; security design review, on the other hand, is a continuous process of reviewing the project for possible vulnerabilities.

It is important to acknowledge that researchers are not reconciled when it comes to the effectiveness of these approaches. At first Xiong and Lagerström (2019) found that threat modelling lacked a common ground with even the definition not being unified across the sources. This highlights a great number of threat-model approaches that could be beneficial for the project, but do not provide a solid conclusion on its success rate. The second point mentioned is analyzed in a work done by Yu et al. (2016) which analyzes code reviews done on a popular open-source platform, GitHub and found that in general, code reviewers can help with providing quality code with fewer bugs. Although, an older study by Edmundson et al. (2013), focusing on the effectiveness of security code review found that there was no evidence that manual reviews resulted in more secure software. The two different results are inconclusive as the methodologies are not identical and the questions asked focus on slightly different aspects (bugs vs security vulnerabilities). Nonetheless, there can be a case built that these two together can enhance the security of the code, providing another building block towards achieving common information security.

### 4.2.2 Considering Ethical and Cultural Approach to Writing a Framework

Policies, frameworks, technologies and legislations can at times threaten human rights, be it through stripping users from their privacy or through enabling censorship. That can be avoided, if possible; therefore Access Now—a non-profit organisation working with digital human rights – created a set of guidelines and ideas to follow when creating laws and policies (Pírková et al., 2020). With 26 recommendations, split into state regulation, self-regulation, and co-regulation, these can be used to build a policy framework for governing the platforms. Some of the recommendations that are worth mentioning for this work are:

a. Making automated systems as transparent as possible.
b. Publish information about how these systems are used and make the procedures behind their application.
c. Make the systems available for independent auditing.
d. Ensure that consent [from the user] can be revoked in an easy and streamlined manner.
e. Notify users of any changes in these rules and ensure they are explicitly accepted by users before they can be applicable.
   "Inform users about the collection and use of their data [...]
f. Issue a transparency report.

These are just a few recommendations that speak on the issue discussed in this work and should be considered when developing both high-level policies as well as the software that will be used in the initiative.

## 4.3  Role of Blockchain in the Policymaking

There are many implementations of blockchain, each with a different goal. Some, such as Bitcoin and Ethereum, were made with cryptocurrency in mind; some others, such as Hyperledger Fabric and IBM Blockchain or R3 Corda, are built to provide enterprise solutions for companies – from the finance sector to supply-chain management (Lawton, 2021). These technologies propose different approaches; nonetheless, each of them has a few similarities that build a typical blockchain. The proposed work should not specify which one of these should be picked up as a tool to enforce as that could limit the policy; it should be compliant with the technology chosen. Instead, it should highlight the purpose of blockchain and draw from the main concepts of blockchain to provide a provenance solution.

Figure 3 presents a simplified graph of how the proposed blockchain network works. Nodes (computers connected to the network) store all information necessary; nodes communicate with each other (P2P connection) and reach the consensus for validating the transaction (blue line and all the other grey lines connecting the nodes). Users both publishers (left side) and regular social media platform users (right side) interact with the social media platform by creating and consuming content. As is proposed above, it does not have a centralised node, which could avoid censorship imposed by one of the parties engaged with the network. With that, immutability (which has been mentioned on multiple occasions in this work) is the key element to that solution. The lack of trust within the nodes makes sure that the content stored on the network is not manipulated by any of the parties.

The immutability comes together with decentralisation. Each node has a copy of information stored on another one. This property allows redundancy in case one of the contributors goes offline or tries to modify the system.

Another aspect is cost. With the initial idea of decentralised blockchain, nodes (or 'minors' in some solutions) are incentivised to provide the service by gaining a share from a transaction. This, sometimes called 'gas' adds to the transaction. Most current social media platforms are free to use the data that is being monetised. The framework should take into consideration this factor and, perhaps, work to avoid the payment. Gas price is not a constant variable (Lewis, 2018) and is dependent

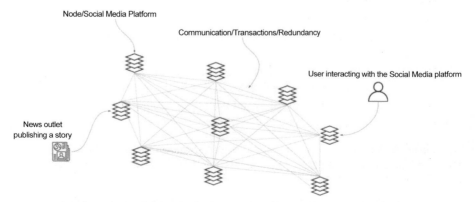

**Fig. 3:** An example of a blockchain network built to provide a news provenance.

on the number of transactions. This could result in spikes of prices when a crucial public event occurs, resulting in some news being delayed or not being published due to the high price.

Considering that nodes are formed by the social media platforms which are required to join the network, these platforms do not receive monetary incentives as is done with the cryptocurrency. In that case, the price for a transaction can be either removed or at least set upfront, depending on whether the system will allow other users and companies to join the network as well.

### 4.3.1 Privacy Complications (Considering GDPR)

The premise of blockchain states that information uploaded to the blockchain cannot be removed (immutability mechanism). Out of an original need for book-keeping transactions, this mechanism could cause legal problems from the privacy legislation around the world. One of these regulations is European GDPR, which applies to every company that operates in the EU territory, serving European customers (Wolford, 2018). Despite this work focusing on the American market (with the focus on Section 230 legislation), social media platforms operate around the world, serving millions of people and complying with different regulations. GDPR is one of the first regulations of its kind and serves as a great example of a direction which other governments are also heading.

There is not a lot of resources on GDPR compliance with blockchain. One of the papers that summarises the current status quo is the 2019 paper by Hofman et al. (2019) which talks about the current information governance techniques used in blockchain technologies. In its conclusion, however, the paper does not bring a lot of practical solutions to the table. Both the tool and the regulations are relatively new and not many companies and academics are still working on it. Another work is done by Politou et al. (2020) which explores how the blockchain can drop the immutability feature while keeping the same level of security and trust as with immutability. Both papers highlight that the 'right to be forgotten' of GDPR is a crucial bottleneck. While there are some exemptions from that paragraph (such as archiving for public interest and historical events), social media posts could not fall under that scheme. Politou et al. (2020) additionally outline that both private and public keys stored on the network can be considered as personal information. The work studies two main options for that issue – bypassing the immutability and removing it.

It is difficult to state what information would be included on the network and how it should be managed. However, knowing how the solution can raise some privacy concerns, the policy should outline the basic guidelines for protecting one's privacy and ensure compliance with local privacy laws, such as GDPR.

## 4.4 News Provenance Framework Proposal

This section presents the work done upon the data presented in this research. To address the issue of misinformation on social media, a framework of governance is presented to establish what the platforms should do to combat the issue and how it should be managed. The framework also considers a centralised authority acting as a centralised entity to oversee the social media platforms and their contribution to the initiative. State stakeholders are not omitted, as they create a legal framework that could change how the framework is constructed. Blockchain plays a crucial role, as discussed in Section 4.3 and is used as a base for the system creation that could track the origin of the news posted on social media platforms. Smallwood (2014) provided a guideline for writing the information governance policy with best practices and considerations. Moreover, the previously mentioned recommendations from Access Now were included to make sure that the result is ethical.

---

**News Provenance Network Framework**

1.   Introduction

1.1   Misinformation online appears to be an ever-growing problem. Although the issue itself is not a new concept, the appearance of social media and the use of algorithms to distribute and amplify the content have made the issue more apparent and more dangerous for societies. To help better manage the issue, there is a need to allow better source tracking. This policy draft is a bridged version of multiple stakeholders that are considered in the issue and propose a high-level policy for governance of the initiative that ought to run this initiative.

1.2   To do so, social media platforms, governors and other specialists should come together to manage the provenance of the news posted on social media. News is text, image, audio, and video content published online by news outlets, companies and high-profile people (also known as influencers).

2.   Scope

2.1   This collaboration outlines the roles and responsibilities of each party, the liability and the technical overview for implementation. Every participant (that is, every social media platform and the governors) shall respect this policy and ensure each party.

2.2   The framework provides guidelines for network implementation and connecting social media platforms for storing the metadata of news published on them.

3.   Network Specification

3.1   To provide a technology that can track the provenance of content posted on social media, a blockchain platform is to be presented.

3.2   The network requires contributors (nodes) that store the database. The database is copied across different nodes to ensure trust and redundancy.

3.3   The database is made from blocks that include algorithmically signed entries that form a chain of information.

3.4    The network facilitates the immutability properties of blockchain to ensure trust and ensure that no modifications to the data stored at rest are made.

3.5    Each platform participating in the system facilitates the blockchain network to publish metadata of all news posted on their platform.

3.6    For each new news, the system must check whether the news has appeared on the network already and append the information in a manner that is clear to understand for the end-user.

3.7    The implementation must be easy to use for the end-users, enabling them to verify the news origin.

3.8    The system must ensure the privacy of an individual. It should not store any personal information (known as PII) on the ledger.

3.9    The network is publicly available, which means everyone can join as a node and read transactions on the network.

3.10    The transactions are done only on social media platforms to ensure there are no third-party actors on the network and lower the risk of any manipulations.

3.11    The validity of transactions is agreed to by so-called consensus algorithms (also known as mechanism or protocol).

3.12    The authority outlines the technical specification of a consensus.

3.13    The algorithm must be respected by each node in the network. Non-compliance will result in denying access to participate in the network.

3.14    The algorithm's technical requirements are outlined by the authority and implemented by the social media platforms and the community.

3.15    The algorithm should consider the environmental impact of the network and its footprint on energy consumption.

3.16    All development for the network must consider a security-first approach, including software review and security design principles.

4.    Roles and Responsibilities

The key players and their roles in the policy are outlined in the segment.

4.1    Social Media Platforms

4.1.1    Social Media Platform (SMP) is every platform that is registered as a legal company that serves a public Internet platform with user-generated content, regardless of its reach. A public platform is understood as a platform that allows people to register on the side without invitation. The opposite to it is a private platform, such as a company's intranet.

4.1.2    The responsibilities of an SMP include maintaining the network by serving as a node that stores data and runs the consensus algorithms.

4.1.3   The SMP may not change the consensus algorithms by any means unless decided by the authority.

4.1.4   The SMP dedicates 2% of its development capacity to contribute to the software development of the network.

4.1.5  The SMP can appoint a consultant to work with the authority to provide technical and business expertise.

4.2   Governors

4.2.1   Governors are understood as local and/or state governments that are implementing laws considering online platforms, misinformation and any other regulations that might impact the initiative. Their decisions directly impact the policy's direction and development.

4.2.2   Governments can appoint representatives to help coordinate project development between the authority and the governors.

4.3   Authority

4.3.1   The authority is an independent organization that oversees the initiative of the network.

4.3.2   The authority is represented by a mix of legal representatives, platform representatives and academics.

4.3.3   Member's duty lasts for four years after which another member has to take the current place.

4.3.4   The authority is sponsored by the government and donations from people as well as organisations are received.

4.3.5   The authority oversees the initiative by actively running development planning. The authority has the power to decide which features, improvements and bug fixes are to be implemented and decide on the priority.

4.36   The authority must be ethical with the decisions that it makes, keeping in mind the goal of the initiative.

4.37   The authority is responsible for publishing a yearly transparency report, issuing any changes in the system, rate of adaptation, and any other information that could be considered crucial for the end-user. The report ought to be accessible online to everyone.

4.4   Community

4.4.1   The community are the volunteers that contribute to the project by reporting issues and requesting features.

4.4.2   The community can audit the source code and take part in the source code development.

---

5.  Compliance and Regulatory Environment

5.1  The initiative is subject to the laws and regulations of countries in which the policy and platforms operate.

5.2  All participants must actively reach cybersecurity maturity by complying with the framework provided by the Department of Homeland Security.

5.3  Social media platforms will be subject to independent auditing for confirming compliance with the policy.

5.4  All software developed for the initiative must be provided in an open-source manner allowing independent auditing.

6.  Review and Approval

6.1  The policy must be reviewed every two years to ensure that any new law requirements and technological advances are included.

---

## 4.5  Framework Proposal Analysis and Discussion

This sub-section breaks down the framework proposal from the previous section, the reasoning being that each paragraph is described to prove the benefit of the decision. The framework focuses on a high-level information governance policy that could be used as a base for further work on this topic.

The solution presents a non-profit organisation whose role is to govern the social media platforms to ensure that these platforms work together to combat online misinformation. It is important that the organization overseeing the initiative is not working underneath some government or any other organization that might impose a bias in the decisions that would shape the system. The governance is included in a form of written policies that are enforced on these platforms. This work does not focus on the operational side of such an organization, but purely on the information governance part presenting the draft policy called 'News Provenance Network Framework'.

The policy is divided into main segments (find synonyms): (1) Introduction, (2) Scope, (3) Network Specification, (4) Roles and Responsibilities, (5) Compliance and Regulatory Environment, (6) Review and Approval. Segment 4 is one of the key elements of that work. It specifies four main parties that should take part in the initiative and on what they should do. These are social media platforms without which their digital expertise, and the fact that they serve millions of people, the project would be unsuccessful. It is important to include them so that the network that is later proposed is emended in their systems. The policy states that these platforms should also allocate some of their resources to help build and maintain the network. This allocation should be proportional to the size of the platform's business so that the small players do not have to sacrifice their work for that initiative. Without forcing these platforms to build the network, the initiative would have to rely either on an open-source community or the organization appointed to run the network would have to spend a tremendous amount of money on hiring software engineers, who are still in high-demand causing salaries to skyrocket (Pham, 2021). It is important that these platforms do not have the right to change any technical specifications of the network – whether that is a consensus algorithm, including or modifying the content of the transaction, etc., otherwise, this power could be potentially abused, either intentionally or unintentionally. However, the platform can appoint a representative with technical and business expertise to advocate the platform's needs.

Following the roles, governors are included as a main touch point to the law. Countries may have different laws on online illegal content (Section 230 in the US), misinformation and privacy regulations (such as GDPR in the EU). Each of these bills or regulations can impact the consensus and other technical requirements of the project. Hence, allowing governing representatives to reach a mutual agreement is a crucial key for ensuring the project runs as it should. The main body for the initiative, called the 'authority' will oversee the whole project. It should gather the platform representatives, the governors, as well as the academics to work on the project. The authority must steer the project – the development, the maintenance. This body should make sure that the platforms comply with the standards they are obligated to comply with as well as making sure no one breaks the rules.

The project should run in an open-source manner, enabling the power of the community. The code for the network should be publicly open, allowing independent audits and contributions from other engineers as per recommendations from Access Now. Although there is no evidence on whether the open-source project provides better security or not (as mentioned in 4.2.1), considering that the platforms are forced to allocate their resources for the development, this solution can bring the best of both open- and closed-source solutions. Additionally, the development of the project should be run in the security design approach, facilitating points described in 4.2.1.

A blockchain network cannot run without nodes that would act as a distributed ledger. In a typical cryptocurrency solution, the network would incentivise ledgers by offering a financial incentive for participating in the network (running the algorithms, etc.). With that, there is a transaction cost associated. However, as described previously in 4.3, this cost should be avoided as it is not a constant variable. Therefore, the network should mostly rely on the ledgers in the form of the platforms that will not receive any monetary incentive for the transactions. The other concern is whether to allow other entities (private organisations, other non-profits, governments, even regular users) that enable network participation. On the one side, it allows for greater network distribution and greater trust, on the other, these entities should be incentivised to run these networks. They do not consider that scenario.

The method of implementation is not included in the framework. Nonetheless, it specifies a few important requirements. Firstly, platforms must cross-check the network for the existence of a news post to prevent sharing misinformation cross-platform. It does not specify the method, just the result – users must be informed and should be able to verify the news by themselves.

Additionally, the network should take into consideration privacy regulations. This is specified in the policy in the part that covers the network requirements. The policy does not paint what is included in the transaction and what is stored on it. It does point out that any PII should not be included on the network. Although that is particularly difficult to achieve – storing information about the origin of the news can be linked to its author, place, etc., and it is an important part of this governance that cannot be overlooked.

The consensus algorithm is also not outlined in the policy as this is a strictly technical part of the network. Many different solutions can be implemented and proposition of one can slow down the system's improvements.

Finally, one of the last segments covers the compliance part of the policy. The decision was made to include only the CMM as a requirement for the platforms and leave out any other security framework as each platform might use a different approach and for some, complying with the full ISO standardization might be too costly. Instead, CMM, as described in the previous sections, is a tool that allows a clear understanding for reaching the goal of maturity. The platforms should aim to reach the highest level (level 5); however, as that is difficult, it should be an overarching goal of the network. The proposal includes a scheduled review of it by the authority, making sure it is always up to date and compliant with other regulations.

## 4.6 Legal and Ethical Considerations

The decision of managing the origin of things appearing on social media and letting the information be open to anyone could face some legal and ethical challenges. Though this research does not evaluate a full spectrum of those issues, some are important to address. Some of the questions that were raised while developing the framework are: (1) Should the social media platforms be forced by law to join the project? (2) Should the project work across nations and how should that be enforced? (3) If the project works across multiple jurisdictions, how does it make sure that it obeys all the regulations? (4) Is storing social media metadata on the publicly available database ethical? (5) Would an implementation of blockchain in the policy prevent other innovative tools from addressing the issue?

(1) There is a debate on whether self-governing companies do enough to protect society from a variety of harmful content. An online article by Elghawaby (2018) states that governments should use their power to provide better regulations over social media platforms. In contrast, Samples (2019) presents an argument against it, proving that it could result in breaking the right of free speech. However, the proposed solution does not act as a country but as a separate entity that could provide the solution. The framework also does not censor the content; rather, it monitors it.

(2/3) Although Facebook is registered as a company in the US and in Ireland (among other countries), it works worldwide as long as the connection is not blocked. Therefore, the framework should provide a solution that could work across different countries. In the end, it is for the government to decide whether or not to allow access to the platform or ask for some adjustments in the way it operates.

(4) 4.3.1 provides an example of GDRP that answers the ethical issue. The framework must respect the privacy of the users and the technology can enable it. As long as the stored data does not reveal any personal information, this should not be a concern.

(5) The introduction of blockchain into the framework may prevent any other technology to elevate how the system works. However, this research aims at considering how blockchain can be used in the selected field. Whether there is another better tool could be addressed by other researchers.

## 5.  Conclusion and Future Work

The research aimed at proposing a governance policy for social media platforms to ensure the cross-platform news provenance solution that is a part of a fake-news fight. The research first digs through existing literature, building an understanding of the overall issue. From there, it becomes obvious there is no unified solution for tackling particularly the issue of misinformation. Status quo of Section 230 talks about the liability of predefined illegal content, but not misinformation. The proposals introduced in 2020 briefly touched the issue. Some platforms are trying to do their best and align their business with the ethics of fake news, and some collaborate with the European Union to better self-govern. There is also plenty of technical solution that can, not only prevent, but also detect misinformation, but that is only done in a theoretical work. Machine learning deployed by the platforms results in a lot of false positives, hence it might not be the optimal solution.

With that, the research defines blockchain and the way social media platforms work by creating a general flowchart of a social media post cycle in which it specifies algorithms that push the content to more people. Based on that, the research investigates the role of information governance to better understand how to create a governance framework for the social media platforms and includes the role of CIA triad, information security frameworks and CMM. This results in the framework proposal and discussion. The proposed solution states there should be a non-profit organisation overlooking the social media platforms and requires participants to use a blockchain network to manage the news source. The idea of blockchain was also built upon the existing solutions proposals. With that, the research considers privacy, legal and ethical issue that might arise from using the proposed solution.

The researchers wants other researchers to use this piece to further develop the solution as it only presents the theoretical approach. Not only the framework but also the use of blockchain should be tested. Such work requires researchers specialising in multiple fields – ranging from information governance to software engineering, with ethical researchers included. A proof-of-concept could be developed in collaboration with the mentioned parties to assess whether the proposed solution (1) slows down the spread of misinformation, (2) nudges users to check the credibility of the news,

(3) enable the cross-platform system that does not overwhelm the network infrastructure and the available computing resources.

As the research only covers the governance part, there is a need to explore the technical aspect of the approach. A recommendation for other academics and researchers is to focus on a technical solution using blockchain that will incorporate the policy in its design. Fighting fake news is a complex topic and requires researchers to look further into the ethics of the proposed solution, thereby answering the question of whether it is ethical to provide such a solution or whether it would be better to go a step further with providing a prevention tool.

# References

Alharahsheh, H.H. and Pius, A. (2020). A review of key paradigms: Positivism vs interpretivism. *Glob. Acad. J. Humanit. Soc. Sci.*, 2: 39–43.

Angius, N., Primiero, G. and Turner, R. (2021). The philosophy of computer science. *In*: Zalta, E.N. (ed.). *The Stanford Encyclopedia of Philosophy*. Metaphysics Research Lab, Stanford University.

Barker, D. (n.d.). *Online Safety Bill published in the UK* [WWW Document]. Pinsent Masons. URL. https://www.pinsentmasons.com/out-law/news/online-safety-bill-published-uk (accessed 7.19.21).

Bondielli, A. and Marcelloni, F. (2019). A survey on fake news and rumour detection techniques. *Inf. Sci.*, 497: 38–55. https://doi.org/10.1016/j.ins.2019.05.035.

Cabral, S. (2021). Covid 'hate crimes' against Asian Americans on rise. *BBC News*.

Carnegie Mellon University, the Johns Hopkins University Applied Physics Laboratory L.L.C. (2020). Cybersecurity Maturity Model Certification (CMMC). *Version 1.0.*

Chen, Q., Srivastava, G., Parizi, R.M., Aloqaily, M. and Ridhawi, I.A. (2020). An incentive-aware blockchain-based solution for Internet of fake media things. *Inf. Process. Manag.*, 57: 102370. https://doi.org/10.1016/j.ipm.2020.102370.

Cinelli, M., De Francisci Morales, G., Galeazzi, A., Quattrociocchi, W. and Starnini, M. (2021). The echo chamber effect on social media. *Proc. Natl. Acad. Sci.*, 118: e2023301118. https://doi.org/10.1073/pnas.2023301118.

ConsenSys. (n.d.). *A Blockchain Glossary for Beginners* [WWW Document]. ConsenSys. URL. https://consensys.net/knowledge-base/a-blockchain-glossary-for-beginners/ (accessed 7.24.21).

Cornell Law School. (2018). 47 U.S. Code §230—Protection for private blocking and screening of offensive material. *LII/Legal Information Institute*.

Department of Homeland Security. (2014). Best Practices for Planning a Cybersecurity Workforce White Paper.

Dollarhide, M. (2021). *Social Media Definition* [WWW Document]. Investopedia. URL. https://www.investopedia.com/terms/s/social-media.asp (accessed 8.27.21).

Edmundson, A., Holtkamp, B., Rivera, E., Finifter, M., Mettler, A. and Wagner, D. (2013). An empirical study on the effectiveness of security code review. pp. 197–212. *In*: Jürjens, J., Livshits, B. and Scandariato, R. (eds.). *Engineering Secure Software and Systems, Lecture Notes in Computer Science.* Springer Berlin Heidelberg, Berlin, Heidelberg. https://doi.org/10.1007/978-3-642-36563-8_14.

Elghawaby, A. (2018). *Social Media's Self-regulation isn't Enough* [WWW Document]. *Cent. Int. Gov. Innov.* URL. https://www.cigionline.org/articles/social-medias-self-regulation-isnt-enough/ (accessed 8.23.21).

Eugen, P. and Petru, D. (2019). Exploring the New Era of Cybersecurity Governance, 6.

European Commission. (2021a). *Code of Practice on Disinformation|Shaping Europe's Digital Future* [WWW Document]. URL. https://digital-strategy.ec.europa.eu/en/policies/code-practice- disinformation (accessed 6.28.21).

European Commission. (2021b). *Reports on April Actions and Continuation of the Monitoring Programme—Fighting COVID-19 Disinformation|Shaping Europe's Digital Future* [WWW Document]. URL. https://digital-strategy.ec.europa.eu/en/library/reports-april-actions-and-continuation-monitoring-programme-fighting-covid-19-disinformation (accessed 6.28.21).

Facebook Inc. (2017). *Facebook—Resources* [WWW Document]. Investor.fb.com. URL. https://investor.fb.com/resources/default.aspx.

Facebook Inc. (2020). *Here's How We're Using AI to Help Detect Misinformation* [WWW Document]. URL. https://ai.facebook.com/blog/heres-how-were-using-ai-to-help-detect-misinformation/ (accessed 7.5.21).

Gartner (n.d.). *Definition of Information Governance—Gartner Information Technology Glossary* [WWW Document]. Gartner. URL. https://www.gartner.com/en/information- technology/glossary/information-governance (accessed 8.12.21).

GCHQ. (2021). Ethics of AI: Pioneering a New National Security (White paper).

Guidi, B. (2020). When blockchain meets online social networks. *Pervasive Mob. Comput.*, 62: 101131. https://doi.org/10.1016/j.pmcj.2020.101131.

Hasan, H.R. and Salah, K. (2019). Combating deepfake videos using blockchain and smart contracts. *IEEE Access*, 7: 41596–41606. https://doi.org/10.1109/ACCESS.2019.2905689.

Hofman, D., Lemieux, V.L., Joo, A. and Batista, D.A. (2019). The margin between the edge of the world and infinite possibility: Blockchain, GDPR and information governance. *Rec. Manag. J.*, 29: 240–257. https://doi.org/10.1108/RMJ-12-2018-0045.

Jeevanjee, K., Lim, B., Ly, I., Perault, M., Schmeling, T., Vattikonda, N. and Zhou, J. (n.d.). All the Ways Congress Wants to Change Section 230 [WWW Document].

Johannesson, P. and Perjons, E. (2014). Research strategies and methods. *In*: *An Introduction to Design Science*. Springer International Publishing, Cham, pp. 39–73. https://doi.org/10.1007/978-3- 319-10632-8_3.

Johnson, A. and Castro, D. (2021). How other Countries have Dealt with Intermediary Liability, Information Technology and Innovation Foundation.

Kerr, Á. (2017). *Facebook Addresses Fake News Globally* [WWW Document]. Facebook Addresses Fake News Glob. URL. https://www.facebook.com/journalismproject/facebook-addresses-fake-news-globally (accessed 7.5.21).

Kietzmann, J.H., Hermkens, K., McCarthy, I.P. and Silvestre, B.S. (2011). Social media? Get serious! Understanding the functional building blocks of social media. *Bus. Horiz.*, 54: 241–251. https://doi.org/10.1016/j.bushor.2011.01.005.

Koren, S. (2019). *Introducing the News Provenance Project* [WWW Document]. Medium. URL. https://open.nytimes.com/introducing-the-news-provenance-project-723dbaf07c44 (accessed 7.6.21).

Kosseff, J. (2018). *The Twenty-six Words that Created the Internet* [WWW Document]. Jeff Kosseff. URL. https://www.jeffkosseff.com/home (accessed 6.26.21).

Koumchatzky, N. and Andryeyev, A. (2017). *Using Deep Learning at Scale in Twitter's Timelines* [WWW Document]. URL. https://blog.twitter.com/engineering/en_us/topics/insights/2017/using-deep-learning-at- scale-in-twitters-timelines (accessed 7.12.21).

Lawton, G. (2021). *Top 9 Blockchain Platforms to Consider in 2021* [WWW Document]. SearchCIO. URL. https://searchcio.techtarget.com/feature/Top-9-blockchain-platforms-to-consider (accessed 7.24.21).

Lewis, A. (2018). *The Basics of Bitcoins and Blockchains: An Introduction to Cryptocurrencies and the Technology that Powers them.* Mango Publishing, Coral Gables.

Meland, P.H. and Jensen, J. (2008). Secure software design in practice. *In*: *2008 Third International Conference on Availability, Reliability and Security, presented at the 2008 Third International Conference on Availability, Reliability and Security*, IEEE, pp. 1164–1171. https://doi.org/10.1109/ARES.2008.48.

Moran, C. (2019). *Why We're Making the Age of our Journalism Clearer at the Guardian* [WWW Document]. The Guardian. URL. http://www.theguardian.com/help/insideguardian/2019/apr/02/why-were-making-the-age- of-our-journalism-clearer (accessed 8.28.21).

Murica, E.A. (2020). *Section 230 of the Communications Decency Act: Why California Courts Interpreted it Correctly and what that says about How we should Change.* Loyola Los Angeles, Law Rev.

Naeem, S.B., Bhatti, R. and Khan, A. (2020). An exploration of how fake news is taking over social media and putting public health at risk. *Health Inf. Libr. J.* https://doi.org/10.1111/hir.12320.

Nakamoto, S. (n.d.). Bitcoin: A Peer-to-Peer Electronic Cash System, 9.

Naumov, M. and Mudigere, D. (2019). *We are Open-sourcing a State-of-the-Art Deep Learning Recommendation Model to Help AI Researchers and the Systems and Hardware Community Develop New, More Efficient Ways to Work with Categorical Data* [WWW Document]. URL. https://ai.facebook.com/blog/dlrm-an-advanced-open-source-deep-learning-recommendation-model/ (accessed 7.12.21).

Ochoa, I.S., de Mello, G., Silva, L.A., Gomes, A.J.P., Fernandes, A.M.R. and Leithardt, V.R.Q. (2019). FakeChain: A blockchain architecture to ensure trust in social media networks. *Commun. Comput. Inf. Sci.*, 105–118. https://doi.org/10.1007/978-3-030-29238-6_8.

Pham, T. (2021). *Council Post: Analysing the Software Engineer Shortage* [WWW Document]. Forbes. URL. https://www.forbes.com/sites/forbestechcouncil/2021/04/13/analyzing-the- software-engineer-shortage/ (accessed 8.30.21).

Pírková, E. and Pallero, J. (2020). *Access Now, 2020, 26 Recommendations on Content Governance—A Guide for Lawmakers*. Regulators and Company Policy Makers.

Politou, E., Casino, F., Alepis, E. and Patsakis, C. (2020). Blockchain mutability: challenges and proposed solutions. *IEEE Trans. Emerg. Top. Comput.*, 1–1. https://doi.org/10.1109/TETC.2019.2949510.

Proenca, D., Vieira, R. and Borbinha, J. (2016). A maturity model for information governance. *In: 2016 11th Iberian Conference on Information Systems and Technologies (CISTI), Presented at the 2016 11th Iberian Conference on Information Systems and Technologies (CISTI)*, IEEE, Gran Canaria, Spain, pp. 1–6. https://doi.org/10.1109/CISTI.2016.7521480.

Reidenberg, J.R., Debelak, J., Kovnot, J. and Miao, T. (2012). Section 230 of the Communications Decency Act: A Survey of the Legal Literature and Reform Proposals. *SSRN Electron. J.* https://doi.org/10.2139/ssrn.2046230.

Rosen, G. (2021). Community Standards Enforcement Report, First Quarter 2021. *Facebook.* URL. https://about.fb.com/news/2021/05/community-standards-enforcement-report-q1-2021/(accessed 7.5.21).

Rosenthol, L., Parsons, A., Scouten, E., Aythora, J., MacCormack, B., England, P., Levallee, M., Dotan, J., Hanna, S., Farid, H. and Gregory, S. (2020). The Content Authenticity Initiative—Setting the Standard for Digital Content Attribution.

Samples, Jo. (2019). Why the government should not regulate content moderation of social media. *Cato Insitute Policy Anal.* https://doi.org/10.1163/2210-7975_HRD-9985-20190065.

Saunders, M.N.K., Lewis, P. and Thornhill, A. (2007). *Research Methods for Business Students.* 4th ed., Financial Times/Prentice Hall, Harlow, England; New York.

Shang, W., Liu, M., Lin, W. and Jia, M. (2018). Tracing the source of news based on blockchain. *In: 2018 IEEE/ACIS 17th International Conference on Computer and Information Science (ICIS), Presented at the 2018 IEEE/ACIS 17th International Conference on Computer and Information Science (ICIS)*, IEEE, Singapore, pp. 377–381. https://doi.org/10.1109/ICIS.2018.8466516.

Shao, C., Ciampaglia, G.L., Vaol, O., Yang, K., Flammini, A. and Menczer, F. (2018). The spread of low-credibility content by social bots. *Nat. Commun.*, 9: 4787. https://doi.org/10.1038/s41467-018-06930-7.

Smallwood, R.F. (2014). *Information Governance: Concepts, Strategies, and Best Practices.* Wiley CIO Series, Wiley, Hoboken, New Jersey.

Smith, A. (2018). Attitudes toward algorithms used on social media. *Pew Res. Cent. Internet Sci. Tech.* URL. https://www.pewresearch.org/internet/2018/11/16/algorithms-in-action-the-content-people-see-on-social-media/ (accessed 7.19.21).

Song, G., Kim, S., Hwang, H. and Lee, K. (2019). Blockchain-based notarisation for social media. *In: 2019 IEEE International Conference on Consumer Electronics (ICCE), presented at the 2019 IEEE International Conference on Consumer Electronics (ICCE), IEEE, Las Vegas, NV, USA*, pp. 1–2. https://doi.org/10.1109/ICCE.2019.8661978.

Tallon, P.P., Ramirez, R.V. and Short, J.E. (2013). The information artifact in it governance: Toward a theory of information governance. *J. Manag. Inf. Syst.*, 30: 141–178. https://doi.org/10.2753/MIS0742-1222300306.

Tankovska, H. (2021). *Facebook: Daily Active Users Worldwide* [WWW Document]. Statista. URL. https://www.statista.com/statistics/346167/facebook-global-dau/ (accessed 6.26.21).

Twitter Inc. (n.d.). *COVID-19 Misleading Information Policy* [WWW Document]. URL. https://help.twitter.com/en/rules-and-policies/medical-misinformation-policy (accessed 7.27.21).

Valente, M. (2019). *What is Proof of Authority?* Coinhouse. URL. https://www.coinhouse.com/learn/what-is-proof-of-authority/ (accessed 7.6.21).

Veiga, A.D. and Eloff, J.H.P. (2007). An information security governance framework. *Inf. Syst. Manag.*, 24: 361–372. https://doi.org/10.1080/10580530701586136.

Vincent, J. (2020). *YouTube Brings Back More Human Moderators after AI Systems Over-Censor* [WWW Document]. The Verge. URL. https://www.theverge.com/2020/9/21/21448916/youtube-automated-moderation-ai- machine-learning-increased-errors-takedowns (accessed 7.5.21).

Vosoughi, S., Roy, D. and Aral, S. (2018). The spread of true and false news online. *Science*, 359: 1146–1151. https://doi.org/10.1126/science.aap9559.

Wardle, C. (2017). *Fake News. It's Complicated* [WWW Document]. First Draft. URL. https://firstdraftnews.org/articles/fake-news-complicated/ (accessed 1.1.21).

Wolford, B. (2018). *What is GDPR, the EU's New Data Protection Law?* [WWW Document]. GDPR.eu. URL. https://gdpr.eu/what-is-gdpr/ (accessed 7.28.21).

Wylie, C. (2019). Mindf*ck: Inside Cambridge Analytica's Plot to Break the World. Profile Books.

Xiong, W. and Lagerström, R. (2019). Threat modelling—A systematic literature review. *Comput. Secur.*, 84: 53–69. https://doi.org/10.1016/j.cose.2019.03.010.

YouTube, Tubefilter. (2019). Hours of video uploaded to YouTube every minute as of May 2019.

Yu, Y., Wang, H., Yin, G. and Wang, T. (2016). Reviewer recommendation for pull-requests in GitHub: What can we learn from code review and bug assignment? *Inf. Software Technol.*, 74: 204–218. https://doi.org/10.1016/j.infsof.2016.01.004.

# 2

# The Forensic Investigation of Misinformation on Social Media

*Natasha Omezi, Stefan Kendzierskyj\* and Hamid Jahankhani*

## ABSTRACT

Digital platforms, connectivity, the ubiquity of technology, the increase of information and the prevalence of Online Social Networks (OSN) have overcome traditional challenges and roadblocks, such as physical borders and the constraints of time and distance. This has made the distribution and sharing of information a lot easier and quicker, delivering messages to a wider audience which of course can have immense benefits. However, it also means that public perception of reality can be more easily influenced and distorted by a small number of individuals through the dispersion of misinformation and disinformation. The growing use of social media to the point that it is considered normative and is ingrained in almost every sphere of modern life, including social, business, personal, etc., means that the proliferation of any news, particularly fake news, is highly likely.

The COVID-19 pandemic saw the effect of misinformation with large-scale impacts: a misinformed public and misrepresented people, organizations and events. Identifying misinformation has consequently emerged as a critical task. A further deterrent would be the investigation of the source of misinformation and the consequential prosecution of propagators of social media misinformation.

Northumbria University London, UK.
Emails: natashaomezi@gmail.com; Hamid.jahankhani@northumbria.ac.uk
* Corresponding author: stefan@cyfortis.co.uk

## 1. Information Age Background

The Information Age, which began around the 1970s, is still going on today. Also known as the Computer Age, Digital Age or New Age, this era has brought about a period in which people can access information and knowledge easily (*History of Technology*, n.d.). The Information Age, also known as the Age of Entrepreneurship, can also add another name to its list: The Age of Misinformation. The consequences of this age are a misinformed public, misrepresented people, organizations and events, as evidenced in a few world events, including Brexit, Cambridge Analytica (US 2016 elections), Pizzagate, US 2020 elections and the COVID-19 pandemic, to mention a few.

11 March 2020, the day the World Health Organization (WHO) declared the COVID-19 outbreak – a pandemic – the virus had gone viral, spreading worldwide! The *Merriam-Webster Dictionary* defines pandemic as 'occurring over a wide geographic area and affecting an exceptionally high proportion of the population' (Merriam-Webster, n.d.). A convergence of virology with virality – the virus itself spread very rapidly and so did the information and misinformation about the outbreak, causing panic among the public (*Journal of Travel Medicine*, 2020).

The impact of COVID-19 on society has been unprecedented and unimaginable and the impact of misinformation was equally as damaging, causing confusion and fear, and thereby hampering the response to the outbreak. Dr Tedros, the Director General of WHO, on the topic of the coronavirus said, "Misinformation on the coronavirus might be the most contagious thing about it."

The COVID-19 pandemic highlighted a spate of global issues: inequality, injustice, falsehoods and most of all, misinformation and disinformation. Previously, elections, celebrity gossip, etc., were considered to have unleashed the worse of misinformation, fake news and disinformation. However, none of these have trumped the misinformation that was unleashed on the world at the peak of the global pandemic. COVID-19 introduced to the world, not only a virus, but an information vacuum at a time of deep fear and uncertainty – what can only be described as 'a perfect storm for disinformation' (Bhulai et al., 2021).

The ubiquity of social media made it easier to spread or even create COVID-19 falsehoods, making the work of public health officials and governments increasingly difficult. At no time was the ingenuity and creativity of our time evidenced more than during the pandemic. Memes, images, videos, information with a bit of truth to outright lies, were all evidenced at the peak of the pandemic. Cybercriminals were equally as active, particularly with targeted and sophisticated phishing scams exploiting pandemic concerns, such as unemployment, welfare benefits and stimulus packages. As of 15 May, 2020, the UK's cybercrime agency had uncovered 7,796 phishing emails linked to COVID-19 (IT Governance, 2020). The world battled the virus and misinformation alike in an effort to restabilize the ecosystem. At the time of writing this research, misinformation had moved on from the source of the COVID-19 virus to the impact of taking the vaccine. 'Evidence'-backed misinformation, claiming a global agenda, permeated social media and other extreme views, leading to people being too afraid to take the vaccine.

The growing use of social media to the point that it is considered normative and is ingrained in almost every sphere of modern life, including social, business, personal, etc., means that the proliferation of any information including false information is highly likely. We now have social media to cover every sphere of life and some examples are as follows:

- **Facebook** – for family and friends
- **Instagram** – for creative images, follow celebrities and other people of interest
- **TikTok** – which took off particularly during the pandemic, to display video editing skills and to participate in a variety of challenges – all captured by video
- **LinkedIn** – to present professional prowess and get involved in professional discussions, recruitment and more
- **Twitter** – gained even more popularity with Donald J. Trump as President
- **Parler** – also another social media platform which has a reputation for spreading 'falsehoods and hateful comments'
- **Gab.com** – considered to be a far-right platform

A lot that has appeared out of Parler and Gab.com, to point out a couple, can be classified as disinformation. There is a plethora of conspiracy theories that have spread from these platforms. This was made most prolific during the pandemic when we saw COVID-19-related conspiracy theories. The 'Black Lives Matter' protest was just one of the civil unrests that were empowered by social media during the pandemic.

## 2. False Information: Misinformation, Disinformation and Fake News

Information, according to Peter Hernon, is defined as organized, timely and accurate data (processed data) that is arranged for a purpose (Hernon, 1995). The commonality of misinformation, disinformation and fake news lies in the fact that they can all be classified as false information, as they lack the 'accuracy' that true information possesses (Tilbury, 2017). However, the distinguishing factor between misinformation, disinformation and fake news lies in intent.

### 2.1 Fake News

Consuming news has always been the traditional method of informing the public about current affairs and how it may affect them. With the evolution of technology and explosion of the Digital Ae, the way we use, digest and interact with information has changed. News can be international, national or local and all serve to inform the general public about the ongoing events through different media, including social media. What is accepted as news, the current method of news consumption and the corresponding sources of news, have all undergone a radical change. There has been an increase in news consumption, speed of dispersion and reach due to technology.

The increase in consumption of digital information has led to the increase in proliferation of news: good, bad, and fake.

The issue of 'fake news' is not new as the world has always experienced propaganda and politically-aligned bias, purporting to be news. It has been around for as long as there have been writing mechanisms. Propaganda, shock headlines, fearmongering or smokescreens, for instance, have always existed (European Broadcasting Union, 2018). However, this activity has taken on new forms, hugely magnified by the ubiquity of social media. Current understanding of fake news ranges from political satire to deliberate misinformation, the motives for which vary considerably, including financial and ideological. The common thread is that it serves to influence the reader through the use of inaccurate information or as Gu et al., put it: '*the manipulation of public opinion to affect the real world*' (Gu et al., 2017). Allcott and Gentzkow define fake news as '*news articles that are intentionally and verifiably false and could mislead readers*' (Allcott and Gentzkow, 2017). However, according to the UK parliamentary report on disinformation and 'fake news', there is no agreed definition of the term 'fake news' as it is applied to various types of false information, including fabricated content, manipulated content, impostor content, misleading content, false context of connection and satire/parody (www.parliament.uk, 2019). Another analysis observes that fake news comes in multiple variants (*The Telegraph*, 2021) including, but not limited to:

- Commercially-driven sensational content
- Nation state-sponsored misinformation
- Highly partisan news sites
- Social media itself
- Satire or parody

Additionally, there are news stories emerging from mainstream media outlets that turn out to be hoaxes or mistakes, although published with good intentions. It is the variety of motives and definitions that makes fake news particularly difficult to counter.

Other known synonyms for fake news include disinformation campaigns, cyber propaganda, information warfare, etc. Disinformation and misinformation are two other terms which have been used interchangeably with fake news but differ slightly.

Despite the fact that the term 'fake news' has been made a lot popular in recent times, it has actually been covered extensively by other academic literatures in political science, computer science, psychology, etc. Adam Berinsky, in his study on healthcare reforms, carried out experiments on political misinformation and posits that rumours acquire power through familiarity and that attempting to quash rumours through direct refutation could actually facilitate their diffusion, as merely repeating a rumour increases its strength, even in the '*context of debunking misinformation with a strong correction*' (Berinsky, 2015).

The changing habits of news consumption means that there is a higher tendency for people to assimilate news as seen on social media, which also enables the wide dissemination of fake news. Fake news is a unique problem because it exists in so many parts. Its roots and the reasons for which it spreads are myriad and complex. Consequently, one of the reasons it has been able to proliferate so easily is due to the fact that the onus of responsibility does not clearly fall in one place (Jain, 2018).

Wu et al., have categorized additional types of misinformation, such as urban legend, unverified information, rumours, crowdturfing, spam, trolls, hate speech and cyber-bullying (Wu et al., n.d.).

## 2.2 Misinformation

Misinformation is defined as 'the inadvertent sharing of false information' and is different from disinformation which is considered to be deliberate. Fake news lies somewhere in between as it is considered not to be tied to a larger agenda (disinformation) but may have financial motives. Misinformation can affect all aspects of life and can inadvertently sway public opinion, even after being debunked. For instance, in 2016, during the United Kingdom's EU Referendum, the Vote Leave campaign claimed that the UK would save up to £350m a week, by leaving the EU. The campaign also purported that these funds would be redistributed to the British National Health Service (NHS). This was later debunked as a 'clear misuse of official statistics' by the UK Statistics Authority. However, a published poll found that nearly half the British population believed this to be true, and voted 'Leave' accordingly, showing that even when information is proven to be misinformation, it could continue to shape society's attitudes towards a given topic (*The Independent*, 2018). Thus, misinformation can be inadvertently shared (i.e., not with malicious intent), due to believing a falsehood. This example, classified as misinformation, could also be categorized as disinformation, as the intention deliberately to deceive is hard to prove or disprove.

Misinformation generally is not malicious and is not spread maliciously; however, the impact may lead to unintended consequences. For instance, the tweet below shows a tweet that was shared in the aftermath of Hurricane Harvey in 2017 which was a devastating Category 4 hurricane described as a 'catastrophic rainfall disaster' (Resnick, 2017). The tweet showed a shark on the flooded streets of Texas. Whilst this was not spread maliciously, it compounded an already stressful situation with fear. It has also been observed that hoaxes go viral during natural disasters. All the elements for virality are in place – uncertainty, heightened emotions and curiosity about what is happening.

This 'shark on the freeway' was an image that had been online for years and made appearances during Hurricane Irene (in 2011) and Hurricane Sandy (in 2012), but still managed to fool Fox news, who later apologized (*USA TODAY*, 2017).

## 2.3 Types and Sources of Misinformation

According to UNESCO's handbook on journalism education and training, misinformation can generally be categorized at a high-level into the following common types (UNESCO, 2018):

- **Wrong Time/Wrong Place** – The most common type of misleading visuals where old visuals are re-shared with new claims about what they depict. These can be easily debunked, but not easily pulled back once in circulation.
- **Manipulated Content** – Content that has been digitally manipulated using photo or video editing software.
- **Staged Content** – Original content that has been created or shared with the intent to mislead, such as deepfakes and just outright false information.

## 2.4 Deepfakes

Deepfakes were originally employed in the pornography industry where it referred to the process of inserting celebrities' faces into pornographic scenes, usually without their knowledge. It is now much more widespread across all spectra of society, including the political arena. Chesney and Citron define deep fakes as '*highly realistic and difficult-to-detect digital manipulations of audio or video*' (Chesney and Citron, 2019).

## 2.5 Disinformation

Disinformation, as defined by the *Oxford Dictionary* is '*false information that is intended to mislead, especially propaganda issued by a government organization to a rival power or the media.*' Analysts generally agree that disinformation is always purposeful and is not necessarily composed of outright lies or fabrication. This is where the power of disinformation lies: it can be composed of mostly true facts taken out of context or blended with inaccuracies and falsehoods to support the intended message. Disinformation also has the added characteristic that it is always part of a larger plan or agenda (National Endowment for Democracy, 2017).

The case of the alleged crucifixion of a three-year-old boy by Ukrainian soldiers is a classic example of disinformation. On 12 July, 2014, viewers of Russia's Channel One (a main State-run television station) watched a woman at a refugee camp near the Russian border being interviewed. She claimed to have witnessed a squad of Ukrainian soldiers nail a three-year old boy to a post. Allegedly, after torturing the boy to death for several hours, they tied his mother to the back of a tank and dragged her through the square. It turned out that the story was a complete fabrication that had not been fact-checked by the journalists. The story had been inspired by a political scientist with ties to the Kremlin, who had posted a similar story on Facebook. By the time the Kremlin connection was uncovered, the damage was done: the report had been run on Channel One and the story had gone viral on social media (*Moscow Times*, 2014). This was just one example of Kremlin-backed disinformation deployed during Russia's annexation of Crimea. Similar tactics were employed by the Kremlin on the United States, particularly during the lead up to the 2016 presidential elections. The Kremlin, by no means, have the monopoly on disinformation campaigns: social media networks and digital tools are being leveraged to spread falsehoods, narratives and distortions to shape public perceptions and undermine trust in the truth (Nemr and Gangware, 2019). States and individuals can easily spread disinformation at speeds information has not previously been spread, with potentially serious impact due to the proliferation of social media platforms.

Shu et al., described fake news as '*news with intentionally false information*' (Shu et al., 2018). The Digital, Culture, Media and Sports (DCMS) published a report *Disinformation and 'Fake News'* in July 2018, in which it was proposed that 'disinformation' should be used instead of 'fake news'. This, they purported is because 'fake news' had been used to describe content that a user might dislike or disagree with and consequently dismiss. They further proposed the definition of disinformation as '*the deliberate creation and sharing of false and/or manipulated information that is intended to deceive and mislead audiences, either for the purposes of causing harm, or for political, personal or financial gain.*' This was subsequently accepted by the UK Government (www.parliament.uk, 2019).

There is an additional category of 'fake news' called 'mal-information'. This has been described by the United Nations Educational, Scientific and Cultural Organization as '*information that is based on reality, used to inflict harm on a person, social group, organization or country.*' (UNESCO, 2018).

For the purposes of this research, the definition of fake news will be that proposed by the UK Government, i.e., '*the deliberate creation and sharing of false and/or manipulated information that is intended to deceive and mislead audiences, either for the purposes of causing harm, or for political, personal or financial gain.*'

For the purposes of this topic, the following are ruled out as 'fake news':

- Unintentional reporting mistakes, e.g., the report that Donald Trump had removed the bust of Martin Luther King Jr. from the Presidential White House.
- Conspiracy theories (difficult to verify and already strongly believed by the perpetrators of such theories).
- Rumours not originating from a news article.
- Incorrect statements by politicians.
- Misleading reports that are not outrightly false [in other circumstances, this could be considered fake news].
- Satire (However, taken out of context, some satirical comments have been perpetrated as news and could also be defined as fake news). For instance, in 2016 the now-defunct website, wtoe5news.com, reported that Pope Francis had endorsed Donald Trump's presidential candidacy. This story was shared more than a million times on Facebook, but what was not included, was the disclaimer on its 'About' page which stated that it was a '*a fantasy news website. Most articles on wtoe5news.com are satire or pure fantasy*' (Allcott and Gentzkow,

2017). The researcher is of the opinion that of all the different types of misleading content, satire can be the most unintentionally misleading as disclaimers can be intentionally or unintentionally ignored.

The term 'fake news' will be used interchangeably with 'disinformation' and 'misinformation' in this document and may also be just referred to as 'false information' as an overarching umbrella.

The impact of fake news has been observed most notably in the 2016 United States elections that saw Donald Trump sworn in as the President of the United States. Even though politics and elections are not the only areas that have been impacted by fake news, the US elections caught everyone's attention, as well as the Cambridge Analytica scandal.

In studying the impact of fake news, Berinsky points out that repetition of rumours can augment their 'fluency', and therefore increase the likelihood of individuals accepting misinformation as truth (Berinsky, 2015). However, Bartels' research on 'The Political Impact of Media Exposure' concluded that media exposure only had a minimal impact on political opinion and that the resulting change was negligible. This, he posits, is not because media is not persuasive, but because most individuals would have already had strong political leanings or views prior to being exposed to any media. He points out that media-effects analysts should focus on individuals with 'new' or 'uncrystallized' opinions (Bartels, 1993). The researcher agrees with this as this was evidenced in the Cambridge Analytica scandal where the target audience were those that had no strong political leanings or were 'sitting on the fence', as it were.

In assessing the impact of misinformation, e.g., fake news, Flynn et al., discuss how political misconceptions can undermine people's ability to form meaningful opinions by distorting public debate, thereby impacting democracy (Flynn et al., 2017). Kuklinski et al., seemingly well ahead of their time, as far back as 2003, unwittingly predicted events leading up to the 2016 US elections, highlighting the issue of misinformation in the political arena amongst American citizens and inferring that widespread information could lead to collective preferences far different from what it would have been if people were correctly informed (Kuklinski et al., 2003). The misinformation of the general public, though not a new phenomenon, appears to be on the increase due to the ubiquity of technology. The dissemination of misinformation in the form of fake news is considered one of the greatest threats in modern times to freedom of expression, independent debate and fair journalism. The result is weakening public trust in governments and other authorities, sparking social unrest (Olszowski, 2021).

## 3. Social Media

Digital platforms, connectivity, the ubiquity of technology, the increase of information and the prevalence of Online Social Networks (OSN), on the one hand have overcome traditional challenges and roadblocks, such as physical borders and the constraints of time and distance, making the distribution and sharing of information a lot easier. On the other hand, it means public perception of reality can be more easily influenced and distorted by a small number of individuals through the dispersion of misinformation and disinformation. The growing use of social media to the point that it is considered normative and is ingrained in almost every sphere of modern life, including social, business, personal, etc., means that the proliferation of any news, particularly fake news is highly likely. McGonagle, in his article, 'Fake News: False Fears or Real Concerns?', is of the position that fake news has always existed but that the 'game-changing factors' are: '*the sophistication with which fake news is being produced; the scale on which it is being produced, and the speed and effectiveness with which it is being disseminated*' (McGonagle, 2017).

Defining social media does present its own challenges due to the broad variety of stand-alone and built-in social media services currently available. However, the *Merriam Webster Dictionary* defines social media as '*forms of electronic communication (such as websites for social networking and microblogging) through which users create online communities to share information, ideas, personal messages, and other content (such as videos).*' By design, social media is Internet-based and gives users quick electronic communication of content. It is this speed that enhances the propagation of all types of information, including misinformation.

## 3.1 Types of Social Media

Social media comes in many different forms, although when the phrase 'social media' is used, most people think about Facebook first. Facebook is just one type of social media. The idea that social media can be defined simply by their ability to bring people together has been seen as too broad, as this could be applied to any form of communication. However, there are four common features, as identified by Obar and Wildman:

- Social media services are mainly Web 2.0 Internet-based applications
- User-generated content is the lifeblood of social media
- Individuals and groups create user-specific profiles for a site or app designed and maintained by a social media service
- Social media services facilitate the development of social networks online by connecting a profile with those of other individuals and/or groups (Obar and Wildman, 2015).

Social media is, therefore, not limited to social networks, like Facebook, but can be grouped roughly into various types (Kakkar, 2020; Aichner and Jacob, 2015):

- Social networks, e.g., Facebook, Twitter, LinkedIn, Google+
- Media sharing networks: Instagram, Snapchat, YouTube, TikTok
- Discussion forums: Reddit, Quora, Digg
- Bookmarking and content curation networks: Pinterest, Flipboard
- Consumer review networks: Yelp, Zomato TripAdvisor
- Blogging and publishing networks: WordPress, Tumblr, Medium, Boing Boing

- Social shopping networks: Polyvore, Etsy, Fancy
- Interest-based networks: Goodreads, Houzz, Last.fm
- Collaborative projects: Wikipedia, Mozilla
- Social gaming: World of Warcraft, Mafia Wars

The list above is by no means exhaustive and there may be differing opinions on the classification, in spite of which it is clear that the social media has had a positive effect on society, such as reinforcing free speech, facilitating the flow of ideas across various boundaries, such as societal, geographical, etc. (Niklewicz, 2017). It has played and continues to play a positive role in political and social developments allowing, for example, the mobilisation of pro-democratic movements, e.g., Egypt 2011, Ukraine 2013–2014 and the BLM marches, in 2020, instigated by the killing of George Floyd. The video showing his murder went 'viral' on social media, sparking an unrest that spread globally. In 2014, West Africa witnessed the largest Ebola outbreak since 1976. Amidst the fear and uncertainty, there were the usual rumours and misinformation as initially there had been no approved options for treating Ebola. Misinformation on the use of salt water to prevent and treat Ebola went viral on social media, resulting in fatalities. The Centre for Disease Control deployed health communicators to West Africa, to support ministries of health in deploying and disseminating science-based messages. Social media was the chosen medium for most of this information as it has the potential to spread information fast, effectively combating the false information being circulated via the same medium.

## 3.2 Social Media—Proclivity for Misinformation

In spite of the positive attributes of social media, there are a variety of characteristics that increase the proclivity of the spread of misinformation on social media and it lies primarily in the differences between social media and traditional media. Social media displays characteristics different from traditional media (e.g., newspapers, TV, radio broadcasting, print magazines, etc.) in a variety of ways, including reach, frequency, usability, quality, etc. The other differences (Roy, 2016) are:

i. Information from social media reaches a maximum and more varied audience, while traditional media reaches a targeted audience.

ii. Changes to social media can be made once published, making it more versatile than traditional media, which cannot be changed once published.

iii. Information from social media is released immediately, while press times can cause delays with traditional media.

iv. Social media encourages a two-way conversation, while traditional media is one-way.

Critical to the development of efficient detection algorithms and tools for early detection methods, is the understanding of how false information proliferates on social media platforms and why it succeeds in deceiving readers.

## 3.3 Echo Chambers

The existence of social media bubbles, also known as echo chambers, is a high factor leading to the successful deception of its consumers. Echo chambers are groups of users who, consciously or unconsciously, consume the same content and are not presented with alternative information or opinions. This is due to the algorithms employed by social media platforms in an effort to guide the advertising that users might see. Based on a user's reading habits, additional similar content is presented to the user. This effectively means that opinions held by an individual can be reinforced. For instance, extreme right-wing militants will see extreme right-wing content; and radical left-wing users will be surrounded by content posted by like-minded individuals, thus reinforcing their belief-system. An example of this was seen in the 2021 storming of the United States Capitol. Called to action by President Trump, thousands of his supporters gathered in Washington DC in support of his false claim that the 2020 election had been stolen by the 'radical-left Democrats'. He demanded that Mike Pence and Congress reject Biden's victory. He sent out tweets following this speech. His supporters stormed the Capitol, breaching police perimeters because they believed that they would lose their country if they did not fight for it (instigated by Trump's speech). This resulted in five known deaths (directly or indirectly) with 138 police officers and many others injured.

## 3.4 Bots

This is another phenomenon increasing the spread of misinformation on social media. Bots are 'automatic profiles', i.e., special programmes that masquerade as genuine profiles managed by human beings. They can send mass content, share or retweet selected items at rapid speeds, reacting to pre-programmed word sequences and hashtags. They can also follow each other, thereby further increasing the appearance of authenticity. The main goal of a bot is to fill social media platforms with messages targeting pre-programmed people groups. Much of the misinformation spread on social media is done by bots. Twitter and Instagram are particularly susceptible to them.

Originally, (ro)bots were developed to perform repetitive and mundane tasks, such as organising and cataloguing content. However, over time, bot functionality extended to customer service tools (chat bots) and social media interactions. There are now a variety of functions, ranging from harmless web crawlers to more malicious bots that are used to spread spam or disinformation.

Additionally, bots have been used to push polarising messages to voters throughout the United States and Europe. Social media companies, such as Twitter, Facebook and Google, have increasingly become concerned about the proliferation of bots on their platforms and have taken several steps to remove these accounts. There are a number of incentives to remove 'bad' bots from online spaces as they not only undermine the quality of legitimate user interactions, but also the quality of user data that is sold to advertisers who want to reach the real consumers (Bradshaw, 2020).

### 3.5  Regulatory Framework for Social Media

With increasing concern about harmful content and activity online, including cyber-bullying, self-harm and the use of groups spreading misinformation to stop people from taking the COVID-19 vaccine, for instance, there has been an increased outcry by many, including parliamentary committees, academics to introduce statutory regulation. These groups argue that self-regulation by Internet companies is not enough to keep users safe (Woodhouse, 2021). Technology and social media companies monetise our attention, encouraging users to click through fake information (click-bait). When enough users click through, the content creators generate income. Therefore, attention-grabbing headlines, ranging from distorted truths to outright fabrications, are spread via social media. There needs to be additional regulation for the spread of this type of false information. Customers in retail shops in the UK, for instance, know that if an item on the shelf has a price tag, the item has to be sold at that price. The onus is on the retailer to ensure their tagging is accurate. Nowadays, food retailers are under obligation to disclose all ingredients particularly following incidences, such as the 'Pret-a-Manger' incidence, where a young girl died from eating a sandwich which did not have all the allergens written on the packaging. In the same vein, news headlines and other attention-grabbing headlines, should accurately indicate the content, otherwise face some type of penalisation or measures to corrective actions.

### 3.6  Social Media Platforms and Big Tech Responses

Recent progress, in terms of corrective action, was demonstrated when both Twitter and Facebook banned Trump from their platforms for two years in the wake of content that was posted and following actions made from the US Capitol riots. Facebook has gone further to state that it would no longer give politicians 'immunity for deceptive or abusive content based on their comments being newsworthy' (BBC News, 2021).

Facebook have also put out at a statement on their website about their increased fight against false information (Facebook, 2017).

With the increased awareness of the proliferation and dangers of false information, the susceptibility of social media, to being the channel combined with social media platforms joining the fight against misinformation and the potential for legislation arising, could see the rise in persecutions due to the investigation of misinformation.

## 4.  Forensic Investigation Guidelines—ACPO Principles

Digital forensic science focuses on the recovery and investigation of material found in digital devices related to cybercrime. With the exponential growth in data, the performance of digital forensic investigators and their tools used are becoming increasingly important. Artificial Intelligence, inter-connected networks, the 'smart'-lifestyle – all fundamentally depend on data. Consequentially, any successful investigation would be highly dependent on the data retrieved, and the tools and processes used would therefore have to be relevant and cutting edge. Additionally, for forensic investigations, these processes need to be considered forensically sound. In the course of time, as the world has become more digital, investigations have gone from 'paper and cabinet files' to data and data storage devices. With the proliferation of digital misinformation, mal-information and all forms of false information, the requirement to be able to investigate accurately is pertinent.

## 4.1 Definition of Digital Forensics

In attempting to define what digital forensics is, Mark Politt posits that there is no single answer to this question, but that it is a series of tasks and processes in investigation (Politt, 2004). However, Ricci Ieong describes digital forensics investigation as '*a process to determine and relate extracted information and digital evidence to establish factual information for judicial review*' (Ieong, 2006). Kruse and Heizer set out the three A's of computer forensics as:

(1) **Acquire** the evidence without altering or damaging the original data.
(2) **Authenticate** that your recorded evidence is the same as the original seized data.
(3) **Analyse** the data without modifying the recovered data (Kruse and Heiser, 2002).

The Association of Chief Police Officers (ACPO), now called the National Police Chiefs' Council (NPCC), developed guidelines for computer investigations and electronic evidence, which are still currently in use.

## 4.2 Current ACPO Forensic Guidelines for Computer-based Evidence

The current ACPO forensic guidelines for the investigation of computer-based evidence, are as stated below (ACPO, 2012):

- **ACPO Principle 1:** No action taken should change data held on a digital device including a computer or mobile device that may subsequently be relied upon as evidence in court.
- **ACPO Principle 2:** Where a person finds it necessary to access original data held on a digital device, the persons must be competent to do so and able to explain their actions and the consequent implications on the digital evidence to the Court.
- **ACPO Principle 3:** A record of all actions that have been applied to the digital evidence should be created and preserved in such a way that an independent third party forensic expert should be able to follow or examine those processes and reach the same conclusion.
- **ACPO Principle 4:** The individual in charge of the investigation has the overall responsibility to ensure that these principles are followed.

In order to cover crimes involving websites, forums and blogs, the ACPO guidelines recommend the proposed method for copying a website and it is to visit the site and record the relevant pages using video capture software in order to ensure visible representation of how they looked originally. The guidelines also recommend that where there is difficulty in capturing evidence by visiting the site, a request can be made to the Internet hosting service provider in order to recover evidence of who has created the web page or posting (ACPO, 2012). This could be the first step in ensuring the forensic investigation of fake news, which is usually posted on web forums, blogs, social media, etc.

The outcome of previous research is that it is possible to develop guidelines for the forensic investigation of fake news, but not in its pure form as the current ACPO guidelines stand (Omezi and Jahankhani, 2020). However, the guidelines will be subject to caveats as they will have to be adapted according to type, i.e., fake news (text); fake news (images); fake news (videos). Investigating social media misinformation will be subject to being split into these categories, as well.

Investigating misinformation could follow these steps/processes:

1. Fact Checking – is it true or false?
2. Can the original source be found?

## 4.3  Fact Checking

There are currently a plethora of fact checkers covering various aspects of misinformation. Fact checkers focus on multimedia (e.g., web and social media) or text (news and journalism). Misinformation from social media can follow these same pseudo categories and some fact checkers focus only on debunking fake news, such as BBC Reality Check, FactCheck.org, PolitiFact, etc.

### 4.3.1  Investigating Fake News

This could start off with the pulling together of all news fact checkers and running the suspected misinformation by this database. This will determine whether it is true or false and additionally could also provide some context as to how it came into being. For instance, it could be an aberration of a true story. Fact checking analysis should be able to reveal this.

### 4.3.2  Investigating Images

Certain fact checkers, such as Fotoforensics.com, eyewitnessproject.org, Truepic, etc., can be used to investigate and detect alterations to images (Omezi and Jahankhani, 2020). However, it has to be noted that were an image has been put together with deceptive intentions from the start, this process would not work, as there would be no alterations. For instance, taking a picture of two people from a certain angle could appear different to what the exact scenario was.

### 4.3.3  Investigating Videos

Fact checkers, such as InVid, REVEAL Project FP7, etc., can detect doctored videos, including deep fakes.

*4.3.4 Investigating the Source*

For images and videos, there are various methods of doing this, including examining hidden data in the file, such as EXIF data which can reveal GPS location, owner name and other personal details. However, this information may not 'survive' resizing, cropping, compression, etc.

As in all investigations, forensic or otherwise, success lies in the piecing together or various and sometimes unrelated evidence.

# 5. Conclusion

It is clear that the speed of information data exchange, huge amounts of traffic and abundance of channels to disseminate information will inevitably increase the difficulty in separating fake information from reality. The large-scale impact of information: a misinformed public, misrepresented people, organisations and events, is a challenge that cannot go unchecked without dire societal consequences. Identifying misinformation has consequently emerged as a critical task. There is currently a race to improve fact-checking capabilities and many are moving on to Artificial Intelligence.

Artificial Intelligence (AI) is often proposed as a solution to fake news, due to its effectiveness in flagging, blocking and removing online content. In areas, such as organised crime and terrorism, for instance, there has been progress in applying AI and machine learning computational models to tackle the spread of harmful content. Automating responses to misinformation/fake news is more difficult, as it can be subjective at times and not quite as clear cut. Computational responses can be used to identify instances of harmful, fake or conspiratorial content going viral and flagging them for action. However, review by human editors should always remain a part of the take-down process, for it to make sense.

Social media, by its very nature, lends itself to being the biggest propagator of false information. The connectivity of social media, the fact that users feel safe in their various networks, means that people are less cynical and reserved about sharing news they have received from loved ones, or just people they are connected to. Psychologically, people feel close to people they are digitally connected to. It is this false sense of connectedness that is a contributing factor to the speed in dissemination of misinformation. Add to this, the added layer of echo chambers, where people who have the same views are linked together and share information, and it is easy to see why social media is such a propagator of misinformation. Propagators of disinformation campaigns can programme bots to target particular groups and to increase the spread of false information.

In considering social media and misinformation, the situation is not completely dire as there are still laws that can be applied to protect individuals from harmful content, such as hate speech, harassment, etc. However, there needs to be better enforcement of existing legal structures.

With social media, we are in a learning phase. Throughout history, society has had to update its regulations and laws to limit the bad and reinforce the good, and this is the current state of affairs with social media.

While identification and prevention of the spread of misinformation could act as a deterrent, a further deterrent would be the investigation of the source of misinformation and the consequential prosecution of propagators of social media misinformation.

Tools, such as InVid, TruePic and a plethora of other tools, can be used to investigate false information in the form of digitally manipulated images, videos, etc.

Undoubtedly, getting to the point of prosecutions may take a long time, as it has to be proven that laws have been contravened, regulations breached, etc. Carrying out successful investigations will be dependent on a number of factors. This research is positioned for further work to take place in the implementation of forensic guidelines to investigate social media misinformation.

# References

ACPO. (2012). *ACPO Good Practice Guide for Digital Evidence*, London: Metropolitan Police Service.

Aichner, T. and Jacob, F. (2015). Measuring the degree of social media use. *International Journal of Market Research*, 57(2): 257–275.

Allcott, H. and Gentzkow, M. (2017). Social media and fake news in the 2016 Election. *Journal of Economic Perspectives*, 31(2): 211–236.

Bartels, L.M. (1993). Messages received: The political impact of media exposure. *The American Political Science Review*, 87(2): 267–285.

BBC News. (2021). *Facebook Suspends Trump Accounts for Two Years* [Online]. Available at: https://www.bbc.co.uk/news/world-us-canada-57365628; https://www.bbc.co.uk/news/world-us-canada-57365628 [accessed 7 August, 2021].

Berinsky, A.J. (2015). Rumours and health care reform: Experiments in political misinformation. *British Journal of Political Science*, pp. 1–22.

Bhulai, R., Nemr, C., Ragnet, M. and Thompson, E. (2021). *Fanning the Flames: Foreign State-sponsored Disinformation in the Time of COVID*. s.l.: Disinfo Cloud.

Bradshaw, S. (2020). *Responding to Fake News through Regulation and Automation* [Online]. Available at: https://www.carter-ruck.com/insight/fakes-news-authentic-views/responding-to-fake-news-through-regulation-and-automation/; https://www.carter-ruck.com/insight/fakes-news-authentic-views/responding-to-fake-news-through-regulation-and-automation/ [accessed 22 Sep., 2021].

Chesney, R. and Citron, D. (2019). *Deepfakes and the New Disinformation War—The Coming Age of Post-truth Geopolitics* [Online]. Available at: https://www.foreignaffairs.com/articles/world/2018-12-11/deepfakes-and-new-disinformation-war; https://www.foreignaffairs.com/articles/world/2018-12-11/deepfakes-and-new-disinformation-war [accessed 28 Nov., 2019].

European Broadcasting Union. (2018). *'Fake News' and the Information Disorder.* Brussels: EBU.

Facebook. (2017). *Working to Stop Misinformation and False News* [Online]. Available at: https://www.facebook.com/formedia/blog/working-to-stop-misinformation-and-false-news; https://www.facebook.com/formedia/blog/working-to-stop-misinformation-and-false-news [accessed 29 July, 2021].

Flynn, D., Nyhan, B. and Reifler, J. (2017). The nature and origins of misperceptions: Understanding false and unsupported beliefs about politics. *Advances in Political Psychology*, 38(S1): 127–150.

Gu, L., Kropotov, V. and Yarochkin, F. (2017). *The Fake News Machine: How Propagandists Abuse the Internet and Manipulate the Public.* s.l.: Trend Micro.

Hernon, P. (1995). Disinformation and misinformation through the Internet: Findings of an exploratory study. *Government Information Quarterly*, 12(2): 133–139.

*History of Technology* (n.d.). *Information Age: A Collaborative Effort* [Online]. Available at: https://historyoftechnologyif.weebly.com/information-age.html [accessed 3 July, 2021].

Ieong, R.S. (2006). FORZA—Digital forensics investigation framework that incorporate legal issues. *Digital Investigation*, 3S: S29–S36.

IT Governance. (2020). *Catches of the Month: Phishing Scams for June 2020* [Online]. Available at: https://www.itgovernance.co.uk/blog/catches-of-the-month-phishing-scams-for-june-2020; https://www.itgovernance.co.uk/blog/catches-of-the-month-phishing-scams-for-june-2020 [accessed 27 September, 2020].

Jain, L. (2018). *The Technologies that are Tackling Fake News* [Online]. Available at: https://www.itproportal.com/features/the-technologies-that-are-tackling-fake-news/; https://www.itproportal.com/features/the-technologies-that-are-tackling-fake-news/ [accessed 14 April, 2019].

*Journal of Travel Medicine*. (2020). The panic of social media panic travels faster than the COVID-19 outbreak. *Journal of Travel Medicine*, pp. 1–2.

Kakkar, G. (2020). *What are the Different Types of Social Media?* [Online]. Available at: https://www.digitalvidya.com/blog/types-of-social-media/; https://www.digitalvidya.com/blog/types-of-social-media/ [accessed 10 June, 2021].

Kruse, W.G. and Heiser, J.G. (2002). *Computer Forensics: Incident Response Essentials.* Indiana: Pearson Education.

Kuklinski, J.H. et al. (2003). Misinformation and the currency of democratic citizenship. *Journal of Politics*, 62(3): 790–816.

McGonagle, T. (2017). Fake News': False fears or real concerns? *Netherlands Quarterly of Human Rights*, 35(4): 203–209.

Merriam-Webster. (2019). *Definition of News* [Online]. Available at: https://www.merriam-webster.com/dictionary/news?utm_campaign=sd&utm_medium=serp&utm_source=jsonld; https://www.merriam-webster.com/dictionary/news?utm_campaign=sd&utm_medium=serp&utm_source=jsonld [accessed 2 November, 2019].

Merriam-Webster (n.d.). *Pandemic* [Online]. Available at: https://www.merriam-webster.com/dictionary/pandemic" https://www.merriam-webster.com/dictionary/pandemic [accessed 26 August, 2020].

*Moscow Times*. (2014). *State Run News Station Accused of Making up Child Crucifixion* [Online]. Available at: https://www.themoscowtimes.com/2014/07/14/state-run-news-station-accused-of-making-up-child-crucifixion-a37289; https://www.themoscowtimes.com/2014/07/14/state-run-news-station-accused-of-making-up-child-crucifixion-a37289 [accessed 9 August, 2021].

National Endowment for Democracy. (2017). *Issue Brief: Distinguishing Disinformation from Propaganda, Misinformation and 'Fake News'* [Online]. Available at: https://www.ned.org/issue-brief-distinguishing-disinformation-from-propaganda-misinformation-and-fake-news/; https://www.ned.org/issue-brief-distinguishing-disinformation-from-propaganda-misinformation-and-fake-news/ [accessed 29 June, 2021].

Nemr, C. and Gangware, W. (2019). *Weapons of Mass Desruction: Foreign State-Sponsored Disinformation in the Digital Age.* s.l.: Park Advisors.

Niklewicz, K. (2017). *Weeding out Fake News: An Approach to Social Media Regulation.* Brussels: Wilfried Martens Centre for European Studies.

Obar, J.A. and Wildman, S. (2015). Social media definition and the governance challenge: An introduction to the special issue. *Telecommunications Policy*, 39(9): 745–750.

Olszowski, R. (2021). *Combating Fake News with the use of Collective Intelligence in Hybrid Systems.* Cordoba, Spain. ISBN: 978-0-9998551-6-4, ISSN: 2767-9640.

Omezi, N. and Jahankhani, H. (2020). Proposed forensic guidelines for the investigation of fake news. pp. 231–265. *In*: Jahankhani, H., Akhgar, B., Cochrane, P. and Dastbaz, M. (eds.). *Policing in the Era of AI and Smart Societies.* s.l.:Springer.

Politt, M. (2004). *Six Blind Men from Indostan.* s.l., Digital Forensic Research Workshop.

Resnick, B. (2017). *Why Houston's Flooding got so Bad, According to Storm Experts* [Online]. Available at: https://www.vox.com/science-and-health/2017/8/29/16216568/hurricane-havery-houston-flooding-experts; https://www.vox.com/science-and-health/2017/8/29/16216568/hurricane-havery-houston-flooding-experts [accessed 10 July, 2021].

Roy, B. (2016). *Social vs. Traditional Media: Has the Battle Already Ended?* [Online]. Available at: https://apps.prsa.org/Intelligence/Tactics/Articles/view/11445/1124/Social_vs_Traditional_Media_Has_the_Battle_Already#.YQ3EwYhKhyw; https://apps.prsa.org/Intelligence/Tactics/Articles/view/11445/1124/Social_vs_Traditional_Media_Has_the_Battle_Already#.YQ3EwYhKhyw [accessed 7 August, 2021].

Roy, B. (2016). *Social vs. Traditional Media: Has the Battle Already Ended?*. [Online] [accessed 8 August, 2021].

Shu, K., Mahudeswaran, D., Wang, S. and Liu, D.L.A.H. (2018). *FakeNewsNet: A Data Repository with News Content, Social Context and Dynamic Information for Studying Fake News on Social Media.* s.l.: Research Gate.

*The Independent*. (2018). *Final Say: The Misinformation that was Told about Brexit During and After the Referendum* [Online]. Available at: https://www.independent.co.uk/news/uk/politics/ final-say-brexit-referendum-lies-boris-johnson-leave-campaign-remain-a8466751.html; https:// www.independent.co.uk/news/uk/politics/final-say-brexit-referendum-lies-boris-johnson-leave-campaign-remain-a8466751.html [accessed 4 July, 2021].

*The Telegraph*. (2021). *Fake News – What Exactly is It and How You can Spot It* [Online]. Available at: https://www.telegraph.co.uk/technology/0/fake-news-exactly-donald-trump-rise/; https://www. telegraph.co.uk/technology/0/fake-news-exactly-donald-trump-rise/ [accessed 13 July, 2021].

Tilbury, J. (2017). *Technology (and the Internet): Mitigating Fake News – A Systematic Literature Review of Disinformation, Misinformation and Fake News Propagation and Detection mechanisms in Social Media.* s.l.: s.n.

UNESCO. (2018). *Journalism, Fake News & Disinformation: Handbook for Journalism Education and Training*, Paris: UNESCO.

*USA TODAY*. (2017). *Hurricane Harvey: That Shark Photo is Fake—and Part of a Bigger Problem* [Online]. Available at: https://eu.usatoday.com/story/news/nation/2017/08/29/hurricane-harvey-shark-photo-fake-and-part-bigger-problem/612601001/; https://eu.usatoday.com/story/news/ nation/2017/08/29/hurricane-harvey-shark-photo-fake-and-part-bigger-problem/612601001/ [accessed 10 July. 2021].

Woodhouse, J. (2021). *Regulating Online Harms.* London: House of Commons Library.

Wu, L., Morstatter, F., Carley, K.M. and Liu, A.H. (n.d). *Misinformation in Social Media: Definition, Manipulation and Detection* [Online]. Available at: https://www.kdd.org/exploration_files/8._ CR.10.Misinformation_in_social_media_-_Final.pdf; https://www.kdd.org/exploration_files/8._ CR.10.Misinformation_in_social_media_-_Final.pdf [accessed 10 July, 2021].

www.parliament.uk. (2019). *Parliamentary Business* [Online]. Available at: https://publications. parliament.uk/pa/cm201719/cmselect/cmcumeds/1791/179104.htm#_idTextAnchor001; https://publications.parliament.uk/pa/cm201719/cmselect/cmcumeds/1791/179104.htm#_ idTextAnchor001 [accessed 14 April, 2019].

# 3

# Data Protection and Privacy in the Ambient Assisted Living System for Patients with Mild Cognitive Impairment*

*David Josef Herzog*

## ABSTRACT

The demographic change with an ageing population and lengthening active life creates an additional demand for healthcare. The combination of telemedicine, electronic health records, smart home technologies and the Internet of Things form the background for the affordable home-based healthcare component. Ambient Assisted Living (AAL) is a developing part of the modern healthcare system. As a technology-reach area, it has specific data protection issues. Healthcare records have high priority. The current chapter presents an overview of the topic and relevant results of an online questionnaire for healthcare stakeholders regarding patient's privacy in AAL for people with mild cognitive impairment.

## 1. Introduction

Ambient Assisted Living is a health-oriented extension of the smart home system. The cyber-physical space encompasses sensors, actuators, networks and computing devices. Sensors' reach data collection environment is coupled with networks and empowered with data processing computing units, which enable the possibility to

University Fernando Pessoa, Praça 9 de Abril, 349, Porto, Portugal-37491.
Email: herzogs@gmail.com
* The results of group comparison from the response on the online questionnaire for healthcare stakeholders.

support a patient and to keep healthcare stakeholders informed about the immediate health condition and the current medical history (Acampora et al., 2013). Permanent and wearable sensors of different types are included for registering vital signs, positioning, security and domestic environment control. Networks, from Body Area Networks (BAN) to external connections, cover different designated areas and facilitate data transmission. All data is provided to computing units. They can be represented by smartphone, tablet, laptop, PC on the patient's side and server on the service-provider side. Solutions as Edge computing and Fog computing are also used to speed-up data transfer and processing in order to shorten the distance between sensors and the cloud. AAL system also can include smart devices, ranging from domotics to smart medical gadgets (Rashidi et al., 2012). COTS, commercial off-the-shelf systems, are often proposed to lessen the price tag of the AAL system and allow customization. In the COTS systems, Single-Board Computers (SBC) are often used for the combination of network and computing applications. The system is run with help of a number of software applications and environments, united by middleware. Data protection and privacy are fundamental principles for AAL exploitation. Every element of AAL handling data can be vulnerable to leaks or loss. The health condition of the patient also has to be considered from the data protection and privacy view angle.

Mild Cognitive Impairment, MCI, or Mild Neurodegenerative Disorder (MND), is a cognitive condition with a stable level of intellectual functions, declined from normal and measured by IQ, which is between 70 and 85 (Kaplan and Sadock, 2020). While MCI can be transitory between normal cognition and dementia, this pathology may stay on for years and the condition, in some cases, can improve. Patients in the older age group are more prone to have MCI and dementia. According to WHO, there is a quickly growing number of patients with dementia and MCI (WHO, 2021). Currently, 55 million people worldwide suffer from dementia only. The projection is 75 million in 2030 and 132 million by 2050. While dementia is a condition which often requires permanent personal supervision and often institutionalization of the patient, MCI gives an opportunity for relatively independent living. The ambient assisted living system for MCI patients has to include specific measures for privacy, security and data protection.

## 2.  Data Protection in AAL—The Field Review

The health data is supposed to have high sensitivity level. The Ambient Assisted Living system handles a significant amount of the information and shares it with several stakeholders. Despite the efforts to support end-to-end security in the AAL system, for example, by eXtensible Access Control Language (XACML) (Vlamings and Koster, 2010), there are multiple issues that require solution before the AAL system will be claimed safe and secure.

The AAL system is based on the smart home and IoT. One of the important issues is the preference of wireless solutions for the convenience of the end-users: patients and caregivers. Besides technical problems with limited computational and energy capacity, these create difficulties for data protection and full-fledged encoding.

There are potential security issues: attacks on secrecy, authentication, silent attacks on service integrity and attacks at network availability or DoS (Marques et al., 2017). The DoS attacks can be performed on several layers: physical, link, network, transport and application.

There are several steps in the data handling processes, which are connected to data protection and security. Every step is connected to a certain layer in the architecture (Koutli et al., 2019). Authentication and authorization, integrity, privacy is related to the Application and Network layers.

Confidentiality, encryption involves, in addition, the Physical layer, while trust is related to the Network layer.

There are three security levels in the WBAN IEEE 802.15.6 standard: unsecured level 0; authentication only, level 1; authentication and encryption, level 2 (Rashidi and Mihalidis, 2012).

The Security in IoT can be conceptualized as a number of principles: mutual authentication, anonymity, non-traceability, no verification/password table, session key agreement, perfect forward secrecy and attack resistance (He and Zeadally, 2015).

The IoT AAL systems include a lot of devices with the necessity to recognize each other (Čaušević et al., 2017). This matter together with the frequent necessity to use wearable sensors prone to battery failures and with limited encoding capabilities make AAL a safety-critical system for unintentional risks and intentional threats. For example, insulin and medication infusion pumps are vulnerable to attack, with an immediate effect.

In the IoT, the devices often communicate with each other by means of the Internet. In addition, sensors, which collect information from the environment, are reachable from outside (Hail and Fisher, 2015). While the end-to-end principle is widely accepted, Information-Centric Networking (ICN) can be a partial solution for data protection in the AAL. ICN is based on the Named Data Objects (NDO), where objects keep their names regardless of location, storage or means of coping and communication (Ahlgren et al., 2012). In some ICN designs name and data, integrity can be verified without a Public Key Infrastructure (PKI). There are proposals to employ the InterPlanetary File System (IPFS), blockchain and smart contracts for trustless transactions in the AAL (Mkpa et al., 2019). Another solution is to use fog computing in the privacy and security-driven AAL architecture (Dmitrievsky et al., 2019). The fog and edge computing shorten the connection link for part of the data in the IoT or AAL; hence, making it safer. In addition to it, the gateway data aggregation with PKI encryption-decryption is proposed (Doukas et al., 2012).

There is a strong requirement by the end-users to control the data (van Heek et al., 2017). The privacy problem is exacerbated by the obtrusive nature of AAL, generating an enormous volume of sensitive information and location systems tracking (Beresford and Stajano, 2003). There are two approaches to privacy issues (Hong and Landay, 2004): the first is built on the framework development; the second is based on the end-user capacity to control personal information and user anonymity. Some authors advocate an institutional approach rooted in the recurrent patterns of social roles and relationships.

Several principles are applied to the privacy issues in data handling (Koutli et al., 2019). Privacy by design has to orient on: data minimization, data anonymization, distributed data storage and processing, standardization, encryption and Right to be Forgotten, to name just the main ones.

There are some concerns about the Right to be Forgotten in AI-powered AAL (Villaronga et al., 2018). One of the solutions is PAML, Privacy-Aware Machine Learning. The other is Long Short-Term Memory (LSTM) Encoder-Decoder for Deep Learning (Psychoula et al., 2018).

# 3. AAL Projects

Ambient assisted living is seen as one of the main methods of healthcare supervision for many home-based independent senior adults and partially-able patients. In recent years, numerous AAL concepts were proposed and numerous projects were implemented and tested.

There is no clear convention on what is called the AAL system, AAL project or AAL platform. The platform can be the basis for several projects, as OpenAAL or UniversAAL. Project is often an original concept with implementation and several variations. Systems can be understood as parts of the whole AAL, described above, when it is also a combination of subsystems. The detailed description makes it clearer but does not fully remove the difference in the terminology used. For example, AALIANCE project is a combined effort of several stakeholders to develop a number of AAL frameworks (http://www.aaliance.eu).

AAL systems may differ in the complexity, type of targeted pathology, technical solutions, level of security, the involvement of stakeholders, price of implementation and support and a number of other parameters (Memon et al., 2014). In order to describe typical AAL systems, several projects were chosen to represent more or less standard solutions.

## 3.1 CASAS

One of the best-known long-term AAL projects is CASAS. The project is run in the Center for Advanced Studies in Adaptive Systems (CASAS) of the Washington State University. There are numerous publications made by WSU researchers about smart cities, smart home technologies, AAL healthcare applications.

CASAS concentrates on the MCI and dementia patients. ADL and IADL are registered by the non-invasive sensor networks and analyzed by reasoning agents (Rashidi and Mihailidis, 2013). There are works produced by the Center, where ADL recognition is enhanced by smartphone sensors, additional context-aware reasoning with coupled HMM. The method is applied for the multi-person condition (Roy et al., 2016).

CASAS is often mentioned not only for its research but also as a source of one of the most comprehensive datasets (http://casas.wsu.edu/datasets) of ADL, data collection tools, synthetic sensor-based data, created with the help of machine learning (ML) (Dahmen and Cook, 2019).

## 3.2 PERSONA

European AAL project PERSONA (Perceptive Spaces prOmoting iNdepentent Aging) encompasses a number of technological initiatives, focused on the creation of affordable, fully-fledged, flexible and scalable AAL environments. The main purpose is to provide a comfortable environment for independent senior citizens. Assisted living is perceived as a physical, technical, social support for patients and relatives. PERSONA support can be extended and be available in part, outside the residential home, in the community environment.

The PERSONA works with various sensors: embedded, positioning sensors, smart textiles and can be interacted by LCD touchscreens and voice recognition (Colomer et al., 2014). In PERSONA, environment computational devices have distributed computing power by using gateways (Tazari et al., 2010). However, proposed 3D posture registration by Time-of-Flight (ToF) cameras reduces privacy, overloading the system without significant achievement in the quality of service (QoS) or clinical necessity.

## 3.3 SOPRANO

Service-oriented Programmable Smart Environments for Older Europeans (SOPRANO) is an international European project. The goal is to address the demands of the ageing population for independent living and create a comfortable smart environment with abilities to support, to predict and to react in the case of an emergency.

A number of sensors are used to monitor safety and activity: temperature sensor, smoke alarm, RFID, magnetic and positioning sensors. The system is built to inform about falls, home emergencies, health status, physical and social functioning. A number of reminders help to maintain the medication regime and daily routine. SOPRANO is focused on iterative user involvement There is an ability to control electric appliances with remote control, as well as the system itself (Bierhoff et al., 2013). SOPRANO is partially developed by the Fraunhofer Research Organization, as well as a number of other projects (AMIGO).

## 3.4 AMIGO

Ambient Intelligence for the Networked Home Environment (AMIGO) is an international collaboration project. The main idea behind it was to integrate electronic and electric devices in the smart home for implementing it in the most appropriate integral way and simplify control. Interoperability of devices includes PC and mobile phones. AMIGO was first oriented on the fully functional technologies, which helped to control domotic devices, security and bill payments. In the process of development, other functions were added to be more acceptable for aged people with partial disabilities (Baquero et al., 2012).

AMIGO might be recognized as not fully functional AAL with pre-elements of IoT. The project was finalized in 2008 and its findings became part of the UniversAAL system.

### 3.5  MPOWER

The project was initiated more than a decade ago and has objectives to build Service-Oriented AAL Architecture (SOA), inter-operable with Google Health. MPOWER register activities and emergencies, communicate with healthcare services and allow audio and voice interaction. Electronic health records (EHR) utilize Extensible Stylesheet Language Transformations (XSLT). XML is suitable for the used SOAP protocol (Mikalsen et al., 2009). Interoperability is one of the main purposes of the MPOWER middleware. Additional functions are sensors' information with context awareness, security service and medical information service.

### 3.6  OASIS

OASiS is an Object-centric, Ambient-aware, Service-oriented Sensornet programming framework for WSN applications. It is a European international project for independent elderly life. The aim is to integrate all relevant areas of activity into automated services' platform: e-work, e-learning, transport, domotics and healthcare. OASIS helps to regulate the social and physical activity, monitor the environment, advice on nutrition, control and report vital signs. The home environment has sensors for activity and movement monitoring (Bekiaris and Bonfiglio, 2009).

Reaction to physical change initiates the services' response. Modular, autonomous, object-oriented, ambient-aware applications are run on the basis of graphs of services (Koutsoukos et al., 2008).

### 3.7  UniversAAL

The UniversAAL open platform and reference Specification for Ambient Assisted Living (SAAL) include best parts of other projects: AMIGO, GENESYS, OASIS, PERSONA, SOPRANO, MPOWER (Ram et al., 2013). An integrated part of the SOPRANO, the openAAL platform, also provides components for the UniversAAL. UniversAAL allows stakeholders, including relatives, to enter the system, yet security is one of the platform's objectives.

### 3.8  eCAALYX

Complete Ambient Assisted Living Experiment (CAALYX) is an original European project. It includes three subsystems: the Roaming Monitoring, the Home Monitoring and the Central Care Service. The home system has numerous sensors, domotic devices, computing units and communication channels, VoIP and video contact through the TV set. Home system, besides monitoring the health condition and reporting emergency issues (fall, etc.), has the ability to control devices, schedule daily activities and support necessary contacts (Boulos et al., 2007).

The roaming monitoring system is a wearable device, wearable sensors and WBAN plus mobile phone with GPS. This subsystem is functional indoors and outdoors.

The central care system has computing units with soft and UI for healthcare staff. It is connected with two other subsystems over the Internet and helps to establish telemedical care via direct contact with a patient and technical control.

eCAALYX is built on the Android platform and iOS application was considered. While smartphone role is important, battery life, inappropriate handling, unwanted updates and system reloads have to be considered.

## 3.9 Dem@Care

Dem@Care is long-term European AAL project for people with MCI and dementia, their relatives and involved healthcare professionals. The system is adapted to the specific needs of people with memory loss and cognitive impairment. At the same time, Ambient Intelligence (AmI) and pervasive computing allow ADL registration and partial analysis. Dem@Care collects enough information to present datasets online: http://www.demcare.eu/results/datasets.

ADL is recognized primarily through the sensors: motion sensors, smart plugs, sleep monitor. There are also IR camera, a depth camera and wearable RGB camera. There are a number of typical scenarios recognized by a depth camera, with Complex Activity Recognition (CAR), for example, standing, walking, sitting. Microcomputers in a number of nodes are attached to the camera. IR camera has Human Activity Recognition (HAR): eating, drinking, reading, watching TV, writing, taking medications. Information is recognized and compared with the normal/abnormal dataset. There is also a wearable wireless microphone. The speech is analyzed by Offline Speech Analysis (OSA) (Stavropoulos et al., 2014).

Other Dem@Care dataset experiments are concentrated on the motion behavior of patients with AD (Bian et al., 2018). In addition to mentioned sensors, there are Gear4 Sleep Clock, Aura Sleep Sensor, UP24 wrist accelerator, tags. All are integrated into the DemaWare2 framework (Stavropoulos et al., 2017).

The Dem@Care project is an impressive application of ambient technology and IT for patients with AD and MCI. Datasets are the foundation for further research and development. However, there are some reservations in connection with extensive use of cameras and microphone, which can undermine the patient's privacy.

## 3.10 SAAPHO

Secure Active Aging Participation and Health for the Old (SAAPHO) is AAL project with user-centred design (UCD). The Android-powered tablet is the dialogue entrepot for the user. Touch Screen is chosen for easy operation by tech novice. The decision is based on questionnaires (http://www.aal-europe.eu/projects/saapho).

The health-monitoring data is stored in the Health Intelligent Server (HIS). There is a Historical Calculation Health Service, which allows to follow up changes in controlled parameters: blood pressure (BP). glucose level, weight. All fluctuations are registered and those outside of the norm are indicated by the system. Besides the report to the healthcare stakeholder, the system can address these issues by automatic recommendations for the medication intake or nutrition advice (Ahmed, 2017).

### 3.11  BelAmI

Bilateral German-Hungarian Collaboration Project on Ambient Intelligence Systems (BelAmI) is an AAL for use in home care. The system is well conceptualized on a general level. The practical lab was run to prove the concept of the Ambient Home Care Systems (AHCS). At the basis of the system are placed the number of principles, when AAL with AmI is embedded, pervasive, invisible; context-aware; anticipatory; adaptive; mobile; heterogeneous and hierarchical (Kleinberger et al., 2007).

There is a proposed element of the AAL, RFID-supplied system for the food-freshness monitoring, smart refrigerator. Another application is a smart ECG system (Havasi and Kiss, 2008).

BelAmI AAL is oriented on enhancing comfort and autonomy, and at the same time is able to handle emergency data. It can register activity, position and report about important events: change in the registered vital signs, security alert, medication non-compliance. As a system, it has the ability for the self-optimization, self-configuration and self-maintenance (Nehmer et al., 2006).

### 3.12  Other AAL Projects

Ambient assisted living had been proposed decades ago and in the last few years, many frameworks and systems were put for scrutiny. While most of the projects are run in limited time settings, some of them, for example, CASAS, Dem@Care, UniversAAL are developing further.

There is no scope to go through all the proposed schemes thoroughly; however, some of them can be mentioned, especially when they have certain notable solution or novel approach.

**PersonAAL** is an ongoing project, focused on online applications and capable to assist the patient in the AAL environment. One of the directions for the project is End-User Development with frameworks, such as 'IF This Then That' (IFTTT) and TARE (Topology Adaptive Re-kEying scheme) platform for IoT (Corcella et al., 2019). PersonAAL allows personalization and detection of the anomalous behavior (Manca et al., 2017).

**DOREMI** is focused more on the social and psychological aspects. It monitors heart rate (HR), number of steps by DOREMI wristband, weight and balance by balance board, the position through the sensors and social activity with help of a smartphone. DOREMI developed stimergy signatures monitoring to holistically register caloric balance, ADL and socio-psychological activity (Palumbo et al., 2016).

**UbiCare** is a low-cost AAL system, where contextual registration of ADL is made through the numerous sensors and IoT items. For privacy reasons, cameras and microphones are excluded. There are no PC, laptop or smartphone as computing units. All data and connections are handled by Arduino microcomputers and Xbee, ZigBee modules (Dasios et al., 2015).

**AMICA** is a telemedical AAL project, concentrated on the home-based Congestive Obstructive Pulmonary Disease (COPD) patients. It features wearable sensors for the ECG and microphone for the pulmonary sounds registration (Gaspar et al., 2015).

**gAALaxy** is a current project, which bundles together existing solutions for AAL and smart home with cloud-based middleware. The project is market-oriented (Ates et al., 2017).

There are different center points for AAL systems. DynAMITE and SENSATION-AAL are recognised as agent-based, while EMBASSI, MAP, SmartKom are monolithic intelligent systems (Byrne et al., 2018).

**AMIVital** is oriented on the development of a business model for AAL; VAALID is concentrated on the computing and engineering tools; REMOTE is designed for people with chronic conditions, but living at a distance from the healthcare providers and CogWatch is specifically focused on the group of patients, suffering from apraxia (Colomer et al., 2014).

A wide range of European projects is listed at the portal http://www.aal-europe. eu/projects, while many AAL platforms are members of the national programs. Austrian ModuLAAr (a modular and scalable AAL system as lifestyle element for silver-ager up to assisted living), West-AAL, ZentrAAL, RegionAAL, WAALTeR and Smart VitAALity have regional division and some specific characteristics (Byrne et al., 2018).

Other projects feature some specific aims. ALICE is designed for patients with visual impairment, DIET4Elders on ADL monitoring and support, EDLAH on object location, ELF@Home on fitness, FEARLESS – emergency situations, WIISEL is focused on the gate and ADL analysis, while MOBISERV is a personal robotic system (Nani et al., 2010).

## 4. Comparative Analysis

Descriptive analysis of the whole set results gives sufficient information for the following analysis and preliminary conclusions. A more profound way is to divide the set into groups and make a comparative analysis. For comparison, descriptive and correlation analysis is informative. Correlation for non-parametric data can be found with help of Mann-Whitney-Wilcoxon test and Kruskal–Wallis test (Kvam and Vidakovic, 2007). Mann-Whitney-Wilcoxon Test checks the equality of two ordinal sets of data. Sets can be of unequal size. MWW test calculates 'unbiased' U parameter. It checks the equality of distribution and the supposed independence of

sets. $U = N_x N_y + N_x \dfrac{(N_x + 1)}{2} - \sum R_x$ where $N_x$ is set X, $N_y$ is set Y and $R$ is the sum of ranks. Precision of the test is lower with significant difference between sets. There is a possibility for type II error in this case.

Kruskal-Wallis test or one-way rank analysis of variance (ANOVA) calculates H parameter to test the mutual dependency of datasets. KW test is designed for two or more sets. The size of datasets can be unequal because the calculation does not involve paired comparison.

$$H = \frac{12}{n(n+1)} \sum_{x=1}^{m} \frac{R_x^2}{n_x} - 3(n+1)$$

where $n$ is certain dataset power, $m$ is number of groups, $R_x$ is rank of $x$ and $x$ is number of the dataset.

Two or more samples are compared. Big differences between sets size can cause type I error, giving false positive results.

# 5. Research

## 5.1 Method

Medical and social requirements for the AAL are formulated at the conceptual stage. There are several ways to find answers, theoretical and practical. Any route gives only partial vision. The needs of caretakers and healthcare stakeholders are collected through questionnaires and expert suggestions. The process can be iterative, mixed and include detailed recommendations. The best approach is to try to encompass all these raised problems in one research to weigh and compare information between sub-questions. In conditions of limited research, complex questionnaire for healthcare stakeholders is the easiest way to obtain necessary preliminary answers. Web-based questionnaire is easy to deliver worldwide. In current research, Google Forms-based questionnaire was used.

## 5.2 Reliability

Questionnaire was tested on several runs before wide implementation. Reliability of the questionnaire is checked in Jasp 0.14.0.0. – for scaled questions. The values in the questionnaire are: for Cronbach's it is 0.920; for McDonald's it is $\alpha \omega$ 0.934; for Guttman's 2 it is 0.932. Values above 0.9 may reflect (a) redundancy of the $\lambda$ test—there are specially added questions in some dimensions to recheck values of the responses, (b) multidimensionality of the test. 15 questions with opposite scales and negative results in the table were excluded from analysis.

## 5.3 Focus Group

The Ambient Assisted Living system design has to be based on the opinion of the main stakeholders: healthcare professionals, technical stakeholders, administrative stakeholders and patients. Every opinion group is important, and the opinion has to be assessed appropriately.

Healthcare professionals represent a specific cross-section of society with a skilled understanding of patient's needs in specific conditions. Years of focused training and practice give a wealth of information about the needs and problems of home-based patients. Still, there is a range of possible opinions, dictated by professional view, personal experience and wide scope of technical, social and organizational knowledge.

This study is based on a complex questionnaire. The questionnaire is presented to the healthcare workers, mainly medical doctors. In order to achieve the best possible combination, heterogeneous groups of medical professionals from different countries are included. In order to obtain as much and as wide information as possible and to keep the sample big enough despite complexity of the questionnaire, all specialists with finished medical education or clinical psychology diploma were considered.

The respondents were reached via web of personal contacts and with help of social media. The main reason was to eliminate subjective element of self-report about profession and professional experience.

More than three hundred medical specialists were contacted in the USA, Canada, UK, the Netherlands, Germany, Switzerland, Sweden, Greece, Israel, Armenia, Ukraine, Belarus and Russian Federation and asked to answer the questionnaire. Around 120 agreed to participate, of whom 60 answered all the questions. Those who did not finish the questionnaire named several reasons for it: unknown topic, the length and complex nature of the questionnaire, heavy workload and shortage of time because of the COVID-19 pandemic. Country name was removed from the questionnaire for reasons of required anonymity. However, there was no informally registered difference in the approach of specialists, depending on the country of practice or residence.

Age and gender were collected for statistical necessities. The age was from 21 to 63, with the average age of 49.9 years.

**Table 1:** Age and gender structure.

|  | Number | Minimal-Maximal | Mean, Years | Median | Mode |
|---|---|---|---|---|---|
| **Age** | 60 | 21–63 | 49.9 | 50 | 50 |
| **Gender: F** | 29 | 21–60 | 49.0 | 50 | 50 |
| **Gender: M** | 31 | 42–63 | 50.7 | 50 | 49 |

## 5.4 Groups

There are several principles of group formation. The main idea is an ability of comparative analysis with potential counterpart groups in accordance with created thematic axes. In the current research potential groups for comparative analysis are listed below:

1. The group of psychiatrists, neurologists, geriatricians, family doctors, medical psychologists.

2. The group of respondents who have professional experience with MCI dementia and patients.

3. The group with hospital work/experience. Another grouping: family and visiting specialists vs non-visiting.

4. The group of mentioned clinical experience.

5. The group of IT proficient and advanced users.

6. The group of university-educated medical specialists.

### 5.4.1 Psychiatrists and Close Specialists

There were nine psychiatrists and narcologists, three neurologists, two geriatric consultants, one family doctor and three clinical psychologists between respondents. It would be reasonable to unite them as most competent in understanding and treatment of MCI condition. The group can be narrowed into psychiatrists only, Psy group, N = 9; psychiatrists, neurologists and geriatricians, PNG group, N = 14; psychiatrists, neurologists, geriatricians and associated professionals, such as clinical psychologists and GP, N = 18. The potential counterpart groups are described in the table below:

**Table 2:** Groups.

| Members of the Group | Size of the Group | Abbreviated Name | Average Age, Years | Main Counterpart Group |
|---|---|---|---|---|
| Psychiatrists, neurologists and geriatricians | N = 14 | PNG | 52.2 | Non-PNG |
| All respondents other than PNG | N = 46 | Non-PNG | 49.2 | PNG |
| Psychiatrists | N = 9 | Psy | 53.1 | Non-PNG Non-PNG&AP |
| Psychiatrists, neurologists, geriatricians and associated professionals, such as psychologists and GP | N = 18 | PNG&AP | 52.0 | Non-PNG&AP |
| All respondents other than PNG&AP | N = 42 | Non-PNG&AP | 49.0 | PNG&AP PNG Psy |

There are a number of statements on which these groups' MWW test p-value is less than 0.05, with Vovk-Sellke maximum p-ratio (MPR) 2.46 and above. There are also statements with p-value for MWW from 0.05 to 0.1 and KW p-values often less than 0.05. Statements with p-values between 0.05 and 0.1 for MWW test and higher than 0.05 for KW test are excluded from further investigations. For current chapter, three relevant statements were chosen:

(1) Section 9, statement E) 'Video camera and microphone can be used in AAL for patients with mild cognitive impairment. for communication only.'

(2) Section 12, statement C) 'Patient's health and privacy are equally important in AAL.'

(3) Section 12, statement F) 'Emotionally sensitive patients are not advised to live in a home with the AAL system.'

### 5.4.1.1  Psychiatrists vs Non-PNG and Non-PNG & AP Groups

**Table 3a** showing main descriptive for Psy group and MWW&KW results for Psy vs Non-PNG (p-value 1) and Psy vs Non-PNG&AP (p-value 2).

| Statement | Mean Psy | Median Psy | Mode Psy | More Positive or Sceptical | MWW p-value 1 | KW p-value 1 | MWW p-value 2 | KW p-value 2 |
|---|---|---|---|---|---|---|---|---|
| (1) | 4.1 | 3 | 1 | + | 0.067 | 0.041 | 0.083 | 0.123 |
| (2) | 4.2 | 5 | 2 | – | 0.009 | 0.006 | 0.007 | 0.008 |
| (3) | 3 | 2 | 2 | – | 0.034 | 0.037 | 0.024 | 0.051 |

**Commentary**

Respondents from the group Psy are positively disposed towards the AAL system for MCI patients. In some statements (1) they have a more positive outlook with fewer limitations than counterparts. Statement (2) shows primary concerns with patients' health, which is seen as more important than privacy in the group. Statement (3) reflects experience with emotionally sensitive patients and assurance that AAL system is suitable for them.

### 5.4.1.2  Psychiatrists, Neurologists and Geriatricians, PNG vs Non-PNG

**Table 3b** showing statements used from the previous section.

| Statement | Mean PNG | Median PNG | Mode PNG | More Positive or Sceptical | MWW p-value | KW p-value |
|---|---|---|---|---|---|---|
| (1) | 4.3 | 3 | 1 | + | 0.038 | 0.033 |
| (2) | 4.9 | 5 | 2 | – | 0.018 | 0.013 |
| (3) | 5.4 | 5 | 4 | – | 0.860 | 0.253 |

**Commentary**

The PNG group shares an opinion with Psy group in comparison with differences in non-PNG specialists on statements (1) and (2).

### 5.4.1.3  Psychiatrists, Neurologists, Geriatricians and Associated Professionals PNG&AP vs Non-PNG&AP

Associated professionals include GP and clinical psychologists.

**Table 4:** PNG&AP vs Non-PNG&AP.

| Statement | Mean PNG&AP | Median PNG&AP | Mode PNG&AP | More Positive or Sceptical | MWW p-value | KW p-value |
|---|---|---|---|---|---|---|
| (1) | 5 | 4 | 1 | +/– | 0.153 | 0.123 |
| (2) | 5.4 | 5 | 5 | –/+ | 0.065 | 0.059 |
| (3) | 4.8 | 4.5 | 2 | –/+ | 0.896 | 0.920 |

## Commentary

There is some skepticism shown for statement (2). Health and privacy are not seen by respondents as equally important.

### 5.4.2 Respondents with Experience of Contact with MCI and Dementia Patients

Responses were allowed on more than one option. Groups are formed in accordance with the sole answer or first answers in the table. There are:

1. 49 respondents who have professional or outside duties contact with MCI or dementia patients. This number includes 35 respondents with routine contacts, 11 with main experience in the specialised institutes and three respondents with main experience outside of duties.
2. 11 respondents have primarily rare or no contact.
3. 35 respondents have contact as part of a medical routine.
4. 11 respondents have claimed main experience with institutionalized or home-based patients.

Three respondents' primary experience as outside of duties.

The following groups are formed:

(1) Routine medical experience (RME) with MCI patients, N = 35;
(2) Institutional experience and with home-based patients (IE), N = 11;
(3) Medical and institutional (MIE) experience, N = 46 (RME+IE, 35+11);
(4) Rare or no experience with MCI patients (NoE), N = 11;
(5) Experience (any) with (Ex) MCI patients, N = 49.

**Table 5:** Respondents with experience of contact with MCI and dementia patients.

|  | Size of the Group | Abbreviated Name | Average Age | Main Counterpart Group |
|---|---|---|---|---|
| Routine medical experience | N = 35 | RME | 50.5 | NoE No-MIE |
| Institutional experience | N = 11 | IE | 48.8 | Non-IE NoE |
| Medical and institutional experience | N = 46 | MIE | 50.1 | No-MIE |
| Rare or no experience with MCI patients | N = 11 | NoE | 48.8 | IE Ex |
| Experience (any) with MCI patients | N = 49 | Ex | 50.1 | NoE |
| No medical and institutional experience | N = 14 | No-MIE | 49.2 | RME MIE |
| No institutional experience | N = 49 | Non-IE | 50.1 | IE |

5.4.2.1 Relevant Statements

There are a number of statements on which these groups MWW test p-value as less than 0.1, with Vovk-Sellke maximum p-ratio (MPR) 1.6 and above. Every statement showed the required p-value at least once in one paired comparison.

(1) Section 12 A) 'Patient's health is more important than privacy issues in AAL.'

(2) Section 12 F) 'Emotionally sensitive patients are not advised to live in a home with the AAL system.'

In Table 6 is shown MWW p-value for every paired comparison.

**Table 6:** MWW paired comparison results.

| Statement | RME vs NoE | Ex vs NoE | MIE vs No-MIE | RME vs No-MIE | IE vs Non-IE | MIE vs NoE | IE vs NoE | Pairs with p-value > 0.1 |
|---|---|---|---|---|---|---|---|---|
| (1) | 0.106 | 0.145 | 0.052 | 0.052 | 0.952 | 0.109 | 0.313 | MIE vs No-MIE RME vs No-MIE |
| (2) | 0.128 | 0.133 | 0.036 | 0.068 | 0.424 | 0.080 | 0.072 | MIE vs No-MIE RME vs No-MIE MIE vs NoE IE vs NoE |

**Table 7:** Significant groups' paired comparison by statements.

| Statement | Pairs with p-value > 0.1 | MWW p-value | KW p-value | Relevant Mean | Relevant Median | Relevant Mode | More Positive or Skeptical |
|---|---|---|---|---|---|---|---|
| (1) | MIE vs No-MIE | 0.052 | 0.051 | 6.6 | 6 | 5 | –/+ |
| (1) | RME vs No-MIE | 0.052 | 0.051 | 6.5 | 6 | 5 | –/+ |
| (2) | MIE vs No-MIE | 0.036 | 0.036 | 4.4 | 4 | 4 | –/+ |
| (2) | RME vs No-MIE | 0.068 | 0.066 | 4.5 | 4 | 5 | –/+ |
| (2) | MIE vs NoE | 0.080 | 0.079 | 4.4 | 4 | 4 | –/+ |
| (2) | IE vs NoE | 0.072 | 0.067 | 4.1 | 4.5 | 6 | –/+ |

**Commentary**

Groups with routine medical experience and institutional experience are more concerned about privacy. Majority of groups with relevant medical and institutional experience give less support to the statement (2) 'Emotionally sensitive patients are not advised to live in a home with the AAL system.'

*5.4.3 Hospital and Non-hospital Experience*

11 respondents marked visiting or family medicine as the only option. 2 – ambulance service only; eight medical research or other activities; two hospital non-clinical;

22 hospital clinical only; 15 – hospital clinical experience with other experience. Groups can be formed as follows:

1. Hospital experience only, HEO, N = 22 respondents.
2. Hospital experience plus, HEP, N = 15 respondents.
3. Hospital experience united, HEU, N = 37 respondents, 1)+2).
4. Non-hospital main clinical experience only, NoH, N = 13 respondents.
5. Non-clinical or hospital non-clinical main experience only, NoCP N = 10 respondents.
6. Non-hospital main experience plus, NoHP N = 23 respondents, 4)+5).

**Table 8:** Hospital and non-hospital experience.

| Members of the Group | Size of the Group | Abbreviated Name | Average Age | Main Counterpart Group |
|---|---|---|---|---|
| Hospital experience only | N = 22 | HEO | 49.1 | HEP NoH |
| Hospital experience plus | N = 15 | HEP | 50.3 | HEO NoH |
| Hospital experience united | N = 37 | HEU | 49.6 | NoHP NoCP |
| Non-hospital main clinical experience only | N = 13 | NoH | 51.3 | HEO HEP |
| Non-clinical or hospital non-clinical main experience only | N = 10 | NoCP | 49.2 | HEU |
| Non-hospital main experience plus | N = 23 | NoHP | 50.4 | HEU |

### 5.4.3.1 Relevant Statements

There is a significant number of statements, on which these groups MWW test p-value is less than 0.06, with Vovk-Sellke maximum p-ratio (MPR) 2.18 and above. A level slightly higher than 0.05 is chosen for the KW test p-value differences. Every statement showed the required p-value at least once in one paired comparison.

(1) Section 8 H) 'AAL system for patients with mild cognitive impairment elements and devices have to be fully designed by specially designated engineering company.'
(2) Section 9 E) 'Video camera and microphone can be used in AAL for patients with mild cognitive impairment for communication only.'
(3) Section 12 A) 'Patient's health is more important than privacy issues in AAL.'
(4) Section 12 B) 'Privacy is more important than the patient's health in AAL.'
(5) Section 14 C) 'Patient's health and privacy are equally important in AAL.'

## 5.4.3.2 Groups Comparison

**Table 9:** MWW p-values for paired hospital experience groups in given statements.

|     | HEU vs NoHP | HEO vs HEP | HEO vs NoHP | HEU vs NoH | HEU vs NoCP |
|-----|-------------|------------|-------------|------------|-------------|
| (1) | 0.027 | 0.210 | 0.010 | 0.036 | 0.179 |
| (2) | 0.055 | 0.023 | 0.430 | 0.009 | 0.824 |
| (3) | 0.497 | 0.017 | 0.093 | 0.557 | 0.643 |
| (4) | 0.590 | 0.016 | 0.169 | 0.078 | 0.256 |
| (5) | 0.159 | 0.181 | 0.054 | 0.091 | 0.683 |

**Table 10:** Groups paired comparison with p-value less than 0.06 in MWW.

| Statement | Pair with p-value Less than 0.06 | MWW p-value | KW p-value | Relevant Mean | Relevant Median | Relevant Mode | More Positive or Sceptical |
|-----------|------------|-------------|------------|---------------|-----------------|---------------|----------------------------|
| (1) | HEU vs NoHP | 0.027 | 0.026 | 8.3 | 9 | 10 | +/– |
| (1) | HEO vs NoHP | 0.010 | 0.010 | 8.8 | 10 | 10 | +/– |
| (1) | HEU vs NoH | 0.036 | 0.035 | 8.3 | 9 | 10 | +/– |
| (2) | HEU vs NoHP | 0.055 | 0.054 | 6.4 | 8 | 8 | +/– |
| (2) | HEO vs HEP | 0.023 | 0.022 | 5.6 | 6.5 | 8 | –/+ |
| (2) | HEU vs NoH | 0.009 | 0.009 | 6.4 | 8 | 8 | +/– |
| (3) | HEO vs HEP | 0.017 | 0.016 | 6 | 5 | 5 | –/+ |
| (4) | HEO vs HEP | 0.016 | 0.016 | 5 | 5 | 5 | +/– |
| (5) | HEO vs NoHP | 0.054 | 0.053 | 7.5 | 8.5 | 10 | +/– |

**Commentary**

a. Three formally significant pairs' comparisons consist of HEO vs HEP testing. The hospital experience only (HEO) group usually holds a more sceptical position. Statements (2) and (3) demonstrate less sureness in the proposed approach. Statement (4) is negative and the HEO group supports them more. The group with hospital and external medical experience is more positively disposed towards AAL system and AAL system for MCI patients in most of the statements.

b. All groups with hospital experience are more medically astute and positive towards AAL system and AAL system for MCI patients than groups without hospital or clinical experience, as shown in statement (2). Technically these groups are also more on the side of fully-fledged technical development in the AAL system, as shown in statement (1). Answers on statement (5) appear more balanced than in the case of groups with psychiatric and associated medical experience.

*5.4.4  Clinical Experience*

51 respondents have direct clinical contact with patients, while nine have rare, indirect or no contact. Five out of nine have or had indirect medical contact, one respondent – personal administrative. One respondent claims no contact with patients. One – personal medico-technical. There are two groups of 51 and nine respondents.

**Table 11:** Clinical experience groups.

| Members of the Group | Size of the Group | Abbreviated Name | Average Age | Main Counterpart |
|---|---|---|---|---|
| Direct clinical contact with patients | N = 51 | CLEXP | 50.1 | NoCLEXP |
| Rare, indirect or no contact | N = 9 | NoCLEXP | 48.9 | CLEXP |

There are three statements, where p-value is lower than 0.1:

(1) Section 8, I) 'AAL system for patients with mild cognitive impairment is better to build from ready Commercial-Off-The-Shelf (COTS) elements and devices.'

**Table 12:** CLEXP vs NoCLEXP comparison.

| | MWW p-value | KW p-value | Mean 1 | Median 1 | Mode 1 | Mean 2 | Median 2 | Mode 2 | More Positive or Sceptical |
|---|---|---|---|---|---|---|---|---|---|
| (1) | 0.076 | 0.075 | 6.9 | 7 | 5 | 8.3 | 9 | 10 | –/+ |

**Commentary**

a. The difference between the two groups is related to statements with the technical load. There is no difference on all questions with emphasized healthcare components.

b. Group with clinical experience is consistently more sceptical about the possibility to make a COTS-based system.

*5.4.5  IT Proficiency*

Five respondents defined themselves as professional IT users, two – semi professional, 13 – advanced users. 40 defined themselves as normal or occasional users.

(1) Respondents with professional and semi-professional skills, PROF, N = 7.

(2) Respondents with advanced skills, ADV, N = 13.

(3) Combined group of respondents with professional and advanced skills, PROFADV, N = 20.

(4) Respondents with normal skills and occasional use of IT, NORMOC, N = 20.

**Table 13:** IT proficiency groups.

| Members of the Group | Size of the Group | Abbreviated Name | Average Age | Main Counterpart |
|---|---|---|---|---|
| Professional and semi-professional IT users | N = 7 | PROF | 49.6 | NORMOC ADV |
| Advanced IT users | N = 13 | ADV | 47.5 | NORMOC PROF |
| Professional and semi-professional with advanced users | N = 20 | PROFADV | 48.3 | NORMOC |
| Normal and occasional IT users | N = 40 | NORMOC | 50.7 | PROF ADV PROFADV |

### 5.4.5.1 Statements

(1) Section 8, K) 'Devices in the AAL system for MCI patients have to be only or mostly wired because it is hard to remember about charging all the batteries.'

(2) Section 9, C) 'The video camera and microphones are too invasive to be used 24 hours a day/seven days a week as AAL sensors for patients with Mild Cognitive Impairment.'

(3) Section 9, D) 'Video cameras and microphones can be used in AAL only for emergency.'

### 5.4.5.2 Groups Comparison

**Table 14:** IT proficiency—groups comparison by statements.

| Statement | PROF vs NORMOC | ADV vs NORMOC | PROFADV vs NORMOC | ADV vs PROF |
|---|---|---|---|---|
| (1) | 0.988 | 0.018 | 0.069 | 0.084 |
| (2) | 0.042 | 0.328 | 0.069 | 0.185 |
| (3) | 0.045 | 0.803 | 0.226 | 0.084 |

**Table 15:** IT proficiency—groups comparison by statements with p-value less than 0.1.

| | Group Pairs | MWW p-value | KW p-value | Relevant Mean | Relevant Median | Relevant Mode | More Positive or Sceptical |
|---|---|---|---|---|---|---|---|
| (1) | ADV vs NORMOC | 0.018 | 0.017 | 4.9 | 5 | 5 | −/+ |
| (1) | PROFADV vs NORMOC | 0.069 | 0.068 | 5.8 | 6 | 7 | −/+ |
| (1) | ADV vs PROF | 0.084 | 0.077 | 4.9 | 5 | 5 | −/+ |
| (2) | PROF vs NORMOC | 0.042 | 0.040 | 8.4 | 9 | 10 | +/− |
| (2) | PROFADV vs NORMOC | 0.069 | 0.068 | 7.5 | 8 | 8 | +/− |
| (3) | PROF vs NORMOC | 0.045 | 0.043 | 8.3 | 9 | 10 | +/− |
| (3) | ADV vs PROF | 0.084 | 0.077 | 6 | 7 | 7 | −/+ |

**Commentary**

a. Proficient users are more concerned with the invasive nature of video cameras and microphones, as seen in statements (2) and (3).

b. There is an interesting difference between professional and advanced users. Sometimes it manifests as separate concern about the statement, as seen in statement (2). In the number of cases the difference is significant, as in statement (3).

### 5.4.6 *Level of Medical Education*

40 medical doctors and two dental medicine doctors form a group of 42 specialists. 11 nurses, four paramedics and three clinical psychologists form a group of 18 respondents. While clinical experience is not a direct equivalent to the level of formal medical education, formal education may not fully reflect medical knowledge.

**Table 16:** Level of medical education—groups.

| Members of the Group | Size of the Group | Abbreviated Name | Average Age | Main Counterpart Group |
|---|---|---|---|---|
| 40 MD and 2 DMD | N = 42 | UNIM | 51.4 | Non-UNIM |
| Nurses, paramedics and clinical psychologists | N = 18 | Non-UNIM | 47.4 | UNIM |

#### 5.4.6.1 Statements

(1) Section 9, E) 'Video camera and microphone can be used in AAL for patients with mild cognitive impairment for communication only.'

#### 5.4.6.2 Comparison, MWW and KW Tests

**Table 17:** Comparison, MWW and KW tests for UNIM vs Non-UNIM.

| | MWW p-value | KW p-value | Mean 1 | Median 1 | Mode 1 | Mean 2 | Median 2 | Mode 2 | More Positive or Sceptical |
|---|---|---|---|---|---|---|---|---|---|
| 1) | 0.094 | 0.093 | 5.4 | 6 | 1 | 7 | 7.5 | 8 | –/+ |

**Commentary**

The UNIM group demonstrates more versatility in the understanding of video camera and microphone usage in AAL system for MCI patients.

# 6. Discussion

The results of the questionnaire reflect the specific experience of every formed group. The most involved professionals with psychiatric, geriatric and neurological knowledge and practice are positively disposed towards the possible implementation of the AAL for MCI patients. They are less concerned with the emotional sensitivity and privacy of patients and put the health of the patient before privacy. However, a wider group of professionals with experience with MCI patients, especially those with hospital experience, value privacy more. It can be connected to the nature of the hospital environment. As seen from the groups with wider than hospital experience, these specialists are less concerned with the privacy of the patient at home and more with a possibility to monitor health issues, which is less problematic in the hospital environment. The group with clinical experience is consistently more sceptical about the possibility to make a COTS-based system. Proficient IT users are more concerned with the invasive nature of video cameras and microphones.

There are some limitations to the study but the nature is extensive and reflects on several points about the general AAL and AAL system for MCI patients. There is no possibility to focus on every detail in depth. The number of respondents is relatively modest and the group division sometimes separates quite small groups. Another constrain is the technical nature of some questions, even though they are fully related to the medical context. These questions are asked from the respondents with limited or no serious experience in IT and AAL. Security questions often require deeper knowledge of the area and it is hard to expect it from the average healthcare stakeholder.

# 7. Conclusion

There are multiple issues connected to data security and personal privacy in ambient assisted living. Some health diagnoses, as mild cognitive impairment, add to the difficulty of data management because of the nature of the condition itself. All these problems require thorough research in order to find a number of acceptable solutions. The wide range of research, from the theoretical framework analysis and practical modelling to AAL systems surveys are the way to resolve data protection and privacy problems for all stakeholders.

# References

Acampora, G., Cook, D.J., Rashidi, P. and Vasilakos, A.V. (2013). A survey on ambient intelligence in healthcare. *Proceedings of the IEEE*, 101(12): 2470–2494.

Ahlgren, B., Dannewitz, C., Imbrenda, C., Kutscher, D. and Ohlman, B. (2012). A survey of information-centric networking. *IEEE Communications Magazine*, 50(7): 26–36.

Ates, N., Aumayr, G., Drobics, M., Förster, K.M., Frauenberger, C., Garschall, M., Kofler, M., Krainer, D., Kropf, J., Majcen, K. and Oberzaucher, J. (2017). Assistive solutions in practice: Experiences from AAL pilot regions in Austria. *Studies in Health Technology and Informatics*, 236: 184–195.

Baquero, R., Rodriguez, J., Mendoza, S., Decouchant, D. and Papis, A.P.M. (2012). Funblocks: A modular framework for AmI system development. *Sensors*, 12(8): 10259–10291.

Bekiaris, E. and Bonfiglio, S. (2009, July). The OASIS concept. *In: International Conference on Universal Access in Human-Computer Interaction*. Springer, Berlin, Heidelberg, pp. 202–209.

Beresford, A.R. and Stajano, F. (2003). Location privacy in pervasive computing. *IEEE Pervasive Computing*, 2(1): 46–55.

Bian, C., Khan, S.S. and Mihailidis, A. (2018, May). Infusing domain knowledge to improve the detection of alzheimer's disease from everyday motion behaviour. *In: Canadian Conference on Artificial Intelligence*. Springer, Cham, pp. 181–193.

Bierhoff, I., Muller, S., Schoenrade-Sproll, S., Delaney, S., Byrne, P., Dolničar, V., Magoutas, B., Verginadis, Y., Avatangelou, E. and Huijnen, C. (2013). Ambient assisted living systems in real-life situations: Experiences from the SOPRANO Project. *In: Technologies for Active Aging*. Springer, Boston, MA, pp. 123–153.

Boulos, M.N.K., Rocha, A., Martins, A., Vicente, M.E., Bolz, A., Feld, R., Tchoudovski, I., Braecklein, M., Nelson, J., Laighin, G.Ó. and Sdogati, C. (2007). CAALYX: A new generation of location-based services in healthcare. *International Journal of Health Geographics*, 6(1): 1–6.

Byrne, C.A., Collier, R. and O'Hare, G.M. (2018). A review and classification of assisted living systems. *Information*, 9(7): 182.

Čaušević, A., Vahabi, M., Fotouhi, H., Björkman, M. and Lundqvist, K. (2017). Towards safety, security and reliability of data communication in IoT AAL applications. *B&H Electrical Engineering*, 11: 6–40.

Colomer, J.B.M., Salvi, D., Cabrera-Umpierrez, M.F., Arredondo, M.T., Abril, P., Jimenez-Mixco, V., García-Betances, R., Fioravanti, A., Pastorino, M., Cancela, J. and Medrano, A. (2014). Experience in evaluating AAL solutions in living labs. *Sensors*, 14(4): 7277–7311.

Corcella, L., Manca, M., Nordvik, J.E., Paternò, F., Sanders, A.M. and Santoro, C. (2019). Enabling personalisation of remote elderly assistance. *Multimedia Tools and Applications*, 78(15): 21557–21583.

Dahmen, J. and Cook, D. (2019). SynSys: A synthetic data generation system for healthcare applications. *Sensors*, 19(5): 1181.

Dasios, A., Gavalas, D., Pantziou, G. and Konstantopoulos, C. (2015). Hands-on experiences in deploying cost-effective ambient-assisted living systems. *Sensors*, 15(6): 14487–14512.

Dimitrievski, A., Zdravevski, E., Lameski, P. and Trajkovik, V. (2019, September). Addressing privacy and security in connected health with fog computing. *In: Proceedings of the 5th EAI International Conference on Smart Objects and Technologies for Social Good*, pp. 255–260.

Doukas, C., Maglogiannis, I., Koufi, V., Malamateniou, F. and Vassilacopoulos, G. (2012, November). Enabling data protection through PKI encryption in IoT m-Health devices. *In: 2012 IEEE 12th International Conference on Bioinformatics & Bioengineering (BIBE)*, IEEE, pp. 25–29.

Gaspar, P.D., Felizardo, V. and Garcia, N.M. (2015). A review of monitoring and assisted therapeutic technology for AAL application. *Ambient Assisted Living*, 7–86.

Hail, M.A. and Fischer, S. (2015, December). IoT for AAL: An architecture via information-centric networking. *In: 2015 IEEE Globecom Workshops (GC Wkshps)*, IEEE, pp. 1–6.

Havasi, F. and Kiss, Á. (2007, November). Ambient assisted living in rural areas: Vision and pilot application. *In: European Conference on Ambient Intelligence*, Springer, Berlin, Heidelberg, pp. 246–252.

He, D. and Zeadally, S. (2015.) Authentication protocol for an ambient assisted living system. *IEEE Communications Magazine*, 53(1): 71–77.

Hong, J.I. and Landay, J.A. (2004, June). An architecture for privacy-sensitive ubiquitous computing. *In: Proceedings of the 2nd International Conference on Mobile Systems, Applications, and Services*, pp. 177–189.

Kleinberger, T., Becker, M., Ras, E., Holzinger, A. and Muller, P. (2007, July). Ambient intelligence in assisted living: Enable elderly people to handle future interfaces. *In: International Conference on Universal Access in Human-Computer Interaction.* Springer, Berlin, Heidelberg, pp. 103–112.

Koutli, M., Theologou, N., Tryferidis, A., Tzovaras, D., Kagkini, A., Zandes, D., Karkaletsis, K., Kaggelides, K., Miralles, J.A., Oravec, V. and Vanya, S. (2019, May). Secure IoT e-Health applications using VICINITY framework and GDPR guidelines. *In: 2019 15th International Conference on Distributed Computing in Sensor Systems (DCOSS)*, IEEE, pp. 263–270.

Koutsoukos, X., Kushwaha, M., Amundson, I., Neema, S. and Sztipanovits, J. (2006, October). Oasis: A service-oriented architecture for ambient-aware sensor networks. *In: Monterey Workshop*, Springer, Berlin, Heidelberg, pp. 125–149.

Kvam, P.H. and Vidakovic, B. (2007). *Non-parametric Statistics with Applications to Science and Engineering*, vol. 653, John Wiley & Sons.

Manca, M., Parvin, P., Paterno, F. and Santoro, C. (2017, June). Detecting anomalous elderly behavior in ambient assisted living. *In: Proceedings of the ACM SIGCHI Symposium on Engineering Interactive Computing Systems*, pp. 63–68.

Marques, G., Garcia, N. and Pombo, N. (2017). A survey on IoT: Architectures, elements, applications, QoS, platforms and security concepts. *In: Advances in Mobile Cloud Computing and Big Data in the 5G Era*, Cham, pp. 115–130.

Memon, M., Wagner, S.R., Pedersen, C.F., Beevi, F.H.A. and Hansen, F.O. (2014). Ambient assisted living healthcare frameworks, platforms, standards and quality attributes. *Sensors*, 14(3): 4312–4341.

Mikalsen, M., Hanke, S., Fuxreiter, T., Walderhaug, S. and Wienhofen, L. (2009). Interoperability services in the MPOWER Ambient Assisted Living platform. *In: Medical Informatics in a United and Healthy Europe*, IOS Press, pp. 366–370.

Mkpa, A., Chin, J. and Winckles, A., 2019, June. Holistic blockchain approach to foster trust, privacy and security in IoT-based ambient assisted living environment. *In: 2019 15th International Conference on Intelligent Environments (IE)*, pp. 52–55.

Nani, M., Caleb-Solly, P., Dogramadzi, S., Fear, T. and van den Heuvel, H. (2010). MOBISERV: An integrated intelligent home environment for the provision of health. *Nutrition and Mobility Services to the Elderly.*

Nehmer, J., Becker, M., Karshmer, A. and Lamm, R. (2006, May). Living assistance systems: An ambient intelligence approach. *In: Proceedings of the 28th International Conference on Software Engineering*, pp. 43–50.

Palumbo, F., La Rosa, D. and Ferro, E. (2016, November). Stigmergy-based long-term monitoring of indoor users mobility in ambient assisted living environments: The DOREMI project approach. *In: AI\* AAL@ AI\* IA*, 18–32.

Psychoula, I., Merdivan, E., Singh, D., Chen, L., Chen, F., Hanke, S., Kropf, J., Holzinger, A. and Geist, M. (2018, March). A deep learning approach for privacy preservation in assisted living. *In: 2018 IEEE International Conference on Pervasive Computing and Communications Workshops (PerCom Workshops)*, IEEE, pp. 710–715.

Ram, R., Furfari, F., Girolami, M., Ibañez-Sánchez, G., Lázaro-Ramos, J.P., Mayer, C., Prazak-Aram, B. and Zentek, T. (2013). UniversAAL: Provisioning platform for AAL services. *In: Ambient Intelligence-Software and Applications*, Springer, Heidelberg, pp. 105–112.

Rashidi, P. and Mihailidis, A. (2012). A survey on ambient-assisted living tools for older adults. *IEEE Journal of Biomedical and Health Informatics*, 17(3): 579–590.

Roy, N., Misra, A. and Cook, D. (2016). Ambient and smartphone sensor assisted ADL recognition in multi-inhabitant smart environments. *Journal of Ambient Intelligence and Humanised Computing*, 7(1): 1–19.

Sadock, B.J. (2020). *Kaplan & Sadock's Synopsis of Psychiatry: Behavioral Sciences/Clinical Psychiatry.*

Stavropoulos, T.G., Meditskos, G., Kontopoulos, E. and Kompatsiaris, I. (2014, August). The DemaWare service-oriented AAL platform for people with dementia. *In: AI-AM/NetMed@ ECAI*, 11–15.

Stavropoulos, T.G., Meditskos, G. and Kompatsiaris, I. (2017). DemaWare2: Integrating sensors, multimedia and semantic analysis for the ambient care of dementia. *Pervasive and Mobile Computing*, 34: 126–145.

Tazari, M.R., Furfari, F., Ramos, J.P.L. and Ferro, E. (2010). The PERSONA service platform for AAL spaces. *In*: *Handbook of Ambient Intelligence and Smart Environments*. Springer, Boston, MA, pp. 1171–1199.

van Heek, J., Himmel, S. and Ziefle, M. (2017, July). Privacy, data security, and the acceptance of AAL-systems—A user-specific perspective. *In*: *International Conference on Human Aspects of IT for the Aged Population*. Springer, Cham, pp. 38–56.

Villaronga, E.F., Kieseberg, P. and Li, T. (2018). Humans forget, machines remember: Artificial intelligence and the right to be forgotten. *Computer Law & Security Review*, 34(2): 304–313.

Vlamings, H.G.M. and Koster, R.P. (2010). *AAL Security and Privacy: Transferring XACML Policies for End-to-end Access and Usage Control.* Philips Research.

World Health Organisation. (2021). *Global Status Report on the Public Health Response to Dementia.*

# 4

# Evaluating Countermeasures for Detecting Misinformation Attacks on Stock Exchange Market

*David Manford* and *Hamid Jahankhani**

## ABSTRACT

Top concern for investors in today's stock exchange market is market manipulation, despite the rapid and strong reaction from regulators when such practices are observed. Quite evidently, existing systems in the business for detecting fraudulent activities on the stock exchange are based on a set of rules derived from professional expertise. It is necessary in the current stock exchange market to have scalable machine learning algorithms that can assist in the detection of market manipulation operations. Misinformation may be purposely inserted into the news that is being spread by the business press that may have an impact on stock market values. A continuous surge in stock prices, spurred by misplaced optimism, may be followed by the release of fake news stories. With technological advancements sprawling in present economic environment, high frequency traders are increasingly utilising bots to influence the stock market in order to earn quick profits. In this article, the researchers will provide an overview of the current work being done to detect certain types of fraudulent activities. Practically, the vast majority of fraudulent acts are based on actual digital misinformation and this study will objectively examine how this may be recognized and dealt with or eradicated rapidly using cutting-edge information security event-handling tools. This research will investigate the pragmatic usage of advanced machine learning techniques for misinformation attacks and the countermeasures that will

Northumbria University London, UK.
* Corresponding author: Hamid.jahankhani@northumbria.ac.uk

be necessary to mitigate this danger. In addition to technical detection systems, recommendations for regulatory compliance will be evaluated as well as the training and measures that users must undertake to help recognize disinformation attacks.

# 1. Introduction

Throughout this research, the words disinformation and misinformation will be interchangeably used.

Several researches have shown that Online Social Networks (OSNs) have increased rapidly over the years. Hence, social media has shaped the digital world to such a point that it has become indispensable (Mehmet, 2017) and is now a dominant source of information. Further research has shown that in the USA, social media is the main source of news (Edson et al., 2018) and has changed the way people ingest news. This over-reliance on online news has its advantages and disadvantages. The first advantage is speed; online news is phenomenally fast. The key disadvantage is that not all online news is reliable.

Considering how quite easy it has become to produce and disseminate news via OSN, fake news and cyber-attacks have also simultaneously increased. In particular, assault on financial news that impacts the stock markets and influences price and stock market direction, which indirectly affect world economies and individual's livelihood has become prevalent.

Cyber-attacks on stock exchange markets can occur through various methods. Predominantly, they occur via identity theft, data theft or data manipulation, disruptive malware, emerging technologies (e.g., blockchain, cryptocurrency and AI) and misinformation. Cyber-attacks that use disinformation to influence stock prices of listed firms, or prices of forex currency pairs and other digital financial instruments, have increased to worrying proportions (Newman et al., 2013). Apparently, attackers manipulate stock market prices by disseminating false financial information and fictitious rumours using fake websites, social media accounts, or by compromising the security of legitimate websites or social media accounts (Pennebaker et al., 2015). Through deliberate misinformation, prices of financial instruments are manipulated via misleading insider information with the sole purpose of profiting from stock price fluctuations.

Misinformation and its impact on stock exchange markets are positively correlated. The impact is adverse given the investment greed among traders. Greed compounded with the tendency to rely on rumours results in massive losses. Misinformation (also known as fake news) is used to influence stock markets, whereby listed companies hire Public Relations (PR) firms to fraudulently publicize their stocks by posing as financial analysts (Heston and Sinha, 2017). The fake news is then published on trusted financial websites and used to influence financial markets. Resultant effects can be far-reaching since it creates a false sense of urgency that causes investors to panic and make quick investment decisions. Stock market misinformation infiltrates the stock markets when investors searching for investment-specific information fall for financial rumours (University of Göttingen, 2021).

The money bots is also another high-tech tool that traders use in doing high-frequency trading by Artificial Intelligence (AI) at lightning speed, raising the risk involved in money markets as featured in documentary broadcasting (Aljazeera, 2020).

One would agree that when rumours accelerate, they affect price fluctuations of the targeted company shares. Given the rising uncertainty, investors make rushed decisions based on the credibility of the publisher (Jegadeesh and Wu, 2013). Similarly, Twitter bots have been found to manipulate financial markets; for example, bot-generated tweets trigger fluctuation in stock prices, thereby creating market volatility. However, retail investors fall prey to this information and lose money by taking short positions. Misinformation infiltrates the stock market through deceptive investment articles that drive stock prices for certain small firms upwards while eroding public trust in professional financial analysis (Verónica et al., 2018). The emergence of disinformation and AI-generated media has sparked widespread concern about how they might be used and disseminated. So far, the majority of attention has been focused on how disinformation could endanger national politics, individual citizens and organizations. In contrast, little research has been done on how misinformation may affect the financial system. Fake news is not a new phenomenon in the finance sector. Deception crimes, such as scam, falsification and price exploitation are prevalent in all economies. Based on the objectives set out, this research is aimed at developing safeguards against malicious attacks against the Stock Exchange market via misinformation (De Beer and Matthee, 2021). Today's highly technologically-advanced trading environment makes it impossible for companies using automated trading strategies to compete with traditional investors. Current trading strategies employ advanced technology and as a result, the trading process has been stripped of human involvement. This kind of machine algorithm does not rely on human expertise. Instead, it uses pre-programmed computers loaded with mathematical formulas to rapidly detect trends before even a basic investor has the chance to detect or notice. Subsequently, the robot's strategies can be altered on the fly and the robot can place orders instantly. Businesses that have recently resorted to market manipulation tactics to increase their profits may have crossed ethical boundaries.

Many researches have shown that it is not difficult to predict that the most common cyber-attacks are financially motivated (Goldman and McCoy, 2015), while IT crimes, which are defined on judicial records as cyber extortion or fraud, are more dynamic, fast, easy, effective, profitable and difficult to detect, will invariably turn to misinformation. Other researches have also shown that if cyber attackers target a bank, central bank, or the entire financial system, it poses a national security risk. Misinformation and synthetic media can encourage and make large-scale attacks on financial infrastructure more likely.

Fake news has already wreaked havoc on national elections, the reputations of individuals and organizations and has had a negative impact on citizens in the COVID-19 pandemic. For example, Choras et al. (2021) cited fake news about alleged medicines in the United States and Brazil and its impact on the population affected. Because of the rapid advancement of this technology, it is becoming increasingly difficult to determine whether visuals or sounds are real or not.

## 1.1  Stock Market Cybercrime

Although the notion of financial cybercrime is relatively straightforward, a portion of financial cybercrime is characterized by the three major stock market breaches listed below (Neyret, 2020):

1. **Insider trading** is a practice that, according to Article L. 465-1 of the Monetary and Financial Code, consists of a person 'making use of inside information by carrying out for themselves or others, either directly or indirectly, one or more transactions or by cancelling or amending one or more orders placed by this same person before they are in possession of the inside information, involving financial instruments issued by this issuer or financial instruments to which such inside information pertains.' Inside information is defined in Article 7 of Regulation (EU) No. 596/2014, paragraphs 1 to 4, mainly as 'specific information that has not been made public, which relates, directly or indirectly, to one or more issuers, or to one or more financial instruments, and which, if made public, would be likely to have a material effect on the price of the financial instruments in question or the price of related derivative financial instruments.'

2. **Price falsification**, which, according to Monetary and Financial Code Article L. 465-3-1, is 'the act, by any person, of carrying out a transaction, placing an order or engaging in conduct that gives or is likely to give misleading signals about the offer, demand or price of a financial instrument or that fixes or is likely to fix the price of a financial instrument at an abnormal or artificial level' and/or 'the act, by any person, of carrying out a transaction, placing an order or engaging in conduct that affects the price of a financial instrument, by employing fictitious devices or any other form of deception or contrivance.'

3. **The spread of erroneous or misleading information**, which is primarily defined by Article L. 465-3-213 of the Monetary and Financial Code, is 'The act, by any person, of disseminating, by any means, information that gives false or misleading indications about the situation or prospects of an issuer or about the offer, demand or price of a financial instrument or that fixes or is likely to fix the price of a financial instrument at an abnormal or artificial level.'

Thus, stock market cybercrime can be defined as all stock market breaches that include a cyber component and are either attempted or committed against or through the use of an information system or communication network. Financial markets, with their complex technology and interconnectivity, are clearly the most vulnerable to stock market cyber breaches. Stock market criminality, even more so than other forms of crime, will hence not be able to evade cyber-crime attacks.

## 1.2  Stock Market Manipulation

The dissemination of disinformation has plagued economies by affecting stock market prices. Misinformation can potentially cause damage to the stock market with the manipulation of stock prices. Cyber criminals are using Artificial Intelligence to alter video statements of influential people, such as CEOs and other VIPs of large known companies (Soare, 2019). One example was when a false tweet had spread through the social media platform, claiming Barack Obama, former President of the United States, had been injured in an explosion, resulting in $130 billion in stock worth being wiped out of the stock market worldwide (Vosoughi et al., 2020). Manipulated media content when distributed, may cause panic in the market with either a company's stock price to plummet or rise, based on the reputation (Soare, 2019). Consequently, Tesla's stock dropped by 6% (Adjer, 2019).

Following a data breach, a call for a Bank of England executive to resign over a security breach surfaced, following the leak of an audio feed containing sensitive information to traders. The audio-feed hijacking benefited high-speed traders, such as currency speculators, who can earn millions of pounds on minute market movements (BBC, 2019). Hence, misinformation can have a significant impact on the value of shares in the stock market. The benefits are immense for those who exploit and the loss is devastating for unsuspecting victims (Mats, 2021).

## 2. Literature Review

Choudhary et al. (2021) conducted a literature review on misinformation detection techniques. The review focused on Machine Learning (ML) detection methods. Specifically, the authors reviewed machine learning algorithms, namely, Naïve Bayes, Convolutional Neural Network (CNN) and LSTM. In addition, other algorithms, such as, neural network and Support Vector Machine, were used to detect and counter fake news infiltration in the stock exchange. Besides the machine learning algorithms, the literature review discussed fake news detection bottlenecks and recommended a combination of diverse machine learning algorithms to enhance detection efficiency. However, Abdullah-All-Tanvir et al. (2020) studied a hybrid model for detecting authentic fake news, utilizing deep learning methods.

Though the study focused on social media, the same techniques can be applied for detecting fake news on financial markets. The hybrid approach is a computational and automated technique that detects fake news using textual analytics. The proposed hybrid model is built on Natural Language Processing (NLP) and machine learning models. The technique draws its superiority from the combination of ML and NLP and has a detection accuracy of 80% based on the Bayesian Classifier. However, it has a detection accuracy of 77% when based on the hybrid neural network architecture.

Similarly, Aphiwongsophon and Chongstitvatana (2018) studied fake news detection, using machine learning algorithms. The study focused on three machine learning techniques, namely Naïve Bayes, neural network, and Support Vector Machine (SVM). The results showed that Naïve Bayes has a detection accuracy of 96.08% while the other two techniques (neural network and Support Vector Machine) have a higher detection accuracy of 99.90%. On the other hand, Ahmed et al. (2020) studied the fake news and opinion spam detection, using text classification algorithms. The study differed from previous studies as it focused on automated detection of misinformation using an N-gram model with a specific emphasis on fake news and user reviews. During the study, a comparison was made between two different features, namely, extraction and machine learning classification techniques. The results showed improved performance when using experimental and fake news datasets as compared to modern techniques.

Dylan et al. (2021) obtained a similar finding while reviewing the literature on the fake news detection approaches. The study recommends machine learning techniques, such as, Naïve Bayes and neural network.

Interestingly enough, Ahmed et al. (2020) investigated fake news detection by utilizing the N-Gram analysis technique alongside machine learning algorithms. The study proposed the combined use of N-gram analysis and machine learning for high accuracy. The research focused on two extraction and machine learning classification methods and concluded that the detection accuracy is high when using Term Frequency-Inverted Document Frequency (TF-IDF). Similarly, the study recommended Linear Support Vector Machine (LSVM) in classification, giving a high accuracy of 92%. However, in another study, Nofer and Hinz (2015) explored the stock market prediction using tweeter as an experimental platform. Using a sample size of 100 tweets, the researcher predicted the stock market returns based on the mood of the social media (Newman et al., 2013). The results showed the significance of mood states of followers on the stock market trading decision. Besides, the study found that a stock market trading strategy depended on the training period and the portfolio grew 36% in just six months.

Similarly, Kamps and Kleinberg (2018) studied the detection of cryptocurrency price manipulations. The investigation explored how the spread of fake news creates cryptocurrency price fluctuations. While studying the cryptocurrency pump and dump, the researcher focused on stock market manipulation in the absence of any regulation. The duo took a classical economic view and proposed the use of an anomaly detection algorithm for detecting irregular trading patterns and activities.

The study findings established the existence of signals that could suggest pump and dump schemes and concluded that fraudulent activities tend to cluster on certain cryptocurrency coins and transactions. Likewise, Lin (2017) studied modern market manipulation techniques with a focus on financial markets. The study reviewed different manipulation techniques, including pump and dump and misinformation. It established that cybernetic manipulation was more lethal as compared with traditional methods. The researcher further posits that misinformation presents insurmountable challenges as it leverages Artificial Intelligence (AI) and machine learning. The study proposes the use of improved intermediate integrity, cybersecurity and simplification of financial market investment strategies.

Analytically, Yayla and Hu (2011) explored information security events and how they affect corporate value. The study focused on information security and its impact on the stock market performance. Furthermore, the research is relevant since compromised systems provide a platform for spreading fake news and misinformation. However, the study links short-term financial market reactions to misinformation on security breaches in the concerned firms. Also, Alexandria (2020) investigated the stock market cybercrime and especially new stock exchange cyber-attacks. While studying online trading-related cyber-attacks, the researcher focused on the modus operandi and challenges of stock market breaches, such as the propagation of false information. The study concluded that misinformation is a modern tool used to perpetrate stock market cybercrime and recommends further research into this grey area.

Furthermore, Lachanski and Pav (2017) explored how the social media mood can be leveraged to predict the financial market. The study suggests that an algorithm that counts the total number of mood words used on social platforms can be used to predict movement in Dow Jones industrial average. Furthermore, it established that a change in online mood is usually followed by a shift in the Down Jones index within a span of up to seven days. This information can inform the prediction of stock exchange movement with a prediction accuracy rate of 87.6%.

Relatively, Wirama et al. (2017) provided a unique perspective on fake news detection. While investigating the stock exchange and how it reacts to the dissemination of misinformation in the Indonesian stock market, the researchers found that rumours were either directly or indirectly published by the sellers as a manipulative tactic to help them sell their stocks at higher prices. Since stock prices can be changed by rumours, traders time them with their trading decisions. To counter the spread of misinformation, the study recommends strict government regulation of financial markets. Equally, Thaher et al. (2021) examined the intelligent detection of misinformation, while targeting Arabic tweets using Hybrid Harris Hawks and machine learning algorithms. The study proposes the use of a smart classification model to detect disinformation, using natural language processing (NLP) algorithms.

Furthermore, the study used machine learning (ML) and Harris Hawk Optimiser (HHO) detection models. Quite significantly, the Bag of Words method was used alongside different feature extraction models. Machine learning algorithms, such as, user profiles and word-based schemes, were also analysed. The findings suggest that Logistic Regression (LR) and Term-Frequency-Inverse Document Frequency (TF-IDF) models recorded the highest detection accuracy. Furthermore, the results showed that feature selection utilizing binary HHO algorithm limited content dimensionality and enhanced algorithmic learning performance. The study concludes that BHHO-LR algorithms have 5% greater performance as compared with results of similar detection algorithms.

To expound the above paragraph further, Arun Kumar (2020) examined fake news detection while utilizing machine learning techniques. The paper investigates how natural language processing algorithms can be used to detect fake news from online sources. The study relied on a text classification approach and employed a total of four classification models. The findings indicate that the LSTM model had the highest detection accuracy. The study experiment examined multiple articles from a single news source. He concluded that once fake news is detected, the source is permanently flagged as a source of fake news. While the technique might have its downsides, De Oliveira et al. (2021) offered a refined detection approach for identifying rumours on social media platforms using Natural Language Processing (NLP) algorithms. The strength of this approach lies in the NLP techniques, such as vectorization, dimensionality and machine learning.

According to the study, human beings cannot differentiate between authentic and fake news and assert that misinformation is a threat to logical facts that underpin stock market operations. Similarly, Kammoun et al. (2019) investigated how stock markets respond to cyber-attacks. While drawing upon a dataset of 3,680 cyber-attacks on five stock exchange markets, the researchers used a hybrid evaluation method to conduct a counterfactual evaluation. The results showed a negative return following the accident date. Both NASDAQ and NYSE posted similar results, even though abnormal returns were negative for French and German firms following the first accident date.

The need for speedy detection of misinformation has become critical. Shu et al. (2019) studied various techniques for collecting, detecting and visualising false information. The research explored the fast detection of fake news on social media platforms, intending to stop further dissemination. Subsequently, the authors recommended a system for fake news detection using a FakeNewsTracker that automatically collects news data alongside its social context and thereafter predicts fake news using visualization methods.

Additionally, Sharma et al. (2020) used machine learning algorithms to detect false news. According to the researchers, fake news has dire implications that include swaying stock market performance. The researchers used Artificial Intelligence to conduct a binary classification of online news sources. Besides, the researchers used natural language processing and machine learning to detect the use of click baits and advertisements in the dissemination of fake news. Using AI, ML and NLP, the researchers were able to classify news as either authentic or fake.

Further research by Carta et al. (2021) examined the interplay between financial events and news tweets. They used hierarchical clustering algorithms to detect financial events, based on news and tweets. The algorithms detected fake news by identifying patterns and clusters of news stories by comparing news from authoritative publishers and related microblogs. The solution was tested on Dow Jones and the Standard and Poor's 500 index time series and was found to be effective in extracting authentic information, based on trending global and financial news. The study utilized the Brexit and COVID-19 datasets.

Complimenting on the above detection research, Alonso et al. (2019) explored the use of sentinel analysis in the identification of misinformation. The study recommended the use of automated detection algorithms. Fake news makes extensive use of sentiments to attract viewers, thus prompting the use of sentiment and text analytics. This fake news detection model makes use of text-based sentiment analysis even though it faces drawbacks, such as multilingualism, bias and multimedia content handling. In a separate, though similar study, Malyshenko et al. (2019) studied the stock exchange anomalies in the face of continuously changing information. While studying the global and Ukrainian stock exchange, the researchers sought to determine the market inefficiencies. The study was randomized and based on a one-to-five-day system of moving averages. It concluded that stock market anomalies underlie collusions at the stock market.

Further research by Seo and Lee (2018) showed that the use of botnets has grown in importance as a security threat on the Internet, and a vast study has been undertaken to detect them in recent years. There are two types of botnet detection: vertical correlation and horizontal correlation. BotHunter is an example of a vertical correlation-based detection system in action. When bi-directional communication flows occur between internal resources and external systems, it is an application that tracks the data exchanges that correspond to a state-based infection cycle and it accumulates evidence of those data exchanges. Horizontal correlation, on the other hand, is concerned with identifying behavioral similarities and correlations between multiple hosts. Other botnet detection tactics have also been recommended.

In the early stages, abnormal behavior traffic is detected with the aim of rapidly eradicating malware-infected systems. However, Seo and Lee, 2018 proposed a method that is distinct from the conventional botnet detection methods. Their study provides a detection mechanism that groups hosts with related behavior and actions, allowing them to determine the IP address of the Command and Control (C&C) server, the duration of the connection and the number of connections, among other parameters. As a result, the proposed approach detects variable command and control channels by tracking communication with the C&C server.

Finally, the present detection techniques are centred on network traffic examination. Recent malware, on the other hand, conceals itself through encrypted command and control traffic or code obfuscation to avoid detection (Seo and Lee, 2018). The proposed detection and elimination methodology makes use of protocol header attribute information to solve challenges associated with examining network traffic payloads.

Regarding cyber-attacks, botnets continue to pose a serious threat and attacks on systems that are specifically designed to be attacked go beyond simple hacking. Using a variety of attack techniques, including malicious code, software vulnerabilities and social engineering techniques, attackers try to make their attacks on existing systems harder to detect by introducing new attack techniques that circumvent security systems, according to Seo and Lee (2018).

According to Bateman (2020), 'the financial threat pose by synthetic media is currently low, so the key policy question is how much this threat will grow over time; however' leading industry experts diverge widely in their assessments.' (Bateman, 2020), maintaining that disinformation is not a new phenomenon in the financial world. Defeasible acts of deceit, such as fraud, forgery and market manipulation pose a persistent threat to every economy.

Furthermore, bad actors are known to incorporate new technologies into their schemes on a regular basis. Because of this, it is worthwhile to consider how novel deception tools, such as deepfakes, could facilitate financial crimes or other forms of financial harm. Bateman (2020) also stated that, 'deceptive synthetic media could be used to inflict financial harm on a wide range of potential targets. Obvious targets include financial institutions, such as banks, stock exchanges, clearing-houses and brokerages – all of which rely on truthful information to conduct transactions— as well as financial regulators and central banks, which oversee general market conditions and combat harmful misinformation. But companies and individuals outside the financial sector also could become targets.'

Researchers and legislators are concerned about misinformation being spread during worldwide democratic campaigns. Both officials and legislators are concerned that deepfake videos will be used to disseminate disinformation and disrupt the democratic process (Metz, 2019). Greengard (2020) has emphasized that 'people are manipulating images and videos portraying "false news" to control public opinion, blackmail and fake video pornography using the AI machine learning platform.'

Similarly, Westerlund (2019) has correctly stated that the popularity of deepfake technology (used to deploy misinformation) has increased, posing a significant cyber-security threat to not only our society, but also to business sectors, our constitutional political system and national security. Journalists and news organizations are struggling to distinguish between deliberate misinformation and legitimate news, eroding citizen trust in the media (Westerlund, 2019).

One would commend Choras' for his research which examines the current state of awareness regarding the detection of fake news in order to identify viable approaches and to identify major concerns and research gaps that could be addressed in future studies. To effectively combat and counter fake news, it is clear that swift and dependable solutions are required. As a result, this article offers a critical assessment of the current state of awareness regarding the detection of fake news and misinformation, as well as potential solutions. It is quite clear that Choras et al. (2020) is advocating that there is still a gap in determining the optimal detection technique for combating deepfake attacks and has noted that fake news can be detected by analysing a variety of digital materials, including images, text, network data and the author's or source's credibility.

Furthermore, given the evolution of misinformation, Lyu and Li (2019) acknowledged the need for additional research and innovation in detection technology. As a result, it is critical to implement solutions that aim to avoid problems in the first place, such as advocating for employee education and awareness training.

Another possibility suggested by Meskys et al. (2020) is for technology companies and governments to consider attempting to enforce penalties and regulations against those who create socially disruptive misinformation. As a result, Westerlund (2020) recommended that workers be trained to distinguish between genuine and falsified information on display.

Golmohammadi et al. (2014) defined price manipulation in securities as the deliberate attempt to deceive investors by affecting or controlling the price of securities or interfering with the fair market in order to profit. Following the findings of this study, it appears that using supervised learning algorithms to identify market manipulation samples by using a labelled dataset based on litigation cases is an effective method of detecting market manipulation. However, because they are trained on a single dataset, a critic may justifiably query the generality of such models.

The need for establishing approaches for methodically synthesizing altered samples that may be merged with real-world market data for training and testing data mining tools for detecting market manipulation is emphasized by the research community. According to Golmohammadi et al. (2014), the application of data mining algorithms in the detection of market manipulation is a relatively new method, but there has been an increase in the number of research works in the last few years to support this claim. Furthermore, early theoretical work demonstrated that there are opportunities for profitable manipulations in the stock market, known as trade-based manipulations, such as wash trades, matched order transactions, runs, collusion and so on.

Consequently, Aggarwal and Wu (2006), expanded on previous theoretical work and conducted empirical research on market manipulation cases in order to gain a better understanding of the dynamics and economics of market manipulation. According to their findings, manipulation is typically associated with increased stock volatility, increased liquidity and high returns during the manipulation period. Aggarwal and Wu (2006) presented proposals for future research to detect market manipulation in the securities market to be carried out in the near future. However, the following are the five categories that have been identified based on specific contributions of the literature on the data mining approach, goals and input data:

1. **Social network analysis:** These techniques are used to identify traders who work together to manipulate the market.

2. **Visualisation:** These visualizations go beyond standard charts, allowing an auditor to connect with market data and identify exploitative patterns.

3. **Rule induction:** These techniques generate a set of rules that can be examined and used by securities market auditors/regulators.

4. **Outlier detection:** These methods are designed to identify observations that are outliers in comparison to the rest of the data (i.e., unknown spike in fraudulent patterns). Additionally, rather than using a predefined threshold to filter out spikes, anomaly/outlier, detection can be used to detect spikes effectively.

5. **Pattern recognition using supervised learning methods:** The purpose of using these methods is to identify patterns that are akin to the trends that are known to characterise fraudulent activities.

An article published by Ross et al. (2012) explains the change in the global market as trades that come in electronic pulses, capital unleashed in hollow spaces, packed with computers operating at full speed and capital released in hollow spaces, packed with computers running at full speed. Human beings are no longer involved in the game; instead, fund managers, traders and investment banks place their entire trust in the hands of complex algorithms managed by computers, with only a minimal amount of human involvement. According to industry experts, High Frequency Trading (HFT) has reduced transaction costs while increasing activity and liquidity on stock exchange floors. However, HFT has also played a central role in a number of shocking US market collapses (Jones, 2013). Computers are competing against one another and against the entire market, executing millions of small, quick trades, each of which yields a negligible return on investment.

Interruptions of the smallest magnitude can mean the difference between profit and loss. It is becoming increasingly difficult for regulatory agencies to detect market abuse as time progresses. Accidents happen in today's market because it is manipulated (Tse et al., 2012). The new generation of financial leaders are programmers developing complex algorithms that are used in high-frequency trading. These algorithms employ a variety of strategies in their pursuit of profits. Computers are looking for stocks that are rising in value in order to profit from them. Another algorithmic threat is the behavioral algorithm, which looks for signs that investors are interested in purchasing a specific stock. High-frequency trading algorithms then purchase the stock and resell it to the original potential buyer for a fraction of the difference between the spot and forward prices (Ross et al., 2012).

The term 'market abuse' refers to a wide range of practices that can be classified as tactics, such as quote stuffing, smoking and layering. These are most commonly employed. At least one company (LLC) in the United States has been sanctioned by regulators for engaging in high-frequency trading (Prewitt, 2012). European policymakers are currently debating whether or not to impose a number of new regulations on high-frequency trading (HFT). The issue is to determine whether high-frequency trading is detrimental to the European markets or not.

Many studies are tailored to the needs of investment banks that employ high-frequency trading strategies or firms that have high-frequency trading firms as clients (Ross et al., 2012). There are some technical obstacles to be considered when determining the impact of high-frequency trading on trades and markets. Datasets are complex, massive and dispersed across multiple trading platforms and across multiple countries. Politicians are concerned about the lack of evidence regarding the benefits and drawbacks of high-frequency trading. They are proposing and planning to take tough measures against high-frequency trading which could include requiring HFT to trade in all market conditions (Jones, 2013).

Critics of high-frequency trading claim that the use of behavior-seeking algorithms makes it more difficult for institutional investors and pension funds to trade large blocks of securities without being detected by computers. Traditional investors and pension-fund managers are well aware that once they begin to trade a large position, they will be identified by computer algorithmic trading, which will then be able to successfully front run the trade. As a result of this problem, fund managers are forced to buy and sell in smaller quantities in an effort to conceal their intentions regarding what they are about to do, which results in higher transaction costs (Jones, 2013).

As high-frequency trading is becoming increasingly important presently, ordinary market participants are being forced to invest in trading technology in order to keep up with HFT traders, resulting in increased costs. The increased importance of high-frequency trading (HFT) has had an impact on traditional investors in more than one way, thus driving traditional investors away from mainstream exchanges and toward dark pools which are managed by brokers and where shares are traded in secret (Jones, 2013).

## 3. Research Methodology

Categorically, the objective of the research methodology is to determine how misinformation-targeting stock exchanges can be detected and suggest countermeasures that can be implemented to prevent future attacks. It will review counter strategies that can be used to stop stock exchange attacks in the future. Hence, this section primarily focuses on combating the infiltration of misinformation into the stock exchange and how it impacts financial markets. Use of qualitative research techniques was informed by the need to collect accurate data and gain in-depth insights on the research topic. Qualitative methods are ideal for capturing factual data from historical or archival documents.

Qualitative research methods were used to collect data that satisfy the inclusion criteria. Non-numerical descriptive data was captured from an archived cyber-attack on stock exchange-related documents. Qualitative data was also collected from historical records obtained from cyber-security data repositories (Vosoughi et al., 2018). Furthermore, the research methodology relied on case studies, historical data and archived stock exchange cyber-security documents. However, the researchers conducted an in-depth study on how attackers use misinformation to infiltrate stock exchanges for the purpose of manipulating stock prices. Several qualitative research methodologies were used to investigate stock exchange cyber security, focusing on misinformation detection and countermeasures (Aggarwal and Wu, 2006). Case study analysis involved the collection and analysis of case studies related to reported incidences of stock exchange attacks. Data was also retrieved from journal articles and other scholarly authoritative sources on the subject.

To accomplish the research objectives, a qualitative study was conducted. Primarily, qualitative research characteristic is most effective with small sample sizes and produces results that are not quantifiable or measurable. Its primary advantage, which also serves as its primary distinction from quantitative research, is that it offers a comprehensive explanation and analysis of a research subject without limiting the research's scope or the nature of contributor responses.

In contrast to quantitative research which uses numerical symbols to represent the world, qualitative research uses primarily linguistic symbols to represent the world (Heppner et al., 1999). Furthermore, the qualitative research method of data collection was chosen over quantitative as the research seeks to observe incidents of misinformation and especially in the area affecting the financial sectors, such as the banks and stock market trading.

## 3.1  Research Approach

The research took an analytical approach where the relevant documents were collected and scrutinized for information. Apparently, its methodology focused on describing the experiences and beliefs of cyber security and stock exchange industry experts. Therefore, the researcher opted for qualitative research due to its efficacy. In addition, it allows for use of multiple data forms and combinations, such as interviews, document analysis and observations, as opposed to reliance on a single data source (University of Michigan, 2018). Furthermore, it permits the breaking down of complex datasets into simple data inferences and is a more communicative approach to research data collection.

## 3.2  Dataset Collection Methods and Tools

Diverse techniques were used to achieve three data collection datasets: misinformation, detection and countermeasures. Qualitative data methods were used to collect non-numeric data that helped the researcher explore the detection and countermeasures used to prevent misinformation from infiltrating the stock exchange. Descriptive datasets were generated from the data captured from cyber-security journals, SIEM, scholarly papers and stock exchange cyber-security reports (Golmohammadi et al., 2015).

The research in this study was also based on the emerging scholarly literature on misinformation infiltrating the stock exchange, as well as articles publicly available on the Internet. Text data and inferences made were holistic and used as a basis for drawing research findings and conclusions. Different folders were created for types of misinformation, countermeasures and detection strategies for ease of computerizing the data collection and analysis process (North Carolina State University, 2020). The qualitative data collection process entailed the use of semi-structured publications in stock exchange market journals while the document study involved analyzing stock exchange security documents and other research material relevant to the study. Circumspectly, the reviewed documents include archived stock exchange cyber-security documents, annual reports and policy documents (Pennebaker et al., 2015).

## 3.3  Sample Selection

Even though many datasets regarding cybercrimes were collected, the concern on this research has now been revised to address the misinformation on the financial sector. In particular, stock exchange data were analyzed to ensure that only a few related datasets cited specifically to main objectives were collected.

## 3.4  Data Analysis

Certainly, the process of qualitative data analysis involved the collection of published articles in reputed journals. Subsequently, text analysis was then used to analyze and make inferences from datasets. Descriptive datasets were retrieved from different stock exchange cyber security, historical and case study documents (University of Michigan, 2018). The collected data includes current statistics on misinformation attacks, types and impacts on the financial markets. Quite importantly, the researcher employed case study analysis where a selected number of case studies on the impact of misinformation on the stock exchange were explored. Besides, inductive analysis was used to understand specific patterns that were essential in confirming findings and gaining a holistic perspective on how misinformation detection and countermeasures were carried out (Pennebaker et al., 2015).

## 3.5 Algorithmic Techniques

Quite evidently, this study used algorithmic techniques to detect disinformation in the stock exchange and its impact on operations. Moreover, it focused on the use of Artificial Intelligence algorithms to detect misinformation, given their accuracy levels. AI algorithms were successfully used in screening and detecting illegitimate bot accounts (Vosoughi et al., 2018). The techniques used were bot-spotting as well as bot-labelling. These two techniques were essential in identifying and shutting down bot accounts. Machine learning algorithms were used to detect and shut down deceptive stock exchange bots, while the combined use of AI and machine learning algorithms were trained, using data from human moderation (Michael et al., 2021). Besides machine learning and AI, pattern recognition was used to spot and flag websites that propagate fake financial investment news.

## 3.6 Research Limitation

The process of data collection and analysis was intensive and involved data gathering from diverse perspectives and capturing diverse experiences from respondents. Collecting data required ample time and so was analyzing it. Secondly, qualitative research requires that researchers explore large datasets to gain insight and deduce from respondent's data. Thirdly, qualitative data is usually descriptive. Given the non-numerical nature of qualitative data, analyzing and interpreting results usually takes longer. Furthermore, the correlation is not necessarily proportionate to causation (Pennebaker et al., 2015). Although causation can be used to support qualitative research findings, proving causality remains a challenge.

Qualitative research is oftentimes inconclusive and requires further research, which is labour- and time-intensive. In addition, qualitative data lacks the replicability that is associated with quantitative data, given the emotional variability of respondents. The theory-based linguistic algorithm uses machine learning to build content classifiers to flag suspicious stock recommendations while providing robust evaluation and simulation of countermeasures (Verónica et al., 2018). To combat misinformation, the algorithm uses theory-based linguistic features and deep learning to improve the effectiveness of classifiers in detecting false information in financial markets.

## 3.7  Ethics and Social Aspects

Data archiving, sharing and reuse ethics are among the ethical and social issues that have been considered. It was determined that the types of data, data archiving, data reuse, researcher and respondent education, data privacy, the anonymity of respondents and appropriate handling of data management challenges, were all taken into consideration in this study (Newman et al., 2013). It also took into account policy development and practices, appropriate data-sharing practices, the protection of researcher and respondent identities, the impact of research on families and society and the ethics of data reuse. When it comes to data reuse, the research looked at policy and practice documents that presented complex ethical situations. Aside from that, the researcher considered the ethical quandaries that arise from financial, technical and social data-sharing procedures (Yang et al., 2020). Furthermore, the researcher focused on developing ethical practices, such as ethical incorporation of future research data into consent forms. Social and ethical implications of data collection, sharing and transmission were put into consideration (Jegadeesh and Wu, 2013). Effective communication and collaboration were used where meetings discussed emerging ethical and social issues.

# 4.  Discussion on the Findings

Social media platforms, such as Facebook and Twitter, have become the norm for the consumption of news and information for many individuals. However, they could also be a platform for spreading disinformation. Online news and posts continue to surface through social media platforms by individuals who share information. They can easily manipulate the content and turn it into fake news. Unfortunately, the information ecosystem is saturated with false information, continuously exploited by threat actors with the means to intensify the spread of disinformation, making it more difficult to discern real from fake.

Stock market misinformation research shows that machine learning algorithms, namely Naïve Bayes, Convolutional Neural Networks (CNN), LTSM and Support Vector Machine can be used to detect and remedy stock market misinformation. However, effective use of these technological frameworks requires the elimination of implementation challenges (Choudhary et al., 2021). Effective detection demands the use of a combination of ML algorithms. However, stock market misinformation can be detected by a hybrid computational model and automated ML techniques. These hybrid models have inbuilt natural ML, Natural Language Processing (NLP) and Bayesian classifiers. However, detection accuracy varies, depending on the framework and algorithms in use. For instance, the hybrid models have a detection accuracy of 77% and rides on short-term memory and neural network architecture (Abdullah-All-Tanvir et al., 2020).

Many researchers have cited machine learning as critical in the detection of misinformation. Though they underscore the use of ML algorithms, namely Naïve Bayes, Neural Network Support (NNS) and Support Vector Machine (SVM). Naïve Bayes and Neural Network Support are the most accurate technological frameworks

(Aphiwongsophon and Chongstitvatana, 2018). Stock exchange misinformation can be detected using automated text classification algorithms based on the N-gram model. However, when used alongside extraction techniques and machine learning classification, the results show significant detection accuracy improvement (Ahmed et al., 2020). However, there is a lack of consensus with regards to detection accuracy since some studies recommend N-gram analysis and machine learning. The proponents of the N-gram technique suggest that when combined with Term Frequency-Inverted Document Frequency (TF-IDF), it yields the highest accuracy levels. Moreover, other findings show that Linear Support Vector (LSV) with a classification accuracy of 92% surpasses popular detection techniques.

Misinformation propagated through social media platforms can lead to stock market manipulation. However, while the current literature shows that trending mood states have a direct impact on stock market predictions and the stock market trading decisions, there is a need for further research (Ahmed et al., 2020). Misinformation does not only affect stock markets but cryptocurrency markets as well. Research has linked misinformation to cryptocurrency market manipulation. The result of the manipulation is pump and dump and ultimately sporadic price fluctuations. Conversely, tightening of government regulations can help remedy stock and cryptocurrency market manipulation (Kamps and Kleinberg, 2018). Certainly, current literature recommends the use of anomaly detection algorithms to detect irregular trading patterns, based on AI and ML. The finding notwithstanding, pump and dump are best detected by identifying the clustering of cryptocurrency transactions. The combined use of AI, ML and DL algorithms to detect stock exchange misinformation yields high detection accuracy (Lin, 2017).

Misinformation is a modern tool used to perpetrate stock market attacks, although further research is needed to thoroughly understand mapping, risks and challenges (Choudhary et al., 2021). Also, stock market research shows that ML and DL can be used to analyze the mood change in social media platforms to influence the stock market movement. Although the social media mood state can be used to predict shifts or price fluctuations in the stock markets, the results are inconclusive (Lachanski and Pav, 2017; Nofer and Hinz, 2015). Further research is needed to establish a direct link between a change in social media mood state and stock market manipulation. Nonetheless, there is conclusive evidence showing that financial markets react to misinformation and hence traders can leverage the reaction for market manipulation. Notwithstanding the impact of misinformation on stock prices, counter-misinformation regulations are required to mitigate stock market exploitation (Wirama et al., 2017).

Hybrid Harris Hawks and machine learning models alongside smart classification models can be used to detect misinformation using natural language processing. However, to achieve high accuracy, Harris Hawk Optimizer (HHO) should be used in combination with bag of words and other modern extraction frameworks, such as content and word-based schemes (Wirama et al., 2017). However, some researchers propose the use of logistic regression (LR) and Term-Frequency-Inverse Document Frequency (TF-IDF) models to achieve high detection accuracy. Accordingly, they assert that these algorithms have higher performance as compared to other detection algorithms. On the other hand, NLP and text classification algorithms can be used to detect misinformation. However, research findings show that text classification models, when used alongside LSTM models, yield high detection accuracy based on the source flagging technique (Abdullah-All-Tanvir et al., 2020).

While NLP algorithms, such as vectorization, dimensionality, quality evaluation and machine learning have proven high textual detection accuracy, hybrid text extraction techniques are effective, counter-factual evaluation frameworks used to distinguish factual from non-factual information. Furthermore, misinformation can be detected using a FakeNewsTracker that deploys ML, DL and visualisation techniques to detect stock market misinformation (Shu et al. 2019).

As gap analysis showed from all the reviews, the use of information security event tools was also a pragmatic approach in detecting misinformation, disseminating misleading data into the stock exchange market. Yayla and Hu (2011) explored information security events and how they affect corporate value. The study focused on information security and its impact on the stock market performance. The research is relevant since compromised systems provide a platform for spreading fake news and misinformation.

Data collection was successful, notwithstanding the various challenges encountered. Data was divided into three datasets, namely detection, countermeasures and deep learning algorithms for detecting misinformation (Heston and Sinha, 2017). Techniques of detecting capital markets targeted misinformation bots, used to manipulate stock prices, were discussed. Keyword-based false information detection uses machine learning models to detect disinformation. Algorithm uses classification models to detect and flag messages using content and linguistic characteristics (University of Göttingen, 2021). The algorithmic detection captures the mood and comprehensibility of the message. To achieve high detection rates, a combination of diverse detection models is used. Such algorithm flags the message using specific mood-defining keywords that would have enticed unsuspecting investors into purchasing a particular stock (Heston and Sinha, 2017).

Once the message is flagged as misinformation, trading on the stock concerned is temporarily suspended. The algorithm then publishes credible information, alerting investors about the suspended trading on the stock and the reasons behind the suspension. Linguistic algorithm analyses the inherent quantifiable attributes, such as grammatical structure and word choice (Golmohammadi et al., 2015). Besides, the algorithm detects the punctuation and text complexity of a news article to deduce its authenticity and trustworthiness. The algorithm has a 76% success rate and a small margin of error as compared to other algorithms.

While linguistic algorithms are associated with a high degree of fake news detection, the challenge lies in training the algorithm with the appropriate datasets (Aggarwal and Wu, 2006); for example, in another research, it was noted that AI accuracy can be infiltrated to give a deceptive result by training the AI using DL algorithm to give wrong information. Jiang et al. (2020) advocates the use of Particle Swarm Optimization (PSO) to overcome the threat of data-poisoning attack by focussing on how data is introduced to the algorithm during the training phase to ensure that high accuracy is maintained.

## 4.1 Detecting and Preventing Misinformation

### 4.1.1 Stock Exchange Infrastructure Architecture and Lab Setup

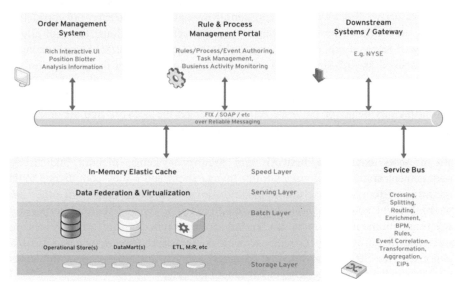

**Fig. 1:** Architecture of a real-world trading platform.

*Source*: https://www.vamsitalkstech.com/architecture/design-and-architecture-of-a-real-world-trading-platform-23/.

Below is the simulated stock exchange lab setup diagram with the aim of targeting the information and data layers systems.

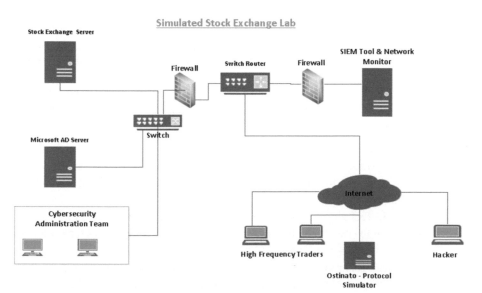

**Fig. 2:** Simulated stock exchange system.

### 4.1.2 Implementing and Detecting Countermeasures

For this research, a commercially available SIEM tool was deployed on a VMware appliance on a lab that consisted of application servers, workstations, virtual networks, active directory system and sample logical datasets to carry out correlation activity across the different log sources and different applications. The tool allows viewing of relevant reports and receive alarms when issues arise. Sample datasets being mocked as real-time data were fed into various parts of the systems for the SIEM's advanced intelligence engine to perform machine analytics, applying multiple real time analytical techniques across all incoming data to spot anomalies and suspicious behavior patterns. Activities across the network and all other data were correlated and analyzed to highlight concerning high-priority events.

Security Information Event Management (SIEM) software gathers, examines and presents data from network and security systems, identity and access management applications, vulnerability management and policy compliance tools, operating system, database and application logs, as well as data from other and external threat sources. Additionally, the SIEM tool is used for monitoring and assisting with the management of user and service privileges, directory services and other system configuration changes, as well as log auditing and review and incident response. The SIEM tool provides detailed security analytics across the entire mocked stock exchange systems environment lab setup.

This section discusses the investigation of the proposed methodology's overall concept, the configuration of the SIEM for detecting the following: using the capabilities of its highly built-in Artificial Intelligence, deep learning and machine learning algorithms and the concept based on the Mitre Att&ck framework.

### 4.1.3 Mitre ATT&CK

MITRE ATT&CK® is a publicly available knowledge base of adversary tactics and techniques derived from field observations. The techniques use various entry vector to gain a foothold through initial access. The ATT&CK knowledge base is used to develop specific threat models and methodologies in the private sector, government, and the cyber-security product and service community.

The Mitre ATT&CK Framework is a collection of techniques used by attackers at some stage in a breach. The ATT&CK matrix breaks the methods down into the following tactics:

- **Initial access:** Techniques that use various entry vectors to gain a foothold. Footholds gained through initial access may allow continued access, like valid accounts and use of external remote services, or may be limited use due to changing passwords.
- **Execution:** Techniques that result in adversary-controlled code running on a local or remote system. Techniques that run malicious code are often paired with techniques from all other tactics to achieve broader goals.
- **Persistence:** Techniques that adversaries use to keep access to systems across restarts, changed credentials and other interruptions that could cut off their access.

- **Privilege escalation:** Techniques that adversaries use to gain higher-level permissions on a system or network. The techniques often overlap with persistence techniques.

- **Défence evasion:** Techniques that adversaries use to avoid detection throughout their compromise.

- **Credential access:** Techniques for stealing credentials, like account names and passwords.

- **Discovery:** Techniques an adversary uses to gain knowledge about the system and internal network. Native operating system tools are often used towards this post-compromise information-gathering objective.

- **Lateral movement:** Techniques that adversaries use to enter and control remote systems on a network.

- **Collection:** Techniques adversaries use to gather information and the source information is collected from that are relevant to following through on the adversary's objectives.

- **Command and control:** Techniques that adversaries use to communicate with systems under their control within a victim network.

- **Exfiltration:** Techniques that adversaries use to steal data from your network.

- **Impact:** Techniques that adversaries use to disrupt availability or compromise integrity by manipulating business and operations processes.

*Source:* https://attack.mitre.org/.

### 4.1.4  Investigation of the Proposed Methodology

- **Insider trading threats**

  Configuration was made to detect any suspicious users based on predetermined users pulled from the Active Directory system. Suspicious datasets of users fed into the system were immediately flagged for attention.

- **Fraud**

  By inspecting the detection of privileged user escalation activities, the lateral movement of data and the file integrity monitoring of file attributes (stock exchange market files) and fraud detection were accomplished. File integrity monitoring is an internal control or process that performs the act of validating the integrity of application software files by comparing the current file state to a known, good baseline, using a verification method between the current file state and a known, good baseline (FIM). A common method of performing this comparison is to compute a recognised cryptographic checksum of the file's initial baseline and compare it to the computed cryptographic checksum of the file's current state.

Detection activities were based on using the tool for pragmatic exercise in detecting the above activities that will likely propagate misinformation in stock exchange information systems.

The following values were checked for any changes to files or configuration items that were not expected. These were credential, privileges and security settings, content, core attributes and size, hash values, configuration values and file attributes and size.

As FIM was the area where the research was critically conducted to find out the effectiveness of the methodology employed, the outcome after fiddling with the stock exchange file system was captured, showing when the files were ***read, modified and added***. The suspicious activities were captured and alarmed, as shown in the images below from the lab test.

**Fig. 3:** Detecting file modification.

- **Behavior anomalies with users**

  Trend analysis was programmed to study the behavior attitude of the subject's use on objects based on roles and responsibilities and any abnormal deviations. The tool had the functionality for monitoring user end-behavior analytics.

- **Compliance violations**

  The tool was set to monitor incoming logs to detect high textual accuracy to distinguish factual from non-factual information textual contents of data not conforming to standard.

- **Disruption to IT services**

  Rules were put in place to detect malware activities where spoofing activities would be detected as well as denial of services (DoS) to suffocate legitimate

**Fig. 4:** Detecting file modification.

users from using the system at the time when perpetrators are hijacking the system to dump misinformation into the system. The tool also has the capability of monitoring the entire network for traffic and packet analysis of know protocols.

### 4.1.4 Network Monitoring (NM) Tool

The NM also has the capability of monitoring the entire network for traffic and packet analysis of know protocols.

The NM can detect malicious content infiltrating the network and extract details, such as the source or destination URL and the file names transferred. It also provides a quick way to analyze smart flow data in order to identify inappropriate activity, such as the use of cloud-sharing applications.

• **Botnets and command and control**

Today's botnet is what is used by high-frequency traders to communicate with inside system through command and control centres. Configuration was made to detect the use of standard ports and legitimate applications that disguise the traffic to avoid detection. The configuration was put in to observe non-http traffic on port 80 and identifies it as legitimate application or suspicious malformed http packet headers.

The NM tool provides detailed security analytics across the entire stock exchange systems environment. The initial analyzed dashboard that displays all the data the network monitor has collected since it was turned on and the timeframe can be adjusted to reflect when the tool began to collect data. This demonstrates the direction of traffic and the type of traffic observed, and a pattern can be observed from here to drill down into the suspicious graph, which may be an indicator of suspicious activity.

**Fig. 5:** Network traffic monitoring.

With the tool's SmartResponse automation capabilities, it was set up to achieve automation for seamless execution of actions at the source of the collected data and alarms to terminate unauthorized activities, such as monitor remote access/Remote Desktop Protocol (RDP) logs and disable unused remote access/RDP ports:

- Implement listing policies for applications and remote access that only permit systems to implement recognized and authorized programmes under an established security policy.
- Audit administrative user accounts on a regular basis and configure access controls according to the principle of least privilege to ensure that new accounts are created by legitimate users.
- Scan the network for open and listening ports and close those that are not required.

### 4.1.5 Education and Training

Providing a platform for educating and training employees on the defences of misinformation attacks could be beneficial in motivating staff to question the validity of an unusual request for payment or network access (Nelson et al., 2020). Also, companies should consider monitoring their social media platforms and websites for misinformation. Individuals need to be aware of the possibility of becoming a victim to various forms of communication fraud. They need to be aware of the importance to verify authenticity of information before taking any action that may result in loss of revenue due to negligence resulting from unawareness of obvious deception.

Furthermore, organizations must assist in the prevention of targeted social engineering and phishing scams by providing end-user awareness and training. Companies need to ensure that employees and stakeholders are aware of potential cyber threats and how they are delivered. Training on information security principles and techniques should also be made available to end users. Employees need to understand the process involved in reporting suspicious transactions and what actions to take to identify threats, including how to initiate mitigation strategies as quickly and efficiently as possible.

As a standard protocol, all employees must undergo Internet security awareness training and be made aware of company policies on the use of electronic devices; for example, computer usage policy and others, like information security policy, records management policy, retention and disposal schedules, archiving policy, data privacy policy, ICT policy, information sharing policy and remote working policy.

### 4.1.6 Legislative and Regulatory Controls

Many research outcomes have shown that having a robust information governance that complements applicable government regulations is a good practice (Selvam and Dominic, 2018). At the very least, there must be information security and data protection policies which ensure data is legally and properly processed.

In addition, compliance with General Data Protection Regulation (GDPR, 2018) is compulsory to ensure that all personal data processed is legal. Additionally, the Computer Misuse Act 1998 must be followed, which safeguards personal data held by organizations against unauthorized access and modification, as well as adherence to Information Technology Infrastructure Library (ITIL) guidelines to protect organization's information asset.

Below is a list of recommended policies/standards that will need to be complied with, to safeguard stock market data:

| Standard Reference | Information about Standard |
|---|---|
| ISO/IEC 27002 Code of Practice | Guidelines for improving security in organizations |
| ISO/IEC 27002 | Information security code of practice and management |
| British Standard 77 99 (ISO 27001) | Security Standard in UK used for implementing IT security process |
| COBIT – Control Objectives for Information Technology | Code of Practice for Information Security and Controls. This is also used for ISMS auditing and certifications |
| SP800-30 National Institute of Standards and Technology (NIST) | Management of risks as recommended by NIST in USA |
| ISO/IEC 27003 | IT system implementation, security management and guidance |
| ISO/IEC 27004 | IT information measurements and techniques |
| ISO/IEC 27005 | IT risk management and security techniques |
| ISO 31000:2009 | Risk management and guidelines standards |
| ISO 31000:2009 | Principles and guidelines of risk management |
| The Committee of Sponsoring Organizations (COSO) | Treadway Commission recommendation on how to deal with the evolution of enterprise risk management to meet the evolving demands of today's businesses |

## 5. Conclusion and Recommendations

The initial purpose of this research was to look into the use of advanced machine learning techniques in deepfake technology attacks and the countermeasures necessary to combat this threat. Additionally, the research was conducted to identify areas requiring legal and regulatory controls as a means of combating deepfake attacks and to assess the necessary steps in education and training for users to detect deepfake attacks.

However, upon further consultation and guidelines with the supervisor, the approved research proposal was slightly changed to objectively examine the implications of disinformation/misinformation, using available technological tools and advances to manipulate the stock market. The research project was carried out with the sole objective of using ISE technological tools in detecting dissemination of misinformation data into the stock exchange system.

However, based on numerous conclusions from literature reviews which focussed on detecting social media fake news as another form of misinformation, there wasn't a concrete detection mechanism currently adopted as a standard framework for stopping stock exchange misinformation. Therefore, there is a big gap in this area of detecting social media misinformation affecting stock exchange market trading systems. Hence, there is future work to be done to establish a proper framework for combating social media misinformation affecting the stock exchange trading market.

On the one hand, the technical research carried out, using the ISE tools successfully, demonstrated how suspicious rogue trader or insider infiltration to disseminate misinformation in the stock market could be stopped. On the other hand, this framework is not widely used due to the fact that the ISE profiled is a commercial product. Hence, it is not widely affordable by many.

Although some specific commercial tools and other simulation products were used, these could be heavily improved upon by using some of the top Gartner quadrant SIEMs, File Integrity Monitoring and Network Monitor commercial tools in providing robust setups/configurations against the propagation of misinformation on the stock market. Detecting misinformation and protecting stock market trading systems must be the ultimate goal to maintain Confidentiality, Integrity and Availability (CIA) of data in the stock exchange trading system.

User awareness training must be a mandatory offering of every organization providing trading systems. Organizational security awareness refers to the knowledge and attitude that members of a company have about protecting the organization's information assets. Organizations must provide formal security awareness training to all employees and this training must be an ongoing process that takes place on a regular basis in accordance with established schedules. Additionally, it must address employees and contractor responsibilities when handling confidential information, including the review of employee Non-Disclosure Agreements (NDA).

Training should also cover topics, such as proper methods for protecting sensitive information on computer systems, such as password policies and the use of two-factor authentication as well as and how to deal with Personal Identifiable Information (PII). Other computer security concerns, such as malware, phishing and social engineering scams should be prominent in such programmes.

According to the European Network and Information Security Agency, 'Awareness of the risks and available safeguards is the first line of defence for the security of information systems and networks' (OECD Security Guideline, 2003).

Organizations must have strong information governance policies in place to govern the use of all related technologies involved in governing the entire organization. Trading organizations must look at the general security protection of the stock exchange trading ecosystem by incorporating in-depth holistic security solutions to thwart any targeted cybercrimes against it. Modern cyber-attacks come in many different ways and forms. Consequently, strong security governance framework must be at the core of every stock exchange trading setup. If cyber criminals compromise trading systems, it's easy to imagine them exploiting the breach by 'artificially' increasing or decreasing the price of their respective sell or buy positions. Typically, this was seen when the Hong Kong exchange suffered cyber-attack in 2019 (FT.com, 2019).

# References

Abdullah Al-Tanvir Mahir, E.M., Huda, S. and Barua, S. (2020). A hybrid approach for identifying authentic news using deep learning methods on popular twitter threads. *In: 2020 International Conference on Artificial Intelligence and Signal Processing (AISP)*, 1–6. doi: 10.1109/AISP48273.2020.9073583.

Aggarwal, R. and Wu, G. (2006). Stock market manipulations. *The Journal of Business*, 79(4): 1915–1953. doi:10.1086/503652.

Ahmed, H., Traoré, I. and Saad, S. (2017). *Detection of Online Fake News Using N-Gram Analysis and Machine Learning Techniques.* ISDDC.

Ahmed, H., Traoré, I. and Saad, S. (2018). Detecting opinion spam and fake news using text classification. *Secur. Priv.*, 1.

Aphiwongsophon, S. and Chongstitvatana, P. (2018). Detecting fake news with machine learning method. *In: 2018 15th International Conference on Electrical Engineering/Electronics, Computer, Telecommunications and Information Technology (ECTI-CON)*, pp. 528–531. doi: 10.1109/ECTICon.2018.8620051.

Call for Bank of England executive to quit over security breach; *BBC News*. https://www.bbc.com/news/business-50849479/. [Online] [accessed 20 July, 2021].

Carta, S., Consoli, S., Piras, L., Podda, A.S. and Recupero, D.R. (2021). Event detection in finance using hierarchical clustering algorithms on news and tweets. *Peer Computer Science.*

Choudhary, M. Jha, S., Prashant, D. Saxena, and A.K. Singh (2021). A review of fake news detection methods using machine learning. *In: 2nd International Conference for Emerging Technology (INCET)*, pp. 1–5. doi: 10.1109/INCET51464.2021.9456299.

De Beer, Dylan and Matthee, Machdel. (2021). *Approaches to Identify Fake News: A Systematic Literature Review.* 10.1007/978-3-030-49264-9_.

De Oliveira, N.R., Pisa, P.S., Martin, A.L., Dianne Scherly, V.D.M. and Mattos, D.M.F. (2021). Identifying fake news on social networks based on natural language processing: Trends and challenges. *Information*, 12(1): 38.

Ghosh, S. and Shah, C. (2018). Towards automatic fake news classification. *American Society for Information Science and Technology, Proceedings of the ASIST Annual Meeting*, 55(1): 805–807.

Golmohammadi, K., Zaïane, O. and Diaz, D. (2015). Detecting stock market manipulation using supervised learning algorithms. *In: DSAA 2014—Proceedings of the 2014 IEEE International Conference on Data Science and Advanced Analytics*, pp. 435–441. 10.1109/DSAA.2014.7058109.

Heston, S.L. and Sinha, N.R. (2017). News vs. sentiment: Predicting stock returns from news stories. *Financial Analysts Journal*, 73(3): 67–83.

Jegadeesh, N. and Wu, D. (2013). Word power: A new approach for content analysis. *Journal of Financial Economics*, 110(3): 712–729.

Kammoun, N., Bounfour, A., Altay Özaygen and Dieye, R. (2019). Financial market reaction to cyber-attacks. *Cogent Economics & Finance*, 7(1).

Kamps, J. and Kleinberg, B. (2018). To the moon: Defining and detecting cryptocurrency pump-and-dump. *Crime Science*, 7(1): 1–18.

Lachanski, M. and Pav, S. (2017). Shy of the character limit: Twitter mood predicts the stock market revisited. *Econ Journal Watch*, 14(3): 302–345.

Lin, T.C.W. (2017). The new market manipulation. *Emory Law Journal*, 66(6): 1253–1314.

Malyshenko, K., Malyshenko, V., Ponomareva, E.Y. and Anashkina, M. (2019). Analysis of the stock market anomalies in the context of changing the information paradigm. *Eastern Journal of European Studies*, 10(1): 239–270.

Mats, D. (2021). A value-driven approach to addressing misinformation in social media. *Humanities & Social Sciences Communications*, 8(1).

Michael, S., Muntermann, J. and Miha, G. (2021). Design principles for robust fraud detection: The case of stock market manipulations. *Journal of the Association for Information Systems*, 22(1): 156. doi: 10.17705/1jais.00657.

Mitre ATT&CK Framework. https://attack.mitre.org/.

Nadejda, K., Love, E., Mattias, S., Larsson, A., Shah Syed, I.H., Myrsini, G., Vasilis, K., Newman, M.L., Pennebaker, J.W., Berry, D.S. and Richards, J.M. (2013). Lying words: Predicting deception from linguistic styles. *Personality and Social Psychology Bulletin*, 29(5): 665–675.

Nofer, M. and Hinz, O. (2015). Using twitter to predict the stock market: Where is the mood effect? *Business & Information Systems Engineering*, 57(4): 229–242.

North Carolina State University. (2020, April). 'Fake news' increases consumer demands for corporate action, *ScienceDaily*, retrieved 2 July, 2021. www.sciencedaily.com/releases/2020/04/200408125519.htm.

Pennebaker, J., Booth, R., Boyd, R. and Francis, M. (2015). *Linguistic Inquiry and Word.* Retrieved 28 April, 2016.

Shu, K., Mahudeswaran, D. and Liu, H. (2019). 'FakeNewsTracker: A tool for fake news collection, detection, and visualization. *Computational and Mathematical Organization Theory*, 25(1): 60–71.

Smith, K.T., Jones, A., Johnson, L. and Lawrence, M.S. (2019). Examination of cybercrime and its effects on corporate stock value. *Journal of Information, Communication & Ethics in Society*, 17(1): 42–60.

Thaher, T., Saheb, M., Turabieh, H. and Chantar, H. (2021). Intelligent detection of false information in arabic tweets utilising hybrid harris hawks based feature selection and machine learning models. *Symmetry*, 13(4): 556.

University of Göttingen. (2021, February). Detecting fake news designed to manipulate stock markets, *ScienceDaily*; retrieved 2 July, 2021. www.sciencedaily.com/releases/2021/02/210201144933.htm.

University of Michigan. (2018, August). Fake news detector algorithm works better than a human, *ScienceDaily*; retrieved 1 July, 2021. www.sciencedaily.com/releases/2018/08/180821112007.htm.

Verónica Pérez-Rosas, Bennett Kleinberg, Alexandra Lefevre and Rada Mihalcea. (2018). *Automatic Detection of Fake News.* Submitted to arXiv.

Vosoughi, S., Roy, D. and Aral, S. (2018). The spread of true and false news online. *Science*, 359(6380): 1146–1151.

Wirama, D.G., Bagus Wiksuana, I.G., Mohd-Sanusi, Z. and Kazemian, S. (2017). Price manipulation by dissemination of rumors: Evidence from the indonesian stock market. *International Journal of Economics and Financial Issues*, 7(1).

Yang Cheng and Zifei Fay Chen. (2020). The influence of perceived fake news influence: examining public support for corporate corrective response. *Media Literacy Intervention, and Governmental Regulation, Mass Communication and Society*, 2020. doi: 10.1080/15205436.2020.1750656.

Yayla, A.A. and Hu, Q. (2011). The impact of information security events on the stock value of firms: The effect of contingency factors. *Journal of Information Technology*, 26(1): 60–77.

# 5

# Profiling and Predicting Malware Threats during COVID-19 Pandemic

*Karishma Hiranna Raghupati* and *Sina Pournouri**

## ABSTRACT

2020 was a year that taught us that events in the real world and cyber security are inextricably linked. According to previous *M-Trends reports*, geopolitical events frequently have an impact on cyber security and in 2020, we witnessed a worldwide pandemic affect business operations and, as a result, the cyber-attack landscape and risk profile of most businesses. Businesses around the world saw attackers take advantage of these unprecedented times as businesses struggled to adapt to the new norm of cyber security. This past year, security practitioners encountered a slew of problems that pushed businesses into unknown territory. A global pandemic reaction to COVID-19 demanded remote employment for a major section of the economy, while ransomware developers targeted State and public organizations in addition to hospitals and schools. Businesses are forced to embrace new technology and rapidly scale beyond their regular development plans (FireEye, 2021). Multiple COVID-19-themed cyber-attacks targeting different categories of businesses were detected in 2020. Looking ahead a year, the world will still be in transition, attempting to adjust to a new economy. Organizations will rethink their cyber-security strategy and shift to more adaptable operational models. This chapter aims to investigate the effectiveness and efficiency of the data-mining specifically classification techniques in predicting malware in the pre- and post-COVID-19 era, to highlight the cyber-security challenges that malware attacks pose to businesses.

Sheffield Hallam University, UK.
* Corresponding author: S.Pournouri@shu.ac.uk

# 1. Background

## 1.1 Malware Categorization

Malware, often known as malicious software, is a software that is designed to infect a computer without the knowledge or agreement of the user. It is essentially a standard term to define all types of threats that might damage a system. The malware basically comprises file infections and stand-alone malware. The malware's goals might consist of gaining access to private networks, data theft, resource utilization, and service disruptions. Malwares are generally disguised as trustworthy software but are intentionally malicious with the ability to remain undetected, propagate through the network, damage or corrupt the system. The most common types are viruses, worms, Trojan horses, backdoors, rootkits, ransomwares, spywares, etc. (bin Asad et al., 2020).

## 1.2 Malware Type

As previously stated, malware, also known as malicious software, is a collection of codes created by cyber-attackers with the purpose of causing harm to other people's information or computer systems. With this context in mind, malware is commonly

**Table 1:** Malware types (Aslan et al., 2020).

| Malware Types | Primary Characteristics |
|---|---|
| **Virus** | • Malware that is most prevalent and well-known<br>• It attaches itself to other programmes to spread |
| **Worm** | • Spreads through the use of a computer network<br>• Unauthorized access is possible<br>• Frequently opens a backdoor in the infected machine |
| **Trojan Horse** | • Appears to be a genuine or trustworthy software, but it is not<br>• It can open a backdoor in the infected machine<br>• Unauthorized access is possible<br>• Command and control to transmit sensitive data to unauthorized party |
| **Backdoor** | • Traditional security methods are bypassed<br>• Allows remote access to the system<br>• Trojans and worms are commonly used to install backdoors |
| **Rootkit** | • Provide attackers with administrative access<br>• Files are hidden from the operating system<br>• It has the ability to merge with other malware |
| **Ransomware** | • Data is encrypted on the target or infected machine<br>• The target or victim has to pay a ransom to receive the decryption keys to open the data |
| **Spyware** | • Transmit sensitive data of target or victim to unauthorized party<br>• Usually used to get access to credit card data or to learn about user behavior |
| **Obfuscated malware** | • Any form of malware obfuscated<br>• Makes detection challenging |

classified as indicated in the table below, based on the primary characteristics and varying effects on the target or victim. An attacker often begins the attack by exploiting a known vulnerability in the system to launch the malware. Vulnerabilities may include buffer overflow, injection and sensitive data misconfiguration. As malware is growing increasingly complex, exhibiting characteristics of multiple types, categorizing them, based on type, is becoming complicated (Aslan et al., 2020).

## 1.3 Malware Family

The malware family is a concept that categorizes malware based on the way it achieves its aim and not on the aim. As is usual in software engineering or development, malware, like any other software, it goes through a continual cycle in which features are added and flaws are repaired. The new sample created may be a variation or a version of the existing family. It is based on their differences from earlier iterations. They are usually from the same family. Grouping the malware into families improves the efficiency of analysis by providing researchers with additional information, apart from the malware type. Categorization based on family is done differently than based on type and it is not possible to fit all malware into a predetermined list of families. Typically, the name of a new malware family is based on strings discovered in samples and follows the Computer Antivirus Research Organization's (CARO) malware naming method (Simpson, 2021).

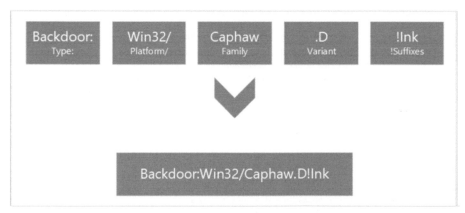

**Fig. 1:** Computer Antivirus Research Organization (CARO) malware naming scheme (Simpson, 2021).

## 1.4 Malware Nature

Malware is divided into two types: first and second generation. The internal structure of the malware does not change for the first, whereas it keeps varying for the second.

The second generation is broadly classified, based on their nature as mentioned in the table below (Dwivedi and Sharan, 2021).

**Table 2:** Malware nature (Dwivedi and Sharan, 2021).

| Malware Nature | Primary Characteristics |
|---|---|
| **Encrypted** | The first camouflage technique in the second generation with the goal of modifying the binary code of the malware. It is often composed of an encrypted body and a decryption code. At every instance of infection, the encrypted malware is encoded differently and a different key is used to disguise the signature. The first encrypted malware was CASCADE followed by Win95/Mad and Win95/Zombie. The primary purpose of encryption was to evade or delay static code analysis. In recent times, TLS encryption is being used, which is making pattern-matching techniques ineffective and creating a requirement for improved and enhanced detection methods. |
| **Oligomorphic** | The drawback of encrypted malware was the discovery of decryption keys. To overcome this, malware was designed to change the decryptor slightly by giving a variety of decryptors rather than a single one. One example is W95/Memorial, which can generate 96 decryptors. Nevertheless, this is not a preferred method by attackers as it can be easily detected by signature-based analyzers. |
| **Polymorphic** | This has two components: one for decrypting the code and the other is the body part. One portion of the body remains the same at each repetition. Due to this, it can be easily detected. Mark Washburn created the first known polymorphic malware, 1260, in 1990. During malware execution, the mutation engine generates a new decryptor by changing the length of NOP, permutation of usage registers and inserting loops in the code that are linked with the encrypted malware body to form a new strain of malware. |
| **Metamorphic** | Known as body-polymorphic at each repetition, resulting in each succeeding version of the code being distinct from the previous one. The malware's essential functionality remains the same by producing a new instance, using obfuscation techniques, instead of a decryptor. Due to the changes, it is difficult to detect by signature-based tools. Very few malwares exhibit real metamorphism, like Win95/Regswap, Win32/Ghost, W32/NGVCK. |

## 1.5 Malware Detection Taxonomy

Recently, there has been a dramatic rise in the amount of scholarly research on malware analysis and detection techniques. During the early stages of development, signature-based detection was extensively utilized and performed efficiently for detecting known malware with known signatures, but was infective for unknown or zero-day malware. Over time, new methods were researched and new models depicts an overview of malware detection methods, characteristics and strategies utilized (Aslan and Samet, 2020).

## 1.6 Current State of Knowledge

There are many research works done in the field of malware prediction using data mining techniques and a few of literatures have been reviewed below to understand the strengths, weaknesses and scope of future works.

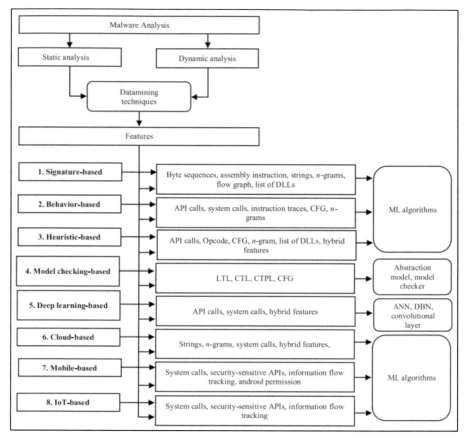

**Fig. 2:** Flow chart of malware detection taxonomy (Aslan and Samet, 2020).

Pournouri et al.'s (Pournouri et al., 2019) research work uses classification data-mining techniques to predict the type of cyber-attack targets. The research is conducted using OSINT; specifically, the dataset obtained from the Hackmageddon Blog by Paolo Passeri from 2013 to 2015, with 2,694 records and each record with nine different features. The data is initially restructured to include only relevant five features and then processed using the open refine tool to remove doubles and ambiguous records, irrelevant records and irrelevant columns and deal with capital and small letters. The research then utilizes classification algorithms, namely, Decision Trees, Naïve Bayes, Support Vector Machine, K nearest neighbour and artificial neural network, as they are considered most effective in prediction. The dataset is divided into training and testing: first for training and second for testing the accuracy of the classifiers using the R (carpet package) programming language. The training includes two parts: the first part is train control that validates the accuracy of classifiers using K fold cross-validation with k set to 10 and the second part is tune grid that validates the reaction to various changes for better accuracy and tangible results. The performance is evaluated using the kappa and accuracy of every classifier; SVM is considered for predicting the target type as it has the highest accuracy of 39.69%. The work next evaluates which variable has the most or least effect on the prediction framework by using Weka inbuilt methods of Information Gainer, Correlation Attribute Evaluator, Classifier Attribute Evaluator and Wrapper Subset Evaluator. The results of the SVM classifier illustrate that the attacker has the greatest influence and the country has the minor effect.

The cybersecurity specialists can benefit from the prediction of the type of targets to build a futuristic comprehensive framework for the business, based on the nature of operations as a certain business can be a more significant target. The OSINT dataset has the advantage of being less costly and can be easily shared without any legal issues. The training process is more precise and robust because of the repetitive cycle of k fold cross-validation.

On the other hand, using OSINT has illustrated disadvantages, like intensive as fully automated tools are not used for restructuring and pre-processing the dataset; it has inconsistencies and noise; and data is not comprehensive due to the missing classified sources. In future, the framework can be tested with more comprehensive datasets, using a fully automated software for data processing. The authors have also proposed to test the framework by eliminating the country of target from dataset and considering time-series analysis to see the variance based on time.

This work is closely related to the proposed framework as it illustrates the benefits of predicting the type of cyber-attack target, using OSINT dataset from the Hackmageddon Blog and the dataset is refined using open refine open source tool. The work specifies that classification techniques are well known and best fit for the prediction model. Also, the proposed framework performs well with malware attack types.

Udayakumar et al.'s (Subbulakshmi et al., 2019) research work's aim is to utilize data-mining classifiers to predict the malware category. The malware dataset was created from PE (Portable Executable) files of top 10 malware categories, using open source PE header analysis tool and including seven features. Then the seaborne python library and correlation graph were used for visualization to see the significance on dataset of removing each feature and this provided the dependent and independent features. The training dataset was made less complicated by deleting the dependent features. Next, the dataset was pre-processed by cleaning irrelevant entries, transforming non-integers to integers and finally reducing or removing irrelevant features using Pandas library in python and a number of functions. The model is trained, using Logistic Regression, K nearest neighbor and Support Vector Machine classifiers giving the accuracy of 74%, 91% and 99% respectively. The logistic regression shows to be unsuitable for predicting the malware category with significant low accuracy. The KNN shows better accuracy with k = 13 without considering the over- and under-fitting. The SVM classifier shows to have improved accuracy and is used for testing dataset.

The malware researchers can benefit from this study to forecast malware in early stages and minimize the loss of hackers trying to exploit the vulnerabilities, by having prevention strategies in place. A fully automated tool is used for visualization or dataset pre-processing and feature selection, which reduce the time and resources considerably. The proposed framework demonstrates that classification performs better than clustering for prediction model.

However, before dataset processing, the actual data extraction from files is complicated and fraught with problems. The dataset is limited only to PE files which is not a comprehensive way to collect data for analysis. The work can be further improved by using different datasets and features. The framework is trained against only three well-known classifiers and need to be tested with other classification techniques (not mentioned why specific classifiers were selected).

This work is closely related to the proposed framework as it works on malware datasets and illustrates that prediction of malware can bring positive change to the business. The work specifies that classification techniques are well known and best fit for prediction model.

Rahman et al. (Rahman et al., 2020) proposed a framework for prediction of attack type, using data-mining technique. The framework is divided into two parts: first detection of attack by extracting patterns from the historical dataset and then second is prediction of attack for future. A publicly available Canadian Institute of Cybersecurity (CIC) intrusion detection systems (IDS) datasets are utilized for this framework. A total of seven separate datasets are used, each dataset having a minimum record of 170366 and maximum record of 692703 and each dataset having 78 attributes without considering the class. The work used J48 Decision Tree because it simplifies the understanding of occurrence of any event with the help of logical rules. An open-source tool, Weka is utilized for running this algorithm with default parameters. The accuracy is measured by comparing the detected patterns with the provided class distribution by CIC in the dataset. The experiment provides the accuracy results for DDOS, port scan and infiltration of approximately 99%. For DDOS, the dataset includes 128027 records and the classifier demonstrates nine patterns for 128018 records. For port scan, the dataset includes 158930 records and the classifier demonstrated 11 patterns for 158917 records. For infiltration, the dataset includes 36 records and the classifier demonstrated two patterns for 26 records. This also demonstrates that the classifier performs with accuracy even when the dataset has an imbalance of class.

The cyber-security specialist can benefit from the prediction of type of cyber-attack by having appropriate countermeasures to protect against cyber-attacks and reduce the impact of cyber-attacks on the business. The publicly available dataset used for this work is massive and extensive, with numerous features to test the efficiency of a framework. The J48 classifier uses logic principles to simplify the comprehension of every event's occurrence and provides high accuracy of 99%. The patterns generated from the proposed framework can be further used to detect analogous type of attack, based on regex patterns.

The framework used only one classifier to predict only three types of attacks (DDOS, port scan and infiltration) with high accuracy. The framework must be tested and trained with other classifiers for more types of attacks. The dataset has numerous features and feature dependency should be performed to obtain a better dataset. The work proposes to test the framework, using cost-sensitive classification algorithms with imbalanced datasets to improvise the prediction if J48 doesn't perform with the expected accuracy.

This work uses OSINT dataset, open-source Weka software for analysis and demonstrates that classification technique is best suited for a prediction model which is closely related to the proposed framework.

Wass et al.'s (Wass et al., 2021) research takes into account the COVID-19 pandemic impact on cyber-security landscape to provide a model that can predict the type of attack, using classification algorithms. The research is conducted by using OSINT; specifically, the dataset obtained from the Hackmageddon Blog by Paolo Passeri from 2017 to 2019 for only countries within Europe, it consisted of 1989 records and each record with 11 different features. The data is initially restructured to include only relevant five features and then processed, using the open refine tool to remove duplicates, irrelevant records and irrelevant columns, dealing with capital and small letters and combining values. The research utilizes classification algorithms, namely Support Vector Machine, Random Forest, K nearest neighbor, Naïve Bayes and neural network. The performance is evaluated using metrics of TP rate, FP rate, Precision, Recall and F-measure and then compared to determine the Random Forest classifier to have higher TP rate (0.675%), lower FP rate (0.216%) and a higher accuracy rate (67.4%). The RF classifier was chosen for validation (COVID-19) dataset to demonstrate TP rate, FP rate and accuracy rate of 0.629%, 0.349% and 62.8%, respectively. Even though the model demonstrates not to be robust, it is effective for certain classes of attacks when evaluated with the validation dataset. Malware, targeted attacks and injection attacks were successfully detected. However, Account Hijacking, DDOS, Phishing, Social Bot and Brutes Forcing attacks were not detected.

In the changing security paradigm with COVID-19, this research paper shows the importance of prediction of the type of attack in assisting business to be prepared for a futuristic approach. The dataset used is from publicly available resource which as mentioned above does not pose any ethical or legal issue when shared or used. The framework worked efficiently in detecting malware attacks.

The publicly available dataset has drawbacks, like limited attacks, imbalanced records per category and some records with unclear category type. To improvise the approach, a more balanced dataset should be used where the records are equally distributed between different types of attacks and malware not being the major number, and more concise dataset with clear categories and not ambiguous classes. The dataset is manually reconstructed and pre-processed and this should be fully automated to pose no constrain on time and resource usage.

This research work is based on pre-COVID-19 period prediction using classification algorithms and publicly available dataset. The Hackmageddon Blog dataset is pre-processed using open-refine open-source tool. The researcher illustrates that classification algorithms perform well in prediction of malware attacks on the proposed model.

Yeboah-Ofori et al.'s (Yeboah-Ofori et al., 2021) research work aims to apply machine learning techniques on Cyber Threat Intelligence (CTI) for the prediction of type of threat specific to the supply chain. The research is divided into three phases, namely threat analysis, threat prediction and controls. The Microsoft Malware

Prediction dataset from Kaggle blog is utilized for this experiment and it consists of 40,000 records and every record has 64 features. The records are from endpoints that are not only Microsoft clients, hence the dataset is exhaustive with various malware attacks. The dataset is initially pre-processed by transforming average columns, removing all NaN (Not a Number) and removing unwanted duplicates to generate a total of 52 columns or features. For the experiment, 10-fold cross-validation optimization algorithm is used to establish the parameter approximation. The metrics used to evaluate the accuracy are TP, TN, FP, FN rates and then the results are compared using ROC-AUC curve. The different machine learning algorithm used in this work are Logistic Regression (LR), Support Vector Machine (SVM), Random Forest (RF) and Decision Tree (DT), which demonstrated accuracy rate of 66%, 62%, 66% and 63%, respectively. Hence it demonstrates that LR and RF are the preferred classifi2ers due to improved Precision, Recall and F-Score. However, when considering only malware, ransomware and spyware attacks, the accuracy rate was improved to 85%.

The advantage of using CTI is that it includes data from various sources, like OSINT and dark web, making the dataset comprehensive. This specific dataset includes malware samples from numerous endpoints that are not only from Microsoft clients. The researcher believes that using CTI can enhance the overall security landscape. The accuracy of framework showed better results for malware prediction compared to other type of attacks.

The overall performance or accuracy of this framework is average and can be improved by pre-processing the dataset to be more appropriate and selecting more suitable features.

Using publicly accessible datasets, this research effort examines machine learning methods for malware sample prediction, which is linked with the framework that will be presented in this research work. The predictive findings illustrate that malware and spear phishing are the most anticipated type of attacks in the supply chain.

## 1.7 Summary

The basic elements of this study – malware and data mining, are investigated and explained clearly. Furthermore, the following, gathered from a careful assessment of previous literature relevant to this study, is based on the four important elements:

➤ *Framework* – First element is a theoretical framework that comprehends the concepts pertinent to the research topic. The papers reviewed here follow a similar predictive framework with same building blocks through different techniques, tools and outputs.

➤ *Type of data* – Second element is the source of collecting data. The data can be obtained from classified or publicly available sources. The papers reviewed have all collected publicly available datasets as they can be easily shared without any ethical concerns.

➤ *Type of analysis* – Third element is the technique used to analyse data for prediction. The papers reviewed have all used data mining algorithms to train and test the proposed framework but with different classifiers.

**Table 3:** Summary of related works.

| Research Paper | Framework | Source of Data | Type of Analysis | Accuracy |
|---|---|---|---|---|
| Pournouri et al. (Pournouri et al., 2019) | Data mining classification techniques to predict the type of targets | Public – Hackmageddon | DT NB SVM KNN ANN | SVM - 39.69% |
| Udayakumar et al. (Subbulakshmi et al., 2019) | Data mining classifiers to predict the malware category | Unknown | LR KNN SVM | SVM - 99% |
| Rahman et al. (Rahman et al., 2020) | Data mining techniques to predict the type of attack | Public – Canadian Institute of Cybersecurity (CIC) | J48 | J48 - 99% |
| Wass et al. (Wass et al., 2021) | Data mining classification techniques to predict the type of attack | Public – Hackmageddon | SVM RF KNN NB ANN | RF - 67.4% |
| Yeboah-Ofori et al. (Yeboah-Ofori, et al., 2021) research | Machine learning techniques on CTI to analyse and predict the type of threat to Cyber Suply Chain | Public – Microsoft Malware Prediction (Kaggle) | LR SVM RF DT | LR & RF - 85% (only for malware type) |

> *Accuracy* – Fourth element is the accuracy of the proposed framework. The papers reviewed have evaluated accuracy using different parameters with some classifiers performing better than others. For the purpose of summarisation of this paper, we give more importance to the classifier with better accuracy for malware detection.

# 2.  Methodology

This study is developed in four phases: Data collection, data pre-processing, data analysis using learning algorithms and results of optimal framework.

## 2.1  Phase 1—Data Collection

This phase focuses on the different available data sources and method followed to collect data. Cyber intelligence cannot be collected from classified sources, like government, due to information sharing restrictions. There are many companies, like Crowdstrike, FireEye and Forcepoint that collect cyber intelligence for their own product enhancement or a service to paid customers. There are many publicly available sources, like SoReL-20M (only Windows Portable Executable files), Kaggle (includes multiple datasets but not updated frequently) and EMBER (only Windows portable executable files).

The source of data utilized for this study is the Hackmageddon Blog that is publicly available and does not have any legal or ethical implications on usage or sharing. It is updated more frequently by the authors' experience in collecting main attacks. It includes raw data in Excel sheet since 2011 and for the purpose of this study, we will use data from 1 January 2015 to 31 December 2019 as pre COVID-19 era (training dataset) and from 1 January 2020 to 31 December 2020 as COVID-19 era (testing dataset).

## 2.2  Phase 2—Data Pre-processing

The data collected from phase 1 consists of 11 features or columns for each record. As this study is based for predicting the type of target, the data will be restructured to remove features or columns that are not relevant. After restructuring, the dataset will be pre-processed to extract records only related to malware, type of target summarization, type of attack summarization, replacing empty values and combine same capital and small letters. There are several open-source tools available for pre-processing, like RapidMiner, Data Ladder, Trifacta and OpenRefine. They vary based on the data format, outliers, clustering, spelling variations, language and other factors (Petrova-Antonova and Tancheva, 2020). The 'open-refine' open-source tool will be used as it meets all the requirements for data pre-processing in this study.

## 2.3  Phase 3—Learning Algorithms

With the careful assessment of related works, the most common classification techniques used in cyber-security prediction framework are Decision Trees, Naïve Bayes, Support Vector Machine, K nearest neighbor, Artificial Neural Network and Random Forest. Below is a brief explanation of how each classifier works.

The 'Decision Tree (DT)' technique is considered one of the familiar approaches for representing classifiers in data classification. It has been used in diverse academic fields for machine learning, pattern recognition and statistics. It is a member of the supervised learning algorithm family and unlike other algorithms, it may be utilized to solve regression and classification issues. The aim of utilizing this technique is to build a model from learning primary decisions from previous data to predict the target class or value. It is a good technique used for grouping. The DT technique is a tree-shaped approach where it starts from the top, called the root and then data is branched into sub-trees to include sub-nodes (or decision nodes) until the last leaf node is obtained with a Boolean value. In this tree, each node represents an attribute, each branch represents a decision and each leaf node represents the result in categorical or continuous values (Charbuty and Abdulazeez, 2021). With DT, the drawback of over-fitting happens when the tree is built in such a way that it precisely fits all the training dataset and the branches include scarce data with stringent rules. This adversely affects the prediction accuracy of samples that are not part of the training dataset. The main reasons for over-fitting are noisy samples, training datasets that are too small, and over-learning. There are various methods for preventing overfitting while creating decision trees, like the pruning and ensemble methods. Pruning is a method where branches where attributes are of less value are cut either from the root or leaf nodes. In the pre-pruning process, at each segmentation, cross-validation error is checked and when the difference is significantly less, the tree is stopped, but this can give rise to under-fitting. In post-pruning, first the entire full tree is created and then less significant branches or branches that do not increase the accuracy are removed (Mehedi Shamrat et al., 2021).

The simple idea behind 'Nearest Neighbor' classification is to categorize observations or samples according to the class of the nearest neighbor. Using more than one neighbor for classification provides enhanced results; so it is referred to as the K Nearest Neighbor (KNN) classifier, where 'k' stands for the number of nearest neighbors used to determine the sample class. It is a supervised learning approach commonly used for the classification process, which involves collecting the existing data and then determining the category of new data based on the closest distance from the existing data. The KNN has many benefits, like it is simple to interpret, can be used with non-linear data due to its non-parametric technique and can be used for both classification and regression (Cunningham and Delany, 2021). The main drawback of using the KNN algorithm is that it stores all the training datasets in the memory at runtime to make predictions about new samples, which makes it significantly slower when handling large datasets and not suitable for environments for rapid prediction. This is why it is also known as Memory-based Classification or Lazy Learning (Cunningham and Delany, 2021).

The 'Support Vector Machine (SVM)' learning algorithm was introduced by Vapnik in 1995 as a kernel-based model to solve issues with classification and regression analysis (Cortes and Vapnik, 1995). In recent years, SVM has been one of the widely used classification algorithms for data mining and pattern recognition due to its remarkable generalisation capabilities, optimum solution and discriminatory capacity. It is a supervised learning technique and can be used for the classification of linear as well as non-linear datasets. The SVM is based on the approach of selecting the best hyperplane that optimally separates the data into various classes with maximum distance, known as 'margins'. Different kernel functions, like polynomial and radial-based, are used to obtain the support vectors (observations on the boundary) and find the maximized margins (Ahmad et al., 2018). SVM has some significant drawbacks, like intensive training time for large datasets due to the algorithmic complexity, feature scaling is required, doesn't perform well with overlapping classes or unbalanced datasets, optimal kernel selection is a complex task, multi-classification needs to be changed to multiple binary classification and is difficult to understand and comprehend unlike decision tree (Cervantes et al., 2020).

The 'Naïve Bayes (NB)' classifier originally appeared in the mid-1990s and was one of the earliest approaches to email filtering. It is commonly used for sentiment assessment, spam filtering and proposal approaches. It is easy, fast, requires fewer training datasets and performs well with multi-class predictions. It is a type of simple probabilistic machine learning model based on the Bayes theorem that makes a strong assumption of feature independence. This is a simple model of classifier represented as feature value vectors, where problem instances are assigned class labels and class labels are taken from a finite set. It is a collection of algorithms used to train, based on a common concept that assumes that for a given class variable, the value of a specific feature is independent of the value of any other feature (Granik and Mesyura, 2017). One of the major drawbacks of the NB classifier is the assumption that with all features, being independent but in real world, it is not practical to get all predictors independent of each other and this degrades the performance (Granik and Mesyura, 2017). Another limitation when using categorical variables is, if a certain category is not present in the training dataset, then the classifier is unable to predict that category because it assigns a 'zero frequency' or zero probability to it. This is overcome by using the smoothing approach, also known as Laplace estimation (Tang et al., 2019).

An 'Artificial Neural Network (ANN)' is a computational model representing the human brain's nervous system proposed by McCulloch and Pitts in 1943 (McCulloch and Pitts, 1990). It is widely used for classification, clustering, pattern recognition and prediction in several domains. It has proven helpful in comparison to regression and statistical models. The high-speed processing in huge analogous operations offered by ANN has increased the demand for study in this area. In numerical patterns, ANN is utilised due to its outstanding input-to-output mappings with high self-learning, fault tolerance, adaptivity and nonlinearity capabilities. In contrast to other algorithms, which may hit a plateau at a certain size and amount of data, neural networks' effectiveness increases as they get larger and work with more data (Berman et al., 2019). An ANN is made up of several processors operating in parallel and organized as layers. Like the human optic nerve, the first layer takes in raw input. Each successive layer receives input from the previous layer and provides output to the next layer. The output is received from the last layer. Each layer is made up of nodes strongly linked to the nodes in before and after layers. Each node has its own set of rules, both programmed and self-learned, and its own knowledge paradigm. Each node then weighs the significance of the input received from previous nodes and assigns the greatest weight to the one that contributes the highest in getting the correct output. The key to neural network effectiveness is the ability to adapt and learn rapidly (Berman et al., 2019). The major drawback with ANN is the Blackbox nature as there is no simple method to describe the model's underlying workings. Another downside is that it mandates data pre-processing and it cannot operate with missing attributes (Abiodun et al., 2018).

Supervised techniques, like classification and regression need training data to create a model. Training data is labelled data where datasets have input feature vectors and target variables. To create a good model, sufficient training data is required. The trained model is then validated, using test data to assess its prediction accuracy. It is critical to thoroughly test the model with enough data to provide accurate predictions in the real world. Data mining experts typically divide the dataset into two subsets: training and test, by dividing the original dataset by a ratio, like 80:20 or 70:30 and using the larger fraction as the training subset. This is also known as the 'holdout' method. A bias may be caused in the split, for example, data points may be grouped in such a manner that one group stays in the training set while the other is in the test set. Due to bias, a single train-test split would lower the model's prediction accuracy. To construct an accurate model, multiple distinct splits of training and test data are required. 'Cross validation', like a linear regression model, uses multiple train-test splits (also known as 'folds') to train the learning model with reduced bias compared to the holdout method. Each fold yields an accuracy metric, like RMSE (root mean squared error) and the overall model accuracy is achieved by taking an average of the RMSE of each fold. Cross-validation techniques may be divided into two categories: non-exhaustive and exhaustive. Non-exhaustive does not compute all possible data splits from the original sample into a training and validation set, but exhaustive tests on all feasible ways to split. Non-exhaustive techniques are the Holdout, K fold CV and Stratified K Fold CV and exhaustive technique is Leave-P-Out cross-validation. A cross-validation technique performance is based on three key criteria: bias, variance and computational complexity. Bias reduces with higher folds preferably closer to dataset size. Variance reduces with smaller folds, but this increases bias. Computational cost increases with folds. A preferable model must have minimized bias and variance and commonly used K value is 10, also known as 10-fold CV (Gunasegaran and Cheah, 2017).

## 2.4 Phase 4—Optimal Framework

The classification techniques can be evaluated, using different metrics and it is vital to understand each metric's evaluation process to know which fits the proposed framework. The majority of these metrics are scalar metrics, while others are graphical approaches. Using scalar metrics is easier, but it can cause issues with imbalanced datasets and graphical metrics providing various interpretations (Tharwat, 2021).

## 2.5 Accuracy

The measurement metrics, like Accuracy (Acc) use both columns of the confusion matrix; however, any change in data distribution impacts the earlier, and not the latter. Acc is defined as below:

$$Acc = \frac{TP+TN}{TP+TN+FP+FN}$$

**Fig. 3:** Accuracy (Tharwat, 2021).

Now consider that the number of negative samples has increased by α times. This will have an adverse effect on Acc. This means that Acc value changes even if the performance does not change.

$$Acc = \frac{TP+\alpha TN}{TP+\alpha TN+\alpha FP+FN} \neq \frac{TP+TN}{TP+TN+FP+FN}$$

**Fig. 4:** Accuracy (Tharwat, 2021)

## 2.6  Receiver Operating Characteristics (ROC) & Area under ROC Curve (AUC)

The Receiver Operating Characteristics (ROC) curve is a graphical representation in two-dimensions to illustrate the connection or trade-off between sensitivity and specificity and the Area Under ROC curve (AUC) indicates the value of the framework aim. The ROC is utilised to strike a balance between benefits (TP) and costs (FP). A classifier with discrete output creates only one confusion matrix and a classifier with continuous output creates a threshold; both create only one point in ROC curve. ROC curve is not affected by change in class distribution as the one ROC curve is created for every class. It is also not sensitive to imbalanced data as the formula is based on same columnar ratio. The AUC value ranges between 0 to 1 but in real, any classifier has value 0.5 or above and it is sensitive to class distribution and error rates.

## 2.7  Precision-Recall (PR) Curve

The most commonly used graphical measurement metrics for evaluating performance of classification techniques is Precision-Recall (PR) curve and has the same idea as ROC showing the connection or trade-off between recall and precision. As a result, the TN value is not required in the PR curve. Since this curve is mostly zigzagged, they are inclined to cross one other more often than ROC curve. A curve that is higher than the other has superior classification performance. Since it is based solely on recall and precision, it tends to overlook the correctly classifying negative samples and is sensitive to imbalanced data.

## 2.8  Data Pre-processing

In this section, first, the dataset details are explained, second, the detailed process of how the data is restructured to remove features not relevant to this study, and finally or third, the detailed process using the open refine tool to pre-process the dataset to extract records relevant to this study is described. The last part of this section shows important statistics from the final processed dataset about trends in malware and the type of targets.

# 3.  Data Restructuring

## 3.1  Initial Dataset

Initially the dataset obtained from the Hackmageddon Blog included 13 features/columns as follows:

- ID – Serial number assigned to each sample
- Date reported – Date when the malware was reported

| ID | Date Reported | Date Occurred | Date Discovered | Author | Target | Description | Attack | Target Class | Attack Class | Cou ntry | Link | Tags |
|----|----|----|----|----|----|----|----|----|----|----|----|----|
| 49 | 23/12/20 | - | 01/11/20 | UltraRank | At least a dozen e-commerce sites | Researchers from Group-IB reveal that a cybercriminal gang known as "UltraRank" has launched a new campaign, targeting at least a dozen e-commerce sites to steal payment card data using a JavaScript sniffer, says security firm | Malicious Script Injection | G Wholesale and retail trade | CC | >1 | https://www.databreachtoda y.com/ultrarank-targets-more-e-commerce-sites-a-15657 | Group-IB, UltraRank |
| 50 | 24/12/20 | - | 23/12/20 | Conti | Sangoma Technologies Corporation | Sangoma discloses a data breach after 26 GB of data were stolen during a recent Conti ransomware attack and published online. | Malware | C Manufactur ing | CC | CA | https://www.bleepingcomput er.com/news/security/freepb x-developer-sangoma-hit-with-conti-ransomware-attack/ | Sangoma Technologies Corporation, Conti, Ransomware |

**Fig. 5:** Initial dataset snippet.

- Date occurred – Date when the malware incident happened
- Date discovered – Date when the malware was initially detected
- Author – Threat to actor conducting the attack
- Target – Name of target on whom the attack is conducted
- Description – Brief description of the attack
- Attack – Type of attack
- Target class – Category of organization to which the target belongs
- Attack class – Category in which attack belongs
- Country – Country to which target belongs
- Link – Weblink with details on the attack
- Tags – Keyword related to the attack

## 3.2 Remove Irrelevant Features

The dataset is reconstructed to remove features irrelevant to this work. Some features have no impact on the actual prediction of the type of target, like ID, description, link and tags. In this study, importance is given only to data reported as the date occurred and discovered, which is not accurate or unknown in most cases; so, it can be removed. Also, the aim is to identify the type of target and not the exact target name; so it can be removed. Now the date reported, author, attack, target class and attack class will be renamed for simplicity as date, attacker, type of attack, type of target and attack category, respectively. Now the reconstructed dataset includes six features/columns as follows:

| Date | Attacker | Type of Attack | Type of Target | Attack Category | Country |
|----|----|----|----|----|----|
| 23/12/20 | UltraRank | Malicious Script Injection | G Wholesale and retail trade | CC | >1 |
| 24/12/20 | Conti | Malware | C Manufacturing | CC | CA |
| 24/12/20 | Pay2Key (Fox Kitten) | Malware | M Professional scientific and technical activities | CW | IL |
| 24/12/20 | REvil AKA Sodinokibi | Malware | Q Human health and social work activities | CC | UK |
| 24/12/20 | ? | DDoS | Y Multiple Industries | CC | >1 |

**Fig. 6:** Reconstructed dataset snippet.

### 3.3  Extract Malware Samples

The initial dataset from 1 January, 2015 to 31 December, 2020 includes 8451 entries or attack samples. From this, only malware samples will be extracted by filtering the column 'Type of Attack' to include only malware, PoS malware, mobile malware, PoS malware so that malware (Carbanak 2.0), malware (Mobile), malware (JS Exploit), malware (DNSChanger), malware/account hijacking, malware (Adwind), malware via Typosquatting, malware (Konni), account hijacking/malware, multiple attack vectors (account hijacking and malware), malware account hijacking remain and remove all the other rows from the dataset.

The final reconstructed dataset has 2517 malware samples and each sample has six features.

### 3.4  Data Pre-processing

The open refine open-source tool is used for data pre-processing in this study. It involves multiple steps as mentioned below:

- *Clustering similar values* – Open-refine tool includes a facet feature, also known as 'cluster', which merges cell values with multiple representations of the same thing and replaces with the same name. The methods used are key collision and nearest neighbor.

- *Summarise 'Type of attack'* – The reconstructed dataset has 15 types of malware attacks which are summarized into only two categories as malware or POS malware. The samples with POS malware are kept as they are and the type of attack for all other samples is renamed as malware.

- *Summarise 'Type of target'* – The reconstructed dataset has 114 types of targets which are summarized into 15 categories.

- *Summarise 'Country'* – Some attacks are targeted to two or more countries and they are summarized to represent as multiple countries. The cell with values '>1, >A, BR SA, BRMX, BRMXUS, CAJP, ESFR, ESPT, ITPL, JP CN, RU KZ, RU US, UKITCA, USITJP, US/CA, US/UK' are all summarized and replaced with the name 'multiple'.

- *Replacing empty values* – Many samples have some features without any value and this needs to be replaced with a value to ensure that classifiers are able to process the dataset without throwing any errors. The features' date, type of attack, attack category and country do not have any empty cells, whereas the empty cells for attacker feature is replaced by unidentified and type of target feature is replaced by unknown.

The final pre-processed dataset has 2517 malware samples and each sample has six features. This sample is segmented into training dataset (pre-COVID-19 era from 1 January, 2015 to 31 December, 2019) of 1585 samples and testing dataset (COVID-19 era from 1 January, to 31 December, 2020) of 932 samples.

## 3.5 Data Statistics

During the pre COVID-19 era from 2015 to 2019, there has been a steep rise of 75% in total cyber-attacks and 911% in malware and only 13% in non-malware attacks. When compared to the COVID-19 era of 2020, the steep rise from 2015 to 2020 has been 130% in total cyber-attacks and 1,231% in malware and only 48% in non-malware attacks. The figure below provides a breakdown of the cyber-attacks in total, malware and non-malware respectively for each year:

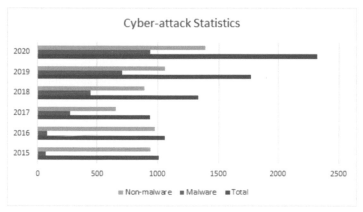

**Fig. 7:** Cyber-attack statistics based on the type of attack from 2015 to 2020.

As per previous figures, as malware attacks have become the majority of cyber-attacks and by concentrating only on malware statistics from 2015 to 2020, it is apparent that the target category or type of target has been shifted for cybercriminals, from individuals to industries. The figure below provides a breakdown of the malware attacks based on the category type for the pre- and COVID-19 era.

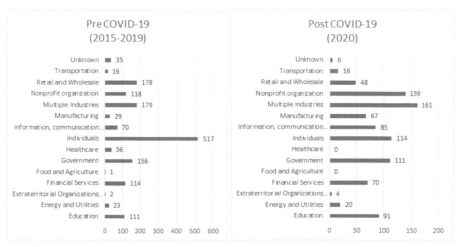

**Fig. 8:** Malware attack statistics based on target category from 2015 to 2020.

Examining the above statistics, it is important to focus dedicatedly on malware attacks and the prediction of the type of targets that cybercriminals are focusing on. Thus the main aim and objective of this study is to predict the malware target category using data mining techniques.

## 3.6 Summary

The final dataset contains 2,241 malware entries segregated into 1585 training samples and 932 testing samples. The data statistics illustrate that the cyber-attack landscape has changed and focus more on malware attacks and the importance of focus is on them specifically. According to this datasets, they have become highest cyber-attacks from 2015 to 2020, with an increase of 1231%. Also, there has been a shift in the type of targets from attacking individuals to industries. Predicting the type of targets specific for malware gives industries or organizations a look forward to defending against malware.

# 4. Data Analysis

In this study, Weka tool is utilised to train, test and validate the model. First, the model is trained with six different classifiers with 10-fold cross-validation on pre-COVID-19 dataset, second, tested with same classifiers on COVID-19 dataset and third, validated using different performance metrics. Then the results are analyzed and compared with the main aim of the research being prediction of the type of target for malwares in the COVID-19 pandemic era.

As explained conceptually in Section 1.6 and 2.3, the model is built to predict the type of target of a malware using J48, RF, KNN, NB, ANN and SVM classification algorithms, by analyzing the data using Waikato Environment for knowledge analysis (WEKA) tool.

## 4.1 Training Phase

### 4.1.1 Cross-Validation Summary

As mentioned earlier, accuracy works well with balanced data but misleads the performance with imbalanced data. Accuracy alone cannot determine the performance of a model. We could have high accuracy but a bad model. Let's say 80% of instances are all in one class, then the model could say everything belongs to that class and it will be right 80% of the time but the model is not efficient and this needs to be done by class balancing.

Cohen's Kappa statistics is used in qualitative experiment. For perfectly balanced data, that is, one class has 50% and the other class has 50% instances, then the likelihood to guess the right class is 50% and Kappa statistics takes this into account to decide how well the model will randomly guess correctly. If this is zero, then everything is randomly guessed and it performs better.

| Correctly Classified Instances | 737 | 46.4984 % |
|---|---|---|
| Incorrectly Classified Instances | 848 | 53.5016 % |
| Kappa statistic | 0.3215 | |
| Mean absolute error | 0.088 | |
| Root mean squared error | 0.215 | |
| Relative absolute error | 78.5356 % | |
| Root relative squared error | 90.8809 % | |
| Total Number of Instances | 1585 | |

*C4.5 Stratified cross-validation Summary*

| Correctly Classified Instances | 739 | 46.6246 % |
|---|---|---|
| Incorrectly Classified Instances | 846 | 53.3754 % |
| Kappa statistic | 0.3274 | |
| Mean absolute error | 0.0876 | |
| Root mean squared error | 0.2132 | |
| Relative absolute error | 78.1441 % | |
| Root relative squared error | 90.1323 % | |
| Total Number of Instances | 1585 | |

*RF Stratified cross-validation Summary*

| Correctly Classified Instances | 727 | 45.8675 % |
|---|---|---|
| Incorrectly Classified Instances | 858 | 54.1325 % |
| Kappa statistic | 0.2993 | |
| Mean absolute error | 0.0886 | |
| Root mean squared error | 0.2127 | |
| Relative absolute error | 79.0478 % | |
| Root relative squared error | 89.929 % | |
| Total Number of Instances | 1585 | |

*KNN Stratified cross-validation Summary*

| Correctly Classified Instances | 736 | 46.4353 % |
|---|---|---|
| Incorrectly Classified Instances | 849 | 53.5647 % |
| Kappa statistic | 0.3169 | |
| Mean absolute error | 0.0849 | |
| Root mean squared error | 0.2125 | |
| Relative absolute error | 75.7708 % | |
| Root relative squared error | 89.8211 % | |
| Total Number of Instances | 1585 | |

*NB Stratified cross-validation Summary*

| Correctly Classified Instances | 743 | 46.877 % |
|---|---|---|
| Incorrectly Classified Instances | 842 | 53.123 % |
| Kappa statistic | 0.3278 | |
| Mean absolute error | 0.1178 | |
| Root mean squared error | 0.2393 | |
| Relative absolute error | 105.1306 % | |
| Root relative squared error | 101.1459 % | |
| Total Number of Instances | 1585 | |

*SVM Stratified cross-validation Summary*

**Fig. 9:** Stratified cross-validation summary (training).

Mean absolute error, root mean squared error and relative absolute error are measurement metrics normally used with regression and not reported in most scientific papers using classification learning models.

Note that the correctly and incorrectly classified instances in the outputs from WEKA in Sections 4.1.1 and 4.2.1 are TP+TN and FP+FN respectively. Then using the accuracy formula from Section 2.4.1, accuracy is equal to correctly classified instances %.

During the training phase, all classifiers provide approximately the same accuracy rate from 45 to 47% with Kappa value ranging from 0.29 to 0.33. With these values being considerably low, it is difficult to predict which classifier will perform better using only the stratified cross-validation summary.

## 4.2 Detailed Accuracy by Class

With recall, given a class, will the classifier detect it? With precision, given the class prediction from the classifier, how likely is it to be correct? F-measure is harmonic mean of recall and precision. Given the value of precision and recall, harmonic mean is closer to the one with lower value and punishes extreme value more. From the above figure, it can be noticed that some F-measure is '?' because the precision is '?'. This is because zero instances were classified for that class and anything divided by zero results in undefined number. The same applies to MCC and both these metrics cannot be used to validate the classifier performance.

The ideal PRC area must be 1, with both high precision and high recall with value of 1. But in real scenarios, this is not the ideal situation and requires a trade-off between the two. The values range between 0.34 and 0.37 which is not an ideal value for a model to perform well.

| TP Rate | FP Rate | Precision | Recall | F-Measure | MCC | ROC Area | PRC Area | Class |
|---|---|---|---|---|---|---|---|---|
| 0.545 | 0.038 | 0.642 | 0.545 | 0.590 | 0.545 | 0.813 | 0.535 | Retail and Wholesale |
| 0.000 | 0.000 | ? | 0.000 | ? | ? | 0.519 | 0.010 | Transportation |
| 0.008 | 0.012 | 0.053 | 0.008 | 0.015 | -0.009 | 0.795 | 0.169 | Nonprofit organization |
| 0.934 | 0.287 | 0.612 | 0.934 | 0.740 | 0.607 | 0.822 | 0.588 | Individuals |
| 0.808 | 0.290 | 0.233 | 0.808 | 0.362 | 0.326 | 0.757 | 0.215 | Government |
| 0.000 | 0.000 | ? | 0.000 | ? | ? | 0.757 | 0.048 | Healthcare |
| 0.034 | 0.006 | 0.400 | 0.034 | 0.062 | 0.089 | 0.738 | 0.212 | Multiple Industries |
| 0.000 | 0.000 | ? | 0.000 | ? | ? | 0.806 | 0.160 | Education |
| 0.158 | 0.019 | 0.391 | 0.158 | 0.225 | 0.214 | 0.604 | 0.159 | Financial Services |
| 0.069 | 0.002 | 0.400 | 0.069 | 0.118 | 0.160 | 0.532 | 0.047 | Manufacturing |
| 0.000 | 0.003 | 0.000 | 0.000 | 0.000 | -0.006 | 0.697 | 0.062 | Energy and Utilities |
| 0.029 | 0.003 | 0.286 | 0.029 | 0.052 | 0.078 | 0.545 | 0.066 | Information, communication technology and internet services |
| 0.057 | 0.004 | 0.250 | 0.057 | 0.093 | 0.110 | 0.673 | 0.113 | Unknown |
| 0.000 | 0.000 | ? | 0.000 | ? | ? | 0.357 | 0.001 | Food and Agriculture |
| 0.000 | 0.001 | 0.000 | 0.000 | 0.000 | -0.001 | 0.356 | 0.001 | Extraterritorial Organizations and Bodies |
| Weighted Avg. 0.465 | 0.130 | ? | 0.465 | ? | ? | 0.758 | 0.349 | |

*C4.5 Detailed Accuracy By Class*

| TP Rate | FP Rate | Precision | Recall | F-Measure | MCC | ROC Area | PRC Area | Class |
|---|---|---|---|---|---|---|---|---|
| 0.539 | 0.026 | 0.727 | 0.539 | 0.619 | 0.587 | 0.831 | 0.567 | Retail and Wholesale |
| 0.000 | 0.000 | ? | 0.000 | ? | ? | 0.510 | 0.010 | Transportation |
| 0.008 | 0.008 | 0.077 | 0.008 | 0.015 | 0.001 | 0.808 | 0.175 | Nonprofit organization |
| 0.915 | 0.274 | 0.617 | 0.915 | 0.737 | 0.601 | 0.835 | 0.613 | Individuals |
| 0.833 | 0.290 | 0.239 | 0.833 | 0.371 | 0.341 | 0.793 | 0.235 | Government |
| 0.000 | 0.000 | ? | 0.000 | ? | ? | 0.767 | 0.051 | Healthcare |
| 0.056 | 0.009 | 0.455 | 0.056 | 0.100 | 0.128 | 0.743 | 0.240 | Multiple Industries |
| 0.000 | 0.003 | 0.000 | 0.000 | 0.000 | -0.015 | 0.815 | 0.165 | Education |
| 0.158 | 0.022 | 0.360 | 0.158 | 0.220 | 0.201 | 0.632 | 0.176 | Financial Services |
| 0.069 | 0.002 | 0.400 | 0.069 | 0.118 | 0.160 | 0.581 | 0.058 | Manufacturing |
| 0.087 | 0.004 | 0.250 | 0.087 | 0.129 | 0.140 | 0.702 | 0.082 | Energy and Utilities |
| 0.057 | 0.014 | 0.160 | 0.057 | 0.084 | 0.071 | 0.562 | 0.067 | Information, communication technology and internet services |
| 0.086 | 0.007 | 0.214 | 0.086 | 0.122 | 0.123 | 0.717 | 0.149 | Unknown |
| 0.000 | 0.000 | ? | 0.000 | ? | ? | 0.321 | 0.001 | Food and Agriculture |
| 0.000 | 0.001 | 0.000 | 0.000 | 0.000 | -0.001 | 0.504 | 0.002 | Extraterritorial Organizations and Bodies |
| Weighted Avg. 0.466 | 0.125 | ? | 0.466 | ? | ? | 0.776 | 0.361 | |

*RF Detailed Accuracy By Class*

| TP Rate | FP Rate | Precision | Recall | F-Measure | MCC | ROC Area | PRC Area | Class |
|---|---|---|---|---|---|---|---|---|
| 0.528 | 0.023 | 0.740 | 0.528 | 0.616 | 0.587 | 0.816 | 0.577 | Retail and Wholesale |
| 0.000 | 0.000 | ? | 0.000 | ? | ? | 0.595 | 0.012 | Transportation |
| 0.008 | 0.009 | 0.167 | 0.008 | 0.016 | 0.022 | 0.808 | 0.179 | Nonprofit organization |
| 0.963 | 0.370 | 0.558 | 0.963 | 0.706 | 0.661 | 0.847 | 0.626 | Individuals |
| 0.782 | 0.285 | 0.231 | 0.782 | 0.356 | 0.314 | 0.786 | 0.212 | Government |
| 0.000 | 0.000 | ? | 0.000 | ? | ? | 0.785 | 0.054 | Healthcare |
| 0.017 | 0.004 | 0.333 | 0.017 | 0.032 | 0.053 | 0.755 | 0.222 | Multiple Industries |
| 0.000 | 0.000 | ? | 0.000 | ? | ? | 0.620 | 0.168 | Education |
| 0.079 | 0.006 | 0.500 | 0.079 | 0.136 | 0.178 | 0.636 | 0.155 | Financial Services |
| 0.000 | 0.000 | ? | 0.000 | ? | ? | 0.704 | 0.045 | Manufacturing |
| 0.000 | 0.000 | ? | 0.000 | ? | ? | 0.767 | 0.040 | Energy and Utilities |
| 0.000 | 0.001 | 0.000 | 0.000 | 0.000 | -0.005 | 0.596 | 0.056 | Information, communication technology and internet services |
| 0.000 | 0.001 | 0.000 | 0.000 | 0.000 | -0.005 | 0.639 | 0.035 | Unknown |
| 0.000 | 0.000 | ? | 0.000 | ? | ? | 0.433 | 0.001 | Food and Agriculture |
| 0.000 | 0.000 | ? | 0.000 | ? | ? | 0.527 | 0.002 | Extraterritorial Organizations and Bodies |
| Weighted Avg. 0.459 | 0.153 | ? | 0.459 | ? | ? | 0.786 | 0.357 | |

*KNN Detailed Accuracy By Class*

| TP Rate | FP Rate | Precision | Recall | F-Measure | MCC | ROC Area | PRC Area | Class |
|---|---|---|---|---|---|---|---|---|
| 0.522 | 0.011 | 0.853 | 0.522 | 0.648 | 0.638 | 0.855 | 0.586 | Retail and Wholesale |
| 0.000 | 0.000 | ? | 0.000 | ? | ? | 0.622 | 0.013 | Transportation |
| 0.025 | 0.010 | 0.167 | 0.025 | 0.044 | 0.038 | 0.814 | 0.175 | Nonprofit organization |
| 0.936 | 0.315 | 0.590 | 0.936 | 0.724 | 0.583 | 0.843 | 0.618 | Individuals |
| 0.833 | 0.304 | 0.230 | 0.833 | 0.361 | 0.330 | 0.803 | 0.235 | Government |
| 0.000 | 0.000 | ? | 0.000 | ? | ? | 0.718 | 0.037 | Healthcare |
| 0.067 | 0.009 | 0.480 | 0.067 | 0.118 | 0.147 | 0.747 | 0.246 | Multiple Industries |
| 0.000 | 0.004 | 0.000 | 0.000 | 0.000 | -0.017 | 0.812 | 0.160 | Education |
| 0.079 | 0.011 | 0.360 | 0.079 | 0.129 | 0.141 | 0.695 | 0.213 | Financial Services |
| 0.000 | 0.000 | ? | 0.000 | ? | ? | 0.735 | 0.044 | Manufacturing |
| 0.000 | 0.001 | 0.000 | 0.000 | 0.000 | -0.003 | 0.759 | 0.044 | Energy and Utilities |
| 0.000 | 0.005 | 0.000 | 0.000 | 0.000 | -0.014 | 0.681 | 0.084 | Information, communication technology and internet services |
| 0.143 | 0.003 | 0.500 | 0.143 | 0.222 | 0.259 | 0.736 | 0.127 | Unknown |
| 0.000 | 0.000 | ? | 0.000 | ? | ? | 0.051 | 0.001 | Food and Agriculture |
| 0.000 | 0.000 | ? | 0.000 | ? | ? | 0.455 | 0.002 | Extraterritorial Organizations and Bodies |
| Weighted Avg. 0.464 | 0.137 | ? | 0.464 | ? | ? | 0.797 | 0.367 | |

*NB Detailed Accuracy By Class*

| TP Rate | FP Rate | Precision | Recall | F-Measure | MCC | ROC Area | PRC Area | Class |
|---|---|---|---|---|---|---|---|---|
| 0.517 | 0.027 | 0.708 | 0.517 | 0.597 | 0.564 | 0.830 | 0.456 | Retail and Wholesale |
| 0.000 | 0.000 | ? | 0.000 | ? | ? | 0.516 | 0.012 | Transportation |
| 0.000 | 0.005 | 0.000 | 0.000 | 0.000 | -0.019 | 0.816 | 0.191 | Nonprofit organization |
| 0.934 | 0.280 | 0.618 | 0.934 | 0.744 | 0.614 | 0.834 | 0.608 | Individuals |
| 0.827 | 0.297 | 0.233 | 0.827 | 0.364 | 0.331 | 0.801 | 0.225 | Government |
| 0.000 | 0.000 | ? | 0.000 | ? | ? | 0.732 | 0.047 | Healthcare |
| 0.067 | 0.009 | 0.500 | 0.067 | 0.118 | 0.152 | 0.769 | 0.238 | Multiple Industries |
| 0.000 | 0.000 | ? | 0.000 | ? | ? | 0.815 | 0.185 | Education |
| 0.167 | 0.025 | 0.339 | 0.167 | 0.224 | 0.198 | 0.669 | 0.151 | Financial Services |
| 0.034 | 0.002 | 0.250 | 0.034 | 0.061 | 0.087 | 0.477 | 0.039 | Manufacturing |
| 0.000 | 0.001 | 0.000 | 0.000 | 0.000 | -0.004 | 0.598 | 0.041 | Energy and Utilities |
| 0.029 | 0.009 | 0.133 | 0.029 | 0.047 | 0.042 | 0.453 | 0.045 | Information, communication technology and internet services |
| 0.143 | 0.004 | 0.455 | 0.143 | 0.217 | 0.246 | 0.752 | 0.109 | Unknown |
| 0.000 | 0.000 | ? | 0.000 | ? | ? | 0.300 | 0.001 | Food and Agriculture |
| 0.000 | 0.001 | 0.000 | 0.000 | 0.000 | -0.001 | 0.215 | 0.001 | Extraterritorial Organizations and Bodies |
| Weighted Avg. 0.469 | 0.127 | ? | 0.469 | ? | ? | 0.773 | 0.348 | |

*SVM Detailed Accuracy By Class*

**Fig. 10:** Detailed accuracy class (training).

Further looking at the ROC area, also known as AUC, the weighted average value is between 0.773 and 0.797, which means that the classifier has 77% to 79% chance to distinguish between classes. However, different classifiers perform differently for individual class. With all classifiers, the ROC area is above 0.77 for classes retail and wholesale, non-profit organization, individuals and education. For class government, all classifiers except C4.5 have a value above 0.77. In addition, the KNN10 classifier provides a higher value for healthcare and the NB classifier provides a higher value for energy and utilities.

## 4.3 Testing Phase

### 4.3.1 Cross-Validation Summary

During the testing phase, all classifiers provided much lower accuracy, approximately between 19.42 to 20.17% and with Kappa value of approximately 0.09. With these values being drastically low, it is difficult to predict which classifier will perform better using only the stratified cross-validation summary.

| Correctly Classified Instances | 182 | 19.5279 % |
|---|---|---|
| Incorrectly Classified Instances | 750 | 80.4721 % |
| Kappa statistic | 0.0912 | |
| Mean absolute error | 0.1076 | |
| Root mean squared error | 0.2471 | |
| Relative absolute error | 90.233 % | |
| Root relative squared error | 98.3482 % | |
| Total Number of Instances | 932 | |

*C4.5 Stratified cross-validation Summary*

| Correctly Classified Instances | 188 | 20.1717 % |
|---|---|---|
| Incorrectly Classified Instances | 744 | 79.8283 % |
| Kappa statistic | 0.0992 | |
| Mean absolute error | 0.1074 | |
| Root mean squared error | 0.2453 | |
| Relative absolute error | 90.1126 % | |
| Root relative squared error | 97.5973 % | |
| Total Number of Instances | 932 | |

*RF Stratified cross-validation Summary*

| Correctly Classified Instances | 183 | 19.6352 % |
|---|---|---|
| Incorrectly Classified Instances | 749 | 80.3648 % |
| Kappa statistic | 0.0913 | |
| Mean absolute error | 0.1079 | |
| Root mean squared error | 0.243 | |
| Relative absolute error | 90.4663 % | |
| Root relative squared error | 96.7003 % | |
| Total Number of Instances | 932 | |

*KNN Stratified cross-validation Summary*

| Correctly Classified Instances | 203 | 21.7811 % |
|---|---|---|
| Incorrectly Classified Instances | 729 | 78.2189 % |
| Kappa statistic | 0.1359 | |
| Mean absolute error | 0.1067 | |
| Root mean squared error | 0.2688 | |
| Relative absolute error | 89.4847 % | |
| Root relative squared error | 106.9849 % | |
| Total Number of Instances | 932 | |

*NB Stratified cross-validation Summary*

| Correctly Classified Instances | 181 | 19.4206 % |
|---|---|---|
| Incorrectly Classified Instances | 751 | 80.5794 % |
| Kappa statistic | 0.0914 | |
| Mean absolute error | 0.1192 | |
| Root mean squared error | 0.2421 | |
| Relative absolute error | 99.9526 % | |
| Root relative squared error | 96.3532 % | |
| Total Number of Instances | 932 | |

*SVM Stratified cross-validation Summary*

**Fig. 11:** Stratified cross-validation summary (testing).

### 4.3.2 Detailed Accuracy by Class

From the above figure, again it can be noticed that some F-measure, precision and MCC is '?' as explained in Section 4.1.2 and these metrics cannot be used to validate the classifier performance.

The weighted average PRC area for all classifiers is approximately 0.2 which is drastically low and indicates that the model will not perform well.

Even the ROC area or AUC is reduced to between 0.684 and 0.712, which means the model has less chance to distinguish classes appropriately. With all the

| TP Rate | FP Rate | Precision | Recall | F-Measure | MCC | ROC Area | PRC Area | Class |
|---|---|---|---|---|---|---|---|---|
| 0.167 | 0.077 | 0.105 | 0.167 | 0.129 | 0.072 | 0.583 | 0.081 | Retail and Wholesale |
| 0.000 | 0.000 | ? | 0.000 | ? | ? | 0.653 | 0.041 | Transportation |
| 0.043 | 0.053 | 0.125 | 0.043 | 0.064 | -0.016 | 0.688 | 0.231 | Nonprofit organization |
| 0.860 | 0.317 | 0.275 | 0.860 | 0.416 | 0.366 | 0.805 | 0.312 | Individuals |
| 0.595 | 0.410 | 0.164 | 0.595 | 0.257 | 0.120 | 0.606 | 0.167 | Government |
| ? | 0.000 | ? | ? | ? | ? | ? | ? | Healthcare |
| 0.006 | 0.005 | 0.200 | 0.006 | 0.012 | 0.005 | 0.808 | 0.428 | Multiple Industries |
| 0.000 | 0.000 | ? | 0.000 | ? | ? | 0.777 | 0.209 | Education |
| 0.043 | 0.032 | 0.097 | 0.043 | 0.059 | 0.015 | 0.552 | 0.088 | Financial Services |
| 0.000 | 0.006 | 0.000 | 0.000 | 0.000 | -0.020 | 0.546 | 0.127 | Manufacturing |
| 0.000 | 0.001 | 0.000 | 0.000 | 0.000 | -0.005 | 0.624 | 0.038 | Energy and Utilities |
| 0.000 | 0.006 | 0.000 | 0.000 | 0.000 | -0.023 | 0.574 | 0.131 | Information, communication technology and internet services |
| 0.000 | 0.001 | 0.000 | 0.000 | 0.000 | -0.003 | 0.876 | 0.279 | Unknown |
| ? | 0.000 | ? | ? | ? | ? | ? | ? | Food and Agriculture |
| 0.000 | 0.000 | ? | 0.000 | ? | ? | 0.429 | 0.004 | Extraterritorial Organizations and Bodies |
| Weighted Avg. 0.195 | 0.104 | ? | 0.195 | ? | ? | 0.684 | 0.222 | |

*C4.5 Detailed Accuracy By Class*

| TP Rate | FP Rate | Precision | Recall | F-Measure | MCC | ROC Area | PRC Area | Class |
|---|---|---|---|---|---|---|---|---|
| 0.167 | 0.054 | 0.143 | 0.167 | 0.154 | 0.105 | 0.604 | 0.113 | Retail and Wholesale |
| 0.000 | 0.000 | ? | 0.000 | ? | ? | 0.657 | 0.034 | Transportation |
| 0.022 | 0.018 | 0.176 | 0.022 | 0.038 | 0.010 | 0.704 | 0.232 | Nonprofit organization |
| 0.842 | 0.322 | 0.267 | 0.842 | 0.406 | 0.351 | 0.816 | 0.363 | Individuals |
| 0.595 | 0.413 | 0.163 | 0.595 | 0.256 | 0.119 | 0.635 | 0.171 | Government |
| ? | 0.000 | ? | ? | ? | ? | ? | ? | Healthcare |
| 0.012 | 0.006 | 0.286 | 0.012 | 0.024 | 0.026 | 0.829 | 0.473 | Multiple Industries |
| 0.000 | 0.000 | ? | 0.000 | ? | ? | 0.756 | 0.196 | Education |
| 0.043 | 0.032 | 0.097 | 0.043 | 0.059 | 0.015 | 0.540 | 0.050 | Financial Services |
| 0.000 | 0.006 | 0.000 | 0.000 | 0.000 | -0.020 | 0.551 | 0.128 | Manufacturing |
| 0.000 | 0.001 | 0.000 | 0.000 | 0.000 | -0.005 | 0.660 | 0.040 | Energy and Utilities |
| 0.118 | 0.047 | 0.200 | 0.118 | 0.148 | 0.090 | 0.598 | 0.133 | Information, communication technology and internet services |
| 0.000 | 0.001 | 0.000 | 0.000 | 0.000 | -0.003 | 0.854 | 0.285 | Unknown |
| ? | 0.000 | ? | ? | ? | ? | ? | ? | Food and Agriculture |
| 0.000 | 0.000 | ? | 0.000 | ? | ? | 0.400 | 0.004 | Extraterritorial Organizations and Bodies |
| Weighted Avg. 0.202 | 0.102 | ? | 0.202 | ? | ? | 0.696 | 0.238 | |

*RF Detailed Accuracy By Class*

| TP Rate | FP Rate | Precision | Recall | F-Measure | MCC | ROC Area | PRC Area | Class |
|---|---|---|---|---|---|---|---|---|
| 0.146 | 0.036 | 0.179 | 0.146 | 0.161 | 0.121 | 0.596 | 0.113 | Retail and Wholesale |
| 0.000 | 0.000 | ? | 0.000 | ? | ? | 0.698 | 0.036 | Transportation |
| 0.014 | 0.013 | 0.167 | 0.014 | 0.026 | 0.006 | 0.730 | 0.251 | Nonprofit organization |
| 0.886 | 0.402 | 0.235 | 0.886 | 0.371 | 0.318 | 0.829 | 0.365 | Individuals |
| 0.631 | 0.421 | 0.168 | 0.631 | 0.266 | 0.136 | 0.680 | 0.184 | Government |
| ? | 0.000 | ? | ? | ? | ? | ? | ? | Healthcare |
| 0.006 | 0.000 | 1.000 | 0.006 | 0.012 | 0.072 | 0.843 | 0.478 | Multiple Industries |
| 0.000 | 0.000 | ? | 0.000 | ? | ? | 0.760 | 0.197 | Education |
| 0.029 | 0.017 | 0.118 | 0.029 | 0.046 | 0.022 | 0.527 | 0.088 | Financial Services |
| 0.000 | 0.000 | ? | 0.000 | ? | ? | 0.591 | 0.134 | Manufacturing |
| 0.000 | 0.011 | 0.000 | 0.000 | 0.000 | -0.015 | 0.733 | 0.051 | Energy and Utilities |
| 0.000 | 0.001 | 0.000 | 0.000 | 0.000 | -0.010 | 0.573 | 0.106 | Information, communication technology and internet services |
| 0.000 | 0.006 | 0.000 | 0.000 | 0.000 | -0.006 | 0.900 | 0.218 | Unknown |
| ? | 0.000 | ? | ? | ? | ? | ? | ? | Food and Agriculture |
| 0.000 | 0.000 | ? | 0.000 | ? | ? | 0.477 | 0.005 | Extraterritorial Organizations and Bodies |
| Weighted Avg. 0.196 | 0.105 | ? | 0.196 | ? | ? | 0.712 | 0.241 | |

*KNN Detailed Accuracy By Class*

| TP Rate | FP Rate | Precision | Recall | F-Measure | MCC | ROC Area | PRC Area | Class |
|---|---|---|---|---|---|---|---|---|
| 0.125 | 0.023 | 0.231 | 0.125 | 0.162 | 0.137 | 0.484 | 0.095 | Retail and Wholesale |
| 0.000 | 0.000 | ? | 0.000 | ? | ? | 0.580 | 0.021 | Transportation |
| 0.000 | 0.000 | ? | 0.000 | ? | ? | 0.748 | 0.295 | Nonprofit organization |
| 0.816 | 0.182 | 0.384 | 0.816 | 0.522 | 0.474 | 0.823 | 0.355 | Individuals |
| 0.036 | 0.029 | 0.143 | 0.036 | 0.058 | 0.013 | 0.659 | 0.180 | Government |
| ? | 0.045 | 0.000 | ? | ? | ? | ? | ? | Healthcare |
| 0.025 | 0.016 | 0.250 | 0.025 | 0.045 | 0.027 | 0.785 | 0.365 | Multiple Industries |
| 0.813 | 0.346 | 0.203 | 0.813 | 0.325 | 0.284 | 0.766 | 0.311 | Education |
| 0.100 | 0.143 | 0.054 | 0.100 | 0.070 | -0.032 | 0.507 | 0.076 | Financial Services |
| 0.149 | 0.045 | 0.204 | 0.149 | 0.172 | 0.121 | 0.647 | 0.128 | Manufacturing |
| 0.000 | 0.001 | 0.000 | 0.000 | 0.000 | -0.005 | 0.515 | 0.032 | Energy and Utilities |
| 0.012 | 0.028 | 0.040 | 0.012 | 0.018 | -0.030 | 0.563 | 0.105 | Information, communication technology and internet services |
| 0.667 | 0.004 | 0.500 | 0.667 | 0.571 | 0.574 | 0.857 | 0.339 | Unknown |
| ? | 0.000 | ? | ? | ? | ? | ? | ? | Food and Agriculture |
| 0.000 | 0.000 | ? | 0.000 | ? | ? | 0.336 | 0.004 | Extraterritorial Organizations and Bodies |
| Weighted Avg. 0.218 | 0.080 | ? | 0.218 | ? | ? | 0.690 | 0.225 | |

*NB Detailed Accuracy By Class*

| TP Rate | FP Rate | Precision | Recall | F-Measure | MCC | ROC Area | PRC Area | Class |
|---|---|---|---|---|---|---|---|---|
| 0.167 | 0.052 | 0.148 | 0.167 | 0.157 | 0.108 | 0.567 | 0.077 | Retail and Wholesale |
| 0.000 | 0.000 | ? | 0.000 | ? | ? | 0.602 | 0.024 | Transportation |
| 0.014 | 0.014 | 0.154 | 0.014 | 0.026 | 0.002 | 0.737 | 0.263 | Nonprofit organization |
| 0.860 | 0.322 | 0.271 | 0.860 | 0.413 | 0.362 | 0.773 | 0.254 | Individuals |
| 0.595 | 0.409 | 0.164 | 0.595 | 0.257 | 0.121 | 0.651 | 0.163 | Government |
| ? | 0.000 | ? | ? | ? | ? | ? | ? | Healthcare |
| 0.019 | 0.006 | 0.375 | 0.019 | 0.036 | 0.050 | 0.816 | 0.404 | Multiple Industries |
| 0.000 | 0.000 | ? | 0.000 | ? | ? | 0.764 | 0.151 | Education |
| 0.057 | 0.075 | 0.058 | 0.057 | 0.058 | -0.018 | 0.567 | 0.085 | Financial Services |
| 0.000 | 0.006 | 0.000 | 0.000 | 0.000 | -0.020 | 0.502 | 0.114 | Manufacturing |
| 0.000 | 0.001 | 0.000 | 0.000 | 0.000 | -0.005 | 0.667 | 0.048 | Energy and Utilities |
| 0.000 | 0.022 | 0.000 | 0.000 | 0.000 | -0.046 | 0.519 | 0.110 | Information, communication technology and internet services |
| 0.000 | 0.000 | ? | 0.000 | ? | ? | 0.896 | 0.152 | Unknown |
| ? | 0.000 | ? | ? | ? | ? | ? | ? | Food and Agriculture |
| 0.000 | 0.000 | ? | 0.000 | ? | ? | 0.416 | 0.004 | Extraterritorial Organizations and Bodies |
| Weighted Avg. 0.194 | 0.102 | ? | 0.194 | ? | ? | 0.686 | 0.209 | |

*SVM Detailed Accuracy By Class*

**Fig. 12:** Detailed accuracy class (testing).

classifiers, the ROC area is above 0.77 for classes individuals, multiple industries, education, unknown and energy. In addition, the J48 provides a higher value for education and the NB classifier provides a higher value for energy and utilities.

# 5. Summary

The table below provides a summary of metrics used to validate the performance of the model by using different classification algorithms for training and testing.

Table 4: Performance metrics summary.

| Classifier | Training/Testing | Accuracy Rate | ROC Area | PRC Area |
|---|---|---|---|---|
| J48 | Training | 46.50% | 0.758 | 0.34 |
| | Testing | 19.53% | 0.684 | 0.222 |
| RF | Training | 46.62% | 0.776 | 0.361 |
| | Testing | 20.17% | 0.696 | 0.238 |
| KNN10 | Training | 45.87% | 0.786 | 0.357 |
| | Testing | 19.64% | 0.712 | 0.241 |
| NB | Training | 46.44% | **0.797** | 0.367 |
| | Testing | 19.85% | **0.729** | 0.252 |
| ANN | Training | 45.68% | 0.786 | 0.368 |
| | Testing | 21.78% | 0.690 | 0.225 |
| SVM | Training | 46.88% | 0.773 | 0.348 |
| | Testing | 19.42% | 0.686 | 0.209 |

The accuracy rate of approximately 45% is low during the training, but it gets drastically reduced to less than half the value of approximately 20% during testing. The F-measure and MCC metrics cannot be used as they are dependent on precision and some classes have zero TP instances. Again, the PRC area was already low during the training which reduced radically during testing, from approximately 0.35 to 0.2. However, the AUC seems reasonably good for overall model of approximate weighted average 0.78 during training, which did not change drastically like other metrics, during testing of approximate weighted average 0.70. When looking at each, the classifiers performed differently in training and testing. During training, all classifiers performed well for classes retail and wholesale, non-profit organization, individuals and education, whereas during testing, all classifiers performed well for classes individuals, multiple industries, education, unknown and energy. In addition, during training, KNN10 performed well for healthcare, whereas during testing, J48 performed well for education. The NB classifier performed well for energy and utilities during both training and testing.

# 6. Evaluation

The purpose of this section is to provide a summary of the discussion around the suggested predictive model as part of this study.

The algorithms that have been used exhibit inadequate characteristics for classifying the dataset under study. These characteristics may be seen in the sensitivity, specificity and accuracy of each of the classifiers, which are all shown in the preceding section. The levels of sensitivity, specificity and accuracy are all exceedingly variable and depend on the class of prediction being made. When compared to the number of instances that are incorrectly categorized, the number of instances that are properly classified is extremely small. By looking at the confusion matrix generated by each classifier, we can see that none of the classifiers could predict the 'transportation', 'healthcare', and 'food and agriculture' classes, which resulted in all of these instances being incorrectly classified into different classes, resulting in a total prediction probability (TP) of zero for these instances. Another example, utilizing the confusion matrix, shows that the majority of instances are incorrectly categorized as 'retail and wholesale', 'individuals', and 'government'. This explains that the attack pattern of certain types of target seems to be a lot like another one making the instances misclassified. This demonstrates that the malware has characteristics to hide the kind of target under investigation. Following from what was covered in the review section, the malware nature varies with each infection, making it unpredictable to anticipate which sector will be attacked by the malware. Due to the ambiguous nature of malware, it is essential to get a more comprehensive dataset to assess the model in greater depth.

In the illustration given in the above section, when the ROC area is utilized as the defining performance metric, the NB classifier earned the highest weighted average score in both training and testing, despite the fact that the accuracy was low in both cases. When compared to the other classifiers employed in the experiment, the NB classifier performed better on a greater number of classes. The NB classifier is probability based; that means that it creates a histogram of all attribute labels that occur in a class and then creates a probability of discrete individual attribute labels given to a class. When an unseen testing dataset is passed through the NB classifier, the class selected for each instance is with the highest probability. It is naïve because it ignores relationships among attributes and performs well in prediction compared to other classifiers. For the purpose of demonstration only, using the weka.classifiers.bayes, NaiveBayes classifier in the 'auto-Weka' function in the Weka tool produced an accuracy of 62.0172% and a ROC Area of 0.933. When the NB classifier's parameters are tweaked, it is possible to enhance the accuracy and overall performance of the proposed data mining model. However, due to time limitations, this was not investigated in a detailed manner in this research.

Based on the literature review and domain knowledge, attributes have been selected for dataset restructuring and pre-processing. This process of feature selection is available in different techniques in the Weka tool, known as 'Select Attributes'. The main components of this are that the attribute evaluator evaluates individual attributes (features) from the perspective of the class or output; and the search method evaluates different combinations of features to provide the best-chosen list. For the purpose of demonstration only, using the 'InfoGainAttribute' attribute evaluator and 'Ranker' search method produced an average merit, with maximum value of 0.936 for 'country' attribute and less than 0.20 for all other attributes used in this work. This means that changing values of this attribute will change the output class, i.e., the type of target. This illustrates the importance to have an automated study of the features and their importance for the output. However, due to limitations of this study, this was not investigated in detail in this research.

## 7. Conclusion

When dealing with big datasets, data mining is the process through which patterns are discovered. Both scientific research involving enormous raw scientific data and businesses collecting statistics and useful information make extensive use of data mining methods. Similarly when it comes to cyber security, data mining has proved to be an invaluable tool for identifying weaknesses and collecting indications for future predictions.

The predictive model was trained by using six different classification algorithms along with 10-fold cross-validation on dataset obtained from the Hackmageddon Blog and then compared using performance metrics, like accuracy, PRC area and ROC area. While it is true that the derived model does not perform well enough to forecast future type of targets, this maybe because it depends on the target country and patterns within a country. All the classifiers have almost the same accuracy value, but NB has higher ROC area and classifies more classes accurately. However, this is reduced considerably when tested against unseen data and hence the resulting model does not perform with sufficient accuracy to be used for prediction of type of target. The proposed model by itself does not perform well but this can be improvised through different approaches as mentioned in the future works.

## 8. Future Work

To improve the performance of the proposed work, future research must be done by acquiring complete and more accurate dataset. As illustrated in previous section, the feature 'country' has a major impact on the output. The performance or accuracy of a classifier can largely improve by having an equal distribution of types of targets instead of favouring individuals because of obvious advantage in sample size. This will have an impact on the classifier since it will have a fair distribution in the TN for each class and will assign TPR and TNR over an equal number of samples per class. This will avoid the shadowing of TP, FP and FN by excessive number of TN. If a balanced dataset cannot be collected, then the model can be tested on imbalanced dataset by using the cost-sensitive classifier with cost matrix or resample dataset by applying the Synthetic Minority Oversampling Technique (SMOTE). Additionally, the created model may be further refined in future work by including additional features and doing more in-depth study into the implications of each feature.

To improve the overall performance, data mining algorithms other than classification techniques can be tested through clustering, image recognition and time series analysis. In addition, the classifiers used here must be tested with different parameters in Weka other than the default settings.

In light of this research, we believe that a shift in cyber-attack strategy is required, from one that is reactive to one that is more proactive, and that this shift should be founded on the development of techniques of anticipatory thinking, rather than the present reactive approach. Because of the significant increase in both the number and diversity of malware in recent years, it is essential to make this change to deal with the cyber-threat environment. Furthermore, the work recommends that further research be conducted on the advantages of adopting a proactive approach to cybersecurity.

# References

Abiodun, O.I., Jantan, A., Omolara, A.E., Dada, K.V., Mohamed, N.A. and Arshad, H. (2018). State-of-the-art in artificial neural network applications: A survey. *Heliyon*, 4(11). doi: 10.1016/j.heliyon.2018.e00938.

Ahmad, I., Basheri, M., Iqbal, M.J. and Rahim, A. (2018). Performance comparison of support vector machine, random forest, and extreme learning machine for intrusion detection. *IEEE Access*, 6: 33789–33795. doi: 10.1109/ACCESS.2018.2841987.

Ahmad, S., Wasim, S., Irfan, S., Gogoi, S., Srivastava, A. and Farheen, Z. (2019). Qualitative v/s. quantitative research—A summarized review. *Journal of Evidence-based Medicine and Healthcare*, 6(43): 2828–2832. doi: 10.18410/jebmh/2019/587.

Aslan, Ö.A. and Samet, R. (2020). A comprehensive review on malware detection approaches. *IEEE Access*, 8: 6249–6271. doi: 10.1109/ACCESS.2019.2963724.

Aslan, Ö., Samet, R. and Tanrıöver, Ö.Ö. (2020). Using a subtractive center behavioral model to detect malware. *Security and Communication Networks*, 2020: 17. doi: 10.1155/2020/7501894.

Berman, D.S., Buczak, A.L., Chavis, J.S. and Corbett, C.L. (2019). A survey of deep learning methods for cyber security. *Information*, 10(4). doi: 10.3390/info10040122.

bin Asad, A., Mansur, R., Zawad, S., Evan, N. and Hossain, M.I. (2020). Analysis of malware prediction based on infection rate using machine learning techniques. *In: 2020 IEEE Region 10 Symposium (TENSYMP)*, IEEE, pp. 706–709. doi: 10.1109/TENSYMP50017.2020.9230624.

Cervantes, J., Garcia-Lamont, F., Rodríguez-Mazahua, L. and Lopez, A. (2020). A comprehensive survey on support vector machine classification: Applications, challenges and trends. *Neurocomputing*, 408: 189–215. doi: 10.1016/j.neucom.2019.10.118.

Charbuty, B. and Abdulazeez, A. (2021, March). Classification based on decision tree algorithm for machine learning. *Journal of Applied Science and Technology Trends*, 2: 20–28. doi: 10.38094/jastt20165.

Cortes, C. and VapniK, V. (1995). Support vector networks. *Machine Learning*, 20: 1–25.

Cunningham, P. and Delany, S.J. (2021). K-nearest neighbour classifiers—A tutorial. *ACM Computing Surveys*, 54(6): 25. doi: 10.1145/3459665.

Dwivedi, P. and Sharan, H. (2021). Analysis and detection of evolutionary malware: A review. *International Journal of Computer Applications*, 174: 42–45. doi: 10.5120/ijca2021921005.

FireEye (2021, April 16). Retrieved from FireEye: https://content.fireeye.com/m-trends/rpt-m-trends-2021.

Granik, M. and Mesyura, V. (2017). Fake news detection using naive Bayes classifier. *In: 2017 IEEE First Ukraine Conference on Electrical and Computer Engineering (UKRCON)*, IEEE, pp. 900–903. doi: 10.1109/UKRCON.2017.8100379.

Gunasegaran, T. and Cheah, Y.-N. (2017). Evolutionary cross-validation. In: *2017 8th International Conference on Information Technology (ICIT)*, IEEE, pp. 89–95. doi: 10.1109/ICITECH.2017.8079960.

McCulloch, W. and Pitts, W. (1990). A logical calculus of the ideas immanent in nervous activity. *Bulletin of Mathematical Biology*, 52: 99–115. Retrieved from https://www.cs.cmu.edu/~./epxing/class/10715/reading/mcculloch.and.pitts.pdf.

Mehedi Shamrat, F.J., Chakraborty, S., Billah, M.M., Das, P., Muna, J.N. and Ranjan, R. (2021). A comprehensive study on pre-pruning and post-pruning methods of decision tree classification algorithm. *In: 2021, 5th International Conference on Trends in Electronics and Informatics (ICOEI)*, pp. 1339–1345. doi: 10.1109/ICOEI51242.2021.9452898.

Muttoo, S.K. and Badhani, S. (2021). An analysis of malware detection and control through Covid-19 Pandemic. *In: 2021 8th International Conference on Computing for Sustainable Global Development (INDIACom)*, IEEE, pp. 637–641. doi: 10.1109/INDIACom51348.2021.00112.

Pournouri, S., Zargari, S. and Akhgar, B. (2019). An investigation of using classification techniques in prediction of type of targets in cyber attacks. *In: 2019 IEEE 12th International Conference on Global Security, Safety and Sustainability (ICGS3)*, IEEE, pp. 202–212. doi: 10.1109/ICGS3.2019.8688266.

Rahman, M.A., Al-Saggaf, Y. and Zia, T. (2020). A data mining framework to predict cyber attack for cyber security. *In: 2020 15th IEEE Conference on Industrial Electronics and Applications (ICIEA)*, IEEE, pp. 207–212. doi: 10.1109/ICIEA48937.2020.9248225.

Simpson, D. (2021, June 1). Retrieved from Microsoft: https://docs.microsoft.com/fr-fr/windows/security/threat-protection/intelligence/malware-naming.

Tang, W., Zhou, Y., Wu, Z., Lu, L. and Li, M. (2019). Naive bayes classification based on differential privacy. *Proceedings of the 2019 International Conference on Artificial Intelligence and Advanced Manufacturing*. Association for Computing Machinery, pp. 1–6. doi: 10.1145/3358331.3358396.

Tharwat, A. (2021). Classification assessment methods. *Applied Computing and Informatics*, 17(1): 168–192.

Udayakumar, N., Subbulakshmi, T., Mishra, A., Mishra, S. and Jain, P. (2019, February). Malware category prediction using KNN and SVM classifiers. *International Journal of Mechanical Engineering and Technology*, 10(02): 787–797; Retrieved from https://iaeme.com/MasterAdmin/Journal_uploads/IJMET/VOLUME_10_ISSUE_2/IJMET_10_02_082.pdf.

Wass, S., Pournouri, S. and Ibbotson, G. (2021). Prediction of cyber attacks during coronavirus pandemic by classification techniques and open source intelligence. *In: Cybersecurity, Privacy and Freedom Protection in the Connected World*. Springer International Publishing, pp. 67–100. doi: 10.1007/978-3-030-68534-8_6.

Yeboah-Ofori, A., Islam, S., Lee, S.W., Shamszaman, Z.U., Muhammad, K., Altaf, M. and Al-Rakhami, M.S. (2021). Cyber threat predictive analytics for improving cyber supply chain security. *IEEE Access*, 1–1. doi: 10.1109/ACCESS.2021.3087109.

# 6

# Research into Modern-day Domestic Abuse and Digital Coercive Control

## Focus on How a Framework could Assist Stakeholders with Technical Evidence Gathering in Order to Incriminate Abusers

*Megan Smith* and *Hamid Jahankhani**

## ABSTRACT

The motivation for the project is to add value to existing literature surrounding domestic abuse and digital coercive behavior in the era of the Internet of Things. Focus is put on creating a framework to assist law-enforcement stakeholders with incriminating abusers and to provide suggestions on how to improve the safety of domestic-abuse victims when it comes to smart home devices. Stakeholders of IoT devices are listed and suggestions regarding the security of devices has been provided. The suggestions have been put against real life case studies to show how they could have prevented a similar situation from happening. The framework that was then created has the ideal scenario step-by-step guidance on how police could assist victims when a crime is reported, particularly if the suggested changes were made to the devices. The aim of this research is to have a framework and the suggestions in place to help victims to feel safer in their own homes. The suggestions do not come without their negative side as having to take into account any new regulations would require going through government processes and with the security of IoT devices already under scrutiny, it would be a lengthy process for the vendors to implement certain new features on the devices. This is something that future work could definitely take a look into.

Northumbria University London, UK.
* Corresponding author: Hamid.jahankhani@northumbria.ac.uk

## 1. Introduction

Domestic abuse and digital coercive behavior are sensitive topics that are sometimes not talked about enough, particularly when you see the statistics of the increase of cases since the coronavirus pandemic. Studying in the world of cyber security, there is often more of a focus on hacking and cybercrimes and with it being a male-dominated subject and the majority of abuse cases being against women, things like domestic abuse are often not considered as something that can be related to cyber security.

The purpose of this chapter is to bring more attention to the topic in the hope that the more literature that is out there surrounding the topic, the more that can be done.

The research carried out consisted of reading into real life scenarios of domestic abuse within a technology format and from this, being able to draw up ideas and recommendations to stakeholders and vendors on ways to improve technology and law-enforcement methods when it comes to technology-facilitated abuse. The data being used throughout the research is qualitative data. It is believed that the use of this method was the most appropriate to the research question and objectives. The conclusions drawn from the research is that it would be beneficial to have a framework in place and for vendors to consider domestic abuse when adapting future devices.

## 2. Literature Review

Nearly 46% of Americans admit to 'stalking' an ex or current partner online by checking in on them without their knowledge or consent and 10% admitted to using an app to monitor an ex or current partner's text messages, phone calls, direct messages, emails, and photos (Hodson, 2020). But often the abusers are not even aware that what they are doing is an example of digital coercive behavior and some of it is even illegal. '*The IoT is a giant network of connected things and people – all of which collect and share data about the way they are used and about the environment around them*' Clark (2016). The IoT can include anything from a smart kettle and remotely controlled heating and air-conditioning units to smart watches, phones and PCs. Basically, anything connected that can be connected to the Internet is part of the Internet of Things. As much as the IoT has improved and made easier people's way of life, it has already created a lot of scenarios in which devices and users can be hacked and abused.

It is expected that there will be 75 billion IoT devices connected to the Internet in 2025 (IoT, 2020). It therefore, comes as no surprise that using technology as a weapon in domestic abuse is on the rise too. Although it is something that is beginning to be addressed, it still has its dilemmas and complications. In a study completed by Comic Relief, 90% of practitioners reported that they saw technology as a risk but felt they did not fully understand how to use technology effectively and safely (Lee, 2019).

A survey conducted by Woodlock et al. (2018) looked at what the specific technologies were that were being mostly used by abusers. The survey was carried out on practitioners who work with abuse victims and the following results show how often they saw the methods of abuse in their clients:

- Text message – 47% of victims
- GPS tracking via smartphone apps – 40% of victims
- Facebook – 37% of victims
- Email – 38% of victims

## 2.1  A Smart City/Society

A smart city is a city that uses technology to provide services and solve city problems. It includes things, such as improving transport, social services and to generally improve the citizens' ways of life (Gorini, 2021). The local governments are able to see real time data of things around the city that might require attention, such as water quality/usage, air pollution and live traffic information. The data can then be collected and used quickly to make improvements that resolve the issues. Navigation apps are even starting to work closely with smart cities so that live traffic data and footage from roadside cameras can be shared between them in order to provide real time traffic updates and avoid delays on roads for emergency services. In New York, reports from the traffic navigation app come four minutes faster than a 911 call, which can be a life-saving amount of time difference (Stober, 2021). Smart cities also allow for the provision of safety measures. Sensors can be used to give early warning signs of floods, landslides and hurricanes, as well as infrastructure problems and leaks (Twiglobal.com, 2021).

So, with all the above being said, a smart city sounds like a positive benefit to any society with only positive outcomes from it, but the concept does not come without its issues. In an article written by Naveen Joshi (2019), it is reported that the following issues are the dark side of smart cities:

**Public education and engagement** – All the efforts at installing a smart city are wasted if the public are not involved or engaged in the progress. Installing a traffic monitoring system would be pointless if the citizens were not technical enough to use the suggested methods. Joshi (2019) reports that even in developed countries, there is a very high percentage of people who are not tech-savvy enough for a smart city.

**Infrastructure** – The infrastructure of setting up a smart city does not come at a low price, sometimes costing countries billions of pounds to set up and then also enduring hefty costs of employment to keep it up and running and maintained. For developing countries, this is not something that would be easy for them to do – relying on investors from other countries to get them up and running. This often means that underdeveloped countries would get left behind as they do not have the funds or the capacity for the equipment and network that is needed.

**Power** – The increase in batteries that would be required to support a smart city and all the IoT devices within it would be huge and almost impossible to keep up with in some countries. The only alternative to this would be to use electricity, fossil fuels, or a completely wireless power solution to power all IoT devices; but any plans for this is still a long way off yet.

**Privacy and Security** – Smart cities would need to collect a lot of data for it to work, such as camera footage and application data. Joshi (2019) reports on how several civil rights activists have already expressed concern about the invasion of privacy. Cyber-attacks are constantly being developed and any data falling into the wrong hands could be catastrophic for the city as well as the fact an attacker could have the ability to bring down the entire smart network.

**Data bias** – Data bias is the final point that has been seen as a dark side of smart cities. Several investigations have been undertaken that show racial discrimination in facial recognition methods that are often used in smart cities by cameras in stores and on the street, with the poorest accuracy consistently found in subjects who are female, Black and 18–30 years old (Najibi, 2020). This is one way in which data bias could be created as any of the data that might be needed to be used in crimes could be inaccurate. Another way in which data bias is created is in the amount of technology that is required to get a smart city up and running; poorer communities within the city are discriminated against if they are unable to keep up with the moving trends and the ability to have technical devices to help contribute towards the smart city.

The relevance of a smart city to this study is that it shows how technology is rising in a much larger scale than personal devices. It adds to the pressure of society to keep up with technology devices and therefore, increases the chances of people using devices in an abusive form. There are pros and cons of the uprise in smart cities, particularly data bias being a major problem when it comes to using the statistics in crime. But, on the other hand, the stronger use of surveillance and monitoring tools can help to create a much safer place to live. If a victim was being stalked, it would not take long for this to become apparent and for them to become incriminated.

Technology company Huawei spoke to the BBC and claimed the following on smart city surveillance: 'It means they can combine their own video surveillance networks with other public and private security systems, as well as vehicle mounted and portable eLTE solutions, to keep a watch for incidents of theft, civic disturbance and unauthorised access. In theory, it means zero blind spots in their surveillance network' (Safe cities: Using smart tech for public security | A Better Connected World | Huawei | BBC Worldwide, 2021).

## 2.2 Technology Facilitated Abuse

A research paper was completed by Harris et al. (2018) in which digital coercive control was looked at in Australia. It was reported: 'There was no pre-existing evidence in Australia that detailed whether technology abuse was a widespread issue in domestic violence and how technology was being used.' They completed a study called SmartSafe and within this they carried out 'in-depth interviews with 30 female victim/survivors, 19 lawyers, 24 domestic violence workers and three magistrates.'

The findings were analyzed and it was discovered that all 30 of the women interviewed, who had experienced domestic abuse, had been abused through technology realms with a significant amount of them having been stalked, using technology methods. The participants involved told the study how they 'were concerned that such harms were not taken seriously by police and that there was not enough support for both practitioners and clients' as reported by Harris et al. (2018). This research provides a significant amount of reassurance that the topic in question is something that does need addressing. Though the research was undertaken in Australia, it could be argued that the UK system is different in dealing with digital coercive behavior and how it is handled by police and stakeholders. The research still holds a lot of value as it shows how many people, particularly women, are receiving domestic abuse in a technical format.

A report written by Woodlock et al. (2018) explains how 'technology-facilitated domestic violence is an emerging issue for social workers and other service providers.' A survey was provided to over 500 practitioners who support domestic abuse victims and it was asked about how abusers use technology as an abuse tactic. Woodlock et al., explained that the response to the survey was the following: 'The findings demonstrate that DV practitioners believe perpetrator use of technology is extensive and has significant impacts on the safety of clients.' The social workers explained that a major issue they are facing is how to help the victims stay safe online from the abuse but still be able to use social media and other technology forms to stay connected to family and friends.

Woodlock also speaks in his research of how domestic violence is not always considered as the crime and stalking offences are often wrongly categorized as 'electronic intrusion' or 'cyber harassment' instead. This further emphasises the need for a framework to be in place so that supporting services and stakeholders are better able to assist victims and incriminate abusers appropriately.

Similar to Harris et al., the study completed by Woodlock et al., was carried out in Australia, potentially leading to an unfair reflection of digital coercive behavior in the UK, but the following literature is from Women's Aid, which is a UK-based charity that highlights that the same problems are being seen worldwide.

Since 2013, Women's Aid has been trying to create awareness regarding domestic violence and the increase of technologies involvement. Laxton (2014) put together a report following a conference that took place to discuss this increasing problem. An online survey conducted on 300 domestic-abuse survivors showed several relevant statistics:

- 45% had experienced online abuse, including social networking sites
- 38% reported being stalked online
- 75% reported concerns that the police did not know how best to respond to online abuse
- 12% who reported to police were not helped at all

Sharon Stratton, a training coordinator at the college of policing, spoke at the conference held by Women's Aid and was quoted as saying, 'Professionals working with or on behalf of victims must ensure that they have the knowledge and capability to support those affected and to prevent further opportunities for re-offending. This requires a coordinated response from support services, the police and criminal justice partners and social media providers, who should be provided with the best training and appropriate resources to respond effectively.'

It is clear from the research conducted by Women's Aid that domestic abuse in the technology age has been an issue much longer than some may suspect. It could be argued that the survey and conference was hosted in 2014 and therefore is no longer relevant or has since significantly improved. This argument is something that is to be considered, as there are no statistics provided till date to show what the cases were like after 2014 and the conference. Despite this, it is clear to see that the cases have since risen again after 2019 due to the consistently rising sale of technology devices and the ever-rising cases of domestic abuse in more recent years due to the COVID-19 pandemic.

The current ongoing worldwide pandemic, COVID-19 has played a part in an increase of domestic violence against women. Jeffrey Kluger (2021) claims that 'domestic violence is a pandemic within the COVID-19 pandemic'. It was reported by the Executive Director of UN Women, Phumzile Mlambo-Ngcuka (2020), that 'globally, 243 million women and girls suffered physical or sexual violence from their partners between 2019 and 2020', which only continued to increase throughout the pandemic. Mlambo-Ngcuka (2020) continued to explain that less than 40% of women who experienced the abuse reported it as a crime or sought any kind of support.

This was no different for the victims being abused through technology means either. Melissa Godin (2020) reported during the pandemic: 'It's much easier to get access to a partner's phone to alter privacy settings, obtain passwords, or install tracking software when people are spending so much time together in close proximity.' Experts from the anti-virus company, Avast (2020) reported that the pandemic has most likely made the problem even worse.

## 2.3 Cyberstalking

Two common tactics used for tech abuse are cyberstalking and tracking. Location tracking devices are very easy to find and use and can be easily disguised by the abuser, if necessary. All modern smart phones have readily available apps that can be easily downloaded on the app stores. Apples Find My iPhone feature provides real-time location tracking that is then stored on the user's account, which can be exploited by the abuser. Stalking apps, also known as stalkerware, can go completely undetected on a device and can track everything from phone calls and text messages to Google searches and location of the user. Avast, a global leader in digital security and privacy products, reveals there has been a 93% increase in the use of spyware and stalkerware apps in the UK since lockdown measures were first introduced (Press.Avast.com, 2021). Avast also reported that the increase in the stalkerware being installed on devices has also been linked to the increase of domestic abuse cases. Other security firms were also able to see an increase in the installation of stalkerware on devices – Malwarebytes reported a 1677% increase globally on spyware installations since COVID-19 began. Kaspersky were also able to backup these statistics as they reported seeing the spyware on thousands of more devices worldwide in 2020 than the previous year (Pozniak, 2020). The statistics are great evidence that the issue of domestic abuse through technology is still very real and something that needs addressing. It has been heightened and brought to light even more over the last two years due to the COVID-19 pandemic accentuating the problem.

## 2.4  *Domestic Abuse in a Smart Home*

Smart homes are becoming more popular with many household items that now have the ability to work remotely or connect back to Internet that would never have been imagined in previous years. According to a report by McKinsey (2017), in 2017 there was 29 million homes in the US that contained at least one form of smart technology, growing at a rate of 31% a year.

The Nest smart thermostat is a device that learns your habits in the home and will create heating or cooling schedules so that it no longer needs to be manual. It also comes with the ability to be able to control it remotely from a phone or tablet so that the heating and hot water can be controlled at the touch of a button whilst on the go.

Phillips Hue created smart lights that allow light bulbs throughout the home to be controlled remotely. They also provide sensors and switches which can be fixed and removed from rooms as needed.

Google provides a full smart home range involving speakers, cameras, sensors, lights and Chromecast devices, all of which can be accessed remotely from a mobile device.

Samsung created an oven that can connect to your home Wi-Fi, allowing users to remotely monitor the oven functions, preheat and change temperatures, set a timer and turn off the oven, all from a smartphone application.

Smart toothbrushes are even in existence. They have a camera on the brush itself, allowing anyone with the app installed on their phone to be able to see photos and videos of inside the mouth of the person using it.

The above items could all be seen as an improvement for society but for domestic abuse victims, all the above can be used against them and there are several cases in which they already have been. In 2018, helplines in America said that 'more people were calling than ever before about losing control of Wi-Fi-enabled doors, speakers, thermostats, lights and cameras. Lawyers also said they were wrangling with how to add language to restraining orders to cover smart home technology' (Bowles, 2018).

Bowles continued to report on how victims of domestic abuse through smart technology have reported how it made them feel like they had been going crazy and losing control of their own home. Before they even realized, they were being abused through those means. She continued to explain that the problem is often that one person in the home takes charge of the technology and sets up everything and knows all the passwords – thus handing them all the power. This research conducted by Bowles is significant in showing the impact smart devices are having emotionally on abuse victims. Although the research was conducted in 2018, there is no reason to believe that the situation is much different now, and if anything, it could be argued that the situation is now worse, as technology is advancing daily and so are the tactics used by hackers and abusers.

## 2.5 Smart Technology in Crimes

There have now been thousands of cases in which IoT devices have been used as a domestic abuse tool. Many go unreported by women and as mentioned previously, many support services do not feel like they have the knowledge or skills to assist the victims. Domestic abuse through technology is a relatively new crime and in 2018, it was reported by Braithwaite (2018) that there had only been one reported case in the UK of a conviction for smart-related device abuse. The *Sunday Times* reported on the case that the husband was an electronics expert and had been using a wall-mounted iPad in his estranged wife's home to eavesdrop into her conversations and hack her social media accounts. Moments after the woman confided in her mother about no longer loving her husband, he turned up at her door and bombarded her with abuse. 'The woman told magistrates that she switched off a camera facility on the iPad and brought in an IT engineer to change the password on the system so that he could no longer access it; but the court heard he still logged in remotely' (Hammersley, 2018). The husband was found guilty of stalking offences.

Smart devices can hold a lot of data and devices, such as Alexa and Google Home that have microphones in them are able to listen and store what they have heard. The devices are always listening to the users, as they are listening out for the 'wake' word, such as 'Alexa' or 'Hey Google' and any command that follows that is stored in the app and can be sent back to Amazon's servers for them to use in order to improve their algorithms and learn more about the user. The commands can also be listened back by the companies for 'human screening' to help improve the device's performance (Clauser, 2019). It is debated how much the devices are hearing outside of the 'wake' word. A study was conducted by Ford and Palmer (2018) in which they carried out an analysis of the Alexa voice service network traffic. Two identical Echo devices were placed in the researcher's home and Wireshark was used over a course of 21 days to monitor the traffic on the devices. Response cards were sent to the Amazon Alexa app and stored in the history settings; the cards contained a transcript of what the conversation involved. Findings in the experiment showed that the device had responded to the researcher when the 'wake' word had not been used. Ford et al., reported: 'All audio recorded and streamed by the Echo Dot(s) were inadvertent, meaning the Echo misinterpreted home audio as the 'wake' word, or it randomly recorded home audio.' Ford et al., went on to conclude that he could not confirm or deny if the devices were always listening, or if they just misinterpreted other words for the 'wake' word.

The devices are also capable of recognising voices. So they know when you are home or not, and maybe even the room you are in due to devices often being named after what room they are in, for example, 'Kitchen Echo' or 'Bedroom Alexa'.

American company, criminal defence lawyer, wrote a report on how a smart home could be called as a trial witness in a court case. A case referred to as 'The

Arkansas Case' was provided as an example. In 2015, James Andrew Bates invited two friends to his house, but when he awoke the next day, one of the friends was found dead, face down in his hot tub. Both James and the other friend denied involvement and claimed they had gone to bed before the time of death. Bates owned an Echo smart speaker and the investigating police issued a search warrant to Amazon for data from the Echo device. 'The Seattle-based tech company twice declined to provide police with the information they requested from the device' (Hern, 2017). It wasn't until Bates volunteered the information over himself that Amazon finally handed over the information. Amazon argued that the Echo would only have listened to its 'wake' words, but it was the chance that the device might have misheard and triggered an accidental recording that the prosecutors were hoping for.

The criminal defence lawyer website went on to explain that regarding homes that have other smart devices, such as thermostats and smart TVs, 'the date and time of use of these systems may be relevant to, say, a person's alibi (if one claims to be out of town when a crime occurs but her smart heating system came on and was overridden by an in-home command, for example). Or the smart TV could show activation and usage during the period.' (Could Your 'Smart House' be called as a Trial Witness? 2016).

In relation to the above, in 2015, the police in Connecticut were able to cite Fitbit records in a murder case against Connie Dabate's husband. Fitbit data was able to show that Connie had been making steps around her home over an hour after the time that he had reported that she had been killed. The husband's lawyers requested for the Fitbit data to be kept out of the trial, bit it was luckily declined by the judge. But over four years later, the trial is still to be completed and the husband maintains his innocence, despite having a story that does not match up to the Fitbit data (Paiella, 2017).

The examples provided above are an example of how smart technologies are easily being used in crimes, but the positive reflection of the above studies is that they are being considered as evidence in court rooms, and lawyers are becoming more aware of what is happening and calling for technology devices to be analysed.

## 3. Research Methodology

Positivism comes up with research questions and hypothesis that can be evaluated and analysed (Thesis mind, 2019). It is believed that this is the closest philosophy to the research that is being conducted as positivism is what defines knowledge solely on observable facts and does not look at other values that might not be relevant or cannot be proved as reliable. The research undertaken is on a very sensitive topic of domestic abuse and digital coercive control and therefore cannot afford to have information that is incorrect or made up that might discredit the topic. The research is solely based on facts and all literature and statements are able to be backed up with references.

The approach of the research is inductive, as it is building on a topic that already exists. Although there is already knowledge that exists surrounding the topic, there is more that can be gained and put together and also other ideas that can be put forward surrounding the topic, such as the frameworks that can be used.

The research is also mainly using qualitative data and this is discussed further in detail under the headings to follow.

The strategy used throughout the research is very much case-study-based as the main aim is to gather a very in-depth understanding of an issue in a real-life setting. The research looks at one particular topic, which is the IoT and the impact it has had on domestic abuse and digital coercive control.

The benefits of using a case-study strategy is that it has allowed the authors to focus solely on one topic and enable deeper understanding of that topic. The opposing side to this is that it does tend to involve some assumptions and has more room for the authors' personal views to have an impact on the study.

The data being used throughout this research is mainly qualitative data. It is believed that the use of this method is most appropriate for the research question and objectives. Due to the nature of the research topic, a lot of the research undertaken involves case studies concerning individual people, businesses and organizations, particularly those involved with the development of IoT devices and victims of domestic abuse. However, some of the data collected is in a quantitative format, such as comparison of statistics, including the increase in amount of IoT devices, increase of domestic abuse cases and the relation between them, as this is also relevant to the research.

The benefit of using mainly qualitative data is that the findings about cases will be true and accurate to that particular case. It also allows for more smaller studies to be looked at as it is simpler and cheaper for the writer, compared to carrying out a large qualitative data study which would be time consuming. The disadvantage of using mainly qualitative data is that due to the complicated nature of the research, something that might work for one case might not work for another. Domestic abuse is a complex topic as is the world of IoT and crime, and there is never going to be one straightforward answer; whereas a report that studies quantitative data can hold more weight with solid statistics that can be measured against and analysed.

The time horizons used for this research are cross-sectional. This refers to the fact that the data is being collected at one point in time. As it is not experimental research, there is no need for data to be collected over a stretched period of time. All literature and articles used are the ones that were found at the time of writing the research.

The materials used for the research included library literature, online forums that allow people to share their own stories, newspapers, magazines and website articles that are reporting on statistics and bringing to light the current issues. News articles and journalists who have reported on real life cases that have been concluded or are still ongoing have been used as case studies to use against the framework. Technology expert's opinions on IoT devices and information from the companies themselves have also been used to provide evidence and fair opinions on the way that the technology works. Materials from all other stakeholders' websites and information pages have also been used, for example, the charities that work with the victims of the abuse to help understand the support they need.

Alan Bryman (2016) states that there are four main areas of ethical principles that need to be considered in social sciences research and these are:

- Whether there is harm to any participants
- Whether there is a lack of informed consent
- Whether there is an invasion of privacy
- Whether deception is involved

These above-mentioned areas were considered throughout the research and as a questionnaire was not carried out and no participants were required for the study, there should be no ethical concerns on that part. Therefore, there was also not a lack of consent as no consent was required at any point throughout the research.

It was decided by the writer that conducting interviews and surveys would not be necessary or appropriate for the research conducted. Due to the highly sensitive topic of domestic abuse in the modern era being discussed, it was not deemed appropriate for the researcher to become involved in real life cases that had potentially not been brought to light by the police services or the media. The anonymity of the victims would be of upmost importance as there would have been considerable concerns from an ethical perspective as to whether the research could go ahead or not.

It was instead decided that existing data was to be used; therefore, all case studies used and statistics recorded are all things that the researcher found through online journal research or through media stories that had already been made public. Any names and details used throughout the research are the ones that can be publicly found already, without further involvement of the writer. Therefore, there was no invasion of privacy or deception involved throughout the process of research.

The sole purpose of this research is to be beneficial to existing research and is in no way biased to either side of the argument. Everything involved in the research is ethically and legally appropriate and aims to provide fairness and truth by citing previous work that adds additional weight to the project.

## 4. Data Analysis and Critical Discussion

Previous parts of the chapter refer to stakeholders; in terms of this research, stakeholders refer to the following information. 'The international standard providing guidance on social responsibility, called ISO 26000, defines a stakeholder as an individual or group that has an interest in any decision or activity of an organization' ASQ (2021).

When it comes to the technology devices themselves, particularly in the IoT, the stakeholders of an IoT device could include:

- **Company executives** – The people who make the decisions at technology companies, can be held accountable if their items are not safe or not provide safe options.

- **Product management** – The people who design and manage the devices.
- **Product engineers** – The people, who create the devices and programme them, could have the ability to input coding and safety features to help keep people safe or be able to raise concerns about things that are missing.
- **Sales team** – The people who would hear customers' concerns and ideas and be able to report back to management and design teams about the devices.
- **The end user customers** – The people who are buying the products.
- **Legal teams** – The people, who would be fighting any court battle that came their way in regard to devices not being used appropriately, would be in their best interest to make sure all devices are used lawfully.

Stakeholders of criminal investigation would include:

- Police force
- Crown prosecution services
- Social services
- Supporting charities
- Other government bodies

All the above could be accountable towards helping the incrimination of abusers using technology.

## 4.1 Stakeholder Responsibility

With the dramatic increase in IoT devices being owned per household, the statistics provided in the literature review, showing the amount of tech abuse that is now taking place, can be of no surprise. The fight for more to be done continues and a lot of responsibility for some of the actions taking place can fall with the stakeholders surrounding the devices.

The purpose of this section of the chapter is to delve further into how stakeholders could contribute better to assisting owners of IoT devices, particularly smart home devices, in feeling safer and to enable a way of assisting victims of domestic abuse, support services and law enforcement in incriminating any abuse carried out.

Use of remotely accessing devices is a common problem that victims have encountered and it usually always happens without the victim knowing that it is happening; further leading to stalking or them being manipulated or made to feel crazy. One solution could be that smart devices should allow for a noise or notification to be created that shows the device is being currently accessed remotely.

A case study that would have been beneficial is the previously-mentioned story in the literature review by Braithwaite (2018) in which a husband was eavesdropping on his wife through a wall-mounted iPad in their home. Moments after the woman confided in her mother about no longer loving her husband, he turned up at her door and bombarded her with abuse. If a solution was in place, like a sound being played when the iPad was accessed remotely, then it would have notified her when the conversation was taking place and could have prevented the abuse that followed the eavesdropping. If things had been escalated further by the husband, a simple notification to alert the wife that someone was accessing the device could have been lifesaving.

The creators of the devices should hold a level of responsibility to be more aware of the abuse that is taking place. Another solution that could be in place is that the vendors of the smart-home devices should provide a level of support to the law enforcement and supporting charities and provide guidelines on how devices work and the hidden features that are available on them as well as having an input towards the training that is provided to the staff.

A solid training plan should be in place for relevant stakeholders to follow. It is mentioned that the support staff looking after the victims need to have correct specialist training to be able to support the victims, and it was previously mentioned in the literature review that relevant charities, which support domestic abuse victims, felt that they do not have enough knowledge about technology in order to help as much as they would like to. Thus given below is an example of some training that could be made readily available and provided to the support teams of these victims.

**IoT training** – Both Microsoft and IBM provide IoT training courses providing a great overview of what they are and how they were.

**IoT security** – For anyone who already knows the basics of IoT, the next level would be an IoT security course. A company called 'IoT Security Foundation' offers a two-day course in which they claim all attendees will know how to secure a connected IoT device from scratch, and be able to discuss main threats and attacks after the course is finished (IoT Security Training – IoT Security Foundation, 2021).

These courses should be provided at the very minimum to the support staff and alongside should be the additional training provided by the smart home vendors. Any staff that are expected to be in a role that is reactive to crimes involving IoT devices should be continually trained on emerging technologies and always receive up-to-date guidance from all vendors when new products are let into the market.

A further solution could be for more regulations to be put in place for owners of home smart devices to require admin accounts for anyone over the age of 18 that is living in the household. The stakeholder, who would need to be responsible for enforcing this action, would be the government. Thus, not making it something easy to put into place, but if it was to be, the smart home vendors would be required to declare on the packaging of the devices that this is the case. Something like this would be not easy to enforce, but it would possibly be a deterrent to abusers if they knew they were not able to hold all the power of a device. The regulation could also be used against an abuser if a report was made by a victim and it was discovered that the devices in the home did not have an admin account for the other tenants of the household. The advantage of all members of the household having an admin account is to be able to self-defend. The literature review mentioned how more and more cases are being seen in which victims are reporting losing control of home devices, such as thermostats, lights, and speakers and there is a study conducted by Dr. Leonie Tanzer, in which she explains 'the perpetrator, who very often is male, is the person who purchases the device and maintains it, giving them control over the admin settings and the environment they are in' (Silva and Franco, 2020). If the victims had an admin account, they are much more likely to be able to get themselves out of an unsafe situation if needed. A case-study example of a situation in which this would have been useful is in the case of a ring doorbell being monitored remotely.

The BBC news reported an incident in October 2020, in which a woman's ex-husband was using her ring-doorbell camera to track her movements. The smart doorbell was able to trigger alerts when there were movements, including people coming and going from the home, which would then be recorded and be able to be watched from the app on a smart phone (Silva and Franco, 2020). The woman reported feeling trapped and if she took the batteries out of the device, it would trigger more of a reaction from the abuser.

There is a chance that if the woman had her own admin account and was able to access the ring doorbell remotely too, then she would have the ability to change the notification settings and be able to delete footage of herself leaving her home if required for her own safety – again potentially being lifesaving in certain situations.

Another solution that would help with the problem of unknown devices being in a home is that a notification is always sent to other devices on the network, to let the users know there is a new device on the network. For example, if an abuser was to buy a camera or microphone and hide it within a home, the victims would receive a notification on their phone or tablet to notify that a new device had been added to the network. This idea has stemmed from the new Apple air-tag device, in which a small key-ring can be attached to your keys to enable them to easily be found if lost. It works by connecting to any apple products that are within close proximity of the device. The device is small and can easily be hidden, making it seem like the perfect tool for tracking and stalking someone, but the air tag sends a notification to the apple device near it, letting the user know that an 'air tag has been found moving with you'. The victim can then disable the tracking of the device if it is unknown to them. This feature is a great example of how Apple as a vendor are paying attention to domestic abuse and stalking offences and are making positive changes within their new devices to stop them being used maliciously. Taking an example from this and incorporating notifications on nearby devices is something that would deter abusers from acting covertly as they would not be able to get away with it.

A fifth suggestion is for smart home devices to have the ability to set up a trigger, or safety word. This word could then either be used to call the police or a friend or relative, or it could be used to alert the device to begin recording or monitoring what is happening in the home. In case studies of physical domestic abuse, particularly when the victims feel that they wouldn't be believed, a feature like this in their smart devices could be what helps them get justice in court. Johnny Depp and Amber Heard had been undergoing a court battle for months over alleged domestic abuse charges, both parties claiming that either was the one who was being abused and public opinions were very much divided over who was telling the truth (Bryant, 2021). In situations like this, a phrase could be set up. Patrick Hearn (2021) suggested that, for instance, you could use a word such as 'pernicious' as a safe word, as it is not something likely to be heard in everyday conversation. A phrase, such as 'add fish fingers to my shopping list' could also be used to trigger an Alexa to start monitoring the actions in the home.

Smart devices are in a perfect position to be able to keep a home and its owners safe. It is likely that extra features, such as trigger words, have already been considered as a feature to be added and it is presumed that there are security issues as to why it hasn't been done yet. There are already a lot of privacy concerns surrounding smart devices and the data that they hold and it is unlikely to be approved to allow them to hold even more.

When purchasing a smart device, the adverts promoting the device, the external packaging and the instructions that display the devices in a very positive light, exclaiming the benefits of what the device can do and the positive capabilities. Another suggestion to assist in the personal safety of smart devices is to include safety labels and precautions in the adverts and packaging of the devices – all capabilities, including any negative ones should be declared on devices, almost as if in the same style as ingredients that are prone to allergies are displayed on food packages. Users, who are less technical and are unaware of the dark side of technology, are more prone to falling victim to being hacked or falling into a trap of digital coercive behavior due to the unknowing of how powerful some devices are and applications that can be installed on them. This includes a lack of understanding of the importance of having secure passwords and admin accounts on the devices.

Figure 1 below shows an example of the kind of security and privacy warning that could be present on an IoT device.

**Security & Privacy Warnings**

Device: xxxxx
Version: xxxxx
Manufacturer: xxxxx

Device features – xxxxx
Feature capabilities - xxxxx

Access control – xxxxx
Security updates – xxxxx

Data collection – xxxx
Data storage – xxxxx
Shared with – xxxxx

**Fig. 1:** Security and privacy warning.

A final suggestion that could help improve the reliability of any evidence extracted from a smart device is that history on devices should be made permanent, or should be moved and stored remotely in case it is needed for evidence purposes. It is very easy for an admin of a device to be able to go into the settings and delete all history. Therefore if a victim got the confidence to report a crime and the history had been deleted by the abuser, then it would give them the ability to gaslight the victim into thinking they were crazy and making up scenarios.

## 4.2 Proposed Framework

Figure 2 shows a proposed framework created by the writer. It shows an initial framework that police and other law-enforcement agencies could use to assist them when a victim approaches them with a domestic abuse or digital coercive behavior case. It is to be presumed that the above suggestions might be in place already in order to be able to show what the best outcome would be if there were solutions and a framework in place.

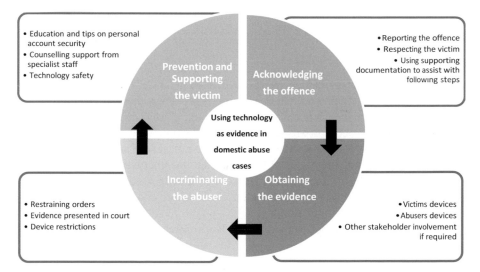

**Fig. 2:** Framework to assist stakeholders with technical evidence gathering in order to incriminate abusers.

It is really important for a framework to be in place, as the literature review shows that victims have previously felt that their abuse was not taken seriously enough or not even reported by the police.

The framework starts with **acknowledging the offence** and with the following sub points:

- Reporting the offence
- Respecting the victim

Use of supporting documentation to assist with the following steps:

**Table 1:** Devices documentations.

| Victim Smart Devices | Abuser Smart Devices |
|---|---|
| **Wearable devices** | **Wearable devices** |
| Fitbit or similar | Fitbit or similar |
| Apple watch | Apple watch |
| Smart clothing | Smart clothing |
| GPS tracker | GPS tracker |
| **Devices that can be carried** | **Devices that can be carried** |
| Phone | Phone |
| Tablet | Tablet |
| **Devices at home** | **Devices at home** |
| Laptop | Laptop |
| PC | PC |
| Smart speaker | Smart speaker |
| Doorbell camera | Doorbell camera |
| Any other smart home devices | Any other smart home devices |

The sub points are an important start to any crime that is being reported. It ensures that all offences reported are acknowledged by law enforcement and is being recorded in their systems and taken seriously. Respecting the victim is also a key element. If a victim is to report that they are being abused or that they think their technology has been compromised, they need to be able to feel like they can trust who they are telling and that they will not be made to feel as if the crime is irrelevant or that they are going crazy. Use of the supported documentation to assist with the following steps, refer to Table 1, in which it will be expected that every device on the list will be considered for examination. Each device could provide evidence or alibis or both parties.

**Obtaining the evidence** encourages the law enforcers to complete the following sub points:

- Victim's devices
- Abuser's devices
- Other stakeholder involvement, if required

This step is the most important from the framework as it is where the main evidence gathering will take place and will ensure that no corners are cut. Victim's devices and abuser's devices refers to Table 1, in which it shows a list of devices that are potential items that the victim or the abuser could have on them or in their home. It is vital that the law enforcements use it as a checklist and check all devices from both sides that might be relevant to the investigation. It can sometimes be overlooked as to what devices might be relevant, as using smart devices as evidence is still a new process to get used to. This, therefore, ensures that nothing is getting overlooked and even if one of the devices or the evidence on the device is not relevant, it is important that it has still been checked. For example, if the victim was physically assaulted whilst at home, the smart devices at home would be able to provide evidence, such as a camera could display footage, a smart speaker might have detected sound, or a ring doorbell could prove that the abuser was also at the home, as well as an attacker's smart watch or smart phone would be able to provide statistics on physical activity and location. Another example is if a victim was being stalked by someone, once the person is located, the smart devices on the person would be able to provide details of the locations being the same as the victims or that the attacker had been near the victim's home on more than one occasion. If the previous-mentioned suggestion was in place, it would also include any recordings that had taken place after the victim had initiated the trigger safety word on a device.

**Incriminating the abuser** is the third step of the framework and includes the following:

- Restraining orders
- Evidence presenting in court
- Device restrictions

This step would involve the same work that police already do, but they would now have the extra evidence required to complete the steps better with help from the framework. The evidence presented in court could be more meaningful to the case and provide extra support needed to get the correct results. This then would initiate restraining orders and device restrictions. Device restrictions refer to the abuser having devices taken away from them or being banned from using certain applications; such as, if the abuser was committing digital coercive control by remotely accessing smart devices in the victim's home, he could have all of the access revoked if the evidence was there to prove he was not using it appropriately.

**Prevention and supporting the victim** is the final step of the proposed framework with the following sub points:

- Education and tips on personal account security
- Counselling support from specialist staff
- Technology safety

This final step will ensure that the victim is looked after, both personally and in terms of the technology. Counselling sessions from support staff will ensure that the victim recovers from what she has been through. The training that the staff undergo is one of the important aspects of this section. The specialist staff will refer to staff who have good knowledge about technology and how to support victims that have been abused through these methods. Education and technology safety will be provided to the victims in terms of an assigned person to assist them, depending on the circumstances, in securing their devices or adding extra features to make them feel safer. For example, if there is a victim of digital coercive control and the abuser was using smart devices in the home to manipulate the victim, then the police or charity would be able to help in securing the home and removing the abuser from all devices and then providing help and support in keeping the victim safe from any further distress. If previous solutions were used, then all support services would be fully kept up to date on emerging technologies and have received guidance from other stakeholders and vendors to enable them to provide the best support possible.

## 5.  Case Studies

*The Guardian* News website (2021) reported that 'three in four domestic abuse cases end without charge in England and Wales' and that '80% of domestic abuse allegations were closed because of lack of evidence or lack of support from the victim prosecute.' Whilst these figures are shocking, it relays the fact that the processes in place are not getting any better and more help is still needed to help prosecute abusers. If it is being reported that there is a lack of evidence to support the charges, then it might need to be considered that more needs to be done to help find the evidence required. This is where technology and IoT devices could be used to benefit victims and the police force where necessary, to prevent evidence getting missed. The following case study is a real life case that has been published publicly online. The previous framework and suggested methods to improve safety of smart devices will be used to see how they could assist with any future domestic abuse cases.

### 5.1  Hannah Clarke Case Study

Hannah was a mother living in Australia, when she and her three children were murdered by her estranged husband in a horrendous attack. It became apparent that she had been suffering domestic abuse and coercive control for many years prior to the murder. The abuse included stalking and technology abuse – the husband would turn up at places where Hannah already was, without any explanation as to how he knew she was there. There were several signs that indicated he had been through her handbag and mobile phone.

Hannah's parents are still campaigning for coercive control to be made illegal in Australia as this is not something that is in place yet, whereas it was made illegal in the UK back in 2015 (Gearing, 2021).

Although it would never be possible to know if things could have been different, it enables us to investigate how the police would look at a similar offence, had it been reported and it was illegal in that country. This is where a framework like the one created would come into play, as it allows some guidance to the police and reassurance for the victim that the specialist staff would be assisting.

*Step 1*: It would begin with the crime being reported, even if it was just a suspicion that the victim felt as if being stalked or her phone had been hacked. The crime would be reported and submitted, and it would always be investigated.

*Step 2*: The devices of the victim would be investigated in a private setting to always ensure the safety of the victim. The victim would be available to provide full access to her devices. So, in this scenario, there should be no need for involvement from external stakeholders of the device. This is at the point in which investigators will have hopefully been able to see if any software or tracking applications were installed on the victim's device. If not, they would continue the investigation on other devices that she may own. If other suggestions were in place, such as code words in any smart devices, then this information will be able to be extracted and used as evidence.

*Step 3*: Any unwanted applications or tracking would be removed from the victim's device and anything found would be used against the abuser, whether in the form of a restraining order or fine/sentence. At home, smart devices could be checked to ensure the victim had admin accounts on them.

*Step 4*: The victim and the abuser are now both known to the services and any further incidents that arise should be taken much more seriously. Fully trained counselling and police support stuff can be provided to the victim as well as help with technology devices and keeping her safe.

The above steps are only the ways the victim could be helped from a technology perspective. They are in no way a reflection of preventing physical abuse or helpful if the abuser is to breach any restraining orders or warnings. The steps provided are to reflect how seriously even the most minor of offences are to be taken. If the abuser was stalking the victim using applications on a phone and this led to murder of the victim, then it could have potentially been prevented if steps before that were taken more seriously.

## 6. Conclusion and Future Work

The original research aim – 'research into modern-day domestic abuse and digital coercive control, with focus on how a framework could assist stakeholders with technical evidence gathering in order to incriminate abusers' – has been achieved. The research shows an array of suggestions on improvements that could be made to IoT devices to make evidence gathering easier when required, for incriminating abusers. Some of the improvements help to deter the crimes from happening in the first place. The framework created could help assist stakeholders with incriminating abusers as it shows a step-by-step method in assisting the victims, right from the point the crime is reported and right until the end and the support they can offer after.

Domestic abuse and digital coercive control are very sensitive subjects that can be difficult to approach and even harder for some people to talk about. The purpose of this research was to throw more light on the issue and to be able to provide suggestions to improving IoT devices.

The stakeholders involved in the creation of IoT devices do not have domestic abuse at the forefront of their mind when creating devices; the main aims are to make them as practical and easy to use as possible in the home in order to make an easier way of life, in the hope that eventually we will not need to lift a finger as technology will be able to do it all. Often the positives and excitement of something new can overlook the cons of the item, like being able to remote control your heating would not have any downsides for anyone who was not personally a victim of domestic abuse, but for other people it can cause hell.

It is strongly believed that IoT vendors and stakeholders should have more involvement with law-enforcement agencies, in terms of being able to give training and assistance to the police and supporting services and charities. This will enable them to receive information that could help them with improving devices' safety features within a home in the future.

Future work that needs to be continued within this research is more in-depth conversations to take place with the stakeholders themselves. Contact needs to be made with supporting charities and social services to gain an even deeper understanding of how they feel and what further support they need with technology. The proposed solutions and framework could be presented to them to gather feedback and then appropriate amendments can be made.

Future work needs to be completed in a more technical arrangement. The suggestions made to improve the security of the devices need to be implemented and tested. Testing can be completed on test devices and a technical write-up made to show how the improvements were implemented. Additionally, it would be good to see if there are any shortcomings in the improvements, particularly if they create any further security implications of the device.

# References

BBC.com. (2021). *Safe Cities: Using Smart Tech for Public Security | A Better Connected World | Huawei | BBC Worldwide*. [Online]. Available at: <http://www.bbc.com/future/bespoke/specials/connected-world/government.html> [accessed 2 September, 2021].

Bowles, N. (2018). *Thermostats, Locks and Lights: Digital Tools of Domestic Abuse* (published 2018). [Online]. Nytimes.com. Available at: <https://www.nytimes.com/2018/06/23/technology/smart-home-devices-domestic-abuse.html> [accessed 7 July, 2021].

Braithwate, P. (2018). *Smart Home Tech is being Turned into a Tool for Domestic Abuse*. [Online]. WIRED UK. Available at: <https://www.wired.co.uk/article/internet-of-things-smart-home-domestic-abuse> [accessed 11 July, 2021].

Bryant, K. (2021). *Johnny Depp's Lawyers Accuse Amber Heard of a 'Calculated and Manipulative Lie' in New Appeal*. [Online]. Vanity Fair. Available at: <https://www.vanityfair.com/style/2021/03/johnny-depps-amber-heard-appeal> [accessed 20 September, 2021].

Clark, J. (2016). *What is the Internet of Things, and How does It Work?* [Online]. IBM Business Operations Blog. Available at: <https://www.ibm.com/blogs/internet-of-things/what-is-the-iot/> [accessed 5 July, 2021].

Gearing, A. (2021). *Queensland Moves to Criminalise Coercive Control after Murder of Hannah Clarke and her Children*. [Online]. *The Guardian*. Available at: https://www.theguardian.com/society/2021/feb/17/queensland-moves-to-criminalise-coercive-control-after-of-hannah-clarke-and-her-children> [accessed 13 September, 2021].

Gorini, M. (2021). *What exactly is a Smart City?* [Online]. Blog.bismart.com. Available at: <https://blog.bismart.com/en/what-is-a-smart-city> [accessed 25 August, 2021].

Harris, B. and Woodlock, D. (2018). Digital coercive control: insights from two landmark domestic violence studies. *The British Journal of Criminology*, 59(3): 530–550.

Hodson, D. (2020). *Digital Domestic Abuse: The Need for International Laws and Protections*. [Online]. Familylaw.co.uk. Available at: <https://www.familylaw.co.uk/news_and_comment/digital-domestic-abuse-the-need-for-international-laws-and-protections>.

Iotsecurityfoundation.org. (2021). *IoT Security Training – IoT Security Foundation*. [Online]. Available at: <https://www.iotsecurityfoundation.org/iot-security-training/> [accessed 8 September, 2021].

Joshi, N. (2019). *Exposing the Dark Side of Smart Cities | Internet of Things*. [Online]. Allerin.com. Available at: <https://www.allerin.com/blog/exposing-the-dark-side-of-smart-cities> [accessed 30 August, 2021].

Kluger, J. (2021). *Domestic Violence and COVID-19: The Pandemic within the Pandemic*. [Online]. Time. Available at: <https://time.com/5928539/domestic-violence-covid-19/> [accessed 14 July, 2021].

Laxton, C. (2014). Virtual world, real fear: Women's Aid report into online abuse, harassment and stalking, *Women's Aid*. Retrieved from https://www. womensaid. org. uk/virtual-world-real-fear.

McKinsey.com. (2017). *There's No Place Like [A CONNECTED ] Home*. [Online]. Available at: <https://www.mckinsey.com/spContent/connected_homes/index.html> [accessed 7 July, 2021].

Mlambo-Ngcuka, P. (2020). *Violence Against Women and Girls: The Shadow Pandemic*. [Online]. UN Women. Available at: <https://www.unwomen.org/en/news/stories/2020/4/statement-ed-phumzile-violence-against-women-during-pandemic> [accessed 5 July, 2021].

Najibi, A. (2020). *Racial Discrimination in Face Recognition Technology - Science in the News*. [Online]. Science in the News. Available at: <https://sitn.hms.harvard.edu/flash/2020/racial-discrimination-in-face-recognition-technology/> [accessed 1 September, 2021].

Pozniak, H. (2020). *Inside the Fight to Rid the World of Abusive Stalkerware*. [Online]. WIRED UK. Available at: <https://www.wired.co.uk/article/stalkerware-spyware-monitoring-apps-uk> [accessed 5 July, 2021].

Press.avast.com. (2021). *Use of Stalkerware and Spyware Apps Increase by 93% since Lockdown Began in the UK*. [Online]. Available at: <https://press.avast.com/use-of-stalkerware-and-spyware-apps-increase-by-93-since-lockdown-began-in-the-uk> [accessed 5 July, 2021].

Silva, S. and Franco, T. (2020). *How Smart Devices are Exploited for Domestic Abuse*. [Online]. BBC News. Available at: <https://www.bbc.co.uk/news/technology-54554408> [accessed 15 July, 2021].

Stober, A. (2021). *You're Already Benefiting from Smart Cities*. [Online]. Medium. Available at: <https://medium.com/waze/youre-already-benefiting-from-smart-cities-34611a89ea4a> [accessed 25 August, 2021].

Twi-global.com. (2021). *What is a Smart City? – Definition and Examples*. [Online]. Available at: <https://www.twi-global.com/technical-knowledge/faqs/what-is-a-smart-city> [accessed 25 August, 2021].

Woodlock, D., McKenzie, M., Western, D. and Harris, B. (2019). Technology as a weapon in domestic violence: Responding to digital coercive control. *Australian Social Work*, 73(3): 368–380.

# 7

# The Issues and the Misinformation that Social Media Creates and in Particular How This is Dealt with in Asia

*Kudrat-E-Khuda (Babu)*

## ABSTRACT

Now, almost all the fake news is spread on social media. As there is no proper fact-checking system, perpetrators target the social media platforms especially on Facebook, Twitter, to spread fake news. Besides, the filter bubble of social media platforms is no longer effective to find out or detect any false news. Some fact-checking institutes have sprung up in different countries and which are trying to fight against false news but these are not enough in comparison to the scale of fake news spread on social media. Some developed countries in Asia including Singapore have developed such tools and take some steps to control the spread of news. Besides, many countries—Bangladesh, India, Malaysia, Taiwan, Singapore, Japan, South Korea, Cambodia, and the Philippines have formulated different legal frameworks in the hope of checking fake news and harassment on social media. But sometimes those laws are misused by the authorities concerned to implement their political agenda and gagging the public opinion criticizing the authorities' misrule and punishing the individual under the laws for being critical against them. Despite those attempts at fact-checking, fake news is still dominating the social media due to low implementation and incapacity of the tools

Professor of Law, Daffodil International University, Dhaka, Bangladesh.
Email: kekbabu@gmail.com

and steps. With the limited and inadequate steps, it is almost impossible to check the millions of fake news generated regularly on the giant social media platforms across the globe. This chapter tries to understand the issues of misinformation on social media and how different countries are dealing with the issues, especially in the Asian region. The purpose of this chapter is to illustrate the features of misinformation on social media. In addition to this, it highlights the typology of this misinformation, the most significant misinformation, and the chronology of the developments. In the chapter, the beliefs in the mistreatment in the daily life of people in Asian countries in the context of the current reality; the prevailing misinformation, superstition about public health, and wrong practices have also been reflected. Also, the issues of correcting misinformation and getting true health information have been mentioned.

# 1. Introduction

Technology has brought a radical change in the life of people across the world. However, modern communication technology has expedited the changes, especially within a decade. Now news from one end of the earth can be collected from the other end within seconds, thanks to modern technology. Social media has brought a revolutionary change in communication technology in this twenty-first century. People are using different platforms and media to communicate with others. Social media, occupying the main place in all the communication platforms has become a very important part of people's life. People's wide access to the Internet and the use of smartphones have played the role of a revolutionary change-maker in modern communication technology. Now all classes and ages of people are using social media platforms for communication, information, and entertainment using their smartphones and other communication devices. Facebook and Twitter are prominent among the different types of social media and Blogs (Alam, 2019). The emerging interests of people worldwide and easy accessibility of the Internet leads to the coining of the term 'social media' (Jin, 2017), which is yet to be defined constructively and exhaustively. Social media is an interactive web 2.0 internet-based application that facilitates the development of social networks online by connecting a profile with those of other individuals and/or groups (Kwon, 2021). Besides, social media is a platform of communication technology in which people can share their thinking, views, opinions, and information in society through the medium of virtual networking systems. Social networking sites permit people to build up their profile under a sophisticated system and sort out the lists of their chosen ones to share connections and views (Popat, 2018). Users log in to the social media platform using an ID by Internet-based software through computers or other electronic devices like smartphones, tabs, smartwatches, etc., social media platforms are used for sharing personal or organizational information, ideas, job vacancies and photos, videos, and any other content. Alongside their views, they can see others' posts, share, comment, and react to them. On some platforms, like using Facebook Messengers, they can be engaged in chat, talk both audio and video, and share evening things including photos, documents, and videos with others.

Now companies, organizations, and advertisers are also crowding at the social media platforms as a marketplace due to their popularity and low cost, and easy availability to reach the target people (Shu, 2019). At the present time, social media sites have emerged as a giant power, keeping the user connected where users are being connected and sharing thoughts and ideas easily. Here, social media users can make a group with their friends, close people, family members, colleagues, classmates to share their views, feelings, sympathy. They can find jobs, even many can do freelance jobs and find people with the same characteristics and interests, and share their thoughts, feelings, and passions and maintain the social network. Social media users have now become habituated to pass all most all of their leisure time engaging in social media (Huang, 2020). Even many users cannot imagine a day without social media. Taking advantage of social media, unscrupulous people have been spreading rumors mainly because of not having censorship or any other measures to make them accountable. There is a measure – the filter-bubble effects – which itself intensify the spread of misinformation, believes numerous users. Amid the massive disturbance, some organizations have developed fact-checking tools and are fighting against the menace globally. Almost every people, irrespective of age, cast, profession, education, and region, use social media right now as a tool of communication, recreation, or information (Shahbaz, 2019). The main reasons behind the widespread popularity and influence of social media are: it is an easy medium; the cost of operation is much lower than all means of communication; it can be operated or used at home, on the street, in the office, or anywhere without going in public; it is very easy to reach more people; whatever the mind desires, whatever is good or bad, can be expressed. Taking these advantages, unscrupulous people spread rumors, fake news, hatred, or conflicts on social media platforms for their interest or political gain.

## 2.  General Concept of Social Media

Social media is rapidly spreading around the world, attracting users and influencing them consciously or subconsciously. Although these platforms were originally designed as tools for free communication and expression, they are now also used as digital weapons and are arbitrarily targeted by the public for vested interests or exploitation in most cases. Social media refers to interactive computer-based technologies through which the spread of information, mutual interaction, sharing of opinions and diverse forms of communication can be executed with hardly any effort (Abe, 2014). Due to the changing role of social media in today's world, a new definition of social media has become important now (Jang, 2014). Social media can be used for sharing information in any format–doc files, photos, videos, infographics, writing, gaming, interacting, video broadcasting, live official meetings, commercial advertisements, reactions, reviews and feedback, and so on. It is being used as a medium for news, social activities, advocacy, training, teaching, medical treatment and even as a strong tool for motivating voters during the elections.

## 3. Detecting Fake News in Social Media: A Few Asian Countries Perspective

Following the Tohoku earthquake and tsunami in March 2011, a nuclear crisis occurred at the Fukushima Daiichi nuclear power facility in Japan. Since the Chernobyl nuclear power plant tragedy in 1986, this disaster has been classified as a Level-7 disaster on the International Nuclear Event Scale, causing global worry and spreading speculations about radiation leaks (Wang, 2018). A bogus graphic depicting a map of radioactive discharge into the Pacific Ocean was displayed at the time. This figure, depicting the wave height of the tsunami that followed, was circulated on social media.

Credit: Guardian Liberty Voice

**Fig. 1:** Symbol of a social media (*Source*: Communications ACM).

**Fig. 2:** Fake news and misinformation abound in Taiwan's recent presidential election, inflaming supporters on both sides (*Source*: cacm.acm.org).

Various social, psychological, and computer science-based institutions have been set up to understand, research and check fake news or propaganda (Ma, 2019). The importance of automated fact-checking methods is increasing due to various programmes, such as data mining, natural language processing, and Artificial Intelligence. The methods that currently prevail are essentially collecting evidence of past events or claimings to identify whether they are real or fake by presenting appropriate data. The new research, and technology have further improved the effectiveness of existing strategies and these models also present data-testing explanations. These methods can be classified into the following four parts:

### i.  Feature-engineering Method

Based on this method, the first data-driven research projects on fake news were started in East and East Asia, using classical features such as temporal (e.g., frequency of spikes over time), structural (density, clustering) to create fake news. Attempts were made, and linguistic (for example, rejection and use of persuasive words) traits were consistently effective during a short term (a few days) and long term (perhaps two months). The feature-based on social interaction can further enhance the performance of the model. Creating features for this stream requires raw data processing to be detailed, biased, and labor-intensive.

### ii.  Matching-based Method

False claims can be identified through feedback from suspicious users, and by false rumor searches and clustering tweets. Textual patterns of cepticism are very effective in verifying actual claims. This method requires a specific manual for rule-based matching. Semantic matching may be a viable approach in this scenario. False statements can be confirmed using generally trustworthy sources like the news media or Wikipedia. An evidence-aware neural attention model may highlight relevant keywords and verify them with assertions..

### iii.  Representation-learning Method

Deep neural networks such as Recurrent Neural Networks (RNN) are used to know the frequency or word embedding to find out the ins and outs of an event based on low-level features. Some rumors are identified through Generative Advertising Networks (GANs). This co-attention network-based model helps to find the correlation between posts and their comments more accurately. Besides, it also automatically identifies which users, sentences, comments, and words containing fake signals.

### iv.  Multimodal Method

Typically, the news was shared on social media in a variety of formats, including text, image, and content. The multimodal data is scrutinised by an automatic fact-checking method. This method uses an RNN-based multimodal feature extraction and fusion model to detect rumors. Adversial neural networks have also been built to detect multimodal fake news by learning the invariant representation of an event. Fake news is checked in the early stages of news transmission using publisher-news relations and user-news interactions in tri-relationship embedding models.

Recently these methods have been technically developed from non-learning-based methods, traditional supervised learning methods, neural representation learning methods. Depending on the content, the data is verified by a combination of multiple forms by taking text or images from a single method. Semantically, earlier methods began with shallow patterns, and manual features were developed using automatic feature learning, which has now further improved fact-checking process by using more sophisticated learning techniques across heterogeneous content and

**Fig. 3:** A map falsely introduced as showing the spread of radioactive seepage from the Fukushima region
(*Source*: cacm.acm.org).

structures (Lee, 2018). For practical applications, those are now relying on a limited set of observations and detecting the contents more accurately instead of employing a massive collection of user responses in the early stage of news propagation. However, these models have some limitations to explain and check all the issues regarding fake news. So, there is a need for new models and fact-checking a process that can address all issues regarding the source of the fake news—identities of users and publishers of the fake news, its topics and types, and social manners. Besides, the research on fact-checking issues is still inadequate. Though the consequence of fake news may be more devastating than an atomic bomb, this issue has not been taken seriously. Both social media authorities and the concerned authorities of respective countries and regions have no effective tools to check the issues. The existing models have many limitations to check current fact-checking issues as there are so many variations on social media content that reflect current dynamics and diversity (Jarman, 2016). Supervised models usually focused on historical events dealing with different types of features because a single representation does not apply to new data and negatively impacts the model's—ability to generalize, as the training set is multifaceted. Usually, most algorithms only search the activities of social media users, evaluate their attitudes and positions. Since the response to all lies is not only shown on social media, these algorithms cannot report the results of feedback published in any other way outside of social media. In addition, users of certain groups deliberately create fake responses to fool or attack other people or groups. Since those responses can come from any user at any time and the information they report is usually very noisy, the existing algorithms cannot make a reliable assessment. The Government of Taiwan has launched a special cell for conducting advanced research in fighting against fake news. Besides, South Korea's National Research Foundation (NRF) and the Japan Science and Technology Agency (JST) also invested in research projects to fight the menace of disinformation. We think that other countries in Asia and the Oceania region will take initiatives to develop resources to fight against fake news.

However, the types and classes of fake news are now changing their courses and are being boarded on new platforms. Alongside Facebook and Twitter, now YouTube and instant messaging (IM) services – Whatsapp and Kakaotalk, IM—are emerging as hotspots of fake news. A survey conducted by the Korea Press Foundation states that 34% of Korean YouTube viewers report that they watched or received videos containing fake news. In 2017, the Open Government Foundation 'g0v' stated that only 46% of chatbot responses on that nation's most popular IM app LINE is correct (Haciyakupoghlu, 2018). It is very concerning that take news on streaming platforms and IM services contain visual content, which is more persuasive than mere text posts. Since people follow social networks and blindly believe, false claim or fake news through IM can strengthen their belief to keep trust in the misinformation. Some techniques like GANs can produce high-quality fake and naked videos of celebrities and politicians to undermine their images. Now intelligent fact-checking chatbots are being developed incorporating GAN to retrieve and generate evidence and explanations of natural language. The Taiwan government has taken a programmes named *Cofacts* which has developed techniques and implemented IM services to detect false information and prevent it from spreading instantly (Zhao, 2015). In the area of social media, big data, and Artificial Intelligence, it is urgent to launch a stronger effort and build up a strong research community to develop appropriate and productive techniques to detect fake news and fight against the menace of miss information.

## 3.1 Abuse of Social Media Puts Asia's Democratic Elections in Jeopardy

The fake news and other misinformation on social media have appeared as a big threat to democracy in Asia. The fake news and other misinformation have now very common due to a string of elections in the region. Voters are being persuaded and motivated through spreading fake news during election time via every type of social media. The elections in Thailand, India, Indonesia, the Philippines, and Singapore are maybe the major example of motivating voters and the overall elections through spreading fake news on social media. In such a situation, a question may arise— whether the problems can be fixed without throttling basic rights like freedom of speech or free thinking? Singapore has made such an attempt and moved a bill incorporating fines for Facebook and other social media platforms if they do not comply with the government's censorship rules. This created a huge outcry and controversy. The bill titled 'The Protection from Online Falsehoods and Manipulation Bill' stated the spread of any type of misinformation that is 'prejudicial' to the security of Singapore is illegal. According to the law, any individual found guilty can face fines of up to 100,000 Singapore dollars (about $73,000), and/or, up to 10 years of imprisonment, and if any company found guilty of spreading 'fake news' will be fined up to one million Singapore dollars (Maida, 2019). Following the enactment of the law, the international rights watchdog, Human Rights Watch has warned that the new law could be misused for 'political purposes' as a tool for flexing muscles.

Like Singapore, all countries in Asia, and the rest of the world have been facing fake news and misinformation and struggling against it with their best efforts. So, everybody irrespective of governments, businessmen, social-political and other organizations are desperately seeking solutions to the technological menace. Though many countries have taken some technological measures, these are not enough to prevent the destructive effects of social media. In the meantime, the voices against the world's giant and dominant tech companies are mounting by the governments of many countries like Singapore. This move will gradually pave the way to change the fundamentals of business models for social media platforms, as well as ensure greater fines on law-breakers. The United States of America (USA), the European Union (EU), and Australia have already taken some regulatory measures against the tech giants to bring them under accountability. The EU has fined Google $1.7 billion. With the fine, one of the world's largest tech companies will have to face a total of $9.3 billion fines since 2017 by the EU (Manzi, 2019). Meanwhile, the US has pulled in the reins of another tech giant Facebook and has brought its data capitalism under accountability. For some scandals including Cambridge Analytica and other accusations of breach of trust and privacy in the US, Facebook is facing criminal charges along with huge criticism and pressure. Asian governments are also watching closely the movements of the EU and the US. However, these issues must be looked at from a more broader perspective and the focus of the digital landscape should be based on political and social values. Scrutinizing the recent situations of the tech giants, and movements and measures taken by different countries across the world, Wendy Hall and Kieron O'Hara of Southampton University in the UK have found out four emerging blocs. These are the libertarian bloc (which is broken); commercial bloc (which is dominated by a handful of tech companies); the European bloc, based on a tough regulation (which is gaining appeal); and the China-style digital authoritarianism bloc.

Asian countries are adopting the policies and ideas from all the four coalitions. Since the 2019 election, governments have been exercising accountability and even authoritarian control over personal rights and privacy. However, despite allegations of vote-rigging and irregularities in vote-counting in Thailand, the opposition Pheu Thai party, which is loyal to former Prime Minister Thaksin Shinawatra, successfully waged a social media movement against the military junta lead government. If the junta lead Palang Pracharat party wants to stay in power, it will have to go for further digital authoritarianism. There was a similar example in the Philippines. The country's powerful President Rodrigo Duterte tried to control the opposition. The fake stories spread on social media, such as Duterte's presidential election victory, is expected to become obsolete. Comparatively, voters in India and Indonesia faced less pressure from their respective governments. This makes the role of social media and its critique even more important. It was true in the case of India, as hate speech on the messaging network WhatsApp has been linked to leaching there. Meanwhile, various organizations and technology-conscious citizens are starting to promote the use of 'fact-checking' algorithms to prevent the spread of misinformation. A new technology called 'Stopgap' helps reduce mass mailing and sets some limitations on social media applications and slowing the spread of fake news. Following the mob lynchings in India, WhatsApp has slapped a limitation on the messaging option and fixed that a single person can be able to forward a message only five times. However, this approach has failed for 200 million users on the Indian subcontinent (Chong, 2019). Another stopgap is now being used to identify and block machines from masquerading as humans—human-like chatbots named 'Bots' acted behind the mass distribution of targeted texts and phone calls in Malaysia' 2018 elections. Through the 2019 elections in Asia, it has been proved that how the business model of social media platforms lacks accountability. The technical measures taken by the authorities concerned of the Asian countries have largely failed to appear as successful tools to check and curb the massive flow of misinformation. The collective failure of the tech companies has given the mandate to the police makers to reuse the remedies that had been rejected terming those as undemocratic. Now the proposal of introducing digital identification numbers of the social media users has gained support from different stakeholders. Scientists in the Western countries are now deeply concerned about the future consequences thinking that if the online robots failed to check the misinformation and identify its sources, democracy could be destroyed.

## 3.2  A Descriptive Analysis of Misinformation Spreading on Social Media during the COVID-19 Outbreak in China

Social media platforms have become popular as a platform for health communication to target patients efficiently amid the lockdowns, restrictions on movement, and huge pressure at the healthcare centers during the COVID-19 pandemic. But taking advantage of this situation, those platforms turned into hotspots for dissemination of misinformation. Some incidents in China can be the best example of such misinformation. For example, WeChat, a common social networking app in China, appeared as the open stage of misinformation on health issues – such as 'chives can kill 99% of cancer cells' and 'rice is the king of junk food'. Usually, misinformation gains momentum and spreads wildly in every critical event or an emergency. So, it is the high time of spreading misinformation or rumor during the coronavirus pandemic.

The first COVID-19 case was first identified in Wuhan of China in December 2019 and the World Health Organization (WHO) declared coronavirus outbreak as a public health emergency of international concern. As the virus spread to different countries threatening global public health the WHO declared it a pandemic. Taking advantage of the pandemic, a large scale of misinformation spread especially about the disease across the globe. Amid the massive spread of misinformation, the WHO has called it 'infodemic,' during the pandemic. The WHO launched an information centre named 'WHO Information Network for Epidemics' to spread authentic information about the COVID-19 among people across the world. Despite that, misinformation spread on social media like viruses that travel with people-to-people and country-to-country faster. Like the COVID-19 pandemic, controlling the infodemic also became the priority during the public health crisis because of its severe negative impact on people. The spread of accurate information can be considered crucial in the degree of crisis escalation and its potential impact. The contest of misinformation, and the ongoing health crisis may accelerate devastatingly if any action regarding the pandemic is taken based on the misinformation. So, like the measures taken to curb the pandemic, the spread of misinformation should be controlled with similar importance and priority. Before designing the strategies to combat the misinformation, it is very crucial to know the characteristics of misinformation on social media and to eliminate the adverse impact of the misinformation.

One of the misconceptions about China is that they have been controlling the pandemic (Cha, 2020). Such misinformation spreads widely during an emergency period, on the social media. Even in this public health scandal, social media has acted as a major vector for spreading misinformation. Comprehending the characteristics of misinformation regarding health issues can be evidence for rebuking and decisively fixing such distortion on social media. Misinformation regarding preventive methods is the mass-talked type of method and types of misinformation related to the daily lives of people are also pervasive, as the results reveal. Besides, social norms and cultural beliefs have an impact on the perception of misinformation, and the effects of the misinformation in the prevailing situation are relevant to the variance of misinformation. Following research results, the health communication strategies for combating misinformation on social media are discussed with credible sources and expert sources. Shortly, combating the misinformation is not a lone effort that can prevent the spread of the infodemic. People from all walks of life and different professions including scholars, journalists, educators and citizens must work together the curb the misinformation.

## 4. Factors Affecting the Spread of False Health Information

Misinformation always grows and spreads in a supportive environment surrounded by illiteracy overloaded with biased information. Misinformation usually grows and spread widely during any emergencies like the COVID-19 pandemic as the public's response to the crisis is very sensitive. Besides, substantial incidents in society and diverse types of information related to the potential subsequent risks also help grow and spreads the misinformation. Different health-related activities have pointed to different factors, which can affect the spread of misinformation about health. According to Rosnow, there are four factors—general uncertainty, outcome-relevant involvement, personal anxiety, and credulity—that can stimulate the spread of misinformation. Misinformation always depends and develops in uncertain situations. When misinformation is transferred from the public to people, they must stay in an uncertain information environment. Besides, people believe in such type of misinformation in which their lives are associated or any other issue that is important to the public. When anyone passes days with anxiety due to certain reasons, they live in any time of apprehensions and in such a situation, they may get or pass any misinformation, especially during the pandemic days, when most people are in anxiety due to health-related issues, financial issues, and many other related crucial issues. It is a good time and situation for the spread of any misinformation as the personal anxiety of people may amplify the transmission of misinformation.

Scholars have found a relationship between anxiety and personal belief. The level of anxiety is largely related to the belief in misinformation. According to Rosnow, credulity is considered a predictor of misinformation spreading. According to experts, two factors—health literacy, and social and cultural factors—can impact people's credulity in the public health domain (Jang, 2018). People decide on public health mostly depending on their health literacy. Health literacy defines the degree of their knowledge in health-related issues in which they can obtain, process, understand, evaluate, and act upon information needed to decide on public health. Usually, this always appears as a complex issue to the public. The public with low health literacy not only believes any misinformation more easily but also have a wrong perception about accurate information. So, they translate any accurate information into misinformation when they pass it among others. According to a previous study health-related behavior is largely influenced by cultural and social factors. As an example, it can be mentioned that any misinformation related to TCM may influence the Chinese people as they have a strong belief in TCM.

Nowadays, health communication has received a huge momentum thanks to the rapid development of social media technologies across the world, facilitating the spread of health-related information intensively. Social media is an ideal place for spreading misinformation about health. Just as misinformation was spread during the Ebola outbreak, so too is false information being spread during the coronavirus pandemic. The spread of misinformation aggravates due to some features of social media. Due to the easy features of social media platforms, people can forward messages to many receivers quite effortlessly with a single click. As a result, misinformation spreads swiftly on social media, producing confusion and undue fear among a large number of individuals.

Individual interest, on the other hand, drives the creation and dissemination of health misinformation. It has been suggested, for example, that some entities are prone to creating internet misinformation on intentionally in order to gain attention or clicks. Misinformation about health usually has a life cycle. The studies on SARS-related misinformation show that the spread of misinformation was speedier than the SARS outbreak. However, in such a situation none of the misinformation prevails for a long time. When certain information is accessible and the public gets an idea about the right information, then misinformation about health cannot exist naturally. At the same time, the anxiety caused by false information is also removed. Though this study persistently stressed the need for the importance of fighting misinformation during the coronavirus pandemic, before developing alternative methods for health communication and misinformation, it is critical to do a thorough investigation into the misinformation.

## 5. The Misinformation and Negative Impacts of Social Media in India during COVID-19

Since the outbreak of the coronavirus in early 2019, the world has been witnessing an unprecedented spread of misinformation and fake news on social media platforms. This misinformation is contributing to paranoia and becoming the barrier to the fight against COVID-19. The developing and worsening situations in India can be a perfect example. The fake news on social media platforms and misinformation—false or inaccurate information—have been dominating the digital information landscape since the inceptions of the social media platforms in the mid-1990s (Cha, 2020). Over time, the susceptibility of people, who are largely habituated with the modern digitalized medium has been deepening especially during any crisis. There is no exception in the case of India. As a developing country, the people in India have to face greater challenges to fight the misinformation and fake news as it has appeared as a global threat which has thrived coupled with the pandemic, because many social media users who do not know much about the evolving technology believe that whatever information they receive through social media are true and share these with their family and friends indiscriminately without verification of its authenticity. Many distrustful mainstream news media also circulate the information after getting this from unconventional alternative sources without verification. Such type of tendency in India's digital periphery has made the situation volatile and vulnerable to the dangers of misinformation, spreading panic among the people during the deadly coronavirus pandemic.

Right now, the COVID-19 situations in India is the worst in the world and facing numerous challenges in its fight in the war against the virus. The Narendra Modi-led government had imposed a 21-day lockdown across the country to curb the spread of infection within communities. The situation turned very grave as the country confirmed over 1,000 deaths daily (Anandabazar Patrika, 202122). However, in the fight against the virus, social media has been playing a contrasting role. People are sharing various information on social media, mostly for helping local communities, the vulnerable, and the elderly. But when that information is re sharing or reposting by fellow friends, families, or mutual friends in the communities in social media, people are being misled. Finally, due to frequent sharing and reposting, the information is being turned into the misinformation which has not relation or similarity with the original post, many times spreading rumours and heightening levels of fear among the pandemic hit people. Due to the easy availability of smartphone and Internet data, Indians, who are second only after the Chinese in terms of active internet users, are incessantly communicating and exchanging purported information about the virus on popular messaging and content apps like WhatsApp, YouTube, and TikTok. Most of the content shared on social media networks are unverified and fake, particularly on the links to COVID-19 and its related advisories (Huang, 2020). For example, a 30-second video on TikTok showed that an individual, wearing a face mask, recommends gargling with salt-and-vinegar mixed hot water as a medication for coronavirus, and at the end of the video, he also urged viewers to share his video for the sake of human health. An individual had claimed that the novel coronavirus was developed in India. Recently a YouTube video, possibly posted from India, went on viral across the world that drinking *gaumutra* (cow's urine) helps recover from the coronavirus. Such types of numerous videos, posts, containing misinformation and fake news spread across social media platforms. In such a situation, the government, mainstream media, and conscious community public join hands to fight against the misinformation alongside their fight against the pandemic.

However, some premature early advisories of the government on COVID-19 also contributed to the misinformation. In January 2020, a ministry of India's Central Government announced using a list of traditional drugs to prevent the COVID-19 infection. According to experts, the announcement might have been to encourage local traditional drug—makers as an objective, but these medicines were untested and had 'no peer-reviewed research. Even, fake information was being spread from India through WhatsApp when the COVID-19 brook out in China last December. As the pandemic lashed heavily in India, world leaders also joined their hands with Indian Prime Minister Narendra Modi to curb the infections. Alongside the struggle against the virus, Modi also has been calling upon the authorities of the social media platforms to ensure correct information regarding the virus. To rein in the misinformation, Modi's government has launched a WhatsApp-based chatbot 'MyGovCoronaHelpdesk' in association with Mumbai-based firm Haptik to respond against the rumors or misinformation. The government also issued an advisory to Facebook, YouTube, TikTok, Snapchat, and Twitter, and other social media platforms to take responsibility for any kind of COVID-19-related misinformation on their feeds. According to the Information Technology Act of India, social media platforms will be accountable under the act for curating fake content on their platform if it breaches the safety of the public. Modi also deployed traditional mainstream media—television, radio, and press—to circulate the government's major decisions on the virus to the public. Appearing on national television a couple of times within a week, he alerted the citizens about the spread of the virus and advised them to maintain physical distancing and avoid rumors to make the 21-day nationwide lockdown a success. He also sent his preventive messages through All India Radio so that the people living in the remotest areas could get the message.

However, the traditional media has been playing a vital role in giving accurate messages to around a billion people who have still no access to the Internet. Modi also praised the role of print media ('stable platforms'). The differences between Indian old and the new media have become clear due to their role at the crucial time when the country is fighting against the biggest global public health challenge in the age of modern technology. Unfortunately, social media could not play its due role, rather it played the counterproductive role, triggering paranoia and creating panic in this war against the global pandemic. Now it remains to be seen whether the traditional media will be able to come back as the trustworthy source of information, and the social media re-appear with self-regulation and content control.

## 6. Asia's Social Media Censors go into Overdrive due to Coronavirus

Some Asian governments have taken some strict legal measures including arrests, fines against the persons for spreading fake news under some laws—in which conscious people have expressed concerned that these types of laws will curb free speech and can also silence dissent. At least 16 people have been arrested in Malaysia, India, Thailand, Indonesia, and Hong Kong for spreading fake news through their posts regarding the coronavirus (Huang, 2020). Besides, the Government of Singapore has been using its notorious law—POFMA—and forcing the media outlets and social media to carry government warnings on their posts and articles saying they contain falsehoods. Lawrence Wong, one of the ministers who is heading a task force formed by the Singapore government to halt the spread of the virus, said 'Fortunately, we now have POFMA to deal with these fake news.' Many things about the coronavirus remain unknown since the virus surfaced in the Chinese city of Wuhan in December 2020. As the death toll has passed 4,636 (at the time of writing), anxiety has been gripping in social media (Huang, 2020). A minister of the then Government of Myanmar rebuked a person for sharing a post on social media recommending eating more onions to beat coronavirus. "What I call the 'moron strain' has created a global, social media-driven panic that is in turn feeding on itself," wrote Karim Raslan in his regionally syndicated column, indicating the challenges for the governments. At least five people were arrested and later released on bail in India's southwestern state of Kerala for their activism on WhatsApp messages, said Aadhithya R, district police chief of Thrissur. Meanwhile, six people were arrested in Malaysia on suspicion of spreading false news. In Vietnam, cyber-censors have been set up to track social media comments relating to the communist government. Under the scanner, at least nine people were fined and three celebrities asked to explain their actions over posts about coronavirus. Thailand's government had set up an 'anti-fake news center' last year. Only dozens of staff of the Centre reviewed nearly 7,600 posts in only four days from January 22–25 successfully (*Anandabazar Patrika*, 2021) and thanks to their vigilance, social posts are being scrutinised and tracked for false news. The authorities already arrested two persons under computer crimes laws at that time. Thailand's Digital Minister Puttipong Punnakanta said their anti-fake news center has been working intensively to verify these rumors. Thailand is among the countries that have formulated tough laws to control social media posts in recent years despite criticism from the human rights bodies that these laws could be used to punish the government's opponents.

In China, security personnel are not allowing the media even to take pictures of the checkpoint at the Jiujiang Yangtze River Bridge as the country is hit by the coronavirus in Jiujiang of Jiangxi province on 4 February, 2020 (Chong, 2019). Right bodies and free-speech advocates expressed concern that the government's campaign against the fake news over coronavirus could help governments extend their control undermining the health campaign. Matthew Bugher, head of Asia Programme for free expression campaign group Article 19, said, "Criminalisation of speech, even if targeted at falsehoods, is highly likely to stifle the real-time sharing of information that is essential during epidemics." China has been imposing censorship on social media heavily and many critics have been saying that local media cannot reveal the actual situation in Wuhan. Eight people were arrested on the allegation of spreading rumors about the infection in early January of 2021. Meanwhile, messaging app WeChat has added tools to help debunk virus rumours. *People's Daily* in China has also introduced a tool to help people verify reports. Amid the spread of fake news and criticism, Western social media companies are also taking steps. The authorities of Facebook, in a rare move, have said it would take down misinformation about the coronavirus.

## 7. What is Fake News and What Impact does It have on Asia?

According to PolitiFact, fake news is 'made-up stuff and masterfully manipulated to look like credible journalistic reports that are easily spread online to large audiences'.

Though disinformation has not prevailed for long, falsehoods can spread more easily and rapidly thanks to social media and messaging apps. The phenomenon has had far-reaching implications around the world, affecting everything–from voter attitudes to ethnic conflict. In Asia, social media is now serving as a news source. It has become the primary source of news, making it particularly prone to the propagation of false information. Myanmar's military allegedly created fake Facebook accounts to spread hatred and misinformation about the minority Muslims in the country as a part of its persecution against the Rohingya community. Facebook conducted a study which showed that the social media platform 'has become a means for those seeking to spread hate and cause harm, and posts have been linked to offline violence'. There is an allegation against the Sri Lankan government that it has also spread misinformation and spread hatred to trigger the communal violence between the Buddhist majority and Muslim minority in the country. Following a rumour spread that the owner of a restaurant laced meals with 'sterilization pills', a mob of zealots destroyed the restaurant and set fire to a mosque. Following a fake news spread on WhatsApp in India, a group of people started catching innocent people accusing their involvement with child kidnappings and beating them to death. Five innocent people were beaten to death in the western state of Maharashtra in July 2018 after a video on slaughtering children to smuggle their organs was spread on WhatsApp (*Anandabazar Patrika*, 2021). In the video, some pictures were used—from a nerve gas attack in Syria—and levelled that the local children are being tortured and murdered after kidnapping them. Philippine President Rodrigo Duterte has been criticized for spreading 'fake news' through media outlets against his government. But there are allegations against Duterte and some Cabinet members, including his former communications assistant secretary, Mocha Uson, that they have been spreading misinformation online.

Like other Asian countries, there are many examples of real-life violence in Bangladesh that erupted from social media-related activism. In most of the cases, hatred and violence were triggered from Facebook in the country. Here are some examples of the major violence attacks that originated from Facebook in Bangladesh. On 29 September, 2012, thousands of religious zealots unleashed violence on the Buddhist community in Ramu Upazila of Cox's Bazar by spreading a rumor that a derogatory remark to the Holy Quran was made on the Facebook page of local Buddhist youth. The zealots also set fire to Buddhist temples and houses, vandalised and looted more than 50 houses there as a sequel of the Facebook post which was later found to be a fake post (*The Daily Star*, 2012). However, the miscreants also attacked Mushurikhola crematorium at Khurushkul village in Cox's Bazar Sadar Upazila. This is not the end, the zealots on the following day attacked and ransacked Buddhist temples and houses in Ukhiya and Tekhnaf Upazilas. They also damaged Hindu temples in the Palongkhali union of Ukhiya. An investigation by *The Daily Star*, the leading English daily in Bangladesh, revealed that the Facebook profile and the picture demeaning the Holy Quran which instigated the violence was fake. Later, it was also found in other media and government reports that the Buddhist Uttam Kumar Barua was innocent and was provoked by someone intentionally. This violent incident portrayed a picture of the consequences of fake news triggered by social media to thousands of people within a very short time. In this case, a group took the opportunity of social media to achieve their nefarious purpose, but before such a big event happened, no one raised any question about the veracity of that Facebook post. By imitating superstition, they had violently unleashed their anger based on false information. As a result, thousands of innocent people have been affected, hurting the traditional religious harmony in the country.

When the people from the Buddhist community were reeling from the devastating incident, just one year later, another violence erupted in the Pabna district of the country on 3 November, 2013, when the religious bigots swooped on the Hindu community in Bonogram area following a fake Facebook post. Thousands of people carried out rampages and ransacked idols and temples, and – at least 25 houses of the Hindu community. A derogatory comment about Islamic Prophet Muhammad (PBUH) was reportedly published from the account of a minority boy named Rajib Saha. Fearing further attack, about 150 Hindu community families had to flee the area. However, it was later revealed that Rjib had no link with the Facebook page or post. Around a year after the incident, another attack was carried on the Hindu community at Bakhsitarampur village of Homna Upazila of Cumilla following a rumour on Facebook in 2014. Around 3,000 people took part in the violent attack on the Hindu community and ransacked at least 28 houses of the minorities following a rumor defaming Prophet Muhammad (PBUH) on Facebook (Newman, 2008). Another violence originated centering a Facebook post at Nasirnagar Upazila in Brahmanbaria on 30 October, 2016. At least 15 temples and 150 houses of the Hindu community people were vandalized, looted, and set on fire in a series of attacks following a Facebook post reportedly mocking a holy site in Mecca.

At least one hundred people including several devotees were injured in the attacks that happened in broad daylight following announcements made during two rallies organized by two Islamic groups—Touhidi Janata and Ahle Sunnat Wal Jamaat. The attacks were triggered by an anti-religious Facebook post from the account of one Rasraj Das, a fisherman. He was arrested after the incident but freed in January 2017 as police found evidence that his Facebook account was hacked or faked by someone else before the posts were uploaded from it. Later, the law enforcers found that it was not the act of the Hindu fisherman. Another person had opened the account with the name and picture of the fisherman and mocked the holy site to take revenge on him. Following another Facebook post reportedly hurting religious sentiments, a marauding mob of people carried out a rampage on the Hindu community at Thakurpara village in Rangpur on 10 November, 2017. At least one person was killed and 20 others were injured when the agitating mob carried out the attack. They also vandalized and set fire to at least 30 houses of the Hindu community (Kudrat, 2021). The law enforcers had to fire rubber bullets and tear gas shells to bring the situation under control. Later, the investigators found that the Facebook account was hacked and the post was created intentionally. Besides, the above-mentioned incidents, there are numerous incidents of violence and harassment, and tortures especially carried out on women and children following activities on Facebook in Bangladesh. Such misuse of Facebook has been continuing since the widespread use of social media platforms especially Facebook in Bangladesh.

## 8.  How are the Asian Countries Confronting Fake News?

The Taiwan government has warned of taking stern against the persons involved in spreading misinformation. As a part of curbing fake news, South Korean police and the country's telecoms regulators have been working jointly. The Bangladesh government has formulated the Information and Communication Technology Act and the Digital Security Act in its attempt to bring the people to book for spreading or doing any evil attempts on social media. Singapore government has developed a website named 'Factually' in 2012 to check facts on social media platforms and has formulated a law 'Protection from Online Falsehoods and Manipulation Act (POFMA)' in October 2019 to bring the perpetrators under the law. The Indonesian government has been holding a weekly briefing on false news since 2018 and amended its Criminal Code of Procedure, incorporating a punishment of six years' imprisonment for spreading fake news in the same year. Taiwan government added a tool on its website of the Executive Yuan to check fake news. The Open Culture Foundation of this country also developed a fact-checking chatbot *Cofacts* in 2018.

In Indonesia, the government is taking legal actions after identifying the people involved in spreading fake news and bringing them to book for up to five years imprisonment. A security guard of a shopping mall was arrested for spreading false news about COVID-19 infections in Hong Kong.

Many people in Singapore say that their government is implementing its new fake news law strictly. About the spread of fake news and its consequences, Nicholas Fang, founder of Singapore consultancy Black Dot Research, said, "Many examples of misinformation, confusing data and outright fake news present a clear and present danger to public safety, health and security." Rights activists and journalists in Singapore have been critical of the weakness of the law and expressed concern over its implementation. "Just because there are relatively more justifiable uses of a #fakenews law, it doesn't mean that the law was well-drafted and can't be an instrument of abuse and oppression," Journalist and activist Kirsten Han commented on Twitter. Despite huge concerns and steps by the governments against fake news, many Asian countries depend largely on social media for information, paving the way for making them vulnerable to the spread of misinformation. However, the matter of 'fake news' came to the discussion largely through the US election in 2016 though it has been wreaking havoc in Asian countries to a large extent. There are many instances of social media rumours and hoaxes that triggered ethnic, religious, and regional tensions, violence, and political confrontation. In 2018, a parliamentary committee in Singapore suggested formulating laws aimed to book both the responsible person for spreading the fake news and technology companies for giving a platform to those fake voices. As per their suggestion, under the law, criminal charges would be brought against people who will involve in spreading fake news. As a drive against fake news, the Indonesian government led by Joko Widodo held weekly briefings on 'hoax news'. A number of people were also detained for spreading misinformation for which extremist Muslim groups tried to escalate ethnic tensions.

# 9. Conclusion

Many rights bodies and civil society members have been expressing deep concerns over the implementation of the laws stating that those acts might gag the freedom of speech in the name of curbing the misinformation. For example, Malaysian Prime Minister Najib Razak passed a law repressive law just a month before the general elections in the country through his predecessor Mohamad Mahathir-led government repealed the law in August 2018. Earlier, Mahathir was investigated under the 'fake news law' as he claimed that his plane was sabotaged before the elections through which he came to power. The Philippines Senate had discussed a bill in 2018 for bringing people under the law for spreading misinformation and targeting government officials. However, that proposal was canceled later. Amid criticism, the Cambodian government has formulated a 'fake news' law in which their convicts of spreading misinformation on social media or websites can be jailed for two years and fined US$1,000. More than a hundred local NGOs issued a statement criticizing the passage of the new law saying that it will be a 'serious threat' to freedom of expression. Meanwhile, amid huge criticism, tech giants Google, Facebook, and Twitter are compelled to announce that they will take measures to fight against fake news. As a part of their initiatives, the social media authorities in cooperation with researchers and fact-checkers have been suspending user accounts and payments to promote content for spreading fake news and dubious content. In Sri Lanka, the Facebook authority decided to start its campaign to delete fake news after rumours that triggered intercommunal violence there. The tech hulk also worked with different local bodies to detect false posts. Facebook also blocked many accounts for their link to the military in Myanmar and spreading fake news against Rohingyas. Besides, Facebook formed teams to check fake news ahead of the elections in India, Indonesia, the Philippines, and Thailand. Finally, the governments of Asian countries will be more interested to choose the best way of preventing fake news by shutting the main switch. As an example, the Indian government has sought suggestions from the country's telecom operators to help find out the way of blocking Facebook and WhatsApp entirely. The Government of India, the world's largest democracy with over a billion people, might follow the reminiscent approach of China by imposing censorship and authoritarian practices. New Delhi has suspended Facebook and the use of Twitter has been suspended 28 times in Kashmir in the last five years, and the access of the social media platform was blocked for five months in 2016 on the allegation that these platforms were being used for anti-social and 'anti-State' movement. So, coming out of such censorship practice, the democratic governments should first try to formulate responsible regulation involving the civil society groups and rights bodies. Besides, until adopting a basic social media business model, such authoritarian and aggressive steps should not be taken by the government in the name of combating fake news. Stuart Russell, the computer scientist at the University of California, Berkeley, and a social media critic, said that at the root of everything lies the issues of 'click-through' advertising. The content of the click-through advertising model has been designed to feeds content to people implanting their interests with the contents. However, Russel said what the algorithms do is to modify behavior by feeding people information that steers them towards predictable extremes. Therefore, the spread of fake contents on the far left and the far right, and the exaggeration of inflammable 'clickbait' contents are designed to enthuse people toward these contents. The measures against fake news in the latest round of elections in Asia have resulted in countermeasures. Expectantly policymakers in the region will work with other stakeholders closely and adopt a smart balance of technology and regulations to settle the evolving issues refraining from curbing the freedom of expression and human rights that undermine the democracy.

# References

Abe, K. (2004). Everyday policing in Japan: Surveillance, media, government and public opinion. *Int. Soc.*, 19(2): 215–231. doi: https://doi.org/10.1177/0268580904042901 [Accessed 25 Dec., 2020].

Alam, S. (2019). Cyber crime: A new challenge for law enforcers. *City Univ. J.*, 2(1): 75–84. http://www.prp.org.bd/cybercrime_files/Cybercrime [Accessed 10 May, 2021].

Cha, M., Gao, W. and Li, C.T. (2020). Detecting fake news in social media: An Asia-pacific perspective. *Communications of the ACM*, 63(4): 68–71. https://doi.org/10.1145/3378422 [Accessed 2 Jan., 2021].

Chong, E. (2019). Kankokuniokerufakutochi Ikkutosourudaigafakutochi Ikkusentānoyakuwari. https://www.econstor.eu/bitstream/10419/224849/1/Cheng-et-al.pdf [Accessed 23 Mar., 2021].

Haciyakupoglu, G. et al. (2018). *Countering Fake News: A Survey of Recent Global Initiatives.* Singapore: Nanyang Technological University. https://www.think-asia.org/handle/11540/8063 [Accessed 11 Feb., 2021].

Huang, Y.H.C. et al. (2020). Mainframes and mandarins: The impact of Internet use on institutional trust in East Asia. *Telecomm Policy*, 44(2): 1–18. https://doi.org/10.1016/j.telpol.2020.101912 [Accessed 25 Jan., 2021].

Huang, Y.C., Lu, Y., Kao, L. and others. (2020). Mainframes and mandarins: The impact of internet use on institutional trust in East Asia. *Telecomm Policy*, 44(2): 1–18. https://doi.org/10.1016/j.telpol.2020.101912 [Accessed 12 Jan., 2021].

Jang, S.M. and Kim, J.K. (2018). Third person effects of fake news: Fake news regulation and media literacy interventions. *Comput. Hum. Behav.*, 80(1): 295–302. https://doi.org/10.1016/j.chb.2017.11.034 [Accessed 23 Feb., 2021].

Jarman, J.W. (2016). Influence of political affiliation and criticism on the effectiveness of political fact-checking. *Commun. Res. Rep.*, 33(1): 9–15. https://doi.org/10.1080/08824096.2015.1117436 [Accessed 31 Mar., 2021].

Jin, Z., Cao, J., Guo, H. and Luo, J. (2017). Multimodal fusion with recurrent neural networks for rumour detection on microblogs. In *Proceedings of ACM Multimedia*, 2017: 795–816. https://dl.acm.org/doi/10.1145/3123266.3123454 [Accessed 13 Jul., 2021].

Kudrat, K. (2021). Cyber security in the global village and challenges for Bangladesh: An overview on legal context. Advanced sciences and technologies for security applications. *In*: Jahankhani, H., Jamal, A. and Lawson, S. (eds.). *Cybersecurity, Privacy and Freedom Protection in the Connected World. Advanced Sciences and Technologies for Security Applications*. Springer, Cham. doi: https://doi.org/10.1007/978-3-030-68534-8_16 [Accessed 12 Jul., 2021].

Kwon, S., Cha, M. and Jung, K. (2017). Rumour detection over varying time windows. *PLoS One.* doi: https://doi.org/10.1371/journal.pone.0168344 [Accessed 4 Apr., 2021].

Lee, S. (2018). The role of social media in protest participation: The case of candlelight vigils in South Korea. *Int. J. Commun.*, 12(1): 1523–1540. https://ijoc.org/index.php/ijoc/article/view/7767 [accessed 29 Jan., 2021].

Ma, J., Gao, W. and Wong, K.F. (2019). Detect rumors on Twitter by promoting information campaigns with generative adversarial learning. *In Proceedings of WWW*, 2019: 3049–3055. https://core.ac.uk/download/pdf/286034841.pdf [Accessed 26 Aug., 2020].

Maida, A. (2019). To Speak Out is Dangerous—Criminalization of Peaceful Expression in Thailand. *Human Rights Watch.* https://www.hrw.org/report/2019/10/24/speak-out-dangerous/criminalization-peaceful-expression-thailand [accessed 1 Jul., 2021].

Manzi, D.C. (2019). Managing the misinformation marketplace: The first amendment and the fight against fake news. *Fordham L. Rev.*, 87(6): 2623–2651. https://ir.lawnet.fordham.edu/flr/vol87/iss6/12/ [Accessed 4 Jan., 2021].

Newman, J.L. (2008). Keeping the Internet neutral: Net neutrality and its role in protecting political expression on the Internet. *Hastings Comm. & Ent. L.J.*, 31(1): 153–172. https://repository.uchastings.edu/cgi/viewcontent.cgi?article=1668&context=hastings_comm_ent_law_journal [Accessed 25 Feb., 2021].

Popat, K., Mukherjee, S., Yates, A. and Weikum, G. (2018). DeclarE: Debunking fake news and false claims using evidence-aware deep learning. *In Proceedings of EMNLP*, 2018: 22–32. https://arxiv.org/abs/1809.06416 [Accessed 21 Mar., 2021].

Shahbaz, A. and Funk, A. (2019). *Freedom on the Net 2019—The Crisis of Social Media*. https://www.rcmediafreedom.eu/Publications/Reports/Freedom-on-the-Net-2019-The-crisis-of-social-media [Accessed 20 May, 2021].

Shu, K., Wang, S. and Liu, H. (2019). Beyond news contents: The role of social context for fake news detection. *In Proceedings of WSDM*, 2019: 312–320. https://arxiv.org/abs/1712.07709 [Accessed 28 Feb., 2020].

The daily *Anandabazar Patrika* (3 May, 2021). *Coronavirus in India*. https://www.anandabazar.com/india [Accessed 12 May, 2021].

*The Daily Star* (Oct. 1, 2012). Buddhist Temples Torched, 50 Houses Smashed—Extremists Linked. https://www.thedailystar.net/news-detail-251955. [accessed 23 Jan., 2021].

Wang, Y. et al. (2018). EANN: Event Adversarial Neural Networks for multi-modal fake news detection. *In Proceedings of KDD*, 2018: 849–857. https://dl.acm.org/doi/10.1145/3219819.3219903 [Accessed 11 Jan., 2020].

Zhao, Z., Resnick, P. and Mei, Q. (2015). Enquiring minds: Early detection of rumors in social media from enquiry posts. *In Proceedings of WWW*, 2015: 1395–1405. https://doi.org/10.1145/2736277.2741637 [Accessed 25 May, 2021].

# 8

# Are We in Trouble? An Exploration on Crime during Natural Disasters and Pandemics

*Bisola Ogunro, Amin Hosseinian-Far\* and Dilshad Sarwar*

## ABSTRACT

The rise of digital business models, social media platforms, and intensified use of cyberspace during the COVID-19 pandemic have inevitably seen respective and associated cyber and cyber-enabled crimes. There have also been fluctuations in other forms of crimes during the pandemic. This chapter provides a critical overview of crime during natural disasters and pandemics. The paper also outlines a comprehensive background on pandemics, natural disasters, and crimes beside attempting to critically review the existing literature on the correlation between these concepts. It then adopts a case study approach to assess the correlation between pandemics and crime using secondary data sources.

## 1. Introduction

At each point in time when there is a pandemic or natural disaster, the way society responds varies from the traditional methods. Oftentimes, survival instinct motivates some individuals to deviate from the traditional, moral, or societal construct of what is right or wrong. This is largely attributable to the enormous effects pandemics, and natural disasters have on daily living - from economic activities, mobility, access to healthcare and social services, interactions, and mental health. Some of these effects

Department of Business Systems & Operations, University of Northampton, NN1 5PH, UK.
Emails: bbogunro@yahoo.com; Dilshad.Sarwar@northampton.ac.uk
\* Corresponding author: Amin,Hosseinianfar@northampton.ac.uk

are directly traceable to the happenings themselves (pandemic/natural disasters), while others are traceable to attempts to salvage the situation in case of natural disasters or limit the spread in case of a pandemic.

Pandemics and natural disasters usually have the same side effects, resulting in high morbidity and mortality rates. These kinds of outbreaks often have economic implications for the country in which they occur. The government is occupied with ensuring that the health system is upgraded to accommodate the effect of the pandemic, likewise in a natural disaster, the government goes into swift action to defend her citizen's life and property. The citizens too come up with several coping mechanisms, while others adjust to their way of living, while still others rebel against the traditional or societal defined crimes. Some unconcerned parties even take advantage of the situation, like taking to sale of fake drugs during a pandemic, ransomware in health institutions, cyber financial crimes, etc.

These draining effects may motivate people to resort to indulging in crimes to make ends meet. Most often than not, pandemics and natural disasters are unplanned; this means that the government is usually not prepared for them and even if prepared, the extent cannot be accurately gauged.

Several authors have worked on the impacts of pandemics on crime and the impacts of natural disasters on crime. Some authors have even suggested that the definition of crime should evolve, be open to negotiation, and be continuously evaluated by states (Sandberg and Fondevila, 2020). Many have attempted to understand if the crime rate changed during a health crisis, why it changed, where the most changes occurred, at what point precisely during the pandemic did the shift begin to happen, what type of crime brought the most significant change, and how much change occurred (Ashby, 2020; Campedelli et al., 2020; Halford et al., 2020; Stickle and Felson, 2020 and Abrams, 2021).

Similarly, other authors such as Prelog (2015), Shabu (2017) and Roy (2010) have written on the impact, the effect and the relationship of crime and natural disasters. While some viewed it from the perspective of security concern, others view it from the perspective of coping mechanism, especially in situations where the State is unable to provide necessary relief to victims, and in some cases, it is not the victims that commit the crime; rather the others who attempt to take advantage of the occurrence. This chapter tries to identify and compare the impacts of pandemic and natural disasters on crime in the UK. Pandemics and natural disasters restrict movement and increase man's survival instinct. These could activate a causal mechanism that could either increase or reduce the crime rate as suggested by criminological theory (Eisner and Nivette, 2020). To further delve into this subject, let us take a look at the various variables being considered (pandemics, crime and natural disaster) and subsequently, find the relationship between them.

Social media has given freedom to anybody with a system and internet connectivity to send information to a great number of individuals worldwide simultaneously with the click of a button. Social media networking platforms help people, organizations, and businesses to connect, promote businesses and are a great source of information however they can leave users exposed to attack. The utilization of social media platforms accompanies significant cybersecurity risks many scams and malicious apps have been developed and have caused severe damages like data breaches, identity theft, phishing, denial of service, password attacks exposing the victims to scammers, hackers, and vulnerable to extortion and fraud. Many individuals and businesses have lost millions to hackers.

## 2. History of Pandemics

Pandemics are diseases with wide geographic extensions, movement that can be traced, high attack rates and explosiveness, minimal population immunity, relatively novel/new, infection, and severity (David et al., 2009).

According to the World Health Organization (WHO), a 'pandemic is the worldwide spread of a new disease to which most people do not have immunity'. Past pandemics have been caused by viruses that originated from animal influenza viruses. Most people confuse pandemics with epidemic; however, both terms refer to two different things. While a pandemic has been defined as the spread of a new disease, an epidemic is when many more cases of a health condition occur than expected in a particular region but do not spread further.

The WHO has the responsibility to declare when a pandemic occurs. WHO does this by monitoring the trend of the outbreaks and engaging expert health professionals for advice. The responsibility, however, to control the effect of pandemics lies within the hands of the country's government, often with external support from other more developed countries or organizations.

### 2.1 Crime

Crime is an act that society deems fit as wrong and frankly disallowed by the public (Thotakura, 2011). It is an intentional act that causes psychological or physical harm to a person, leads to property loss and is contrary to the law. Crime includes homicides, gun assault, aggravated assault, domestic abuse, robbery, burglary, larceny, drug usage, anti-social behavior, arson, child abuse, cybercrime and online fraud, fraud, hate crime, modern slavery, murder or manslaughter, rape and sexual assault, sexual harassment, stalking and harassment, terrorism, violent crime, theft to mention a few. Most crimes are general across the globe, while some are region-specific.

Henry and Lanier (2001) explained crime as defilement of societal custom or rule, which is built through the moral constructs of the society. Crime is seen to bring harm to individuals, society or the moral ideals of society. Therefore, a crime is said to be an act not permissible or allowable in an environment and if committed, it is punishable by law governing that environment. It is, therefore, an act done either intentionally or without legal justification – that contravenes a criminal law, that attracts a predefined punishment (Treadwell, 2013). According to Williams (2021), one out of five persons would be victims of some crime at least once in his or her lifetime. Generally, it is the government's responsibility to provide a formal system and institution to curb crimes, ensure law and order and set up a system that punishes and brings to book anyone who flaunts the set laws of the society.

Crimes are classified into various classes since many laws govern daily life in an environment. Some of the different forms of crime include cybercrime, organized crime, white-collar crimes, sex crimes, hate crimes, violent crimes and property crimes. Under these classes of crimes, there are several other crimes for ease of reference which will be discussed briefly.

## 2.2 Natural Disaster

Natural disasters, such as floods, earthquakes, volcanic eruptions, landslides, hurricanes, droughts, tsunamis, tornados, blizzards, tropical cyclones are natural happenings, as the name suggests, that overpower residents' limited resources and put the safety, welfare, well-being and smooth working and operations of the society at jeopardy and high risk (Gerard, 2002).

According to the United Nations International Strategy for Disaster Reduction (UN-IDSR), a disaster is 'a serious disruption of society's functioning, causing widespread human and material, economic or environmental losses that exceed the capacity of the affected society to cope using only its resources.' There are two types of disasters – man-induced and nature-induced. Man-induced disasters are caused by deliberate human actions like terrorism, political unrest, wars; natural disasters, on the other hand, are disasters associated with natural occurrences (Makwana, 2019).

## 2.3 Pandemics, Disasters and Crime

Natural disasters and pandemics cause fear, anxiety and panic. The first response to a natural disaster or pandemic is to save lives; security is usually not the top priority in times of such an occurrence. However, the distraction creates an opportunity for criminals to strike and take advantage of the situation and unsuspecting individuals, corporate organizations, and even government to enrich themselves. During the Hurricane Katrina in the U.S., hackers were busy creating fake donation websites and soliciting funds for disaster relief that were siphoned off to their own accounts (Wallace, 2021). COVID-19 changed the mode of social interactions and economic activities. Lockdown was imposed by most nations and people had to stay indoors. More people were now compelled to work from home and many more were made to spend much time online. Criminology theory suggests that a lockdown can trigger a causal mechanism that either increases or decreases crime; some crimes are likely to increase while others, reduce (UNODC, 2020).

Roy (2010) wrote on the effect of natural disasters on crimes and concluded that the violent crime rate tends to increase, based on the size of the natural disaster. The conclusions of Roy (2010) contradict the arguments of Paul et al. (1979) who said that crime rates decrease during a pandemic and do not rise despite reduced policing and other formal security measures because of the usual rise in community-based security and crime-management measures. The buildup in the capacity of informal security systems helps curb the rate of criminal activities in the occurrence of a natural disaster by making the cost and risk of committing crime too high.

A widespread reduction in crime rate followed the earthquake that crushed Chile in 2010, in the property crime rate. García (2019) reported that the effects of the earthquake triggered a robust community support that included community tactics of curbing crimes. These results obtained by García (2019) contradict the arguments of the routine activities theory. The routine activities theory states that the rise in the number of susceptible targets and decrease in the capability of security measures leads to an increase in the crime rate after a natural disaster (Cohen and Felson, 1979). The cost of perpetuating crime significantly reduces because of reduced policing and other security measures, as most attention is focused on rescuing victims, building IDP (internally displaced people) camps and settling victims in a secure environment.

Conversely, other studies have also reported a decrease in different types of crimes after a pandemic. Paul et al. (1979) reported a significant reduction in the crime rate following Florida's Hurricane Andrew. Leitner and Helbich (2011), Sammy et al. (2009) and Bailey (2009) reported a drop in violent and property crime following the natural disaster that was studied in various cities. However, Sammy et al. (2009) also reported an increase in violent crime rate, particularly domestic violence. Similarly, even though Bailey (2009) and Leitner and Helbich (2011) reported reductions in the rate of property crimes generally, they both reported a rise in burglaries. This suggests that crime rate increment or reduction during a natural disaster is not homogeneous but rather heterogeneous; while the rate of some crimes increases, the rate of some decreases. All this depends on the several prevailing conditions and the events that follow the occurrence of a natural disaster.

Many reports were presented in the light of the increment and reduction of crime rate related to natural disasters. However, Renee et al. (2017) reported displacement of property crime from the areas affected by floods in Brisbane, Australia, to areas that were not affected when exploring the effect of the January 2011 floods in Brisbane neighborhood. Another case of displacement of crime was reported by Breetzke and Andresen (2018), following the 2010 and 2011 earthquakes in New Zealand. They reported that the rate of crime dropped in the central business district of Christchurch that was affected by the earthquake and a rise was recorded in central business district neighborhoods that were not affected or less affected by the earthquake. This implies a displacement or flight of crime from one location to another.

This also suggests that crime rates in a community's response to natural disasters differs and is non-linear during an increase or decrease, but can also be a displacement or perhaps a total flight away from a region.

## 2.4  Crime during Pandemic and Natural Disaster

Many studies have written on the various effects of COVID-19 and crime rate; however, it is not extensive because we are still grappling with the effects of the pandemic as new variants keep springing up.

McDonald and Balkin (2020) reported the crime rate in four US cities by comparing it to the previous year, while some others restricted their study to certain jurisdictions, like Los Angeles (Campedeilli et al., 2020), Australia (Payne et al., 2020) and Lancashire in the UK (Halford et al., 2020). These studies are limited in coverage and reported declines from minimal to significant in various types of crime across the states covered. Halford et al. (2020) discovered a decrease in non-residential burglary, while Abrams (2021) observed a substantial increase.

Ashby's (2020) study was based on crime variation in 16 US cities within the first two months of the pandemic as compared to historical data. The result was that the divergence was not statistically significant. According to Abrams (2021), there was a considerably more significant divergence in the crime rate, which might have been due to the availability of more data.

In a report on pandemic, social unrest and crime in US. cities by Rosenfeld et al. (2020), the study was carried out in 34 US cities. In the report the rate of homicides increased by 30%, aggravated assault increased by 6%, gun assault increased by 8%, car theft increased by 13%, robbery rate decreased by 9%, the rate of residential burglary reduced by 24%, and non-residential by 7%, drug abuse reduced by 30%, larceny decreased by 16%, and also a significant increase was also reported in the rate of domestic violence in the early years of the pandemic in 2020 as compared to 2019. The report revealed a consistent increase in violent crimes (homicides, gun assault, aggravated assault, domestic violence) and a decrease in the rate of non-violent crimes (robbery, burglary, larceny and drug usage). The report of Rosenfeld et al. (2021) is consistent with the findings of Halford et al. (2020).

The decrease in non-violent crimes during the COVID-19 pandemic in 2020, as reported by Halford et al. (2020) and Rosenfeld et al. (2020), is consistent with the global 50% decrease, reported by UNODC (2020), especially in countries with stricter lockdown policies. It is fair to attribute the decrease in non-violent crimes, such as theft, burglary, drug usage and robbery to the lockdown and social distancing that ensued after the pandemic. With violent crimes (specific focus on intentional homicide), UNODC (2020) reported variations in the reports from various countries. Suggestively, the variations were attributed to variances in the strictness of the lockdown measures placed by the government of the various countries, the high proportion or prevalence of a particular type of homicide in existence before, such as gang clashes and organized crimes, in the various countries and also the socio-economic situation in these countries pre-pandemic.

Contrarily, Yang et al. (2021), in their study of the impact COVID-19 has had on crime, examined criminal damage, robbery, assault, burglary, battery, fraud and theft. They reported an overall significant decrease in the crime rate in Chicago, especially with regards to burglary: both residential and non-residential, battery, fraud, and theft. Again, this can be attributed to the quarantine that restricted the movement of people during the pandemic. Some crimes became factually impossible, especially during the lockdown, making it less probable to commit crimes like theft. Because of the decrease in legal activities, very few individuals were out of home in the heat of the COVID-19 pandemic and this increased the difficulty of perpetuating some crimes and made it easier for law enforcement to record more of certain other crimes.

A decrease in some activities easily explains the decrease in some criminal activities, such as theft. For instance, Jahshan (2020) reported an 85% reduction in traffic for physical retail shops in the US during the pandemic and this is consistent with reports of fewer thefts, such as shoplifting and robbery. The submission of Jahshan (2020) is consistent with the report of Pietrawska et al. (2020) on the significant 24% drop in the rate of shoplifting in Los Angeles. Another example is the 61% reduction in the pickpocketing type of theft in a city in the UK during the heat of the COVID-19 pandemic as a result of the social distancing directives (Gerell et al., 2020).

However, as highlighted by Campedelli et al. (2021) that crimes and/or certain crimes are usually frequent in some neighborhoods as opposed to being distributed randomly in a city, Yang et al. (2021) observed the cluster of battery, burglary, fraud, and theft in some areas of Chicago. Yang et al. (2021) also reported patterns in the occurrence of battery, theft, assault and fraud. They observed an inclination to sensitivity of crimes to events (pandemic-related or not) and policies. One key feature that impacts crime during pandemics and natural disasters is the disruption of daily routines that follow movement restrictions and/or complete lockdown directives.

BAE Systems (2021) surveyed the COVID-19 crime index and reported that 74% of financial institutions increased fraudulent activities during the pandemic, with a mean increase of 29% in fraudulent activity. 51% of the financial institutions surveyed had to upgrade their security firewalls because of remote working. It was a long time-consuming process to hedge against fraudulent activities. Furthermore, 74% of the financial institutions surveyed were disturbed over the increase in cyber-criminal activities relating to the pandemic, while 77% of them were much more disturbed over the predicted rise in the cyber threats for the succeeding year(s). The results obtained open a perspective of institution-related and institution-affected criminal activity. During a pandemic or a natural disaster, not only individuals are affected by the crimes that are perpetuated, institutions (financial, medical, manufacturing and pharmaceutical) are also affected by criminal activities.

However, individuals are unavoidably affected by criminal activities that affect institutions. BAE Systems (2021) reports that three out of four end-users of the financial institution surveyed have observed malicious or fraudulent activities in the previous year, and one out of four end-users are now more scared of cyber fraud than non-cyber fraud. 50% of their end-users have been sufferers of online crime at one time, and 10 out of 50 have experienced online crime in the previous year. The impact of cyber-crime, whether during a pandemic or natural disaster, transcends institutions and individuals to states.

During the 2020 COVID-19 pandemic, cybercrimes and violent crimes (homicides, gun assault, aggravated assault and domestic violence) were perpetuated the most. The most probable causes for this is the economic hardship that follows the occurrence of a pandemic or natural disaster. Organized criminal activities that have been in existence before the pandemic or natural disaster used the rather tragic events as opportunities to perpetuate more crime. Criminal activities that have been happening before, such as gang violence, were aggravated by the psychological trauma of having everything grounded, especially during the lockdown, human-trafficking victims, especially those in confinement by their traffickers and those in domestic servitude (UNODC, 2020; BAE systems, 2021; Campedelli et al., 2021). Similarly, because of the lockdown directives and social distancing that required people to stay at home and work remotely, people now spend more time online than offline, increasing their chances of being targeted for cybercrimes.

Andresen and Hodgkinson (2020) examined crime patterns during the 2020 COVID-19 pandemic in Queensland, Australia and revealed that the rate of crime generally reduced when the total lockdown restriction was enacted and increased as restrictions were relaxed into social distancing. During the initial total lockdown, more people were inside, leaving less of a target for perpetrators of crime. Also, the total lockdown restriction made policing easier for formal institutions that were established to curb crime. Similarly, Felson et al. (2020) reported a drop in the crime rate in Detroit during the first few periods of the social restriction; their study reported a significant drop in the rate of residential burglary, which eventually began to increase as the restriction was relaxed. Also, up to a 60% rise was recorded in the rate of crime in China at the initial stage of the enacted social restriction, which eventually rose higher than the initial levels before the drop, when the enacted restrictions were relaxed (Borrion et al., 2020).

## 3. Theoretical Concept

### 3.1 The Fraud Triangle

The 'Fraud Triangle' was developed by Donald Cressey when he interviewed over 200 embezzlers for his Ph.D. programme in 1953. The fraud triangle was initially a hypothesis of Donald's work. It was targeted at financial crime, especially with individuals that were trusted with finances and ended up violating the trust because of the pressure of a need that was perceived to be un-shareable to anyone else; hence unsolvable by anyone else.

Donald Cressey's Fraud Triangle identifies opportunity as one of the three factors required to perpetrate fraud. Pressure, rationalization and opportunity are the three legs of the fraud triangle, which states that these three things must have been in place for fraud to occur. During a pandemic and natural disaster, these three factors are present.

### i. *Pressure*

Pressure also refers to the motive for perpetrating fraud. Pressure is best described as perceived because it can be real or unreal (Albrecht et al., 2008). Sources of pressure could be social standing, financial, political, non-political, religious belief and examples can vary from health, debt, maintenance of standard of living, family and more (Murdock, 2008; Abdullahi and Mansor, 2015). For every time that fraud is committed, there must be an incentive or motive or pressure that would fuel the heat for the fraud to be committed. The pressure can be financial or non-financial. Lister (2007) stated that pressure could come externally or as a result of occupational stress or personal. This is fairly consistent with the submission of Albrecht et al. (2008)

that pressure can fall into one of the four categories of money related, addiction, employment-related and miscellaneous pressures. Donald Cressey (1953), as described by Kassem and Higson (2017), categorized the perceived pressures that fraud perpetrators consider unshareable and eventually lead to committing fraud into six (six) groups, viz:

1. Inability to fulfil debt obligations.
2. Inability to take care of personal responsibilities.
3. Bad business, unforeseen losses in business that are beyond control. It could be due to macro-economic or micro-economic factors.
4. Lack of access to help. When the fraud perpetrator cannot access people who can help them out of the difficulty they found themselves in.
5. Social or political standing, the standard of living that is above the fraud perpetrator's means.
6. An unhealthy relationship with employer, co-employees, or subordinates.

However, when it comes to crime and natural disasters, there are still motives, pressure, or incentives for committing a crime which may not exactly fall under some of the categories related to Donald's Fraud triangle theory. The pandemic or natural disaster comes with its economic hardships and scarcity of resources for both individuals and the government of affected countries. It is a form of pressure (UNODC, 2020).

## ii. *Opportunity*

According to Cressey (1953), if the risk of being caught is low, the fraud will most likely occur, which can mean that there must be a chance of getting away with it. Opportunity is highly crucial for fraud to occur. During the pandemic of 2020 (COVID-19), many studies reported a drop in the rate of certain crimes, such as robbery, burglary, larceny and drug usage (Halford et al., 2020; Rosenfeld et al., 2020 and Yang et al., 2021). This is easily explained as a drop-in opportunity resulting from the drop in some activities, such as strict lockdown and social distancing policies. Drop-in activities lead to drop-in opportunities. Also, because of the lockdown and social distancing policies, fewer people were active, making policing easier and increasing the risk of getting caught.

However, for some other crimes during the pandemic (COVID-19), especially crimes that can be committed indoors or in isolation, such as homicides, gun assault, aggravated assault, domestic violence, cyber fraud and gang violence, many studies reported a rise in the rate of these crimes (UNODC, 2020; BAE Systems, 2021 and Campedelli et al., 2021).

It could be deduced that during a pandemic or natural disaster, opportunities for some crimes increase while opportunities for other crimes decrease, depending on the measures that the State adopts to either cushion the effect or flatten the curve of the disaster or pandemic.

Simply put, an opportunity is a possibility of finding a way around crime control (Wilson, 2007).

### iii. *Rationalization*

Rationalization is the bridge that connects pressure/motivation to opportunity (Howe and Malawi, 2006). It is the third leg that completes the triad of the fraud triangle. Once the fraudulent action can be rationalized, then the probability of committing fraud is very high. During a pandemic or natural disaster, as at any other time and as with most actions of humans, there has to be a rationalization for the action that is being perpetuated. If the perpetrator of the crime could not rationalize it, then there is a lesser chance of perpetuating the crime. Rae and Subramanian (2008) described rationalization as the explanation for committing a crime or validation of a crime that is about to be committed or that has been committed.

During crises, such as natural disasters, pandemics/endemics, people have many reasons that can be used to justify their actions, such as survival or coping mechanism during the economic hardships that usually follow the crises. This is probably one of the reasons why most governments provide palliatives and bailout funds for both individuals and organizations. These governmental efforts help to take care of economic/ financial justification/rationalization and pressure for committing a crime or at the very least, cushion the effect.

## 3.2 Economic Theory of Crime

Like the fraud triangle, the economic theory of crime explores how the perpetrator of crime justifies committing a crime. The economic theory of crime is traceable to Becker (1968). The economic theory of crime explained that an 'individual committed a crime if the expected benefit acquired from committing the crime outweighs the benefits acquired from engaging in a legal, economic activity' (Becker, 1968; Pyle, 1983 and Roy, 2010).

According to Anupama (2011), individuals who perpetrate crime assume that returns from legitimate work are without risk and small compared with the benefits of committing a crime. Therefore, crime is perpetuated with the motive of exploiting or taking full/complete advantage of a situation and when the perceived outcome outweighs legitimate work. Crime is also perpetuated when the perceived outcome far outweighs the known punishment for committing the crime.

## 3.3 Routine Activity Criminal Theory

The crime rate is often influenced by the lifestyle and behavior of the population (Cohen and Felson, 1979); for example, there would be no cybercrime if there were no computers and the Internet. The routine activity theory is one of the major theories of environmental criminology. It states that there is a possibility for a crime to be committed when there is a motivated perpetrator, accessible target and the simultaneous absence of a capable guardian that could prevent crime (Arelys and Bonnie, 2012). The routine activity theory examines crime from the perspective of an offender. The motivated offender will only commit a crime if he feels it is relatively safe and how he feels it is relatively safe is through the availability of a suitable target in the absence of a capable guardian.

An accessible target, also referred to as a suitable target, can be a person, place, or thing. The capable guardian is usually a human element or anything whose presence can prevent the occurrence of crime. A capable guardian can be a police officer, neighbor, vigilante, CCTV camera, security dog, staff, friend, security guard. A capable guardian might be formal or informal; it might also be effective and non-effective. An example of an ineffective guardian is a neighbor, who is not paying attention, or CCTV is in the wrong direction, and a co-worker who is not trained to detect crime or even stop it. A motivated offender is a perpetrator who sees or looks out for an opportunity to commit a crime. During a crisis, there is often a change in daily routine, lifestyle and behavior of people, which either creates or eliminates opportunities for creating crimes.

## 4. Methodology and Findings

This study was conducted through the lens of critical realism. The ideal of critical realism is appropriate for a thorough analysis of historical trends. This study is not carrying out any experiment; instead, it views how the crime rate has been influenced by pandemics and natural disasters retrospectively. Secondary quantitative data is collected to investigate causal mechanisms of the data obtained and the inherent consequences of both pandemic and natural disasters on the crime rate in the United Kingdom. The axiological structure of critical realism resonates with this study.

The study strategy adopted for this study is the case-study strategy. A case study is carried out by collecting either qualitative or quantitative information or both on the subject matter to be investigated with a particular set of the population (Bryman and Bell, 2011). In this study in, the United Kingdom, the population is being used as a case study. The study investigates how the crime rate is affected by pandemics and natural disasters in the United Kingdom. The study design for this study is an inductive case study.

This study makes use of the mono method. All data collected were collected secondarily and in a quantitative format.

Appropriate, proper and accurate data analysis alongside proper data collection techniques ensure the integrity of data. The data collected for this study is primarily quantitative and were analyzed quantitatively, using a two-tailed paired t-test and graphical representations to arrive at logical conclusions.

The data is obtained from the public domain of the Office for National Statistics and were summarized into annual averages for three years.

i. *2017 represents a period of natural disaster*. The year 2017 witnessed Hurricane Ophelia. Hurricane Ophelia was estimated to have caused over $1.8 billion loss in damages and was the worst storm to be witnessed in the United Kingdom in the last 50 years. Hurricane Ophelia caused much economic disability following its incidence and economic instability is one of the motivators or justification for crime, as discussed in the previous chapter.

ii. *2019 represents a reasonably neutral year*. The year witnessed no natural disaster except for the United Kingdom floods that started in November, towards the end of the year and ended in February 2020.

2020 represents the pandemic year. 2020 witnessed the COVID-19 pandemic, which is still ravaging the globe. In an attempt to curb the spread of the pandemic in 2020, multiple total lockdown protocols were initiated. Economic activities were grounded and the way some businesses were conducted changed, leaving many in a poor economic state.

## 4.1 Method of Data Analysis

The data on crimes from these three years were obtained from the Office for National Statistics website and summarized into annual averages. The categories of crimes that were considered are violent crimes, sexual offences, robbery, theft, criminal damage and arson, drug offences, possession of weapons, public order offences, crimes against society (others) and fraud. The annual averages of these crimes in both the pandemic and the natural disaster year were matched against the neutral year individually, and a student T-test was conducted to know if there is a significant difference in crime rate between these years and the neutral year.

The student's T-test is used to test the significance of differences among two variables. In this study, the paired T-test was adopted because of the association between the data over the years and across different occurrences of either pandemic or natural disaster. The paired two-tailed t-test helped to understand if there is any significant difference in crime between a pandemic/natural-disaster year and a normal year. The significant difference is irrespective of the increase or decrease in crime rate in a pandemic/natural disaster year with a typical year.

The calculated averages were also compared pictorially, via graphs across all crime categories to observe the differences between the years, if the crimes were higher or lower compared to the neutral year. The graphs would help identify crime categories with an increase or decrease in the pandemic/natural disaster year compared to a typical year.

The crime rate was recorded as per 1,000 of the population and 2017 represented the year for natural disaster because of the occurrence of Hurricane Ophelia, which dealt the most significant impact in recent times. There were not many things unusual about 2019; therefore, 2019 was referenced as a normal year. COVID-19 was declared a pandemic by WHO in March 2020. The COVID-19 virus highly impacted 2020 and therefore represented a pandemic-stricken year. 2018 was omitted because the impact of the natural disaster was far less than that of 2017.

The overall result of this analysis is in tandem with the position of Paul et al. (1995), who argued that crime rates decrease during a pandemic. They continued to argue that the crime rate does not rise even at the advent of the reduction of the capacity of policing and other formal security measures because of the usual rise in community-based security and crime-management measures. However, the scope of this study is limited and cannot ascertain if it agrees further with this claim.

A common need during a crisis is survival, which is sought for in different ways and some ways can be perceived as an opportunity to commit a crime, consistent with the second factor in the Fraud Triangle theory (Cressey, 1953). The need for survival was lightened through government support for individuals and businesses when the lockdown measures were enacted in the wave of the pandemic. The government support came through grants and loans; this deflated the pressure of taking care of the essential needs of man. The government support aided in reducing the motivations to commit potential crimes; hence the reduction in the rate of certain crimes recorded in this study.

The significant difference in the rate of violent crime between the years 2017 (natural disaster) and 2019 (normal) seems not to be attributable to the natural disaster as the levels were consistently higher throughout 2019 (normal period) than 2017 (natural disaster) when compared.

We do not have sufficient evidence to attribute the significant difference recorded in the rate of burglary between the natural disaster periods and normal periods because the rate of burglary seems to be higher all through 2017 when placed side by side with 2019. This is hard to pin on the natural disaster (Hurricane Ophelia) that did not occur until October 2017.

The significant all-year low in the rate of burglary in 2020, when compared to 2019, can be easily attributed to the COVID-19 pandemic that impacted the globe for the entirety of 2020 and whose consequence was the placement of UK under some form of lockdown (partial and total) throughout 2020. As a result of the restriction, most individuals were indoors and the ratio of law enforcement officers to people present in public spaces increased, making it difficult to perpetrate crime. The result agrees with the findings of Halford et al. (2020) on the decrease of non-residential burglary during a pandemic. Also, Rosenfeld et al. (2020) reported a 24% reduction in residential burglary and a 7% reduction in non-residential burglary in 34 cities of the United States of America during the pandemic. Generally, Rosenfeld et al. (2021) and Halford et al. (2020) reported a reduction in non-violent crime.

Furthermore, these are consistent with the global 50% decrease reported by UNODC (2020), especially in countries with stricter lockdown policies. Similarly, Yang et al. (2021), in their study of the impact that COVID-19 has on crime, examined criminal damage, robbery, assault, burglary, battery, fraud and theft. They reported an overall significant decrease in the crime rate in Chicago, especially in burglary: both residential and non-residential, battery, fraud and theft. Again, this can be attributed to the quarantine that restricted the movement of people during the pandemic. Some crimes became factually impossible, especially during the lockdown, making it less probable to commit crimes, like theft. Because of the decrease in legal activities, very few individuals were often out in the heat of the COVID-19 pandemic and this increased the difficulty of perpetuating some crimes and made it easier for law enforcement to record more of certain other crimes.

Similarly, Felson et al. (2020) reported a drop in the crime rate in Detroit during the first few periods of the social restriction. Their study reported a significant drop in the rate of residential burglary, which eventually began to increase as the restriction was relaxed.

Also, the significant all-year low in the rate of theft in 2020, when compared to 2019, can be easily attributed to the COVID-19 pandemic that impacted the globe for the entirety of 2020. The same case can be argued for theft as with burglary above. In addition, knowing full well that it is a pandemic and COVID-19 is communicable, and the virus can be easily contracted by touching anything infected and subsequently ingesting it via the nose and mouth, the fear of contracting the virus might have also detracted the perpetrator of the crime from breaking the lockdown restriction and consequently committing the crime. This agrees with the submission of Pietrawska et al. (2020) on the significant 24% drop in the rate of shoplifting in Los Angeles. Similarly, Gerell et al. reported a 61% reduction in the pick-pocketing type of theft in a city in the UK during the heat of the COVID-19 pandemic due to the social distancing directives.

It is difficult to pin the significant difference in the rate of drug offence on natural disasters (Hurricane Ophelia) because the rate of drug offences was low all year round in 2017 (when compared to 2019), and we do not have sufficient data to determine what happened in parts of 2017 when the natural disaster had not occurred.

The significant difference in the rate of other crimes between 2017 and 2019 cannot be attributed to a natural disaster (Hurricane Ophelia) because the rate was low all year round 2017 as compared to 2019, while the hurricane and its impacts were between October and December of the same year. We do not have enough data to analyze and evaluate what was responsible for all-year significant difference in the rate.

Similarly, the significant increase in the rate of fraud offences between 2017 and 2019 cannot be attributed to the natural disaster (Hurricane Ophelia); the same case can be argued as with 'other crimes' above.

To gain further clarity and insights on the aspects of the natural disaster where we did not have enough data to arrive at a concrete conclusion, the last quarter of 2017 was compared with the last quarter of 2019. The differences in the rate of crime in the period of a natural disaster compared with the same period during a normal year are not significant and can just be attributed to chance.

The average crime rate in the examined period also seems less during the natural disaster than in the normal period (Table 1). Also, this might be because data obtained in this study is not specific to areas most affected by the natural disaster but applies to the whole of the UK during the pandemic. Many studies by Roy (2010); Paul et al. (1979); Leitner and Helbich (2011); Harper and Frailing (2012) and Quarantelli (2007). Kwanga et al. (2017) have reported an increase in the rate of crime during a natural disaster.

The low rate of significant difference in crime rates recorded in this study can be attributed to the deviation in the normal routines during normal periods. Much more attention is paid during a crisis than during normal periods. The routine-activity

**Table 1:** Crime rate during natural disaster.

| | Crime per 1000; October–December | |
|---|---|---|
| | 2017 | 2019 |
| Homicide | 163 | 212 |
| Violent crime | 353605 | 423290 |
| Rape | 13438 | 13683 |
| Sexual | 24213 | 23634 |
| Robbery | 20845 | 21829 |
| Burglary | 114904 | 92020 |
| Theft | 395460 | 362574 |
| Criminal damage and arson | 152805 | 134214 |
| Drug offences | 35014 | 43623 |
| Other crimes | 127432 | 138818 |
| Fraud offences | 150893 | 183779 |
| Average | 126252 | 130698 |
| P-value = | 0.61 | |

criminal theory supports this claim. The routine-activity criminal theory developed by Cohen and Felson (1979) established that three factors make crime possible: a motivated perpetrator, a suitable victim and the absence of a competent watch. In a crisis, at least one of the factors is not available for crime to occur. The routines of the suitable victims change, making them unsuitable. Also, there is increased attention by law enforcement and local vigilantes, causing a spike in law-enforcement people density in affected areas in the case of natural disasters and public spaces in case of pandemics.

## 5. Summary of Findings

Crises generally lead to disruptions in routines, non-use or redefined use of public space and affects social interactions. These potential changes in daily living create opportunities for some crimes and block or reduce chances for other crimes. As much as there was no significant difference in the rate of crime during a pandemic and natural disaster in the United Kingdom from the normal time, the study revealed conclusively that the rate of theft and burglary decreased in UK during the pandemic.

However, the results were still inconclusive despite significant results obtained for violent crimes, burglary, drug offences, other crimes against society and fraud offences during the year representing natural disaster. This is because of the presence/continuation of a trend that either increases or decreases during that pre-natural disaster, making it unclear to attribute the difference to the natural disaster or other factors. Other crime categories during the natural disaster period showed no significant difference from normal periods. Aside from theft and burglary, other crime categories showed no marked change during the pandemic.

Balmori et al. (2021) observed a 'U'-shaped pattern; pre-pandemic, during pandemic and post-pandemic, in how crime rates, including theft, were affected by the COVID-19 pandemic in Mexico. They observed that crime rates dropped during the lockdown and rose after the restrictions were relaxed. Balmori et al. (2021) attributed some of the rises, after the lockdown was relaxed, to the resultant job loss and economic hardships that ensued with the lockdown restriction. This claim is supported by past studies (Raphael and Winter-Ebmer, 2001) on how unemployment increases the crime rate. The drop-in crime was attributed to the reduction in opportunities to commit a crime, according to the routine-activity criminal theory and the fear of getting infected, especially relating to crimes that are committed in groups. The UNODC (2021) reported a more than 50% decline in theft and burglary crime across the globe. This was attributed to an actual decrease in crime and a possible reduction in reported cases.

David (2021) also reported a drop in the crime rate in the USA, with a 24% decline in residential burglary. However, he reported a rise in commercial burglary and car theft, a 38% increase in commercial burglary and a more than 2.5-time rise in car theft. The increase in commercial burglary is possibly attributable to the reduction in concentrated activities around commercial properties, making them an easy target. Car theft might also be attributed to less mobility which meant that people left their cars parked outside untouched for extended periods.

Nivette (2021), in their study of 27 cities spread wide across 23 countries, found out that the rate of robbery (which includes theft) did not significantly increase statistically during the pandemic. However, they recorded an 84% reduction in the burglary rate in Lime (the highest decline they recorded). On average, a 28% reduction was recorded in burglary across all cities studied after enforcing the social restriction.

Similarly, Scott (2021) compared the early periods (January to April 4) of COVID-19 pandemic in Chicago, Baltimore and Baton Rouge in 2020 to the same period in 2019, 2018, and 2017 and found that for each of the other years, there was a decline in the rate of total crime, with theft and burglary common across all comparison.

David (2020) examined the crime rate in 25 large US cities during the pandemic and reported an average of 23% decline in the overall crime rate with a massive drop in the rate of theft and burglary.

# 6. Conclusion

Pandemics, crises and natural disasters are often unplanned. When they happen, they throw society off balance economically, socially, psychologically. Countries respond differently and so do individuals. Some resort to crime either for survival or to continue to maintain a certain standard of living as before the crises. Others perpetuate crime to take advantage of the situation, whichever relates. The pandemics, crises and natural disasters create pressure to commit a crime; other factors, including how the government/State responds to the crises, either providing or eliminating opportunities that individuals rationalize it in their minds. While not all crimes increase during a pandemic, some increase while others reduce. Some factors that may influence the type of crime that increases or reduces are region/location and governmental pro-activeness.

A common factor responsible for the drop in the rate of crime, especially theft and burglary during the pandemic, was a reduction in opportunity according to the routine-activity criminal theory—all traceable to a high reduction in population mobility. Generally, many previous studies recorded a decline in the rate of property crime (which includes theft and burglary) as found in this study.

This study and its outcome can be useful to crime agencies to properly guard themselves and the society they protect. Government agencies can also use the outcome to shape government policies and equally help in damage control.

# References

Abdullahi, R. and Mansor, N. (2015). Fraud triangle theory and fraud diamond theory. Understanding the convergent and divergent for future research. *International Journal of Academic Research in Accounting, Finance and Management Sciences*, 5(4, October 2015): 38–45.

Abrams, David S. (2020). *COVID-19 and Crime: An Early Empirical Look.* U of Penn, Inst. for Law & Econ Research Paper No. 20–49. Available at SSRN: https://ssrn.com/abstract=3674032 or http://dx.doi.org/10.2139/ssrn.3674032.

Abrams, D.S. (2021). COVID-19 and crime: An early empirical look. *Journal of Public Economics.* [Online]. 194: 104344. Available at: https://www.ncbi.nlm.nih.gov/pmc/articles/PMC7826063/pdf/main.pdf [Accessed 27 June, 2021].

Albrecht, W.S., Albrecht, C. and Albrecht, C.C. (2008). Current trends in fraud and its detection: A global perspective. *Information Security Journal*, 17; Retrieved from www.ebscohost.com on 11th August 2021.

Andresen and Hodgkinson. (2020). Somehow I always end up alone: COVID-19, social isolation and crime in Queensland, Australia. *Crime Science*, Springer's Nature. https://doi.org/10.1186/s40163-020-00135-4.

Anupama Jacob. (2011). *Economic Theories of Crime and Delinquency.*

Arelys, Madero-Hernandez and Bonnie, S. Fisher. (2012). Routine activity theory. *The Oxford Handbook of Criminological Theory.* Doi: 10.1093/oxfordhb/9780199747238.013.0027. Available online. https://www.oxfordhandbooks.com/view/10.1093/oxfordhb/9780199747238.001.0001/oxfordhb-9780199747238-e-27.

Ashby, P.J. (2020). *Initial Evidence on the Relationship between the Coronavirus Pandemic and Crime in the United States.*

BAE Systems. (2021). *The COVID-19 Crime Index 2021.* [Online]. *Opportunistic and Overpowering.*

Bailey, K. (2009). An evaluation of the impact of Hurricane Katrina on crime in New Orleans, Louisiana, *Technical Report*, unpublished, Applied Research Project for a Master of Public Administration, Department of Political Science, Texas State University.

Balmori de la Miyar, J.R., Hoehn-Velasco, L. and Silverio-Murillo, A. (2021). The U-shaped crime recovery during COVID-19: Evidence from national crime rates in Mexico. *Crime Science*, 10(1). https://doi.org/10.1186/s40163-021-00147-8.

Becker, G.S. (1968). Crime and punishment: An economic approach. *Journal of Political Economy*, 76(2): 169–217. [Online]. Available at: https://www.jstor.org/stable/1830482.

Borrion, H., Kurland, J., Tilley, N. and Chen, P. (2020). Measuring the resilience of criminogenic ecosystems to global disruption: A case-study of COVID-19 in China. *PLoS One.* https ://doi.org/10.20944 /preprints2 02006.0309.v1.

Breetzke, Gregory and Andresen, Martin. (2018). The spatial stability of alcohol outlets and crime in post-disaster Christchurch, New Zealand: Alcohol and crime in post-disaster Christchurch. *New Zealand Geographer*, 74. 10.1111/nzg.12182.

Bryman, A. and Bell, E. (2011). *Business Research Methods*, 3rd ed., Oxford: Oxford University Press.

Campedelli, G.M. and D'orsogna, M.R. (2021). Temporal clustering of disorder events during the COVID-19 pandemic. *Arxiv2021*, Arxiv:2101.06458.

Campedelli, Gian Maria, Aziani, Alberto and Favarin, Serena. (2020). *Exploring the Effect of 2019-NCoV Containment Policies on Crime: The Case of Los Angeles*, 1–49. https://doi.org/10.31219/osf.io/gcpq8.

Cohen, L.E. and Felson, M. (1979). Social change and crime ratetrends: A routine activity approach. *American Sociological Review*, 44(4): 588–608. [Online]. Available at: https://www.jstor.org/stable/2094589?seq=1.

Cressey, D.R. (1953). *Other People's Money*. Montclair, NJ: Patterson Smith, pp. 1–300.

David, M., Gregory, K. and Anthony, S. (2009). What is a Pandemic. *The Journal of Infectious Diseases*.

David, S. Abrams. (2021). Crime in the Time of COVID-19. *The EconoFact Network*.

Eisner, M. and Nivette, A. (2020). *HFG Research and Policy in Brief: Violence and the Pandemic, Urgent Questions for Research*. [Online]. Available at: https://static1.squarespace.com/static/5b293370ec4eb7e463c960e6/t/601d605dfa7dbf24f5aef487/1612537950607/Violence+and+the+Pandemic.pdf.

Eric Halford, Anthony Dixon, Graham Farrell, Nicolas Malleson and Nick Tilley. (2020). Crime and coronavirus: Social distancing, lockdown, and the mobility elasticity of crime. *Soc.ArXiv Papers*, 2020: 1–22.

Felson, M., Jiang, S. and Xu, Y. (2020). Routine activity effects of the COVID-19 pandemic on burglary in Detroit, March 2020. *Crime Science*, 9: 1–7.

García Hombrados, J. (2019). The lasting effects of natural disasters on property crime: Evidence from the 2010 Chilean earthquake. *Social Policy Working Paper*, 12–19, London: LSE Department of Social Policy.

Gerard, March. (2002). *Natural Disasters and the Impact on Health*. The University of West Ontario.

Gerell, M., Kardell, J. and Kindgren, J. (2020). *Minor COVID-19 Association with a Crime in Sweden, a Five-week Follow-up*. Malmo University. https://osf.io/preprints/socarxiv/w7gka/.

Harper, D.W. and Frailing, K. (2012). *Crime and Criminal Justice in Disaster*. Durham, NC: Carolina University Press.

Henry, S. and Lanier, M. (2001). *What is Crime? Controversies over the Nature of Crime and What to do about It*. 10.2307/3089445.

Howe, M.A. and Malawi, C.A. (2006). Playing the ponies: A $5 million embezzlement case. *Journal of Education for Business*, 82(1): 27–33.

Jahshan, E. (2020). Retail footfall declines at sharpest rate in March. *Retail Gazette*. https://www.retailgazette.co.uk/blog/2020/04/retail-footfall-declines-at-sharpest-rate-in-march/.

Kassem, R. and Higson, A. (2017). The New Fraud Triangle. *Journal of Emerging Trends in Economics and Management Sciences (JETEMS)*, 3(3): 191–195.

Kwanga, G.M., Shabu, T. and Adaaku, E.M. (2017). Natural disasters and crime incidence: A case of 2012 flooding in Benue State, Nigeria. *International Journal of Geology, Agriculture and Environmental Sciences*, 5(5): 43–48.

Lister, L.M. (2007). *A Practical Approach to Fraud Risk: Internal Auditors*.

Leitner, Michael and Marco Helbich. (2011). The impact of Hurricanes on crime: A spatio-temporal analysis in the City of Houston, texas. *Cartography and Geographic Information Science*, 38(2, Jan. 2011): 213–221. 10.1559/15230406382213.

Makwana, N. (2019). Disaster and its impact on mental health: A narrative review. *Journal of Family Medicine and Primary Care*, 8(10): 3090–3095. [Online]. Available at: https://www.ncbi.nlm.nih.gov/pmc/articles/PMC6857396/.

Maryville University. (2020). *The Main Types of Crimes: Motivations and Crime Protection*. [Online]. Maryville Online. Available at: https://online.maryville.edu/blog/types-of-crimes/#:~:text=Understanding%20the%20Main%20Types%20of%20Crimes%3A%20Motivations%20and.

McDonald, John F. and Balkin, Steven. (2020). *The COVID-19 Virus and the Decline in Crime.* https://ssrn.com/abstract=3567500.

Murdock, H. (2008). *The Three Dimensions of Fraud: Internal Auditors.* Retrieved on 22 June, 2014, from www.emerald.com.

Nivette, A.E., Zahnow, R. and Aguilar, R. (2021). A global analysis of the impact of COVID-19 stay-at-home restrictions on crime. *Nat. Hum. Behav.*, 5: 868–877. https://doi.org/10.1038/s41562-021-01139-z.

Paul Friesema, James Caporaso, Gerald Goldstein, Robert Lineberry and Richard McCleary. (1979). *Aftermath: Communities After Natural Disasters.* Beverly Hills, Sage Publications.

Payne, J.L., Morgan, A. and Piquero, A.R. (2020). COVID-19 and social distancing measures in Queensland, Australia, are associated with short-term decreases in recorded violent crime. *Journal of Experimental Criminology.* https://doi.org/10.1007/s11292-020-09441-y.

Pietrawska, B., Aurand, S.K. and Palmer, W. (2020b). COVID-19 and crime: CAP's perspective on crime and loss in the age of COVID-19: Crime in Los Angeles and Chicago during COVID-19. *CAP Index*, Issue 19.3.

Prelog, Andrew. (2015). Modelling the relationship between natural disasters and crime in the United States. *Natural Hazards Review*, 17: 04015011. 10.1061/(ASCE)NH.1527-6996.0000190.

Pyle, D.J. (1983). The economic theory of criminal behavior. *The Economics of Crime and Law Enforcement*, pp. 8–28. [Online]. Available at: https://link.springer.com/chapter/10.1007%2F978-1-349-05245-5_2 [Accessed 31 July, 2021].

Quarantelli, E.L. (2007). The myth and realities: Keeping the looting myth in perspective. *Natural Hazards Observer*, 31(4): 2–3.

Rae, K. and Subramaniam, N. (2008). Quality of internal control procedures: Antecedents and moderating effect on organizational justice and employee fraud. *Managerial Auditing Journal*, 23(2): 104–124.

Raphael, S. and Winter-Ebmer, R. (2001). Identifying the effect of unemployment on crime. *The Journal of Law and Economics*, 44(1): 259–283.

Renee Zahnow, Rebecca Wickes, Michele Haynes and Jonathan Corcoran. (2017). Disasters and crime: The effect of flooding on property crime in Brisbane neighbourhoods. *Journal of Urban Affairs*, 39(6): 857–877. doi: 10.1080/07352166.2017.1282778.

Rosenfeld Richard, Thomas Abt and Ernesto Lopez. (2021). *Pandemic, Social Unrest and Crime in US Cities: 2020 Year-end Update.* Washington, D.C.: Council on Criminal Justice, January 2021.

Roy, S. (2010). *The Impact of Natural Disasters on Violent Rime.* [Online]. Available at: http://www.nzae.org.nz/wpcontent/uploads/2011/08/Roy_The_Impact_of_Natural_Disasters_on_Violent_Crime.pdf.

Sammy Zahran, Tara O'Connor and Lori Peek. (2009). Natural disasters and social order: Modelling crime outcomes in Florida. *International Journal of Mass Emergencies and Disasters*, 27(1): 26–52.

Sandberg, S. and Fondevila, G. (2020). Corona crimes: How pandemic narratives change criminal landscapes. *Theoretical Criminology.* sagepub.com/journals-permissions. doi: 10.1177/1362480620981637 journals.sagepub.com/home/tcr.

Scott, S.M. and Gross, L.J. (2021). COVID-19 and crime: Analysis of crime dynamics amidst social distancing protocols. *PLoS One*, 16(4): e0249414. https://doi.org/10.1371/journal.pone.0249414.

Shabu, Terwase. (2017). Natural disasters and crime incidence: A case of 2012 flooding in Benue State, Nigeria. *Journal of Agriculture & Rural Development.*

Stickle, B. and Felson, M. (2020). Crime rates in a pandemic: The largest criminological experiment in history. *American Journal of Criminal Justice.* https://doi.org/10.1007/s12103-020-09546-0.

Thotakura, Dr. (2011). Crime: A conceptual understanding. *Indian Journal of Applied Research*, 4: 196–198. 10.15373/2249555x/MAR2014/58.

Treadwell, J. (2013). *Criminology: The Essentials.* London; Los Angeles: Sage.

UNODC. (2020). *Research Brief: Effect of the COVID-19 Pandemic and Related Restrictions on Homicide and Property Crime World.* [Online]. ReliefWeb. Available at: https://reliefweb.int/report/world/research-brief-effect-COVID-19-pandemic-and-related-restrictions-homicide-and-property.

UNODC. (2021). *Property Crime Brief*, 2020.

Wallace, F. (2021). *How Natural Disasters Affect Cybersecurity.* [Online]. United States Cybersecurity Magazine. Available at: https://www.uscybersecurity.net/how-natural-disasters-affect-cybersecurity/#:~:text=%20How%20Natural%20Disasters%20Affect%20Cybersecurity%20%201

Wickert, Christian. (2020). Routine Activity Theory (RAT). *SozTheo*, Dec. 2020. soztheo.de/theories-of-crime/rational-choice/routine-activity-theory-rat/?lang=en.

Williams, E. (2021). *Hate Crime*. [Online]. *Victim Support*. Available at: https://www.victimsupport.org.uk/you-co/types-crime/hate-crime/.

Wilson, I. (2007). Regulatory and institutional challenges of corporate governance in Nigeria post-consolidation. *Nigerian Economic Summit Group (NESG) Economic Indicators*, April–June, 12(2).

Yang, M., Chen, Z., Zhou, M., Liang, X. and Bai, Z. (2021). The impact of COVID-19 on crime: A spatial-temporal analysis in Chicago. *Isprs. Int. J. Geo-Inf.*, 10: 152. https://doi.org/10.3390/Ijgi10030152.

# 9

# A Critical Analysis of the Dark Web Challenges to Digital Policing

*Olivia Bamsey* and *Reza Montasari**

## ABSTRACT

The dark web constitutes a small part of the deep web, i.e., sections of the World Wide Web content that are not indexed by search engines. As opposed to the surface web content that can be accessed by a standard web browser, the deep web content can only be accessed through special software, such as the TOR browser or Onion Router. Whilst the dark web could be utilised to promote civil liberties, such as free speech, privacy and user anonymity, simultaneously, it is being exploited by criminals for a wide range of illegal activities. For instance, the dark web is frequently used to facilitate crimes related to distributing and viewing illicit pornography; participating in illicit social activities; selling drugs, firearms, hacking tools and services; recruiting and financing terrorists; and engaging with human trafficking. In view of these, this chapter investigates some of the existing challenges that the dark web poses to the digital policing and, where appropriate, offers a number of recommendations to address the stated challenges.

## 1. Introduction

The dark web is a 'layer' of the Internet where online criminal activity thrives and can do so without much interference from law enforcement (Buxton and Bingham, 2015). Both the dark web and online criminal activity are expanding rapidly due to the ever-growing nature of technology in modern times (Davies, 2020). The dark

---

Hillary Rodham Clinton School of Law, Swansea University, Richard Price Building, Singleton Park, Swansea.
Email: 954253@Swansea.ac.uk
* Corresponding author: Reza.Montasari@Swansea.ac.uk

web poses many challenges to policing due to its consistent expansion (Tabachnick, 2019). Technology has not only brought along new crimes, such as revenge porn and malware crimes, it has also facilitated traditional crimes, such as the drug trade (National Police Chief's Council, 2016), all of which are rampant on the dark web (Finklea, 2017). Due to the ever-growing nature of technology, policing is not able to keep up with major issues, such as anonymity on the dark web, in terms of knowledge and technical ability to be able to challenge it (National Police Chief's Council, 2016). In addition to policing methods, the dark web also raises challenges to law as a whole, along with agencies, such as the United Nations international drug control system (Buxton and Bingham, 2015). In view of these pronouncements, this chapter aims to conduct a critical analysis of the challenges associated with policing the dark web. The remainder of the chapter is structured as follows. Section 2 provides a background on the darknet; Section 3 explores the scale of the challenges presented by the dark web; Section 4 examines jurisdictional issues and Section 5 investigates matters related to the user anonymity that the dark web affords; Section 6 discusses issues pertaining to the undercover policing, while Section 7 discusses the shortages of skilled professionals. Finally, the chapter is concluded in Section 8.

## 2. Background

The Internet, which started in 1969, is currently the largest computer network in the world (Goodwill Community Foundation, 2013). It consists of two different areas including the surface web and the deep web (Stjouwerman, 2017). The surface web is accessible through Internet web browsers and search engines, such as Google (Barratt, 2015). In contrast, the deep web can only be accessed through passwords or software, such as TOR. The Internet has been likened to an iceberg (Bergman, 2001), the small tip of which is only visible to the users. According to the same analogy, there is, however, a larger underworld represented by the bottom part of the iceberg. This is called the deep web, which is invisible to the regular Internet users (Bergman, 2001). Whilst not all parts of the deep web are criminalised, the area exploited for criminal activities is known as the dark web (Barratt, 2015), which is the focus of this chapter. Examples of the criminal activities within the dark web relate to child pornography; drug markets; fraud, human and weapons trafficking, spammers and terrorist content (Finklea, 2017; Moore and Rid, 2016). The dark side of the Internet is reported (Rossi, 2015) to be approximately 1000 times larger than the surface web. As well as its use by the criminals, the dark web is utilised by other groups, such as activists and whistle-blowers for a wide range of purposes (Nath and Kriechbaumer, 2015).

For instance, whistle-blowers with a presence on the dark web might be collaborating with either the media or the police for different reasons. Similarly, some individuals might view the dark web as an opportunity to use the Internet with freedom and to avoid State oppression (Gehl, 2014). The main route to access the dark web is through the Onion Router, also known as TOR (Finklea, 2017), which is used to maintain anonymity (Choudhary and Bhagat, 2018). Given that the data sent through TOR are lost in layers of encryption, it will be extremely difficult to locate the source from which the data originated. However, in cases where criminal services on the dark web have been paid for by debit or credit cards, anonymity will no longer be maintained considering the payment details which would identify the individual behind the transaction (Choudhary and Bhagat, 2018). Therefore, in order to obfuscate their activities and transaction details, criminals exploit one of the many types of cryptocurrency with a view to avoiding detection (Polansek, 2016). According to a report as cited by Sharma (2019), as of August 2017, Bitcoin, Monero and Ethereum were the most preferred coins to carry out dark web transactions.

## 3. Challenges of Scale

The National Institute of Justice (2020) have recently highlighted that the dark web is consistently expanding, which poses significant challenges to policing. As a result, it would be very challenging to determine an accurate representation of crimes that take place on the dark web or because of it (Levi, 2017). This lack of ability to establish the true scale of the dark web-related crime is further exacerbated by the fact that many go unreported (Levi, 2017). The FBI Internet Crime Complaint Centre (2016) stated that on average 'for every crime reported to law enforcement, there are six Internet-enabled crimes that go unreported' (p.3), highlighting the extent of the problem. The lack of accurate statistics in relation to the dark web-related crimes has had a significant impact on the law enforcement efforts to combat this phenomenon. As a result, it is difficult for law enforcement to formulate a response that is both most effective and representative of the scale of the problem (The National Institute of Justice, 2020; Goodison et al., 2019).

It is, however, important to note that this lack of accurate statistical data is not limited only to the dark web-related crimes. This is a common problem that is prevalent across other types of crimes too (Goodison et al., 2019). Furthermore, it is difficult to monitor and hold accountable in a proper manner those individuals who have committed crime through the dark web (Davis, 2017; Cox, 2016). It is difficult to control and hold people accountable in the correct way (Davis, 2017; Cox, 2016). A study was carried out by researchers at Monash University (2019) with the aim to gain more of an understanding about how much of the dark web contained illegal content. The study involved them carrying out an unrestricted crawl of 200,000 sites found on the dark web. Of all the 200,000 sites studied, two-thirds of them contained illegal or unethical content. Although it was found that most sites were based on financial crime, a worryingly large proportion of them related to child pornography and drug marketing. Considering the large size of the dark web, this research was a small-scale study even though a large number of sites were analysed.

According to Grimes (2016), it is estimated that for every successfully prosecuted cybercriminal, 100 either scape the justice with no repercussions or receive only a warning at most. The statistics previously used by the FBI Internet Crime Complaint Centre (2016) can be used in support of this, where they estimated that for every reported dark web-related cybercrime, a further six would go unreported. This is evidenced by the case of the take down of two of the largest dark web marketplace sites, known as AlphaBay and Hansa (Europol, 2017). This operation led by the FBI and the Dutch National Police was seen as a huge success. The two market sites had been responsible for over 350,000 illegal trades, reaching over 200,000 users and 40,000 vendors. As there were so many individuals involved with these illegal marketplaces, it would have been an unrealistic goal to arrest and prosecute every single vendor and customer who used the services. According to Penal Form International (2020), there are at least 124 prisons worldwide that are overrun, with there being 11 million prisoners in total. Prison overcrowding causes problems for policing itself as the more prisoners a country has, more of the law enforcement funding budget must be spent holding the prisoners (Price, 2016). Instead, this spending could be targeted at other areas, such as investigating the dark web. Having to place all dark web criminals in prison would cause major difficulties to the criminal justice system worldwide, thus causing challenges to policing. One of the ways in which this issue can be addressed is to prioritise dealing with the biggest offenders. This would necessitate having a focus on finding the leaders behind the biggest selling platforms or the biggest sellers on these platforms. It would also mean that these criminals must be held accountable with the appropriate prison sentence. Other criminals lower down the chain could be given large fines, that are proportionate with their crime. This would eliminate the issue of overwhelming the criminal justice system whilst criminals will still pay for being involved with the dark web.

## 4. Challenges of Jurisdiction

One of the major challenges of policing the dark web relates to jurisdictional matters. Owing to its large scale, the dark web enables users to connect worldwide for a wide range of noble and respectable purposes. However, oftentimes, this connectivity is also exploited by the criminals to commit crime together (Mounteney et al., 2016), This has culminated in major jurisdictional issues when investigating crime that is facilitated either on or due to the dark web (Goodison et al., 2019). There exists a treaty known as Mutual Legal Assistance (MLA) (Home Office, 2013), which is aimed at assisting the issue of differentiations between jurisdictions. However, the MLA itself presents a number of challenges. For instance, countries involved in a cybercrime-related investigation are most likely to have different laws (Vogt, 2017). One of the causes of this disparity concerns the issue of privacy and disclosure of data forbidden by some countries. Another reason pertains to the amount of time that the request for an MLA can take to process (Vogt, 2017). According to the Home Office (2015), contingent upon the circumstances, it can take up to 30 days or longer for the approval of a request. This could interrupt the investigation process, potentially even resulting in the case having to be dropped and the criminal escaping the justice. In criticism of this, the Home Office (2015) noted that the vast majority of cases are accepted within a 30-day time frame.

Similarly, Haasz (2016) states that if there are multiple jurisdictions involved with one specific crime, there can be difficulty in deciding which jurisdiction the suspect will be charged in. For instance, a suspect involved in distributing child pornography could normally reside in one jurisdiction but could have committed the crime in a different district. In addition, the viewers could have received the illicit content in yet another jurisdiction (Haasz, 2016). The suspect would be eligible to be charged in either of the three jurisdictions. Cooperation would be needed between all three jurisdictions to decide where the charge will take place in a timely manner. However, such a cooperation oftentimes does not exist. To address this issue, there needs to be consistent regulations in place across the globe that can be agreed upon (*The Economist*, 2015). This would also entail the sharing and funding of information-sharing strategies across international borders (Goodison et al., 2019). Another solution would be to establish cross-organisation structures aimed at enabling information sharing and co-operation. Similarly, there could be one official organisation tasked with processing all global MLA requests and managing them all in one place, to speed up the process. This organisation would then need to have knowledge of every State's laws and regulations to determine whether the MLA could be approved or not (Goodison et al., 2019).

Further challenges arise when countries do not work well together, resulting in a detrimental impact on their co-operation when policing the dark web. There would be a risk of prosecution if an investigation team in one jurisdiction investigates a cybercrime launched in a different State without their approval (Ghappour, 2016). Brunker (2002) highlights an example of this by referring to criminal proceedings that Russia's Federal Security Service (FSS) launched against a US FBI agent for unauthorised access to computer data whilst the agent was investigating a crime. This inevitably would have interrupted the investigation process and situations such as this could result in the failure of an investigation, as well as criminal proceedings. Russia is a prime example of a country that does not co-operate with other countries on investigating the dark web and cybercrime. Similarly, Martin (2019) highlights the case of Igor Turashev and Maksim Yakubets, Russian men who had close links to Russia's FSS. The two men in question were wanted in the US for aiding the development of the Dridex banking malware, that had been responsible for the loss of at least $100 million across over 40 countries. As the crime had impacted many individuals worldwide, it was expected that all countries would aid the investigation process of this large-scale attack. Although Yakubets is wanted in the US for financial losses in the tens of millions of dollars, Russia has, to date, refused to extradite him to the US authorities (FBI, 2019).

In conjunction with MLA treaties, extradition treaties are also put in place between countries so as to allow the investigating country to charge a criminal, if he resides in a different jurisdiction (Elsea, 2018). However, in accordance with Article 61 of their State's constitution, Russia does not permit extraditing of its citizens, once again highlighting its lack of co-operation in policing the dark web (Harding, 2007). A further example of this is highlighted (Harding, 2010) through a high-profile case of Russia's refusal to extradite one of its citizens, Andrei Lugovoi, who is wanted by the UK government on suspicions of murder in London. Russia's viewpoint on extradition and co-operation in relation to policing the dark web is a problem in itself, as highlighted by Rubenking (2019), stating that Russia is the 'birthplace of the dark web' (para 1). This point is in line with Haasz's (2016) statement about the challenges associated with establishing agreements between different nation-states in relation to investigating a cybercrime that involves multiple jurisdictions. This clear lack of co-operation and MLA's between States will further encourage criminals to commit crimes knowing that there will be little, if any, repercussions for their illegal activities (Goodison et al., 2019). This, in turn, will significantly undermine the efforts to police the dark web.

## 5. Challenges of Anonymity

Another key issue pertaining to policing the dark web results from the anonymising features that the TOR web browsers provide its users with. As previously stated, the TOR browser allows dark web users to maintain complete anonymity, hence enabling criminals to remain undetected by the police (Parliamentary Office of Science and Technology, 2015; Gillespie, 2013). This anonymity, afforded by the TOR browser, renders the challenge of policing the dark web significantly more difficult than policing the surface web (Haasz, 2016). Given that it is not illegal to use TOR, very little can be done to prevent it from being exploited by criminals (Chertoff, 2015). Elaborating upon this, Persi Paoli et al. (2017) state that anonymity is also facilitated through payments that are made by cryptocurrency on the dark web. Users cannot even be identified through payment methods when cryptocurrency is used. The issue of anonymity is further exacerbated by the TOR browser's built-in features that remove traces of users' browsing activities, once the browser is closed. Considering this, it would be almost impossible to recover traces of evidential value for an investigation (Jardine, 2015). However, in cases where investigators have managed to seize the suspect's machine while it was still running, they would be able to recover data from the machine's RAM. Using digital forensic tools, this can be achieved even after the TOR browser has been closed (Montasari and Peltola, 2016).

Whilst solutions to address anonymity on the dark web appear to be far-fetched, there have been cases in the past where dark web users have been deanonymised (Haasz, 2016). An example of this includes the takedown of a child porn website, where Britain, the US and South Korea cooperated to make the operation successful (*The National News*, 2019). The article stated that anonymity was gained by sales being made through cryptocurrency, and even though it does not state this, TOR was probably used by most of the users as this is usually needed to gain access to the dark web (Woolloston, 2020). No further details have been revealed about the methods used to deanonymise the criminals. However, it has been suggested that hacking methods had been probably used, following the statement by the National Crime Agency that they had deployed 'specialist capabilities' (cited in *The National News*, para 16). Although it is understood that this was a serious and harrowing case, it is difficult to understand the rationale for not employing these methods across all dark web cases. In contrast to seeing anonymity only as a challenge to policing the dark web, there is also a number of benefits that the TOR's anonymity feature could offer. For instance, it enables whistle-blowers to report crimes on the dark web without fear of repercussions.

## 6.  Challenges of Undercover Policing

Undercover policing is a successful method of policing that has been used to police the dark web (Haasz, 2016). This method of policing has been in use for a long time. However, in recent years, it has been adapted to be used online to engage with dark web criminals whilst hiding agents' identities (Davies, 2020). Experts in hacking and computer systems are needed to help in the investigation, to be able to access the dark web and to ensure the identities of the officers are consistently hidden (Haasz, 2016). Although this is an effective method of policing, it poses a number of challenges, such as entrapment (Goodison et al., 2019). Entrapment has been defined (Defence Solicitors London, 2018) as a set-up created by law enforcement which results in an individual committing a crime he might not have committed without the provocation from law enforcement. The issue is that there is a risk of criminal proceedings for law enforcement regarding entrapment. This is problematic in particular in the context of the dark web as criminals become more aware of undercover operations (National Institute of Justice, 2020). An example of a case where law enforcement was challenged for entrapment due to an online undercover operation was the *R v Loosely* case, that occurred in 2002 (DLS, 2021). Defendant Loosely was charged for supplying controlled drugs after an undercover officer asked him to make the sale. The judge, Lord Nicholls, disregarded the case as he stated that the law enforcement team involved incited the crime and this should not have happened. Challenging situations such as this often complicate the establishment of appropriate boundaries. Another challenge related to the undercover policing concerns the fact that it could be misused by law enforcement (Davies, 2020).

Relationships formed between covert officers and suspects during the period of undercover policing have raised a number of ethical concerns, so has the use of identities of deceased individuals by the officers for their undercover persona (Dawson and Brown, 2020). This has resulted in the introduction of new regulations under the Investigatory Powers Act 2016 (IPA). The IPA is intended to address inappropriate or unethical behaviour, such as using identities of the deceased individuals (Dawson and Brown, 2020). Whilst the introduction of these regulations has been welcomed, it simultaneously poses challenges to law enforcement. It is believed (Mather et al., 2021) that in cases of child sex offences, a falsified minimal relationship between the undercover officer and the suspect could reveal evidence required to prosecute the suspect.

## 7.  Skills Shortage

Cyber-security skill shortages are also a widespread problem that could have a significant impact on the law enforcement's ability to understand and police the dark web (National Institute of Justice, 2020). According to the former Home Secretary, Amber Rudd, and the Home Office (2018), just 30% of law enforcement teams had up-to-standard technical knowledge. Policing the dark web by underqualified individuals could result in the loss or contamination of important digital evidence. This, in turn, culminates in the dismissal of the case that hinges upon this digital evidence. Preserving digital evidence and acquiring it in a forensically sound manner are a complex undertaking that require both theoretical understanding of, and technical expertise in, a wide range of forensic tools, methods, guidelines, process models and best practices (Montasari et al., 2020; Montasari et al., 2020; Montasari 2018; Montasari et al., 2019a; Montasari et al., 2019b and Montasari, 2017). Digital evidence can readily be contaminated or lost; this is even more prevalent in cyberspace where digital evidence can be very volatile and short lived. This, once again highlights the need for technical expertise in conjunction with a proper understanding of various forensic tools, methods and best practices. A successful prosecution will depend upon digital evidence that has been collected and preserved in a forensically-sound manner.

Rossi (2015) highlights the importance of ensuring that police forces have some degree of technical training as traditional methods of policing that they are accustomed to, cannot be effective when dealing with the dark web. Similarly, Rudd and the Home Office (2015) note that, as the dark web grows and more traditional crimes adapt to the Internet use, policing will also need to adapt with these changes. In their *Policing Vision 2025*, The National Police Chief's Council (2016) recognises that many forms of dark web crimes, such as child exploitation and malware attacks, remain largely unreported, adding that this requires a change. Goodison et al. (2019) suggest that officers trained in traditional policing methods should be provided training by qualified individuals with technical expertise in both the dark web and also traditional policing. Another suggestion would be to introduce the mandatory inclusion of computer science in schools' curricula, considering the fact that cyber security will be a major part of the future of policing.

## 8. Conclusion

In their fight against dark web crimes, law enforcement often encounter numerous challenges, such as those related to technical, ethical and jurisdictional issues. There is a wide range of approaches that could be adopted in order to combat dark web-related crimes more effectively. For instance, both international co-operation and agreed-upon approaches are needed to address jurisdictional matters that arise when combating cybercrime. Similarly, police conduct in the area of undercover policing must take cognisant of the potential abuses of their targets with a view to addressing associated ethical implications. Furthermore, police officers dealing with dark web crimes should be forensically trained in order to ensure that digital evidence is captured and preserved in a forensically-sound manner. This is very important, particularly in criminal cases that rely upon digital evidence. Last, but not least, new generation of cyber security experts must be aspired in order to address the growing shortages of cyber security professionals.

## References

Barratt, M. (2015). A discussion about dark web terminology. *Drugs in Digital Society*. https://monicabarratt.net/a-discussion-about-dark-net-terminology/.

Bergman, M.K. (2001). White paper: The deep web: Surfacing hidden value. *Journal of Electronic Publishing*, 7(1).

Brunker, M. (2002). FBI agent charged with hacking. *NBC News.* https://www.nbcnews.com/id/wbna3078784.

Buxton, J. and Bingham, T. (2015). The rise and challenge of dark net drug markets. *Policy Brief*, 7: 1–24.

Chertoff, M. (2017). A public policy perspective of the Dark Web. *Journal of Cyber Policy*, 2(1): 26–38. doi: 10.1080/23738871.2017.1298643.

Choudhary, D. and Bhagat, R. (2018). The onion routing. *The Symbiosis Institute of Computer Studies & Research.* doi: 10.13140/RG.2.2.10181.09448.

Cox, J. (2016). Study claims dark web sites are most commonly used for crime. *Vice.* https://www.vice.com/en/article/3daqxb/study-claims-dark-web-sites-are-most-commonly-used-for-crime.

Davies, G. (2020). Shining a light on policing of the dark web: An analysis of UK investigatory powers. *The Journal of Criminal Law*, 84(5): 407–426.

Davis, C. (2017). Addressing the challenges of enforcing the law on the dark web. *The University of Utah.* https://law.utah.edu/addressing-the-challenges-of-enforcing-the-law-on-the-dark-web/.

Dawson, J. and Brown, J. (2020). Undercover policing in England and Wales. *House of Commons.* https://commonslibrary.parliament.uk/research-briefings/cbp-9044/.

Defence Solicitors London. (2018). What is entrapment in the UK? *Defence Solicitors London.* https://www.defencesolicitorslondon.co.uk/blog/what-is-police-entrapment-in-uk.

DLS. (2021). Police entrapment is no defence to criminal act. *Swarb.* https://swarb.co.uk/regina-v-looseley-orse-loosely-attorney-generals-reference-no-3-of-2000-hl-25-oct-2001/.

Elsea, J.K. (2018). Mutual Legal Assistance Treaty with the Russian Federation: A sketch. *Congressional Research Service.* https://fas.org/sgp/crs/row/LSB10176.pdf.

Europol. (2017). Massive blow to criminal dark web activities after globally coordinated operation. *Europol.* https://www.europol.europa.eu/newsroom/news/massive-blow-to-criminal-dark-web-activities-after-globally-coordinated-operation.

FBI. (2019). *Most Wanted: Maksim Viktorovich Yakubets.* Available at: https://www.fbi.gov/wanted/cyber/maksim-viktorovich-yakubets (Accessed 27 June, 2021).

FBI Internet Crime Complaint Centre. (2016). Internet Crime Report. *FBI.* 2016_IC3Report.pdf.

Finklea, K. (2017). Dark web. *Congressional Research Service.* Dark Web (fas.org).

GlobalData Technology. (2020). The cyber-security industry must do more to address skill shortages. *Verdict.* https://www.verdict.co.uk/cyber-security-skills-shortage/.

Gehl, R.W. (2016). Power/freedom on the dark web: A digital ethnography of the Dark Web Social Network. *New Media & Society*, 18(7): 1219–1235.

Ghappour, M. (2016). Searching places unknown: Law enforcement jurisdiction on the dark web. *Stanford Law Review*, 69(170).

Gillespie, I. (2013). Cyber cops probe the deep web. Available at: https://www.smh.com.au/technology/cyber-cops-probe-the-deep-web-20131023-2vzqp.html (Accessed: 17/02/2022).

Goodison, S.E., Woods, D., Barnum, J.D., Kemerer, A.R. and Jackson, B.A. (2019). *Identifying Law Enforcement Needs for Conducting Criminal Investigations Involving Evidence on the Dark Web*, RAND.

Goodwill Community Foundation. (2013). What is the Internet? *Learn Free.* https://www.just.edu.jo/~mqais/cis99/PDF/Internet.pdf.

Grimes, R.A. (2016). *Why It's so Hard to Prosecute Cybercriminals.* CSO [Online]. https://www.csoonline.com/article/3147398/why-its-so-hard-to-prosecute-cyber-criminals.html.

Haasz, A. (2016). Underneath it all: Policing international child pornography on the dark web. *Syracuse Journal of International Law and Commerce*, 43(2): 353–380.

Harding, L. (2007). Russian law prevents extradition. *The Guardian.* https://www.theguardian.com/world/2007/may/22/russia.lukeharding.

Harding, L. (2010). Andrei Lugovoi: I will never stand trial in Britain for Litvinenko poisoning. *The Guardian.* https://www.theguardian.com/world/2010/oct/12/andrei-lugovoi-interview-alexander-litvinenko-poisoning.

Home Office. (2013). Mutual Legal Assistance. Gov.uk. https://www.gov.uk/guidance/mutual-legal-assistance-mla-requests.

Home Office. (2015). Requests for mutual legal assistance in criminal matters. Gov.uk. https://assets.publishing.service.gov.uk/government/uploads/system/uploads/attachment_data/file/415038/MLA_Guidelines_2015.pdf.

Jardine, E. (2015). The Dark Web dilemma: Tor, anonymity and online policing. *Global Commission on Internet Governance Paper Series*, (21).

Levi, M. (2017). Assessing the trends, scale and nature of economic cybercrimes: Overview and issues. *Crime, Law and Social Change*, 67: 3–20.

Martin, A. (2019). Cybercriminal charged with stealing £76m while working for Russian intelligence. *Sky News*. https://news.sky.com/story/cyber-criminal-charged-with-stealing-76m-while-working-for-russian-intelligence-11878896.

Mather, J., Ford, S., Pickup, J. and Casebow, M. (2021). Undercover police: Hunting paedophiles. Motion Picture, United Kingdom, *Channel 4*.

Monash University. (2019). Monash IT experts illuminate criminal activity on the dark web. https://www.monash.edu/it/futurist/explore/social-good/articles/monash-it-experts-illuminate-criminal-activity-on-the-dark-web.

Montasari, R. and Peltola, P. (2015, September). Computer forensic analysis of private browsing modes. *In: International Conference on Global Security, Safety, and Sustainability*. Springer, Cham, pp. 96–109.

Montasari, R. (2017). An overview of cloud forensics strategy: Capabilities, challenges, and opportunities. *Strategic Engineering for Cloud Computing and Big Data Analytics*, pp. 189–205.

Montasari, R. (2018). Testing the comprehensive digital forensic investigation process model (the CDFIPM). *In: Technology for Smart Futures*, Springer, Cham, pp. 303–327.

Montasari, R., Hill, R., Carpenter, V. and Montaseri, F. (2019a). Digital forensic investigation of social media, acquisition and analysis of digital evidence. *International Journal of Strategic Engineering (IJoSE)*, 2(1): 52-60.

Montasari, R., Carpenter, V. and Hill, R. (2019b). A road map for digital forensics research: A novel approach for establishing the design science research process in digital forensics. *International Journal of Electronic Security and Digital Forensics*, 11(2): 194–224.

Montasari, R., Hill, R., Carpenter, V. and Hosseinian-Far, A. (2020). Evaluation of the Standardised Digital Forensic Investigation Process Model (SDFIPM). *In: Cyber Security Practitioner's Guide*, pp. 303–363.

Montasari, R., Jahankhani, H., Hill, R. and Parkinson, S. (2020). *Digital Forensic Investigation of Internet of Things (IoT) Devices*. Springer International Publishing AG.

Moore, D. and Rid, T. (2016). Cryptopolitik and the darknet. *Survival*, 58(1): 7–38.

Mounteney, J., Bo, A. and Oteo, A. (2016). The Internet and drug markets. *European Monitoring Centre for Drugs and Drug Addiction*. https://www.emcdda.europa.eu/system/files/publications/2155/TDXD16001ENN_FINAL.pdf.

Nath, C. and Kriechbaumer, T. (2015). The darknet and online anonymity. *Houses of Parliament*. https://post.parliament.uk/research-briefings/post-pn-488/.

National Institute of Justice (NIJ). (2020). *Taking on the Dark Web: Law Enforcement Experts ID Investigative Needs*. US Department of Justice, Office of Justice Programmes and United States of America.

National Police Chief's Council. (2016). *Policing Vision 2025*. Association of Police and Crime Commissioners. https://www.npcc.police.uk/documents/Policing%20Vision.pdf.

Parliamentary Office of Science and Technology. (2015). The darknet and online anonymity. *Postnote*. https://post.parliament.uk/research-briefings/post-pn-488/.

Penal Reform International. (2020). *Global Prison Trends 2020*. Thailand Institute of Justice with the United Nations. https://www.penalreform.org/resource/global-prison-trends-2020/.

Persi Paoli, G., Aldridge, J., Ryan, N. and Warnes, R. (2017). Behind the curtain: illicit trade of firearms, explosives and ammunition on the dark web. *RAND*. https://www.rand.org/pubs/research_reports/RR2091.html.

Polansek, T. (2016). CME, ICE prepare pricing data that could boost bitcoin. *Reuters*. https://www.reuters.com/article/us-cme-group-bitcoin-idUSKCN0XT1G1.

Price, S. (2016). The problem with overpopulation in prisons. *Penn State*. https://sites.psu.edu/ciblog16/2016/02/03/the-problem-with-overpopulation-in-prisons/.

Rossi, B. (2015). Why it's not impossible to police the dark web. *Information Age*. https://www.information-age.com/why-its-not-impossible-police-dark-web-123460505/.

Rubenking, N.J. (2019). The evolution of Russia's dark web. *PC Mag UK*. https://uk.pcmag.com/news/122017/the-evolution-of-russias-dark-web.

Rudd, A. and The Home Office. (2018). *Law Enforcement Crackdown on Dark Web: Home Secretary Speech*. Gov.uk. https://www.gov.uk/government/speeches/home-secretary-speech-on-law-enforcement-crackdown-on-dark-web.

Sharma, R. (2019). *Litecoin Gains Ground on Bitcoin in the Dark Web*. https://www.investopedia.com/news/litecoin-gains-ground-bitcoin-dark-web/.

Stjouwerman, S. (2017). What is the difference between the surface web, the deep web and the dark web? *Security Awareness Training Blog*. https://blog.knowbe4.com/what-is-the-difference-between-the-surface-web-the-deep-web-and-the-dark-web.

Tabachnick, C. (2019). The pitfalls of policing the dark web. *World Politics Review*. https://www.worldpoliticsreview.com/articles/27136/the-pitfalls-of-policing-the-dark-web.

*The Economist.* (2015). Governments grapple with law enforcement in the virtual world. *The Economist*. https://www.economist.com/international/2015/10/08/under-my-thumb?frsc=dg%7Cc.

*The National News.* (2019). Hundreds arrested over child porn website on dark web. *N World*. https://www.thenationalnews.com/world/the-americas/hundreds-arrested-over-child-porn-website-on-dark-web-1.924796.

Vogt, S.D. (2017). The digital underworld: Combating crime on the dark web in the modern era. *Santa Clara Journal of International Law*, 15(1).

Woerner, R. (2015). A call to action: Promoting computer science in schools. *CSO Online*. https://www.csoonline.com/article/2974752/a-call-to-action promoting-computer-science-in-schools.html.

Woollaston, V. (2020). How to access the dark web: What is TOR and how do I access the dark web? *ALPHR*. https://www.alphr.com/technology/1002667/how-to-access-the-dark-web-what-is-tor-and-how-do-i-use-it/.

# 10

# Multimedia Privacy and Security Landscape in the Wake of AI/ML

*Chaminda T.E.R. Hewage,\* Shadan K. Khattak, Arslan Ahmad,*
*Thanuja Mallikarachchi, Elochukwu Ukwandu* and
*Vibhushinie Bentotahewa*

## ABSTRACT

Privacy and security of multimedia content came under scrutiny with the wider application of Artificial Intelligence (AI) and Machine Learning (ML)-based technologies. The issues range from AI/ML-based profiling, creating faceswaps, deepfakes, verifying the authenticity of multimedia content to secure delivery of the content and data-driven network and service management of multimedia applications in next-generation networks. Moreover, advanced AI/ML-based techniques pose a challenge to multimedia content publishers and providers, who are concerned with the unauthorized distribution of their content over the Internet. This chapter provides a comprehensive review of AI/ML-inspired threat landscape and open challenges for multimedia content, service delivery and management. Furthermore, AI/ML-inspired countermeasures for these threats and future directions for embedding AI/ML-based data-driven management approaches for multimedia service delivery are also discussed in this chapter. The main application areas covered in this chapter are deepfakes, digital rights management, AI/ML-driven multimedia network and service management and network-based attacks and defences for next-generation multimedia.

School of Technologies, Cardiff Metropolitan University, Cardiff, United Kingdom.
\* Corresponding author: chewage@cardiffmet.ac.uk

**Section 1**

# 1. Introduction

The Internet of Everything (IoE) bubble generates a vast amount of data which constitutes a larger percentage of multimedia data (e.g., video data is expected to consume 82% of the Internet traffic by 2023, according to Cisco Visual Index (*Cisco Annual Internet Report*, 2021). In the process of responding to the anticipated demand, it is crucial to research, design and develop authentic multimedia content for secure, privacy-preserving and reliable multimedia networks (e.g., sensor networks) and provide necessary processing and storage facilities which will meet the end user's Quality of Experience (QoE). The privacy and security concerns are key challenges for next generation multimedia applications. Some of these concerns originated from AI- and ML-based technologies (e.g., deepfakes); on the other hand, some AI and ML technologies are helping us to tackle these privacy and security implications of multimedia content, as discussed in this chapter.

The AI and ML boom challenges multimedia security and privacy of individuals more than ever. The AI and ML are being used for automated profiling, face swaps and deep fakes. These AI-enabled malicious entities steal Personally Identifiable Information (PII) from multimedia data more easily than humans. There is a need for identification of these malicious entities. Often these require complex algorithms which deploy AI-based building blocks to automate these processes and for adaptation to different contexts. In addition to the technical solutions, there is a need for policies and laws to restrict the use of multimedia-based personal information. The current laws, such as GDPR, may need to be revisited to align with privacy-invasive popular multimedia applications, such as TikTok.

## 1.1 Deepfakes

The use of deepfakes is becoming increasingly widespread. In July 2019, Sensity, a visual threat intelligence company, identified 14,678 deepfakes online and during the period up to June 2020, the numbers had risen to 49,081—an increase of staggering 330% (Walker, 2020).

Realistic audio and video deepfakes can now be made with ease within just a few hours, using deep learning algorithms and with the advancement of technology. The risk of deepfakes is further increased in the light of the virtual workplaces, during the ongoing pandemic. This digital transition increases the use of video conferencing and other digital workplace tools, making way for expanding opportunities for deception, which triggers the tendency to cause severe embarrassment to prominent figures and consequently damage their reputation. Added to that, this technology has the capacity to endanger national security, incite social disorder and destabilise the community.

According to a deeptrace report, 96% of deepfake videos found online in 2019 contained pornographic material (Johnson, 2021). Also, deepfake videos have been used in politics; for example, in 2018, a Belgian political party released a video of Donald Trump giving a speech, calling on Belgium to withdraw from the Paris climate agreement (Johnson, 2021). It turned out be a deepfake and Trump never made that speech. This is just one example of the use of deepfake to create misleading videos to discredit prominent people.

The concerns raised about deepfakes call for important countermeasures to be taken and with that in mind, countries have begun reviewing and revisiting their existing legal systems to stop distribution of deepfake material. As of August 2020, several popular online platforms, such as Facebook, Instagram, Twitter, PornHub, and Reddit have either banned or are in the process of banning deepfakes appearing on their platforms (Farish, 2020). Although social media has indeed begun a campaign against possible deepfakes, they have found it hard to stop the creation of deepfakes in the absence of legal backup to prosecute the perpetrators. Therefore, it is important to promote awareness and have robust legal mechanisms to prevent deepfakes offences.

There are inherent security challenges and personal and privacy implications associated with deepfakes. The use of deepfakes could potentially increase the risk of bullying and put people in dangerous, or compromising situations. The attacker can also manipulate and persuade individuals to share confidential information. The possible consequences would be personal financial losses, change of public opinion and mistrust. One such incident was reported in 2019, in which an energy executive in the UK was scammed out of £200,000 when he responded to an imitating phone call from his boss, asking him to wire money (Best, 2019).

### 1.1.1 Digital Rights Management

Multimedia data over the Internet has seen tremendous growth over the last few years. One of the key drivers behind this trend is the popularity of social media websites and applications (such as YouTube, Instagram, TikTok, etc.), which allow users to get paid for generating multimedia content. For example, over 300 hours of videos are uploaded on YouTube every minute (Li et al., 2019). Many of these videos are copyright protected. Hence, it is important to detect unauthorised uploads. In 2019, YouTube alone spent around US$ 100 million to detect unauthorised uploads, which resulted in generating a revenue of around US$ 3 billion for the content owners (Saadatpanah et al., 2020). Another major driver over multimedia data is the Over-The-Top (OTT) video services (such as Netflix, Amazon Prime Video, Disney+, etc.). Many of these services produce and distribute their own content. However, piracy of such content is a serious concern. For example, it is estimated that Netflix alone could be losing US$ 192 million every month in revenue due to online piracy (Perez, 2019).

Digital Rights Management (DRM) tools facilitate the lawful distribution of multimedia content over Internet. To overcome the challenge of managing, securing and distributing the vast amount of data, content creators and distributors are investing heavily in efficient DRM systems. The global DRM market has been growing at a Compound Annual Growth Rate (CAGR) of 15.3% since 2018 and is estimated to be worth US$ 9 billion by 2026 (Transparency Market Research, 2018). However, despite such huge investments, the revenue lost to online piracy is estimated to reach US$ 51.6 billion by 2022. Therefore, it is important to develop more efficient and automated tools using AI and ML, which can protect the copyrights of online multimedia content.

### 1.1.2 Multimedia Delivery

Today, multimedia traffic dominates the Internet traffic due to the high user demand OTT applications, such as Facebook, Netflix, YouTube, Skype, etc. According to the Cisco Visual Index, multimedia traffic will compose 82% of Internet traffic by 2022 (*Cisco Annual Internet Report*, 2021). Consequently, the high volume of user demand for multimedia services requires both Internet Service Providers (ISPs) and OTT to incorporate novel and innovative solutions for ensuring better service quality as well as user privacy and security (Skorin-Kapov et al., 2018; Barakabitze et al., 2020; Ahmad et al., 2016).

The QoE is a multidisciplinary concept that measures the quality perceived by the user based on the multiple influencing factors, such as application, context, content, system (user device), network and business model (Robitza et al., 2017). While the research community is paving the way to include QoE-aware solutions for network and service management of multimedia services in the next-generation networks, user privacy and security remain open research challenges for both ISP and OTT perspectives (Barakabitze et al., 2020). Moreover, the emerging multimedia applications, such as IoT, Augmented Reality (AR), Virtual Reality (VR), Extreme Reality (XR), etc., have different QoE/QoS and security/privacy requirements on the application as well as network-level that make it challenging to provide an effective network and service management solution in 5G/6G networks (Barakabitze et al., 2020).

### 1.1.3 Study Methodology

The aim of this study is to review privacy and security landscape of multimedia technologies in the wake of AI and ML. The research objectives of this study are listed below:

a. Identification and in-depth analysis of key privacy and security challenges for next generation multimedia applications.

b. Analysis and discussion of addressing multimedia privacy and security, using AI and ML.

The review was carried out by using publicly available secondary data sources that explore and discuss different aspects of AI and ML in multimedia technologies in diverse sectors. The main data sources used in this review are SCOPUS library, Web of Science citation database, ACM library, IEEE Xplorer, Google Scholar and Research gate. A number of keyword searches were used to find relevant studies and reviews necessary to answer the research questions of this study. An exclusion criterion was not used to provide an extensive overview of the issue. In addition to the initial research by the authors, the recommendations contained in previously published research, tutorials, surveys and reviews were used in selecting prominent multimedia privacy and security challenges to focus on this study.

## 1.2 Structure of the Chapter

This chapter is organized as follows: Section 2 discusses privacy concerns of next generation multimedia content with a special focus on deepfakes; digital rights management/video fingerprinting and authenticity of multimedia content are discussed in Section 3; Section 4 elaborates the key AI and ML techniques in multimedia delivery, while future research directions and challenges are discussed in Section 5. Section 6 concludes the chapter. Figure 1 highlights the structure and major contribution of various sections in this chapter.

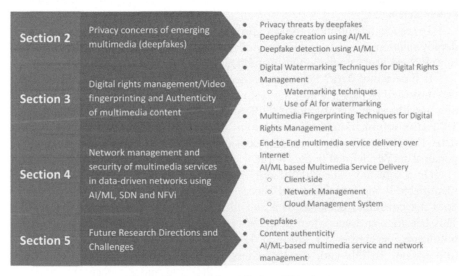

**Fig. 1:** Structure and contribution of this chapter.

# Section 2: Privacy Concerns of Emerging Multimedia (Deepfakes)

## 2. Introduction

Multimedia information should be original (i.e., authentic) and the users should feel safe when consuming multimedia content. With the increase in face-swapping applications and deepfake generators, authenticity of multimedia content is under threat more than ever.

Recent research suggests that famous apps, such as TikTok are in the process of introducing deepfakes into their platforms (TechCrunch, 2021). These emerging apps could harvest a large amount of face data to train their models and to improve the accuracy of this generation applications. In 2019, the Chinese firm was fined a record $5.7m by the Federal Trade Commission (FTC), for mishandling data belonging to juveniles (children). This was followed by a recent legal challenge brought against TikTok by Anne Longfield, the former British Commissioner for Children, over the methods TikTok used to collect and use children's data (BBC News, 2021).

On the other hand, it is possible to use acquired face data for unauthorised face swaps and create deepfakes, which will have a significant impact on privacy and security of the users.

Increasingly, governments around the world are reacting to these privacy-evading applications (e.g., India banning TikTok and USA investigating the privacy issues of TikTok (Matsakis, 2021) and are in the process of enacting laws to minimise the impact of deepfakes. For instance, USA passed the Deepfakes Accountability Act in 2019 which mandated deepfakes to be watermarked for the purpose of identification (TechCrunch, 2021).

To reduce the imminent threat to privacy, future multimedia applications should deploy solutions to verify authenticity of content and in turn, protect user privacy and improve end-user satisfaction or overall Quality of Security (i.e., QoSec).

**Is it personal data?** Some researchers argue that fake images or videos cannot be considered as personal data since it can no longer be attributed to any individual after modification. According to GDPR, personal data does not need to be objective. Subjective information, such as opinions, judgements or estimates can be personal data. Therefore, deepfakes could be considered within the broader classification of personal data as defined in the GDPR.

On a separate issue, GDPR only applies to information which relates to an identifiable living individual and hence, information relating to a deceased person does not constitute personal data and therefore, is not governed by the GDPR. This becomes an issue when deepfakes of deceased individuals, such as popular politicians, celebrities or spiritual leaders are created to provide misleading information. To this end, the legislators are enacting supplementary laws (e.g., Privacy Act of Hungary (Radmilovic et al., 2021) to make it necessary to obtain consent from the heirs of deceased persons.

**Creation of deepfakes:** If we can categorise deepfakes as personal data, processing of personal images or videos needs to be subjected to either informed consent or legitimate interest. If the creators (controllers or processors) fail to obtain prior consent, they are in violation of GDPR regulation.

The consent has to be obtained twice in this case: the consent should be obtained not only from the person in the original video, but also from the person in the fabricated/faked video. The users need to be vigilant when using apps, such as Faceapp, TikTok or any other emerging-face apps and read their privacy notices carefully to understand how their data is used for further processing.

The acquired face data may not necessarily be used for creating deepfakes; rather as training data for their models. Either way, to avoid privacy and security infringements, explicit consent obligation should be enforced on the apps in these categories.

Under GDPR, it is necessary to carry out a Data Protection Impact Assessment (DPIA) to minimise the risk to individuals during processing (ICO, 2021). The use of new technologies (such as creating deepfakes using algorithms, such as Generative Adversarial Networks (GANs)) and collection of biometric data (including face data) are processing activities that require DPIA under the GDPR to minimise the risks to individuals. These measures have inbuilt capacity to protect privacy of individuals who use these new apps.

**Potential solutions:** The use of video fingerprinting and marking the content explicitly as fabricated content would to some extent be a solution to this problem (see Section 3 for more details on fingerprinting). Another popular approach is to probe the provenance of the image and video content to find the origin, for example, by conducting a reverse image search to find a similar content that previously appeared. Recent research also suggests that distributed technology solutions, such as blockchain can provide a solution much needed for screening against fake news, disinformation and deepfakes (Fraga-Lamas and Fernández-Caramés, 2020).

AI and ML algorithms, such as GANs are widely deployed to create true like deepfakes. The collection of sample data through emerging face apps, with or without user consent, have increased the effectiveness of these algorithms by having a large training dataset to train these algorithms. Most of the proposed detection methods are also based on AI and ML (Nguyen et al., 2021). However, it will take considerable time to train these detection models; also embedding these complex detection algorithms in real-time applications and delivery chain will be a challenge.

In similarity to generation of deepfakes, detection algorithms need to go through a training phase, which will result in collecting more user data, which would in turn, infringe user privacy. The subsections below discuss deepfake creation and detection, using AI/ML.

## 2.1 Deepfake Creation using AI/ML

Most of the deepfake creation applications are inspired by deep learning approaches. Deep learning is widely used to represent complex and high dimensional data. The deep auto-encoder is one such deep network, which has been deployed for reducing the dimensionality and achieving compression efficiency (Cheng et al., 2019). One of the first applications of deepfake creation was Fakeapp, which was based on auto-encoder decoder-pairing structure (FakeApp, 2021). The improved versions of deepfake creations inspired by Generative Adversarial Network (GAN) are emerging (Faceswap-GAN, 2021) (CycleGAN, 2021). Furthermore, other forms of AI/ML algorithms, such as multi-task Convolutional Neural Network (CNN) have been introduced to improve stability of face detection and alignment (FaceNet, 2021).

A collection of deepfake creation algorithms is available on GitHub for research and development (Faceswap, 2021). A comprehensive review of deepfake creations is provided in De Lima et al. (2020). Table 1 below highlights some prominent deepfake creation efforts to date.

**Table 1:**  Deepfake creation applications and their features.

| Tool | Features | AI/ML | Link |
|------|----------|-------|------|
| Faceswap GAN (Faceswap-GAN, 2021) | Based on auto-encoder architecture VGG face: adversarial and perceptual loss | GAN | GitHub - shaoanlu/ faceswap-GAN: A denoising auto-encoder + adversarial losses and attention mechanisms for face swapping |
| Few-Shot Face Translation (Huang et al., 2019) | GAN processing of extracted latent embeddings from a pre-trained face recognition model | GAN | https://github.com/sh aoanlu/fewshot-face-translation-GAN |
| Transformable Bottleneck Networks (Olszewski et al., 2019) | CNN models (spatial transformations) using a transformable bottleneck framework (Shih and Zong, 2016) | CNN | https://github.com/k yleolsz/TB-Networks |
| StyleRig (Tewari et al., 2020) | Pretrained and fixed Style GAN via 3D morphable face models. Self-supervised without manual annotations | StyleGAN | https://gvv.mpi-inf.mpg. de/projects/StyleRig |

## 2.2  *Deepfake Detection using AI/ML*

Deepfake detection algorithms came into practice with the introduction of deepfake creation methodologies. Most of the early algorithms were based on imperfections introduced during the image synthesis process. However, the second generation of detection algorithms is inspired by AI/ML (i.e., methods based on deep learning approaches). Most of these algorithms automatically extract salient and image disparities to detect deepfakes (De Lima et al., 2020). The classification models are widely used to determine whether the video is original or fake. However, a large number of original and fake videos are required to train these classifiers. In the early stages of deepfake detection, the unavailability of suitable deepfake videos was a significant challenge. However, deepfake video databases as presented in VidTIMIT database (2021), began to appear in the literature to support further research and development. Early research showed that deepfake detection efforts using face recognition, lip-synching and image quality metrics produced high error rates (arxiv. org., 2021). The deepfake detection in videos can be classified, based on the features exploited by those algorithms (see Fig. 2).

The majority of deepfake video detection algorithms use some sort of deep learning approaches—some are applied in the spatial domain, whereas others are

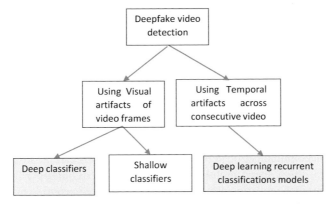

**Fig. 2:** Deepfake detection using spatial and temporal image/video features.

applied in the temporal domain. Table 2 summarises some of these algorithms in detail.

**Table 2:** Recent deepfake detection algorithms.

| Detection Method | AI/ML Technique | Key Features | Temporal/ Spatial Features |
|---|---|---|---|
| Recurrent convolutional strategies for face manipulation detection in videos (Sabir et al., 2019) | Recurrent Convolutional Network (RCN) | RCN and gated recurrent unit cells: Quantifies temporal discrepancies across video frames | Spatial/Temporal |
| Deepfake video detection using recurrent neural networks (Guera and Delp, 2018) | CNN and long short-term memory (LSTM) | CNN: Extracts frame-level features LSTM: Creates a temporal sequence descriptor | Spatial/Temporal |
| Fake video detection using eye blinking (Li et al., 2018) | Long-term Recurrent Convolutional Network (LRCN) | CNN: Extracts face and eye features LTSM: Sequence learning | Spatial/Temporal |
| Deepfake video detection using face warping artifacts (Li and Lyu, 2019) | CNN models | CNN: Artifacts are discovered, based on resolution inconsistency between the warped face area and the surrounding context | Spatial |
| Capsule networks to detect forgedimages and videos (Nguyen et al., 2017) | Capsule networks | VGG-19 network: Extracts latentfeatures Capsule network: Classifies theimages and videos | Spatial |
| 3D head comprises head orientation and position (Yang et al., 2019) | SVM (shallow classifier) | Feature extraction: 68 facial landmarks of the central face region SVM: Classification | Spatial |

## Section 3: Digital Rights Management/Video Fingerprinting and Authenticity of Multimedia Content

## 3. Introduction

Due to recent advances in semiconductor technology, electronic devices, such as mobile phones, tablets and laptops are becoming increasingly affordable. Due to rapid developments in multimedia technology, many of these devices are now equipped with multimedia capture, display and transmission capabilities. Moreover, in terms of telecommunication services, three main trends can be observed over the last few years—high speed mobile networks (such as 4G and 5G (Agiwal et al., 2021) are expanding, covering more area and people), are becoming more affordable and faster (e.g., from 3G to 4G to 5G). As a result of all these factors, multimedia content sharing/distribution over the Internet has seen an explosive growth over the past decade. Unlike in the past, when content was mainly generated and shared by big companies, including television broadcasters, recently there have been two new important players in this regard—OTT service providers (e.g., Netflix, Amazon Prime, etc.) and User Generated Content (UGC) creators. Both OTT service providers and UGC creators generate revenue by creating and sharing/distributing copyrighted content. For example, OTT services earned a total of US$ 106 billion in 2020 (*Digital TV Research Report*, 2021). In the same year, Ryan Kaji, a nine-year-old boy alone earned US$ 29.5 million by creating and sharing content over YouTube (Neate, 2020). Both OTT service providers and UGC creators are faced with the common threat of copyright infringement which can affect their revenues. Therefore, many efforts are currently underway to develop techniques which can efficiently identify and protect copyrighted content.

Digital Rights Management (DRM) tools facilitate the lawful distribution of multimedia content over the Internet. Most of the new DRM solutions are based on a few core approaches, such as digital watermarking and multimedia fingerprinting (Qin et al., 2020). One of the key differences between the two approaches is that watermarking is based on embedding a signal within the content, while fingerprinting is based on extracting a (unique) fingerprint (also called a 'hash') from the content. While both watermarking and fingerprinting have been used since long, the recent advances in Artificial Intelligence (AI) and Machine Learning (ML) offer new opportunities for developing efficient watermarking and fingerprinting schemes for digital rights management. Some of these approaches are discussed in this section.

### 3.1 Digital Watermarking Techniques for Digital Rights Management (DRM)

Digital watermarking (a term coined by Andrew Tirkel and Charles Osborne in 1992) refers to hiding digital information in a career signal (audio, video or image data) and it is typically used to verify the authenticity of a digital content or identify its ownership, facilitating copyright protection (Digital watermarking, Wikipedia, 2021). Digital watermarking belongs to a family of information-hiding techniques, which also include techniques like covert communication, stenography and anonymous communication (Yu et al., 2018).

Digital watermarks are generally divided into three categories, namely, robust, fragile and semi-fragile watermarks. Robust watermarks are designed to withstand various attacks, hence they are mainly used in cases such as copyright protection. On the other hand, fragile watermarks are sensitive to tampering and any attack on the signal may destroy the watermark information. Therefore, they are primarily used in content authentication and tampering-detection applications. Finally, semi-fragile watermarks offer the benefits of both robust and fragile watermarking techniques (Elrowayati et al., 2020) (Yu et al., 2021). Digital watermarks are considered to be a passive protection tool. It just marks the data but does not attempt to control access to the data. Watermarking is used in numerous applications, including areas like source tracking, where a watermark is inserted to the content at each point of the media distribution chain and checked at relevant points to identify its point of origin. Copyright protection, video authentication, video editing software, fraud and tamper detection, content management in social networks and ID card security are some of the common applications (Digital watermarking, Wikipedia, 2021).

The process of generating a watermark (Fig. 3) generally involves inserting the watermark (m) to the image (I) to generate a marked image (J). The receiver can then extract the watermark (m*) from the received image (J*). The goal of the individual components as well as the watermark generation pipeline (within the context of watermarking) is to minimise the difference between the original watermark (m) and extracted watermark (m*) (Elrowayati, et al., 2020).

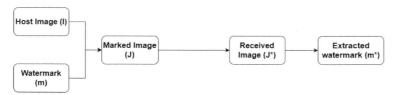

**Fig. 3:** Watermarking pipeline.

### 3.1.1 *Watermarking Techniques*

In addition to the robust, fragile and semi-fragile categories, watermarking can also be grouped into four main categories, based on the domain it is used in (spatial, compressed domain), perceptibility to human vision, extraction process and how the data is inserted into the hosting video (Elrowayati et al., 2020).

Watermarking in the compressed domain is attempted by various methods, typically using the transform blocks and motion vectors. Least Significant Bits (LSB)-based strategies insert the watermark through a bit substitution mechanism. The method is capable of achieving imperceptibility but suffers from robustness as its presence can be revealed using statistical analysis (Shih, 2017). However, the methods to maintain the image statistics to increase the security are investigated in Pevný et al. (2010).

Approaches, such as embedding watermarks on the frequency spectrum, show high security and fidelity (Cox et al., 1997) (Shih and Zhong, 2016) and the work by

Zong et al. (2015) demonstrates that robustness can be improved by embedding the watermark into image histogram.

Kaur et al. (2019) explore the efficient watermarking in the HEVC standard. HEVC uses DCT to de-correlate the residual error that results after the prediction. This work investigates the use of symmetric transforms to embed digital watermarks into appropriate luma transform blocks. In this case, the relationship between the magnitudes of a pair of transform coefficients in a luma transform block is exploited. Extracting the embedded watermark at the decoder is achieved by decoding only the non-zero quantised transform coefficients from a bit stream and the work demonstrates its applicability in real-time applications.

The work proposed in Dai et al. (2003) utilises modifications to motion vectors in MPEG-2 compressed bit streams to embed a digital watermark. In this work, the watermark is embedded within a residual of a large motion vector. The retrieval process at the decoder involves regularising the motion residual with little impact on the decoding speed and perceptual visual quality.

An algorithm for compressed domain digital watermarking on I, P and B frames is proposed in Kang et al. (n.d.). The goal is to reduce the processing time and make the existence of the watermark invisible when comparing the compressed original and watermarked MPEG streams.

Commutative encryption and data hiding algorithm for HEVC are proposed in Xu (2019) as a compressed domain technique which results in minimal visual distortion. The work explores the use of sign of the quantised transform coefficient, sign of the motion vector difference and intra-prediction mode information for this purpose within the HEVC standard.

Videos can be easily manipulated and altered by using techniques like trimming, cropping, recompressing and transcoding. Thus any digital watermark should be robust and imperceptible to the human eye. Hence, determining where to embed the watermark is crucial to the success of the process. In the work proposed in Khmag (2021) 4x4 intra predicted sub-blocks are analysed for spatio-temporal features to select most suitable embedding regions.

### 3.1.2   *Use of AI for Watermarking*

Use of machine learning techniques, such as deep neural networks for image watermarking is becoming prominent with the proliferation of efficient and complex neural network architectures. A primary concern in a watermarking system is to offer imperceptibility of the digital signature to the human visual system and to provide undetectability to computer analysis, i.e., the watermark needs to be robust; meaning the watermark should retain even if the image gets distorted (Cox et al., 1997). In this regard, neural networks are used within different aspects of digital watermarking.

Visible watermarks are prominent in most of the video contents and it is considered a direct and easy method for copyright protection. However, identifying a suitable location for a watermark and ensuring the resistance to editing and other attacks are two of the biggest challenges in this domain. Therefore, determining the embedding position for a watermark is one such area where intelligent NN-based machine learning models are heavily utilised. For instance, Brandão and Jorge (2016) and Jarušek et al. (2015) are utilising the machine learning models to determine the significance of bits of each pixel and GANs to determine the embedding position for the watermark (Tang et al., 2017). A complex use of deep neural networks to hide a full-sized image within an image of the size is proposed by Baluja et al. (Baluja, 2017). The network is jointly trained to distribute the secret image across all available bits rather than the traditional use of LSB of the carrier image. Use of saliency-based visual attention models (Cui et al., 2021) identify embedding regions and distribution of texture complexity is a common approach in these algorithms. Making the process adaptive as proposed in Cui et al. (2021) can reduce the risk of batch removal attacks. Yu and Li (Yu et al., 2021) propose a similar algorithm where texture blocks are divided into multiple patches and are then sorted to identify the blocks which are suited for data hiding.

A neural network to embed a watermark in the DCT coefficient block and a companion network to extract it from the watermarked image is proposed by Li et al. (2019). Robustness of these digital watermarks is identified as a compelling research challenge and Mun et al. (Mun et al., 2019) attempt to integrate attack simulations into the training process to overcome the robustness issues.

Watermark extraction from camera resamples is considered another challenging issue in this domain and work proposed in Zhong et al. (2019), using a DNN, achieve high capacity and high robustness. The experimental results revealing a PSNR of 39.72 dB means a high fidelity in the marked images, i.e., hidden information is not noticeable to the human vision.

Excessive time consumption of watermarking techniques is another issue that needs to be considered. A time-efficient artificial bee colony algorithm is used in Abdelhakim and Abdelhakim (2018) to introduce a watermark-embedding mechanism in the DCT domain.

Watermark's ability to recover under high tampering rates is often considered an important criterion but has often failed to achieve by most of the algorithms proposed in the literature. However, this can be mitigated by seeking an approximate solution to each tampered character-bit group and following a priority assignment of such groups (Zhang et al., 2021), or by reducing the feature dimension as proposed by Ma et al. (2021).

### 3.2 Multimedia Fingerprinting Techniques for DRM

Multimedia fingerprinting is an alternate approach to digital watermarking. One of the limitations of the watermarking approach is that by embedding a signal, the original content is altered, which may result in visual distortion. On the other hand, multimedia fingerprinting offers an alternative DRM approach by extracting a set of features, called a 'fingerprint' or 'perceptual hash', from the content. The fingerprint (or perceptual hash) is then compared with a library of known fingerprints registered by copyright owners. If a match is found, the content is considered to be copyright protected (Agiwal et al., 2021). An important challenge in developing fingerprinting algorithms is to generate perceptually robust, discriminative and compact fingerprints (Agiwal et al., 2021). Perceptual robustness is required so that the fingerprinting algorithm can recognise the content even if the content goes through content-preserving manipulations during distribution (e.g., JPEG compression) or intentional attempts to make them unrecognisable by fingerprinting algorithm (e.g., rotation, scaling, translation attacks). Discriminative capability allows the fingerprints of two visually distinct contents to have a large distance between them. Lastly, compactness requires that the fingerprint should be as short as possible for efficient matching.

Fingerprinting algorithms generally consist of two steps: feature extraction and quantization. Traditional fingerprinting algorithms involve extracting hand-crafted features; on the other hand, AI/ML-based methods rely on neural networks to extract fingerprint features (*Digital TV Research Report*, 2021). Handcrafted features have two main problems: they cannot demonstrate satisfactory robustness against different distortions, and it is computationally impossible to jointly optimise feature extraction and quantisation if they are separately designed, as it is proven to be an NP-hard problem (Monga et al., 2006). On the other hand, AI/ML-based algorithms use neural networks as a hierarchy of feature extractors and allow fingerprinting algorithms to learn features that are both robust and discriminative. By combining feature extraction and quantisation into a unified framework, AI/ML-based algorithms also overcome the limitation associated with traditional fingerprinting algorithms, where the individual steps of feature extraction and quantisation are hard to jointly optimise.

The content identification accuracy and robustness of AI/ML-based fingerprinting algorithms can be optimised by sufficient training. For example, a pre-training algorithm can be added to each layer of a neural network (e.g., a denoising auto-encoder) to train it to reduce the differences between the different representations of the original image and its distorted versions. Similarly, a fine-tuning algorithm can be added to improve the content identification accuracy. In order to make an AI/ML-based fingerprinting algorithm secure, a key-dependent randomisation technique is also added.

While very popular in other computer vision applications, Convolutional Neural Networks (CNN) were not used in early AI/ML-based fingerprinting algorithms. There were two main reasons for this: firstly, the use of CNN made it very difficult to quantitatively analyse the security of the fingerprinting algorithm; secondly, some studies showed that small intensity noise can have a huge effect on the performance of CNN and, hence, that CNN is sensitive to distortion (Rodner et al., 2016). This is an undesirable property in the context of content fingerprinting. For example, copyright-protected files, which use CNN-based fingerprinting algorithm, can be made undetectable by slightly modifying the content. However, recently, it has been found that CNNs with multiple constraints can be efficiently used for content fingerprinting (Qin et al., 2020). This is achieved by not using the CNN to extract features directly but to use it to learn the process of feature extraction through a deep neural network, according to a training target. A fully connected layer is then used to generate the final fingerprint. Two pairs of constraint targets (one each for perceptually identical images and distinct images) are also constructed and then integrated into a total cost function with weight allocation. Such a CNN-based content fingerprinting algorithm can achieve better content identification performance compared to other AI/ML-based and traditional fingerprinting algorithms, using the comparable size of fingerprints. In terms of execution time, such a CNN-based algorithm can be marginally slower than other neural network-based algorithms but substantially faster than traditional methods. It has also been proved to be robust against eight content-preserving attacks, including JPEG compression, Gaussian noise, speckle noise, circular average filtering, median filtering, rotation + cropping, gamma correction and scaling. Lastly, since perceptual robustness and discriminative capability are contradictory requirements, an optimal trade-off between the two is often required to be achieved. This can be done by introducing a training method in which the structure of the training set is set dynamically, i.e., the number of perceptually identical images and the number of perceptually distinct images in the training set can be made dependent on the constraint values of robustness and discrimination.

## Section 4: Network Management and Security of Multimedia Services in Data-driven Networks using AI/ML, SDN and NFVi

## 4. Introduction

The network-enabling technologies, such as Software-Defined Networking (SDN), Network Function Virtualizsation (NFV) and Multi-access Edge Computing (MEC) empowers next-generation networks to exploit softwarisation and virtualisation for deploying efficient network and service management while ensuring privacy and security for multimedia applications (Ahmad et al., 2020) and (Ahmad and Atzori, 2020). The network softwarisation and virtualisation-equipped future networks with programmability, automation of the network functions, control and optimisation, scalability, on-demand deployment, distributive computing, ultra-low latency, high bandwidth and deployment of the network function at network edge (Barakabitze et al., 2021) (Cofano et al., 2017). Furthermore, the network-enabling technologies allow the deployment of data-driven approaches, based on machine learning (ML) and Artificial Intelligence (AI) for network and service management of multimedia services. For example, AI/ML-based data-driven QoE/QoS prediction/ measurement solutions for multimedia services can be deployed on top of SDN controller in the application plane, thus allowing automation to network management and control operations by considering the user-perceived quality (QoE) of multimedia applications. Indeed, the deployment of AI/ML-based service optimisation and security solutions in the next-generation networks open new research opportunities and challenges (Google Edge Network, 2021) and (Schneier, 2007).

The section has the following multi-fold contributions:

1. Firstly, we discuss multimedia end-to-end service delivery and different roles of the major entities in the service delivery.

2. Secondly, we provide an insight into the application of the AI/ML models in the multimedia service in the next-generation networks.

The section is structured as follows: Section 4.1 provides details of the multimedia service delivery, while Section 4.2 investigates the application of the AI/ML in multimedia service and network management in future networks. Section 5.3 discusses the key challenges and future research directions related to AI/ML application in the multimedia service delivery.

## 4.1  Multimedia Service Delivery

Mostly, the multimedia services over the Internet are being delivered in the client-server configuration. Figure 4 represents OTT end-to-end multimedia service delivery which involves the following entities:

- OTT—delivers multimedia services to end users over the Internet. The multimedia contents/services are delivered to users by the OTT media servers/ cloud autonomous domain connected to ISP networks. The OTT media server/ cloud is responsible for serving users' requests with multimedia contents/ services.

- ISP—provides the Internet connection to the end user for utilising services/ applications over the Internet. The ISP network consisting of the core and access

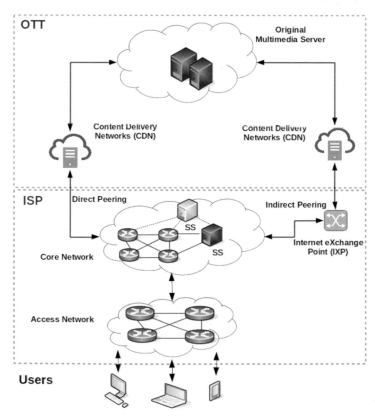

**Fig. 4:** End-to-end multimedia service delivery over Internet.

network connects client-side OTT multimedia applications in the users' devices with the OTT media server/cloud infrastructure.

- Users—utilise the OTT multimedia services delivered over the Internet by connecting to the ISP networks. The client-side of the multimedia services works on users' devices and requests multimedia services from the OTT server/cloud.

The ISP network and OTT cloud infrastructure are connected either by direct peering or by indirect peering, using Internet eXchange Point (IXP). Nowadays, most of the OTT multimedia services use regional Content Delivery Networks (CDNs) to lower the end-to-end latency of the content retrieval/service response. Similarly, some OTT multimedia services collaborate with ISP and use Surrogate Servers (SS) at the network's edge of the ISP to lower the end-to-end latency of the multimedia service delivery. For example, Netflix Open Connect (Netflix, 2021) and Google Global Cache (Google Edge Network, 2021) allow collaborating ISPs to host their surrogate servers, which not only reduce end-to-end delay of the multimedia service but also decrease unnecessary traffic in the ISPs' core network. Both OTT and ISP have different roles in the multimedia service delivery: OTT manages the server and client of the multimedia applications based on the provided network stats, while ISP performs network optimisation and operations based on the application type/usage.

## 4.2 AI/ML-based Multimedia Service Delivery

The next-generation networks based on the network-enabling technologies, such as SDN, NFV and MEC provide a huge opportunity to use AI/ML-based solutions for network management of multimedia applications. Figure 5 shows AI/ML-based data-driven multimedia service and network management in the next-generation 5G/6G networks. The AI/ML-based solution can be deployed in the multimedia

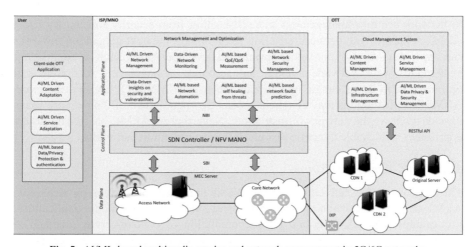

**Fig. 5:** AI/ML-based multimedia service and network management in 5G/6G networks.

service chain in the following places, depending upon the optimisation objectives and roles of the involved entities: client-side OTT application, ISP's network management and operations and OTT cloud-management systems. The rest of the section describes the AI/ML-solution deployment in the multimedia delivery.

### 4.2.1 Client-side

The OTT multimedia services are consumed by users through the client-side implementation of the OTT applications. In the case of traditional multimedia applications, such as VoIP, video conferencing and video streaming applications, the multimedia client application adapts bitrates, video resolutions, video/audio quality based on the estimated network Key Performance Indicators (KPIs). For example, in the case of HTTP adaptive video streaming (HAS), traditionally the client-side adaptation algorithm optimises the content bitrate, server selection and video resolutions by using estimated network bandwidth (Cofano et al., 2017). The AI/ML-based content/service adaptation can be used for the OTT client-side optimization of multimedia services to improve QoE/QoS. Moreover, AI/ML-based solutions for user's data privacy protection and authentication can also be deployed on the client side which may enhance the cybersecurity of multimedia applications.

### 4.2.2 Network Management

The next-generation networks can leverage SDN/NFV-enabled softwarised and virtualised infrastructure for AI/ML-driven network management and optimisation of multimedia services. The AI/ML-based network management solution deployed application plane on top of SDN controller and NFV management and orchestration (MANO), using north/south bound APIs (NBI/SBI) to deliver automation to network management and optimisation by equipping future networks with data-driven network monitoring/insight on network security and vulnerabilities, AI/ML-based QoE/QoS and network faults prediction/measurements, an enhancement to network security management and self-healing from security threats. By using AI/ML solutions with network-enabling technologies, the next-generation networks can apply data-driven approaches toward network operations, such as application-aware/QoE-aware network slicing and resource management. AI-driven cost optimisation to lower capital/operational expenses (CAPEX/OPEX). Furthermore, AI/ML-based solutions may also help predict the requirement of the network usage to scale up/down the network infrastructure. Nevertheless, AI/ML-based data-driven approaches will enable dynamic resource allocation to future networks.

### 4.2.3 Cloud Management System

The OTT provider can empower the cloud management system by deploying AI/ML-driven solutions to optimise the server-side of the multimedia applications. For example, AI/ML solutions for the prediction of content/service demand in different regions across the globe over time may result in delivering higher service quality and effective management of the cloud infrastructure, while lowering the cost for underutilized cloud resources. The data-driven approaches may not only automate the cloud infrastructure management of multimedia in terms of content/ service management but also provide AI/ML-based data privacy and security to the users.

# Section 5: Future Research Directions and Challenges

## 5.1 Deepfakes

There is a constant battle between deepfake creation and detection algorithms based on AI and ML. It is apparent that deepfake detection algorithms are advancing by the day to counter emerging creation algorithm. However, some of these algorithms are based on the imperfections created during the deepfake creation pipeline. Therefore, some of these detection algorithms will fail in the absence of prior knowledge of deepfake creation algorithms. Therefore, future deepfake detection algorithms based on AI/ML should be capable of detecting the deepfake from feature extraction alone.

Another key challenge is the lack of datasets to train deepfake-detection algorithms. Even though there is an apparent increase in openly available deepfake image/s and video databases, more work needs to be done in order to accurately and efficiently evaluate the emerging algorithms. In addition, the distribution networks of multimedia (e.g., Facebook, YouTube) can be equipped with filters and tools to detect deepfakes. Moreover, researchers have suggested techniques, such as blockchain technology to enable immutable metadata during digital content creation. This could be an effective way to deal with deepfakes by blocking the possibility at the multimedia content-creation stage.

In the light of these deepfake-associated risks and threats, the urgency of the need to develop laws and policies could not be emphasised more. However, the biggest issues concerning the development of laws is the fast-growing capabilities of technology and the legal loopholes/gaps in the legislature to regulate online platforms and such technology, like deepfake. The process of revising/updating existing laws and produce legal mechanisms in response to deepfake takes time; therefore, solutions such as blockchain technology should be used to minimise the challenging risks posed by deepfake.

## 5.2 Multimedia Authenticity

1. Generating a common fingerprint representation

Perceptual robustness is an important requirement for content fingerprinting algorithms. Since multimedia content can be subjected to a variety of attacks, it is important that a fingerprinting algorithm should be robust to different types of attacks. However, many fingerprinting algorithms use features which are robust against only a single or limited number of attack types. Hence, an important challenge is to find ways in which different features can be combined to generate a common fingerprint representation (Shamir, 1979).

2. Blockchain-based content authentication systems

Blockchain technology (Blakely, 1979) is a promising tool which can be used to help find, track and monetise digital content. Transparency, decentralization, collective maintenance and trackability are some of the features of blockchain technology which can be useful for content authentication systems (Ukwandu, 2019). Although, there are some commercially available blockchain-based content authentication systems (e.g., (Floris et al., n.d.) (Hantouti et al., 2020), there is lack of available literature in this area. Hence, exploiting blockchain for efficient content authentication is an open research area.

## 5.3  Content Delivery: AI/ML-based Multimedia Service and Network Management

There are many research challenges confronting AI/ML-based multimedia services and network management as data outsourcing continues to gain ground and acceptance because of its economy of scale, use and deployment. This section will be dedicated to discussing some security challenges confronting this domain of service and the adaptability of this service in resource-constrained devices. The use of resource-constrained devices, such as mobile phones, tablet computers and personal digital assistants has become ubiquitous as a result of their mobility, convenience, increase in sophistication and high-speed Internet penetration with 4G and the budding 5G/6G networks.

Currently, the use of encryption mechanisms to safeguard multimedia files outsourced to public storage facilities (cloud storage) has been adjudged to be convenient, common and easily deployable, but the management of encryption key is as tedious and cumbersome as encryption itself (Schneier, 2007). The practice of storage outsourcing has increased computational mobility, thereby making the use of services on high demand convenient, thus bringing to fore the debate about the preference of having strong security as a trade-off to convenience use of services or use of service as a trade-off for strong security of services. Also, for AI/ML to work effectively, privacy is an issue as large datasets are usually required. These not only breed privacy breach, but also social issues bothering the reputation of affected individual or organisation during leakage, theft or cyber-attacks. Some examples include the Cambridge Analytical scandal—Facebook (Cadwalladr and Graham-Harrison, 2021), Clearview Face Recognition scandal (O'Flaherty, 2020) and so on. Furthermore, the use of large datasets in AI/ML makes the deployment, storage and utilization of the services on resource-constrained device a research concern.

Redundancy technology by creating copies of stored multimedia files across multiple storage facilities as currently practised by using data caching technology has been prominent in recent times, as applied in content delivery networks. This practice has been effective but does not in any way mitigate data leakage, outage, theft or damage during attacks or technological hitch as experienced in 27 minutes of Cloudflare outage of 2020 (Graham-Cumming, 2020) and 45 minutes of Fastly outages of 2021 (Hern, 2021). In lieu of this, therefore, a technique that will break data into meaningless granules and store them across multiple storage nodes as objects in such a way that loss, outage or attacks of some nodes will not inhibit the recovery of the original data will be a good research direction. The foundation of the technology had already been established by the works of Adi Shamir (Shamir, 1979) and George Blakley (Blakely, 1979) in 1979, but because their scheme was originally designed to be used in safeguarding encryption keys, the use and application in multimedia files that are usually large and build up to a large-scale data infrastructure has been adjudged not scalable (Ukwandu, 2019).

In lieu of the 4th industrial revolution of 'smart everything', the use of attribute-based encryption that uses the unique attributes of the user to create encryption key for which user's data is encrypted with policy on who is authorised to access data will in no small measure mitigate the issue of privacy of AI/ML data. It also has the capability to provide a user-centric data access design in data structure in such a way that data owner will be able to recognise how the data is used day to day. This also has the capability of self-enforcing GDPR, irrespective of the location data which is domiciled.

### 5.3.1 Secure and Standardized Interfaces for Service and Network Management

The deployment of AI/ML-based data-driven approaches in the multimedia service and network management requires secure standardised interfaces for data monitoring and information exchange among the involved entities (users, OTTs and ISPs), Virtual Network Functions (VNFs), inter/intra slice SDN controller, cloud management systems and NFV MANO for the dynamic resource allocation and automation of network and service management (Floris et al., 2018) and (Hantouti et al., 2020). The extension of the existing web socketing and Remote Procedure Call (RPC) can assist towards the development of standardised and secure interfaces for information exchange for the AI/ML-driven network and service management. Furthermore, the data-driven QoE-aware network management of OTT multimedia applications also requires standardised interfaces for sharing QoE KPIs for QoE monitoring and management (Ahmad et al., 2017) (Ahmad et al., 2017) and (Ahmad et al., 2017).

### 5.3.2 Tradeoff of Monitoring Frequency and Control Plane Traffic

For AI/ML-enabled network and service management of multimedia applications, finding the optimal frequency of the monitoring solutions is an open research challenge as higher monitoring frequency results in higher control plane traffic and large amounts of the data while lower monitoring frequency may lead to affect the prediction accuracy and effectiveness of timely optimisation of the resources (Ahmad et al., 2019). Future research in the direction of the ultra-compressed standardised data representation format can promise a decrease in the volume of the control traffic data. The data monitoring frequency highly depends on the time interval of the optimisation, data/accuracy requirements of the optimisation algorithm and time-period of the optimisation. For example, if the optimisation is occurring at O-RAN near-real-time, the RAN Intelligent Controller (RIC) will require extremely fast and secure interfaces for information retrieval in comparison to optimisation at non-real-time RIC and NFV MANO (Floris et al., 2018).

### 5.3.3  *Computational Requirement Trustworthiness of Data and Self-healing to Threats*

Most of the AI/ML algorithms are computationally expensive and require high computational power. The computational requirements of AI/ML models may also vary, based on the placements, e.g., deployment at MEC will require AI/ML to be less computationally expensive due to limited resources at MEC. Nevertheless, the application of the AI/ML-driven approaches in future networks and service management may require network and cloud infrastructure to be equipped with hardware acceleration (FPGA/GPU processing). Future research is required for optimising the computational complexity of AI/ML models according to the placement and use case. Furthermore, the prediction performance and efficiency of the AI/ML-based data-driven approaches highly depends on the trustworthiness of the underlying dataset. Therefore, further research is needed to perform qualitative as well as quantitative studies on the trustworthiness of datasets for training and testing of the AI/ML models. Indeed, future research is needed on AI/ML solution security from adversarial attacks for self-healing in network automation and management (Benzaid and Taleb, 2020).

## Section 6: Conclusion

This chapter discusses contemporary privacy and security issues related to multimedia content and delivery. It highlights how AI- and ML-inspired technologies help the multimedia technology in preserving privacy and security in emerging application domains. AI and ML technologies can play a bigger role for multimedia in the process of overcoming privacy and security challenges of next-generation multimedia applications, as discussed in the chapter. In contrast to other application domains, AI/ML-inspired technologies are used by both adversaries and controllers for attack and protection, respectively. Therefore, extensive (or further) research and development should be undertaken to ensure that AI/ML are widely used across multimedia applications for tackling privacy invasion and security issues.

## References

Abdelhakim, A.M. and Abdelhakim, M. (June 2018). A time-efficient optimization for robust image watermarking using machine learning. *Expert Syst. Appl.*, 100: 197–210. doi: 10.1016/j.eswa.2018.02.002.

Agiwal, M., Kwon, H., Park, S. and Jin, H. (2021). A survey on 4G-5G dual connectivity: Road to 5G implementation. *IEEE Access*, 9: 16193–16210.

Ahmad, A. and Atzori, L. (2020). MNO-OTT collaborative video streaming in 5G: The zero-rated QoE approach for quality and resource management. *IEEE Transactions on Network and Service Management*, 17(1): 361–374. doi: 10.1109/tnsm.2019.2942716.

Ahmad, A., Atzori, L. and Martini, M.G. (2017). Qualia: A multilayer solution for QoE passive monitoring at the user terminal. *2017 IEEE International Conference on Communications (ICC)*. doi: 10.1109/icc.2017.7997262.

Ahmad, A., Floris, A. and Atzori, L. (2016). QoE-centric service delivery: A collaborative approach among OTTs and ISPs. *Computer Networks*, 110: 168–179. doi: 10.1016/j.comnet.2016.09.022.

Ahmad, A., Floris, A. and Atzori, L. (2017). OTT-ISP joint service management: A customer lifetime value based approach. *2017 IFIP/IEEE Symposium on Integrated Network and Service Management (IM)*. doi: 10.23919/inm.2017.7987431.

Ahmad, A., Floris, A. and Atzori, L. (2017). Towards QoE monitoring at user terminal: A monitoring approach based on quality degradation. *2017 IEEE International Symposium on Broadband Multimedia Systems and Broadcasting (BMSB)*. doi: 10.1109/bmsb.2017.7986131.

Ahmad, A., Floris, A. and Atzori, L. (2019). Towards information-centric collaborative QoE management using SDN. *2019 IEEE Wireless Communications and Networking Conference (WCNC)*. doi: 10.1109/wcnc.2019.8885412.

Ahmad, A., Floris, A. and Atzori, L. (2020). Timber: An SDN-based emulation platform for experimental research on video streaming. *IEEE Journal on Selected Areas in Communications*, 38(7): 1374–1387. doi: 10.1109/jsac.2020.2999683.

Baluja, S. (2017). *Hiding Images in Plain Sight: Deep Steganography*.

Barakabitze, A.A., Ahmad, A., Mijumbi, R. and Hines, A. (2020). 5G network slicing using SDN and NFV: A survey of taxonomy, architectures and future challenges. *Computer Networks*, 167: 106984. doi: 10.1016/j.comnet.2019.106984.

Barakabitze, A.A. et al. (2020). QoE management of multimedia streaming services in future networks: A tutorial and survey. *IEEE Communications Surveys & Tutorials*, 22(1): 526–565. doi: 10.1109/comst.2019.2958784.

BBC News. (2021). TikTok sued for billions over use of children's data—*BBC News*. [Online]. Available at: https://www.bbc.co.uk/news/technology-56815480 [Accessed 25 June, 2021].

Benzaid, C. and Taleb, T. (2020). AI-driven zero touch network and service management in 5G and beyond: Challenges and research directions. *IEEE Network*, 34(2): 186–194. doi: 10.1109/mnet.001.1900252.

Best, S. (2019). Cybercriminals scam £200,000 out of energy firm by using AI to mimic CEO's voice. [Online]. Available at https://www.mirror.co.uk/tech/cybercriminals-scam-200000-out-energy-19167075 [Accessed 2 June, 2021].

Blakely, G.R. (1979). Safeguarding cryptographic keys. *In: Proc. AFIPS*, 48: 313–317.

Brandão, A.S. and Jorge, D.C. (March 2016). Artificial neural networks applied to image steganography. *IEEE Lat. Am. Trans.*, 14(3): 1361–1366. doi: 10.1109/TLA.2016.7459621.

Cadwalladr, C. and Graham-Harrison, E. (June 2021). Revealed: 50 million Facebook profiles harvested for Cambridge Analytica in major data breach. [Online]. Available at https://tinyurl.com/3fmsbxey [Accessed 10 June, 2021].

Cheng, Z., Sun, H., Takeuchi, M. and Katto, J. (2019). Energy compaction-based image compression using convolutional autoencoder. *IEEE Transactions on Multimedia*. doi: 10.1109/TMM.2019.2938345.

*Cisco Annual Internet Report*. (2018–2023) white paper. [Online]. Available at https://www.cisco.com/c/en/us/solutions/collateral/executive-perspectives/annual-internet- report/white-paper-c11-741490.html [Accessed 31 May, 2021].

Cofano, G., De Cicco, L., Zinner, T., Nguyen-Ngoc, A., Tran-Gia, P. and Mascolo, S. (2017). Design and performance evaluation of network-assisted control strategies for HTTP adaptive streaming. *ACM Transactions on Multimedia Computing, Communications, and Applications*, 13(3s): 1–24. doi: 10.1145/3092836.

Cox, I.J., Kilian, J., Leighton, F.T. and Shamoon, T. (1997). Secure spread spectrum watermarking for multimedia. *IEEE Trans. Image Process*, 6(12): 1673–1687. doi: 10.1109/83.650120.

Cui, Z., Qi, W., Liu, Y. and Guo, J. (2021). Research on region selection strategy for visible watermark embedding. *IETE Tech. Rev.* (Institution Electron. Telecommun. Eng. India), 38(1): 5–16. doi: 10.1080/02564602.2019.1711208.

CycleGAN [Online]. Available at: https://github.com/junyanz/pytorch-CycleGAN-and-pix2pix [Accessed 9 June, 2021].

Dai, Y., Zhang, L. and Yang, Y. (2003). A new method of MPEG video watermarking technology. *In: International Conference on Communication Technology Proceedings, ICCT*, 2: 1845–1847. doi: 10.1109/icct.2003.1209886.

De Lima, O., Franklin, S., Basu, S., Karwoski, B. and George, A. (2020). *Deepfake Detection using Spatio-temporal Convolutional Networks*. arXiv preprint. arXiv:2006.14749.

*Digital TV Research Report*: Global OTT TV and Video Forecast (2021). [Online]. Available at: https://www.digitaltvresearch.com/products/product?id=321 [Accessed: 27 June, 2021].

Digital watermarking—Wikipedia. [Online]. Available at: https://en.wikipedia.org/wiki/Digital_watermarking [Accessed 17 June, 2021].

Elrowayati, A.A., Alrshah, M.A., Abdullah, M.F.L. and Latip, R. (2020). HEVC watermarking techniques for authentication and copyright applications: challenges and opportunities. *IEEE Access*, 8: 114172–114189. doi: 10.1109/ACCESS.2020.3004049.

FaceNet [Online]. Available at https://github.com/davidsandberg/facenet [Accessed 9 June, 2021].

Faceswap. (2021). *Faceswap: Deepfakes Software for all*. [Online]. Available at: https://github.com/deepfakes/faceswap [Accessed 9 June, 2021].

Faceswap-GAN [Online]. Available at: https://github.com/shaoanlu/faceswap-GAN [Accessed 9 June, 2021].

FakeApp. (2021). *FakeApp*. [Online]. Available at: https://www.malavida.com/en/soft/fakeapp/ [Accessed 9 June, 2021].

Farish, K. (2020). The legal implications and challenges of deepfakes. [Online]. Available at: https://www.dacbeachcroft.com/en/gb/articles/2020/september/the-legal-implications-and-challenges-of-deepfakes/ [Accessed 25 May, 2021].

Floris, A., Ahmad, A. and Atzori, L. (2018). QoE-Aware OTT-ISP collaboration in service management. *ACM Transactions on Multimedia Computing, Communications, and Applications*, 14(2s): 1–24. doi: 10.1145/3183517.

Fraga-Lamas, P. and Fernández-Caramés, T.M. (March–April 2020). Fake news, disinformation, and deepfakes: Leveraging distributed ledger technologies and blockchain to combat digital deception and counterfeit reality. *In: IT Professional*, 22(2): 53–59. doi: 10.1109/MITP.2020.2977589.

Google Edge Network. https://peering.google.com [Accessed 7 June, 2021].

Graham-Cumming, J. Cloudflare outage on July 17, 2020. [Online]. Available at https://tinyurl.com/7z8tjf4x [Accessed 5 June, 2021].

Guera, D. and Delp, E.J. (2018, November). Deepfake video detection using recurrent neural networks. *In: 2018 15th IEEE International Conference on Advanced Video and Signal Based Surveillance (AVSS)*. IEEE, pp. 1–6.

Hantouti, H., Benamar, N. and Taleb, T. (2020). Service function chaining in 5G & beyond networks: Challenges and open research issues. *IEEE Network*, 34(4): 320–327. doi: 10.1109/mnet.001.1900554.

Hern, A. (2021). What caused the internet outage that brought down Amazon, Reddit and Gov.uk? [Online]. Available at: https://tinyurl.com/ss3kjpu7 [Accessed 25 May, 2021].

Huang, M.Y., Mallya, X., Karras, A., Aila, T., Lehtinen, T. and Kautz, J. (2019). Few-shot unsupervised image-to-image translation. *In: Proceedings of the IEEE International Conference on Computer Vision*, pp. 10551–10560.

ICO. (2021). Data protection impact assessments/ICO. [Online]. Available at: https://ico.org.uk/for-organisations/guide-to-data-protection/guide-to-the-general-data-protection-regulation-gdpr/accountability-and-governance/data-protection-impact-assessments/ [Accessed 9 June, 2021].

Jarušek, R., Volna, E. and Kotyrba, M. (2015). Neural network approach to image steganography techniques. *In: Advances in Intelligent Systems and Computing*, 2015, 378: 317–327. doi: 10.1007/978-3-319-19824-8_26.

Johnson, D. (2021). What is a deepfake? *Everything You need to Know about the AI-powered Fake Media*. [Online]. Available at https://www.businessinsider.com/what-is-deepfake?r=US&IR=T [Accessed 20 May 2021].

Kang, K.P., Choi, Y.H. and Choi, T.S. (2004). Real-time video watermarking for MPEG streams. *Lect. Notes Comput. Sci. (including Subser. Lect. Notes Artif. Intell. Lect. Notes Bioinformatics)*, vol. 3046 LNCS, No. PART 4, pp. 348–358. doi: 10.1007/978-3-540- 24768-5_37.

Kaur, G., Kasana, S.S. and Sharma, M.K. (May, 2019). An efficient watermarking scheme for enhanced high efficiency video coding/h.265. *Multimed. Tools Appl.*, 78(9): 12537–12559. doi: 10.1007/s11042-018-6791-x.

Khmag, A. (June 2021). A robust watermarking technique for High-Efficiency Video Coding (HEVC) based on blind extraction scheme. *SN Comput. Sci. 2021*, 24, 2(4): 329. doi: 10.1007/s42979-021-00729-y.

Li, D., Deng, L., Gupta, B. Wang, H. and Choi, C. (April 2019). A novel CNN based security guaranteed image watermarking generation scenario for smart city applications. *Inf. Sci. (Ny)*, 479: 432–447. doi: 10.1016/j.ins.2018.02.060.

Li, Y. and Lyu, S. (2019). Exposing deepfake videos by detecting face warping artifacts. *In: Proceedings of the IEEE14 Conference on Computer Vision and Pattern Recognition Workshops*, pp. 46–52.

Li, Y., Chang, M.C. and Lyu, S. (December, 2018). Inictu oculi: Exposing AI created fake videos by detecting eye blinking. *In: 2018 IEEE International Workshop on Information Forensics and Security (WIFS)*. IEEE, pp. 1–7.

Li, Y., Wang, D. and Tang, L. (2019). Robust and secure image fingerprinting learned by neural network. *IEEE Transactions on Circuits and Systems for Video Technology*, 30(2): 362–375.

Ma, Y., Xu, J., Zhang, Y., Liu, F. and Luo, X. (2021). Vector separability measurement based fast feature selection for detecting images information hiding. *IETE Tech. Rev.*, (Institution Electron. Telecommun. Eng. India), 38(1): 56-71. doi: 10.1080/02564602.2020.1766999.

Matsakis, L. (2021). TikTok, Under Scrutiny, Distances Itself from China. *WIRED*. [Online]. Available at: https://www.wired.com/story/tiktok-under-scrutiny-china/ [Accessed 9 June, 2021].

Monga, V., Banerjee, A. and Evans, B.L. (2006). A clustering-based approach to perceptual image hashing. *IEEE Transactions on Information Forensics and Security*, 1(1): 68–79.

Mun, S.M., Nam, S.H., Jang, H., Kim, D. and Lee, H.K. (April, 2019). Finding robust domain from attacks: A learning framework for blind watermarking. *Neurocomputing*, 337: 191–202. doi: 10.1016/j.ncucom.2019.01.067.

Neate, R. (December, 2020). Ryan Kaji, 9, earns $29.5m as this year's highest-paid YouTuber. *The Guardian*: UK ed. [Online]. Available at: https://www.theguardian.com/technology/2020/dec/18/ryan-kaji-9-earns-30m-as-this-years- highest-paid-youtuber [Accessed 27 June, 2021].

Netflix. http://paperpile.com/b/ZTAM3t/mDLl. Netflix [Online]. Available at https://openconnect.netflix.com [Accessed 7 June, 2021].

Nguyen, H.H., Yamagishi, J. and Echizen, I. (May, 2019). Capsule-forensics: Using capsule networks to detect forged images and videos. *In: 2019 IEEE International Conference on Acoustics, Speech and Signal Processing (ICASSP)*. IEEE, pp. 2307–2311.

Nguyen, Thanh Thi, Nguyen, Quoc Viet Hung, Nguyen, Cuong M., Nguyen, Dung, Nguyen, Duc Thanh and Nahavandi, Saeid. (2021). *Deep Learning for Deepfakes Creation and Detection: A Survey*. [Online]. Available at: http://export.arxiv.org/pdf/1909.11573 [Accessed 9 June, 2021].

O'Flaherty, K. (2020). Clearview AI, The Company whose Database has Amassed 3 Billion Photos, Hacked. [Online]. Available at https://tinyurl.com/42vyvjyn [Accessed: 2 June 2021] https://tinyurl.com/42vyvjyn.

Olszewski, K., Tulyakov, S., Woodford, O., Li, H. and Luo, L. (2019). Transformable bottleneck networks. *In: Proceedings of the IEEE/CVF International Conference on Computer Vision*, pp. 7648–7657.

Perez, S. (2019). Netflix may be losing $192 million per month from piracy, cord-cutting- study claims. *Tech Crunch*, 2019. [Online]. Available at: https://techcrunch.com/2019/02/27/netflix-may-be-losing-192m-per-month-from-piracy- cord-cutting-study-claims/ [Accessed 4 May, 2021].

Pevný, T., Filler, T. and Bas, P. (2010). Using high-dimensional image models to perform highly undetectable steganography. *In: Lecture Notes in Computer Science (including subseries Lecture Notes in Artificial Intelligence and Lecture Notes in Bioinformatics)*, vol. 6387 LNCS, pp. 161–177. doi: 10.1007/978-3-642-16435-4_13.

Qin, C., Liu, E., Feng, G. and Zhang, X. (2020). Perceptual image hashing for content authentication based on convolutional neural network with multiple constraints. *IEEE Transactions on Circuits and Systems for Video Technology*.

Radmilovic, I.K., Bereczki, T. and Liber, A. (2021). *Hungary Adopts National GDPR Supplementing Legislation—Lexology*. [Online]. Available at: https://www.lexology.com/library/detail.aspx?g=3e045c27-67c6-43a5-a5e8-a0a30a07612b [Accessed 9 June, 2021].

Robitza, W. et al. (Nov. 2017). Challenges of future multimedia QoE monitoring for internet service providers. *Multimed. Tools Appl.*, 76(21): 22243–22266.

Rodner, E., Simon, M., Fisher, R.B. and Denzler, J. (2016). Fine-grained recognition in the noisy wild: Sensitivity analysis of convolutional neural networks approaches. *arXiv preprint*. arXiv:1610.06756.

Saadatpanah, P., Shafahi, A. and Goldstein, T. (2020, November). Adversarial attacks on copyright detection systems. *In: International Conference on Machine Learning*, pp. 8307–8315.

Sabir, E., Cheng, J., Jaiswal, A., AbdAlmageed, W., Masi, I. and Natarajan, P. (2019). Recurrent convolutional strategies for face manipulation detection in videos. *In: Proceedings of the IEEE Conference on Computer Vision and Pattern Recognition Workshops*, pp. 80–87.

Schneier, B. (2007). *Applied Cryptography: Protocols, Algorithms and Source Code in C.* John Wiley & Sons.

Shamir, A. (1979). How to share a secret. *Commun. ACM*, 22(11): 612–613.

Shih, F.Y. (2017). *Digital Watermarking and Steganography: Fundamentals and Techniques.* 2nd. CRC Press.

Shih, F.Y. and Zhong, X. (June, 2016). Intelligent watermarking for high-capacity low-distortion data embedding. *Int. J. Pattern Recognit. Artif. Intell.*, 30(5). doi: 10.1142/S0218001416540033.

Skorin-Kapov, L., Varela, M., Hoßfeld, T. and Chen, K.-T. (2018). A survey of emerging concepts and challenges for QoE management of multimedia services. *ACM Transactions on Multimedia Computing, Communications, and Applications*, 14(2s): 1–29. doi: 10.1145/3176648.

Tang, W., Tan, S., Li, B. and Huang, J. (Oct. 2017). Automatic steganographic distortion learning using a generative adversarial network. *IEEE Signal Process. Lett.*, 24(10): 1547–1551. doi: 10.1109/LSP.2017.2745572.

*TechCrunch.* (2021). ByteDance & TikTok have secretly built a deepfakes maker—*TechCrunch.* [Online]. Available at: https://techcrunch.com/2020/01/03/tiktok-deepfakes-face-swap/ [Accessed 9 June, 2021].

*TechCrunch.* (2021). DEEPFAKES Accountability Act would impose unenforceable rules—but it's a start—*TechCrunch.* [Online]. Available at: https://techcrunch.com/2019/06/13/deepfakes-accountability-act-would-impose-unenforceable-rules-but-its-a-start/ [Accessed 9 June, 2021].

Tewari, A., Elgharib, M., Bharaj, G., Bernard, F., Seidel, H.P., Perez, P. et al. (2020). StyleRig: Rigging StyleGAN for 3D control over portrait images. *In: Proceedings of the IEEE/CVF Conference on Computer Vision and Pattern Recognition*, pp. 6142–6151.

Transparency Market Research, Digital Rights Management Market Global Industry Analysis, Size, Share, Growth, Trends, and Forecast 2018–2026 (2018).

Ukwandu, E. (2019). RESCUE: Evaluation of a Fragmented Secret Share System in Distributed-Cloud Architecture. [Online]. Available at: https://core.ac.uk/reader/286268510 [Accessed 22 May, 2021].

VidTIMIT database. [Online]. Available at: http://conradsanderson.id.au/vidtimit/ [Accessed 9 June, 2021].

Walker, A. (2020). Deepfakes and legal implications: Seeing is not believing. *A Uniquely Challenging Issue.* [Online]. Available at: https://talkingtech.cliffordchance.com/en/ip/other/deepfakes-and-legal-implications--seeing- is-not-believing.html [Accessed 20 May, 2021].

Xu, D. (2019). Commutative encryption and data hiding in HEVC video compression. *IEEE Access*, 7: 66028–66041. doi: 10.1109/ACCESS.2019.2916484.

Yang, X., Li, Y. and Lyu, S. (May, 2019). Exposing deep fakes using inconsistent head poses. *In: 2019 IEEE International Conference on Acoustics, Speech and Signal Processing (ICASSP)*. IEEE, pp. 8261–8265.

Yu, X., Wang, C. and Zhou, X. (October 2018). A survey on robust video watermarking algorithms for copyright protection. *Appl. Sci.*, 8(10): 1891. doi: 10.3390/app8101891.

Yu, Z. and Li, F. (2021). High-capacity constructive steganography using optimal texture block synthesis. *IETE Tech. Rev.* (Institution Electron. Telecommun. Eng. India), 38(1): 36–45. doi: 10.1080/02564602.2020.1780961

Zhang, Z., Yao, H., Xiang, Z. and Cao, F. (2021). Self-embedding watermarking algorithm under high tampering rates. *IETE Tech. Rev.* (Institution Electron. Telecommun. Eng. India), 38(1): 17–25. doi: 10.1080/02564602.2020.1838349.

Zhong, X. and Shih, F.Y. (Aug. 2019). A robust image watermarking system based on deep neural networks. *IEEE Trans. Multimed.* doi: 10.1109/TMM.2020.3006415.

Zong, T., Xiang, Y., Natgunanathan, I., Guo, S., Zhou, W. and Beliakov, G. (May 2015). Robust histogram shape-based method for image watermarking. *IEEE Trans. Circuits Syst. Video Technol.*, 25(5): 717–729. doi: 10.1109/TCSVT.2014.2363743.

# 11

# An Explanation on Social Media

*Ramsha Ateeq*[1] and *Umair B. Chaudhry*[2,*]

## ABSTRACT

The research problem under consideration investigates the methods and important factors that regulate cyber abuse and how social media can be governed globally. This requires a clarification on the description and working of social media. The social media technologies are digital platforms, applications and services that support convergence of in-depth social communication, interpersonal interaction, content sharing, community formation, collaborative opportunities and work. It incorporates several modalities, such as text, photographic images, sounds and videos.

To leverage the multiple opportunities offered by social media, the previous researches and practices have mainly focused on the positive aspects of this technology. However, its 'dark side' presents enormous repercussions for individuals, politics, businesses, communities, industries and society as a whole. The multidimensionality of this negative side encourages cyber abuse which includes cyberbullying, addictive use, trolling, fake news, online witch-hunts and privacy abuse. Along with that, the umbrella term of 'cyber abuse' encompasses online abusive interpersonal communication, such as stalking, exposure to pornography and sexual solicitation. This chapter aims to critically discuss it all.

## 1. Introduction

Kietzmann et al. (2011) created the Honeycomb Model to review social media influence and effectiveness. This model is constituted of seven key building blocks,

---

[1] Northumbria University London, UK.
[2] Queen Mary College, University of London, UK.
* Corresponding author: Umair.Chaudhry@northumbria.ac.uk

which the companies and businesses can analyse, evaluate and act upon the area of interest to formulate business strategies, perform specific functions and constitute the business model accordingly.

The afore-mentioned blocks refer to the extent to which users can communicate, share content, reveal locations, make relationships, know the reputation of other users, form communities and reveal identities. Contrary to this, each block contains consequences and negative implications as well. The 'Conversations' block refers to the communication between users. Different platforms, such as Twitter, Instagram, LinkedIn and Facebook enable one to converse with functionalities, such as 'Like', 'Reply', 'Direct Message' and 'Comment' but it can also ignite witch-hunts and chatbots mimicking human behaviour and conversation to pollute conversations with misleading conversations and spams.

Exchanging, distributing and receiving of the content is covered under the 'Sharing' aspect. The fundamental risk associated with sharing content is that it can be shared without requiring permission from the content owner of Intellectual Property Rights (IPR). The 'Presence Functional Block' refers to knowing the location of other users online or in the real world. Social media platforms use the Internet Protocol (IP) address information to track locations from mobile devices and check-in declarations but this allows users to be tracked without awareness and consent, making it directly tied to concerns pertaining to safety, protection and invading the privacy. The 'Relationships' building block concerns the extent to which individuals relate to each other. The online relationships bring along deleterious consequences that include stalking, online harassment and cyberbullying (Supreme Assignments, 2020) (Worrall et al., 2021). Reputation is the degree to which users can influence others by holding a distinct identity in social media environment – how users display competence, demonstrate social norms, attract, inspire and fascinate others. Sharing or uploading an inappropriate content can destroy one's reputation and influence the audience in a wrong way. The 'Groups' building block ascribes the functionality of creating circles of communities concentrated around a common interest or practice. Suppose, on Facebook, people were to participate in closed or open groups for socialising, self-status seeking, entertainment and for seeking information. The negative side of this block reveals the 'ingroup-outgroup bias'. People define themselves as social groupings (ingroup identity) and find themselves in an echo-chamber in which their own thoughts and beliefs are reinforced, resulting in polarised discussions of gender and racial inequality (D'Souza et al., 2020).

## 2. Data Privacy on Social Media

Society is making a substantial amount of personal information available online, but still there is an expectation of privacy. Sometimes, people falsely like to determine who can access private data and how it can be used. OSN service providers collect this data to provide personalized services and use it for commercial purposes and share it with third parties, which may lead to privacy leakages. Data retrieval and data privacy are two growing disciplines of computer science. Sometimes while designing solutions for information retrieval for data analysis, privacy issues are overlooked but data privacy restricts information-retrieval techniques to protect sensitive data.

The location-based networks, often referred to as 'geosocial networking', reveal the user's location that pose a challenge to privacy and LSBN, such as stalking. Data can be scrapped easily from geo-location applications and the user's activities can be monitored. Another issue is default settings of 'opt-in' vs 'opt-out' wherein the forum requires a user to sign in to a specific service to receive benefits. Hence, the provider gets access to the user's personal data. Moreover, there are approximately 50,000 applications associated with Facebook. Even if the Facebook provides protection, these third-party applications might not be safe and as a result they can be infected with a malicious code, such as Koobface worm. Additionally, cyber criminals can attack personal devices by hacking social networking sites.

Gross violation also includes the cloning attack, which is the creation of bogus accounts with a faux profile of victim to win trust over their friends. Moreover, web bugs, also known as clear GIFS, invisible GIFs and Beacon GIF are file objects placed on a web page to act as spyware to monitor user behaviour (Vivekanandarajah, 2019). There are no clear guidelines to ensure data privacy matters while carrying out research because the social media content is analysed by advanced and automated methods (Identity Theft Resource Centre, 2020).

According to the US social media account privacy 2018 statistics, 45% of the respondents reported to have all their accounts in private state while 19% claimed to have all of their accounts completely public (Iwendi et al., 2020).

## 2.1: Ethical Challenges

There are five categories of ethical dilemmas, explained in the book, *Digital Dilemma: Exploring Social Media Ethics in Organisations*, that can occur for practitioners responsible for social media accounts in companies. Firstly, 'role dilemmas' that is, having multiple roles, create confusion regarding ethical responsibilities, for instance, whether an employee is active online in a professional or personal capacity. Secondly, 'tempo dilemmas' can take place because the exchanges in social media happen at a very fast pace that enhances the chances of making mistakes. Third one is 'integrity dilemma' that concerns the commitment to personal and moral values while representing an organisation online and being pressured to act against personal values to support the company's objectives. 'Speech dilemmas' are associated with decisions about what to express and what to with hold while being in online environment. Lastly, the 'competence dilemma' occurs when the social media specialists exploit competence gaps for their advantage with minimal risk of detection.

The social media professionals are not as strongly equipped with ethical guidance as the journalists and editors. Hence, the 'navigation wheel' can offer a solution. The framework consists of six questions – law, identity, morality, reputation, economy and ethics. The priority depends upon the decision-maker and the next step is to identify the most relevant questions and then using the arguments derived from the questions to make a foundation for deriving a decision ((Department for Education, 2017).

The ethical concerns also arise while conducting research. For instance, in a research investigating the relationships between victims and perpetrators and among victims and bystanders ethical concerns are triggered, questioning respondents to recall psychological and physiological experiences of social media bullying. This can be ethically controversial. Moreover, due to ethical constraints when participants are not questioned sufficiently, investigation of longitudinal studies that examine the long-term effects of cyber bullying is hindered (Statista, 2021).

Online bullies get a perverse sense of contentment, called gratification, by inflaming and enraging people. It reflects the extent of civility and ethics prevailing in today's society (Linvill et al., 2019). Social media holds a huge potential for research in public health, but this networked data available online is riddled with ethical encounters and there is no apparent consensus to handle the data in an ethical manner. The key issues include privacy, confidentiality, anonymity, data management and security, authenticity, rapid changes in social media environment, voluntary participation, informed consent and minimal harm (Hudders et al., 2021).

A mental health therapist, Roy Huggins claim that social media is a great platform for counselling patients and communicating with other therapists, but it entails ethical concerns, such as oversharing client's personal details which is against the HIPPA privacy rule. The 'contact me' pages on therapists' websites reroute client's personal enquiries to form third-party services that result in breach of confidentiality. Furthermore, reviews are required on social media platforms from patients, thus exposing their mental health condition to all the users in the online environment (Kastrenakes, 2018).

Another ethical problem arises when young-aged tormenters are charged with harsh criminal charges that even result in jail terms. Adequate research is required on cyberbullying regulations before declaring a child guilty. The convictions should be concluded on the intentions of oppressors as in many cases these victims are unaware that their comment will be counted as an illegal activity (Al-Saren et al., 2021).

## 2.2 *Effects of Social Media Hacks*

Social media hacking can cause identity theft that involves a hacker taking unauthorised control of social media platforms. The orchestrated actions can manipulate the social behaviour that appears to be initiated by the users; the acts can be offensive, can contain sensitive information or spread untrue personal information and more that can have repercussions with friends, family and even the employer. Beyond this, access to forums can result in access to other synced accounts. Any application or website which has been used to sign up or login via Facebook, Twitter and Google connection can be taken over. Social media hacking can inject malware and snare other victims as well, sending malicious links in private messages or posting it on profile that can attract friends and followers to open it (Strickland and Dent, 2017). This eventually forwards malware to that user's account or can attain personal details from them.

The third-party tools can be proved to be a great security threat. When the Twitter and Instagram accounts of National Football Team were hacked, the criminals got access through third-party platform and they compromised the email account of one of the employees and targeted a tool that was used to measure the engagement. Since the entire team used that tool to monitor data on posts and tweets, the breaking in proved to be very successful (Strickland and Dent, 2017).

If a phished link is not taken down from a trusted brand, it can cost a loss of millions of clients and reputation as they get hi-jinxed by relying on a big name. The longer the post is available on account the greater is the strain imposed on financial resources and struggles of marketing and public relations team to alleviate the reputation damage (Baccarella et al., 2018). Hacking attacks can cause depression, anxiety and PTSD as the consequences can result in losing jobs, suicides and broken marriages. Few people relate to the pain of being sexually abused and 70% refuse to trust even their close relatives after being cyber attacked (Copy Keeper, 2020). The psychological effects of false influence and misinformation have been given very little attention. It is suggested that this is also a form of cyber threat known as 'cognitive hacking'. It is predicated on the distribution of disinformation at an unprecedented speed and the cognitive vulnerability of the audience to accept false news because it attracts existing anxieties and fears (Barnhart, 2020).

The attack on government officials and celebrities' social media accounts is one of the trending news of the 21st century. Since 2019, there has been 43% enhancement in social media fraud attacks. In May 2016, Linkedin was compromised and as a consequence, it exposed 117 million credentials. In 2017, Vevo was hacked by a phishing attack that led to data exfiltration of 3.12 terabytes. Similarly, in August 2017, Slack fell victim to hacking and half a million in Ether coins got stolen.

Threat Intelligence consultant, Bethany Keele suggests that according to the 2020 threat trends, there are three top most motivations to target social networking websites. To begin with, extreme financial gains; that is, in July 2020 when the Twitter was targeted through a spear-phishing attack. The accounts for Barack Obama and Elon Musk were used for bitcoin scam. The next motive is to target a large number of people by hacking their accounts. For instance, in the Roblox hacking incident in early 2020, hackers gained access to gaming accounts to spread pro- Trump election propaganda. Lastly, social media forums provide vector for cyber warfare. It is used by State-backed and nation-states' cybercriminals to disorder, influence and act on political motives against foreign governments. The US government threat intelligence agencies confirmed the interference of Russia in US presidential elections of 2016 by spreading fake information. According to Microsoft, they participated actively in campaigns to disrupt the 2020 elections as well (Harrison and Leopold, 2021).

## 3. Internet Laws, Cyber Abuse and Misinformation Control

For the smooth execution of any system laws, regulations and defined procedures are indispensable as they provide approved guidelines for carrying out activities along with the fear of being accountable and paying hefty penalties if found guilty.

## 3.1  Regulations by Social Media

Social media forums provide the feature to unfriend, block and report the abusive people from making any kind of connection. It also facilitates with community guidelines and safety and help centres advise adoption of steps that are necessary to stop cyber abuse (Department for Education, 2018). Sometimes users are reluctant to complain or report due to anxiety and fear of their bully but Facebook allows to report bullying on behalf of others. A team reviews the complaints to decide if the reported posts violate policies. It is also trying to implement the functionality to find and block the words that are considered hateful in the comments on their posts (Jones, 2021) (Bauer, 2020).

The community standards released by Facebook state the list of official rules regarding the permitted types of users and posts. It breaks down the unacceptable content into six categories, viz., objectionable content, safety, violence and criminal behaviour, integrity and authenticity, content-related requests and respecting intellectual property (Haselton, 2021).

Most social media services expect their users to be at least 13 years of age to comply with the COPPA law in USA and GDPR in UK. According to these laws, organisations operating online services are restricted to collecting personal information of individuals under 13 years of age with parental consent. The forums have full rights to delete an underage account if found with fake age (Kvalnes, 2020).

Recently, Facebook decided to remove content violating policies and disabled the accounts of users who repeatedly broke the rules. Additionally, the policies are tested on regular basis with safety experts and required changes are made. According to the new policy, people will be protected from intimidation and mass harassment from multiple accounts that cause heightened risk of online consequences; for instance, government dissidents and direct messages or comments on personal posts. Along with this, pages, groups and accounts created for State-linked and adversarial networks will get removed; such as closed private groups created by State-sponsored organisations for coordinating mass postings on rebellious accounts.

The harassment and bullying policy differentiates between private individuals and public figures to facilitate freedom of expression and legitimate public disclosures among the public. Degrading and sexual comments or activities are removed. The Instagram and Facebook policies are developed after consultations with global stakeholders, such as human rights experts, free speech advocates, women's safety groups, public figures, representatives of LGBTIQ and many more (Ethics Sage, 2019).

According to Instagram's moderation policy, an alert with objectionable stories, comments and posts are created for users with a warning to remove it; while users have the right to appeal regarding the moderation decisions (Ramasubbu, 2021).

YouTube, Twitter and Facebook have come to an agreement with European Commission regarding a Code of Conduct on countering illegal hate speech online. They aim at sharing the best practices with other Internet and social media platforms, effectively reviewing processes for illegal hate speech and taking the lead in controlling its spread. The *Hate Crime Report 2017* suggested otherwise. The Home Affairs Committee was critical over social media and technology companies, like Facebook and YouTube, for being too far from taking enough measures to tackle illegal content and abide by the law. Additionally, it also objected to the lack of transparency with Facebook, YouTube and Twitter refusing to reveal the number of employees hired for user's safety or the funds spent on public safety initiatives due to 'commercial sensitivity' (Zivkovic, 2021). Facebook also claims to aim at further development in Artificial Intelligence, augmented and virtual reality to help build tools to support growth of small businesses, create new jobs and compete with larger companies (Di Minin et al., 2021).

The moderation of content cannot rely merely upon technology; human resources are required for maintaining the balance and maximum accuracy. YouTube put offline the human moderators during the pandemic but the AI filters failed to match the required precision. They relied on Machine Learning systems to flag the hate speech and misinformation content and remove it automatically. But, this led to a significant enhancement in incorrect video removals. Between 2020 April and June, the number of videos removed were estimated to be 11 million, that is, double the usual rate. Among this, 320,000 of the takedowns were appealed and half of them were reinstated. YouTube chief product officer, Neal Mohan told the *Financial Times* regarding the power of machines and ML algorithms definitely having significance as 50% of content from the 11 million was removed without any view and the other 80% had less than 10 views when they got removed (Roca and Christie, 2018). Hence, both human beings and machines are required in an adequate balance to achieve the most accurate results (Galpin, 2021).

It is of extreme importance to keep the moderators financially, physically and mentally sound as they are the first-line defenders against potential trauma to the user base. Facebook hired more than 15,000 moderators and most of them are contracted through third-party firms, indicating that they do not enjoy the same benefits as the company's salaried employees. Thus the company faces criticism at employees being forced to watch gruesome content for hours, leading to post-traumatic stress disorder and brutal working conditions. The *Wall Street Journal* described that being a Facebook moderator was the worst job in technology as the breaks were restricted, phone usage was limited and exceptionally strict NDAs were imposed. In 2020, due to mental health implications, Facebook paid $52 million to tens of thousands of moderators in class-action lawsuit. The moderators also complained that, despite spending most time on content moderation that affected their output, they were punished if they tried to contact the policy team (Meijer, 2018).

Facebook CEO, Mark Zuckerberg was questioned by a US representative about the measures undertaken by Facebook for regulating online hate. In response, the former replied that despite having policies against bullying, it was difficult to police cyber abuse content because it was not clearly illegal. Moreover, he presented several possible changes in the US Internet legislation, such as increased transparency for SM forums, defined standards for addressing illegal material and laws for providing protection to smaller SM platforms against heavy regulations and lawsuits (Gordon, 2021).

## 3.2  Regulations by USA

Research suggests that half of the students in US have received hurtful comments online and 10% to 20% of them have experienced online bullying regularly. Meanwhile, approximately 70% students report about frequently being witness to online harassment. The question that arises is what can be an appropriate approach to tackle cyber abuse besides reporting the offender to the social media platform? Legal ramifications can arise from cyberbullying and to control the consequences, lawmakers are drafting and creating cyber-abuse laws.

Sexting is considered as an online abuse if the sexts are exchanged between minors for it is considered as child pornography. Even the person taking pictures and sending them willingly will be charged with distributing child pornography material (Lepper, 2021). The federal government has not passed any law at the national level; hence each state is responsible for creating and implementing its own legislation. Different states have specific age-group limits for inflicting punishment; for example, Connecticut punishes teenagers between 13 to 15 years of age for sending inappropriate images of themselves and 13 to 17 for receiving and not reporting this to the concerned authorities. In Louisiana, everyone is prohibited until the age of 17 from sending or keeping explicit photographs, while Texas allows sexting among children who have an age difference of two years and are dating.

Punitive actions are taken against a minor (less than 18-years old) by trial through the Juvenile Justice System and penalties are imposed, such as a strong verbal warning, community service and counselling, fine of $60, report to a probation officer, detention in a specific placement location. The adult penalties include incarceration, a fine that might exceed $5000, probation and getting registered in the State sex-offender registry for a minimum term of ten years (PHYS.ORG., 2021).

If someone experiences online hate due to race, national origin, sexual orientation, gender, religion or disability, then discrimination is reported under the Discriminatory Harassment and Federal Civil Rights Laws. A significant number of cases are prosecuted as harassment. Consequently, few cases are concluded in the civil court while others receive warrants on criminal charges and prosecution for hate crimes, violations and impersonation under the Computer Fraud and Abuse Act (CFAA). If the school is federally funded and the harassment falls under discriminatory harassment and federal civil laws, such as Title IX and Section 504, then it is required from them to address cyber incidents and impose disciplinary procedures, even if the cyberbullying happens outside the school grounds. It is required from school districts to submit all records about bullying to the US Department of Education which then includes this data in its Civil Rights Data Collection (CRDC) survey that is conducted annually.

The federal government has not passed any cyberbullying legislation and requires each state to write and enact its own laws. Some states have developed policies, laws and regulations while others have established model policies for school districts. Meanwhile, only a few states categorise bullying as a criminal offence. Consequently, New York's Dignity for All Students Act (DASA) requires school districts to develop and implement policies for cyberbullying, report procedures for all types of bullying, conduct employee training and hire a DASA coordinator to address any issues with staff, students and parents.

Ohio introduced the Jessica Logan Act when Logan committed suicide after getting trolled online for her nude pictures circulated in her high school. In response, Ohio law authorities expanded the existing bullying policies and included both online and incidents on school buses as well. It also warned students against engaging in any kind of bullying as it could result in suspension from school while the concerned institutes would suggest strategies for anonymous reporting and provide protection from retaliation to the person reporting the incident (VerSprite, 2021).

### 3.3 Regulations by European Union and United Kingdom

The government of UK does not consider cyberbullying as a crime in itself but an individual's actions might be considered as a criminal offence under different Acts. Protection from Harassment Act 1997 states it to be criminally charged if a person harasses another person, for example, by sending abusive emails to cause distress. The perpetrator can receive imprisonment of up to six months and if found committing the same offence on two occasions, the punishment could go to up to five years or imposition of a financial penalty or both. According to Malicious Communications Act 1988, if a person sends indecent or grossly offensive communication, threats or false information to create a situation of distress and anxiety for the recipient, then it is considered a grave offence and the guilty person is liable to face prison up to six months or a fine of £5000 or both.

Section 127 of the Communication Act 2003 declares it as an illegal act to use the electronic communication network to send an indecent, menacing or obscene character message. A bully can receive up to six months in jail, or a fine or both. The Obscene Publications Act 1959 makes it a felony to publish an obscene article with the intention to deprave and corrupt the reader and other people interacting with it. It also includes circulating, projecting and transmitting the article or data in it. Section 5 of the Public Order Act 1986 affirms that any abusive or threatening behaviour in writing or visual representation is an offence. With regards to cyber abuse, a situation where a mobile phone is used to alarm or harass other individuals, it is considered an an offence. Under the Computer Misuse Act 1990, it is illegal to hack someone's personal computer or online accounts.

The workplaces are experiencing an enhanced amount of cyberbullying. One out of five employees claim to be bullied that results in extreme stress. Collectively, the bullying at the workplace costs approximately £2 billion a year due to sick pay and less productivity. This issue can be covered by the Health and Safety at Work Act 1974, under which it is the employer's duty to provide employees with a safe working atmosphere. If any employee faces cyber abuse using the company's infrastructure, computer or any equipment, then it is the employer's duty to provide protection to the working staff. Additionally, Safer Internet Day is observed yearly in UK to promote the safest ways for Internet usage and emphasise on safer online activities. It aims to discourage cyberbullies and bring together online communities to prevail against unacceptable online behaviour (Local Solicitors, 2021).

The Education and Inspections Act 2006 relates more closely to cyberbullying (Galpin, 2021). Section 89 states that to discourage all forms of bullying, schools must make good behaviour a part of school policy and communicate it to all students, parents and staff. It also entitles the head teacher to control the behaviour of pupils even when they are off the school premises (Department for Education 2017). It gives the legal power to a staff member to control the conduct of pupils by confiscating, retaining or destroying any items as a disciplinary penalty, such as, if the prohibited item a pornographic image, it should be disposed of immediately or handed over to the police in case it amounts to a specified offence. Law provides defence against staff provided they act lawfully. Moreover, parents should be informed too, though it is not a mandatory requirement (Department for Education, 2018).

In UK, the white paper on 'Online Harms' calls for establishing an accountability framework for any oversight committed by the tech companies. This would be overseen by an independent regulator endowed with effective enforcement powers and reporting requirements. The online safety regulatory framework will clearly define the responsibilities of companies to keep the users safe (Department for Media Culture and Support, 2020). The regulator will have the authority to hold senior executives personally responsible if their company fails to limit the distribution of harmful content (Browne, 2020). Additionally, there are organisations, such as the National Bullying Helpline, National Society for the Prevention of Cruelty to Children (NSPCC) and Anti-Bullying Alliance which offer emotional help and practical advice to victims of cyberbullying.

The implementation and passage provided by General Data Protection Regulation (EU) 2016/679 regulates the law on data privacy and protection for all within EU and European Economic Area and export of personal data, services and goods outside these territories dealing with EU subjects. The legislation addresses the issues of online harassment, identity theft and cyberbullying. This privacy legislation mandates the mechanism of clear consent to ensure the users understand with whom their data is being shared and the purpose behind it. Thus, the data cannot be collected without the user's consent and he or she can also request for deleting and altering his or her data (Meijer, 2018).

The GDPR also affects Facebook advertising with remarketing ads that follow the visitors from a product/service website to Facebook and vice-versa. The legislation adds extra requirements for EU customers who would have agreed to process their data via an existing sign-up or disclaimer in the advertisement. As of January 2020, it was reported that $126 million penalty was imposed on different companies for GDPR violation (Barnhart, 2020).

## 4. Significance of Frameworks

The following frameworks can be implemented to govern the functionalities of government and social media companied and to assure if they are in accordance to the required security measures. The application of these frameworks will provide globally recognized benchmark to measure the success or failure ratio of a company.

## 4.1 ISO 27001

The GDPR is in effect from some time but companies are still struggling to accomplish the requirements as the instructions are not clear. The international information security standard ISO 27001 can help to comply with GDPR as they both contain guidelines regarding the management of sensitive data. It addresses several practices such as personal data encryption, formal risk assessment and pseudonymization, recovery from incidents, confidentiality, availability, ensuring resilience, and integrity of systems and services, ensuring the security of processes by regular assessment of technical and organizational measures (Irwin, 2020). ISO 27001 is strongly recommended as it holds the credibility to be the only auditable International Standard that explains the requirements of an Information Security Management System (ISMS). All social media platforms can control cyber abuse when they have an effective control over the cyber security, this will allow the platforms to recognize and resolve security threats and conduct annual risk assessment as well (Irwin, 2021).

## 4.2 COBIT-19

The organizations specially the social media companies and government can implement COBIT-19 framework, this IT Management framework can provide assistance in development, organization and implementation of governance strategies. It also concentrates on risk management and security issues related to governance such as cloud computing, cyber security and digital formation. With the use of this framework organizations can identify the procedures, policies, processes, infrastructure, ethic, culture, organizational skills and behaviours to formulate an Information Governance System (White, 2019).

# 5. Social Media Forensics

Though the laws are passed, but the court of law requires evidence in order to proceed on the social media crimes, such as photo morphing, hacking, cyberbullying, link baiting, shopping and dating scams. Social Network Forensics plays a key role in conviction of a suspect. It is a technique to locate the source of electronic evidence in an unhampered manner while observing all the laws. The evidence collection must adhere to the terms of service agreement of social media platforms which defines the nature of data that an investigator can gather and manipulate.

The following are the three stages in Social Network Forensics:

## 5.1 Evidence Identification

It involves the identification of all social media accounts associated with the subject, including the identification of friends and family in the accounts. Moreover, it is required that the forensic examiner document contains all the sources of proofs along with how and when they were discovered.

## 5.2 Collection

Various methods can be used for collecting electronic evidences, such as manual documentation, open-source tools (HTTrack), screen scrape, forensic recovery, content subpoena, commercial tool (X1) and Web service (page freezer). Additionally, for acquisition of evidences from smartphones forensic tool kits are available to access the internal memory of smartphone and capture a logical image of all the files in it. The files are then further analysed for gathering evidences.

## 5.3 Examination (Organisation)

The collected files require specific tools to decode and view the contents in them. After decoding, a huge amount of user data, such as call logs and messages history, etc., are collected. A large bank of social media communication footprints is provided to the forensics examiner. The obtained artefacts are examined and correlated with the case under consideration.

Mobile devices are used by 90% of users to access social networking forums that make these devices the biggest repertoire of evidences but mobile devices pose a challenge to forensic investigators as the data is updated regularly, leading to a rapid loss of evidences. Moreover, extracting evidences from the mobile phones using custom tools becomes difficult because of the closed source operating system of smart phones and frequent OS releases by the vendors. As a result, the forensic professionals face challenges to keep abreast of the methods of examination and latest tools (Incognito Forensic Foundation, 2019).

## 6. Machine Learning Techniques for Controlling Disinformation and Fake News

The cases reported on social media need to be analysed. To identify the areas that need maximum attention are highlighted by creating visual representation of data by using Data Analytics. Once the areas are recognized, the social media policing teams take steps, like blocking, banning and holding the perpetrators to prevent online bullying. Continuous monitoring of the behaviour of three billion active users is not possible with traditional data analytics but advancements in big data help to create Artificial Intelligence speech recognition systems for identification of abusive and unacceptable words in the written speech (Praveena and Smys, 2017). Latest Data Analytics identify data patterns more efficiently and in significantly less time using Machine Learning technique and then patterns are used to capture the offenders (Sai, 2021).

Online harassment draws attention due to its intense negative social influence. Therefore, the identification of bullying messages has gained attention of many researchers. Consequently, research has been developed to design and develop an effective method for detection of abusive messages by combining natural language processing and Machine Learning.

Several Machine Learning algorithms, like Naive Bayes, Decision Tree, Vector Machines for Support (SVM) and Random Forest are among the proposed cyberbullying models. For analysis of four Machine Learning algorithms, two distinctive elements, such as Bag-of-Words (BOW) and term frequency-inverse text frequency (TF-IDF), are used, along with emotions, sentiments and personalities as the features for detection improvement. Previously, several Machine Learning-based works had been carried out for cyber abuse detection, such as for contextual and sentimental features of a sentence, an algorithm with a bag-of-words was proposed but it showed an accuracy of barely 61.9%. Moreover, a project known as Ruminati, conducted by Massachusetts Institute of Technology, employed the Support Vector Machine for cyberbullying detection on YouTube comments. The research was combined with common sense reasoning by adding together social parameters through the application of probabilistic modelling. The results improved to show 66.7% accuracy. Another language-based online harassment-detection technique showed 78.5% success with the usage of algorithms instance-based Trainer and Decision Tree.

The online bullying-detection framework consists of two major parts: NLP (Natural Language Processing) and ML (Machine Learning). In the first phase, datasets comprising of harassment messages, texts or posts are collected and prepared for the ML algorithms by using NLP. The ML algorithms are then trained by the processed datasets for cyberbullying detection on social media, including Twitter and Facebook.

## 6.1 Methodology

The researcher of the above-mentioned study used the following methodology:

- **Natural Language Processing:** Unnecessary characters, like numbers, stemming, stop-words, tokenisation and punctuation, etc., are removed to clean the social media content before the application of ML algorithms on the comments and prepare the text for the detection phase. After pre-processing, the two important elements of text BoW and TF-IDF are prepared. In BoW phase, the raw text is incapable of working directly with ML algorithms. For this reason, before the application of algorithms, the text must be converted to numbers or vectors. Then, for the next phase, this processed data is transformed to BoW. The TF-IDF statistically measure the relevancy of a word to a document during the collection. Equal priority is given to all the words in BoW, but in TF-IDF, the importance depends on the frequent occurrence of words as they classify more efficiently.

- **Machine Learning:** Several Machine Learning algorithms, like Naive Bayes, Decision Tree, Vector Machines for Support (SVM) and Random Forest are among the applied approaches. For a specific public cyberbullying dataset, the highest accuracy classifier is discovered. The first classifier is Decision Tree that provides both regression and classification. It is a tree-like structure where a condition is represented by each internal node and a decision from each leaf node. The class having the target is returned by the classification tree, while the predicted value of an input is yielded by a regression tree.

- **Naïve Bayes** is based on Bayes theorem. The algorithm quickly resolves the classification problems of binary and multi-class to predict on the object's probability by using the formula $p(y|X) = p(X|y) \times p(y)/X$. Here, y denotes class variable and X is the dependent feature vector of length $n$. Multiple decision-tree classifiers are found in Random Forest Classifier. Individual prediction is given from each tree and the final output is based on the maximum votes of prediction. Lastly, Support Vector Machine can be applied in regression and classification; that is, in both. In an infinite-dimensional space, it constructs a set of hyperplanes and the implementation of kernel transforms the input data space to the required form. For instance, linear kernel takes the dot product of two instances by the formula $K(x, xi) = sum(x * xi)$. Consuming less time than other algorithms, it produces more accurate results (Islam et al., 2020).

In another research it was found that all types of cyberbullying can be summarised into text format if the words are implied or explicit. When profane words are used with negative emotions, it can create 11 explicit expressions, while detecting cyber abuse in implicit speech identification is a challenging job as there are no foul words in cynical or ironic phases. Moreover, the methods inspired by Deep Learning and Machine Learning have increased the online-bullying detection accuracy but the advancement is limited by the lack of standard datasets. For this purpose, the user comments dataset for labelling is applied by capturing the real-time scenario of kind or deliberately abusive words and crowdsourcing.

For cyberbullying detection, social media platforms should use a meta-analytic approach for identification, text classification and personalised text-based cyber stalking. Furthermore, other initiatives were concentrated upon, for finding author identification, such as digital forensics. Moreover, DL algorithms were applied for the construction of prediction models after dataset extraction with three-word embedding structure, namely vector initialisation, GloVe and Sense-Specific Embedding Word (SSWE). To cater to the attacks on Arabic language, Sataiku DSS and Weka were used as they support Arabic language. The experiment was based on real-time dataset and by implementing Naïve Bayes and SVM classifiers used for prediction, positive results were obtained. In another experiment, by considering a dataset of 69,874 tweets after mapping the tweets to vectors with Glove's open source word embedding, 93.7% accuracy was achieved with deep Convolutionary Neural Networks.

A classifier was identified in Wiki-Detox dataset to produce a result approximately equivalent to three human resources calculated by ROC curve and Spearman correlation field. The model construction was based on three dimensions: architectural model (Logistic Regression vs Multi-Layer Perception), sort of mark (distribution of one-hot vs empirical) and sort n-gram (word vs char), using the classifiers they identified the harassment.

In another contribution, prediction researchers used Deep Bidirectional Long Short-Term Memory (BLSTM) and linguistic methods for evaluating results for prediction on the Kaggle dataset. Parts of speech were taken into account to track the type of pattern being followed by normal and abusive tweets. Subsequently pre-processing steps, like text cleansing, tokenisation, stemming, Lemmatisation and stop words were removed. Then four Deep Learning models were applied to obtain the results from the experiments, namely BLSTM, Gated Recurrent Units (GRU), Long Short-Term Memory (LSTM) and Recurrent Neural Network (RNN). Using these models, empirical analysis was carried out to determine the performance and effectiveness of these algorithms. Finally, a comparison between them showed that BLSTM model secured high accuracy and $F1$-measure scores in detecting insults in social commentary (Iwendi et al., 2020).

SkyNews reports that in Britain, 150 schools have started to use the AI tool, known as AS Tracking, developed by STEER Company. It involves students to take an online psychological test. It requires peers to imagine a space in which they feel comfortable and then asks a series of abstract questions. In response, the children can scale the question from 'very easy' to 'very difficult'. The STEER Company then compares the results obtained with the psychological model and flags the students requiring attention in the teacher dashboard. The co-founder claimed a significant 20% decrease in self-harm since the introduction of this tool in college. AI helps in web-filtering, self-harm alerts and cyberbullying monitoring. SN Technologies Corporation is one step ahead, as their AI solution uses the facial recognition for tracking 'blacklisted' students from videos obtained from surveillance cameras installed in schools (Zivkovic, 2021).

Deep Learning and Machine Learning are an effective technology to fight against rumours faced at individual as well as at international level. During COVID-19 pandemic, a very large amount of rumours spread like wild fire on social media, leading to a manic situation among the population, apart from market disorder and dramatic effects on people's well-being and mental health. In open platforms, manual detection by the authorities is extremely challenging. Therefore, to combat rumours in the early stages, the researchers conducted several studies on intelligent methods utilisation for fake news detection, mainly the ML and DL methods. DL algorithms superseded ML as they do not require pre-processing, feature engineering process and showed superior enhancement in various fields, without requiring human assistance. To further investigate, a novel Hybrid Deep Learning Model based on Long Short-Term Memory (LSTM) and Concatenated Parallel Convolutional Neural Networks (PCNN) was proposed. On ArCOV-19 dataset, the experiments were conducted on 3,157 tweets. Among them, 1,480 were rumours while 1,677 were not rumours. The model illustrated a superior performance in terms of accuracy, recall, precision and F-score. To select the appropriate scheme, word-embedding layers were investigated. For this purpose, the influence of static word embedding, such as word2vec, FastText and GloVe on the proposed model was explored (Al-Sarem et al., 2021).

## 7. Influencers and Unconscious Decisions

Apart from technologies, there are some human-based aspects that strongly influence the working of the social media. In the past decade, social media influencers or micro-celebrities established a strong identity by creating attractive social media profiles that strongly impact the follower's decision making. Therefore, advertisers approach them frequently to endorse products and services. This marketing tactic is called 'influencer marketing'. The forecasts suggest that influencer market search is expected to reach $15 billion by 2022 (Hudders et al., 2021).

Cyberbullying is considered as a significant con of influence as the accounts contain a significant ratio of hackers (Hassan et al., 2018). There are specific forums, such as Lipstick Alley supporting cyber abuse that aims at bringing down the celebrities and influencers alike with minimal or no censorship (Copy Keeper, 2020).

Influencers and social media platforms hold the responsibility to post responsible content as it can have a direct impact on the followers' wellbeing. For this purpose, in 2019, Instagram teamed up with an anti-cyberbullying charity, Cybersmile, to campaign for anti-bullying week from 11th to 15th November. Instagram influencers, Zoella Founder of ZOE Sugg, comedian Mo Gillgan and Cheesie King collaborated in a campaign and talked about their experiences in cyber bullying. The partnership aims to take on the people who use banter as an excuse for online harassment (Bold, 2019).

## 8. Conclusion

*The Literature Review* aimed at finding the various aspects that contribute effectively in triggering cyber abuse and the solutions to eradicate it. The background first investigates at building the understanding of social media and how it facilitates and attracts individuals in all aspects of personal and professional life. It consists of seven building blocks that illustrate the negative aspects behind every element of the Honeycomb model. As cyberbullying has reached the level where it cannot be rectified and controlled without authorised governance, it has led to the study of laws and regulations that are being implemented in USA, EU and UK. Social media platforms are also taking revolutionary steps to tackle this adversity. While digging through the laws, it becomes obvious that the number of laws directly catering to online hate are very few in number and all laws require much stronger implementation to provide a secure online environment. Governance can be further strengthened with the implementation of globally recognised frameworks, such as ISO 27001 and COBIT-19.

It also defines the technical aspect of controlling online harassment by using Machine Learning algorithms, which contribute a great deal, but using it alone is not an optimal solution as it has its own limitations that needs to be catered. Hence, all participating entities, like government, law authorities, software developers and researchers, social media forums and educational institutes are formulating the strategies to fight this apprehension, concentrating more on theoretical measures rather than on implementation specifically the laws and detecting and reporting system on social media.

# References

Al-Sarem, M., Alsaeedi, A., Saeed, F., Boulila, W. and Ameerbakhsh, O. (2021). A novel hybrid deep learning model for detecting COVID-19-related rumours on social media based on lstm and concatenated parallel CNNs. *Appl. Sci.*, 11(17). doi: 10.3390/APP11177940.

Baccarella, C.V., Wagner, T.F., Kietzmann, J.H. and McCarthy, I.P. (2018). Social media? It's serious! Understanding the dark side of social media. *Eur. Manag. J.*, 36(4): 431–438. doi: 10.1016/j.emj.2018.07.002.

Barnhart, B. (2020). *GDPR and social media: What marketers need to know*. https://sproutsocial.com/insights/gdpr-and-social-media/ [Accessed 18 Nov., 2021].

Bauer, D. (2020). *What is the Cost of a Social Media Account Hack?* https://www.zerofox.com/blog/social-media-account-hijacking-cost/.

Bold, B. (2019). *Instagram Teams up with Cyber Smile for anti-bullying Cyber Campaign*. https://www.prweek.com/article/1665377/instagram-teams-cybersmile-anti-bullying-influencer-campaign [Accessed 25 Nov., 2021].

Browne, R. (2020). *Facebook is creating 1,000 new jobs in the UK*. https://www.cnbc.com/2020/01/21/Facebook-is-creating-1000-new-jobs-in-the-uk.html [Accessed 2 Dec., 2021].

Chan, T.K.H., Cheung, C.M.K. and Lee, Z.W.Y. (2021). Cyberbullying on social networking sites: A literature review and future research directions. *Inf. Manag.*, 58(2): 103411. Doi: 10.1016/j.im.2020.103411.

Childnet. (2018). *Age Restrictions on Social Media Services*. https://www.childnet.com/blog/age-restrictions-on-social-media-services/ [Accessed 2 Nov., 2021].

Copy Keeper. (2020). *Cyberbullying—A New Epidemic For Social Media Influencers?* https://copykeeper.wordpress.com/2019/12/13/cyberbullying-a-new-epidemic-for-social-media-influencers/ [Accessed 18 Dec., 2021].

Davis, A. (2021). *Advancing Our Policies on Online Bullying and Harassment*. https://about.Facebook.com/news/2021/10/advancing-online-bullying-harassment-policies/ [accessed 5 Nov., 2021].

Department for Education. (2017). Preventing and Tackling Bullying. *Gov. Uk*, p. 19. [Online]. Available: https://assets.publishing.service.gov.uk/government/uploads/system/uploads/attachment_data/file/623895/Preventing_and_tackling_bullying_advice.pdf%0Ahttps://www.gov.uk/government/publications/prev enting-and-tackling-bullying.

Department for Education. (February, 2018). *Searching, Screening and Confiscation*. [Online]. Available: https://assets.publishing.service.gov.uk/government/uploads/system/uploads/attachment_data/file/67441 6/Searching_screening_and_confiscation.pdf.

Department for Media Culture and Support. (2020). *Online Harms White Paper*. [Online]. Available: https://www.gov.uk/government/consultations/online-harms-white-paper/online-harms-white-paper.

Di Minin, E., Fink, C., Hausmann, A., Kremer, J. and Kulkarni, R. (2021). How to address data privacy concerns when using social media data in conservation science. *Conserv. Biol.*, 35(2): 437–446. doi: 10.1111/cobi.13708.

Djuraskovic, O. (2021). *Cyberbullying Statistics, Facts, and Trends (2021) with Charts*. https://firstsiteguide.com/cyberbullying-stats/ [Accessed 19 Oct., 2021].

D'Souza, N., Forsyth, D. and Blackwood, K. (2020). Workplace cyber abuse: Challenges and implications for management., *Pers. Rev.*, 50(7-8): 1774–1793. doi: 10.1108/PR-03-2020-0210.

Ethics Sage. (2019). *Cyberbullying and Emotional Distress*. https://www.ethicssage.com/2019/09/cyberbullying-and-emotional-distress.html [Accessed 5 Dec., 2021].

Gordon, S. (2020). *6 Things Every Teen Needs to Know About Sexting*. https://www.verywellfamily.com/things-teens-do-not-know-about-sexting-but-should-460654 [Accessed 25 Oct., 2021].

Galpin, S. (2021). *Aldenham Prep School Cyber Bullying Policy*. https://aldenhamprep.com/wp- content/uploads/2020/10/20-APS-Anti-Cyber-Bullying-Policy-September.pdf [Accessed 20 Nov., 2021].

Gordon, S. (2021). *Understanding the Legal Ramifications of Cyberbullying*. https://www.verywellfamily.com/cyberbullying-laws-4588306 [Accessed 6 Dec., 2021].

Harrison, K. and Leopold, A. (2021). *How Blockchain can Help Combat Disinformation*. https://hbr.org/2021/07/how-blockchain-can-help-combat-disinformation [Accessed 8 Dec., 2021].

Haselton, T. (2018). *Here's Facebook's once-secret list of content that can get you banned.* https://www.cnbc.com/2018/04/24/Facebook-content-that-gets-you-banned-according-to-community- standards.html [Accessed 4 Nov., 2021].

Hassan, S., Yacob, M.I., Nguyen, T. and Zambri, S. (2018). Social media influencer and cyberbullying: A lesson learned from preliminary findings. *Proc. Knowl. Manag. Int. Conf. 2018*, No. July, pp. 200–205.

Hudders, L., De Jans, S. and De Veirman, M. (2021). The commercialization of social media stars: A literature review and conceptual framework on the strategic use of social media influencers. *Int. J. Advert.*, 40(3): 327–375. doi: 10.1080/02650487.2020.1836925.

Huggins, R. (2018). *2018's Top 5 Social Media Ethics Issues, According to Roy.* https://personcenteredtech.com/2018/12/20/2018-top-5-social-media-ethics-issues/ [Accessed 7 Nov., 2021].

Identity Theft Resource Centre. (2020). Recent Social Media Hacks are Proving Just How Dangerous They Are. https://www.idtheftcenter.org/post/recent-social-media-hacks-are-proving-just-how-dangerous-they-are/ [Accessed 30 Oct., 2021].

Incognito Forensic Foundation. (2019). *Application of Social Media Forensics to Investigate Social Media Crimes.* https://ifflab.org/application-of-social-media-forensics-to-investigate-social-media-crimes/ [Accessed 5 Dec., 2021].

Irwin, L. (2020). *How ISO 27001 helps you achieve GDPR compliance.* https://www.itgovernance.eu/blog/en/how-an-iso-27001-compliant-isms-helps-you-comply-with-the- gdpr [Accessed 20 Nov., 2021].

Irwin, L. (2021). *5 benefits of ISO 27001 certification.* https://www.itgovernance.eu/blog/en/benefits-of-iso-27001-certification [Accessed 20 Dec., 2021].

Islam, M.M., Uddin, M.A., Islam, L., Akter, A., Sharmin, S. and Acharjee, U.K. (April 2020). Cyberbullying detection on social networks using machine learning approaches. *2020 IEEE Asia-Pacific Conf. Comput. Sci. Data Eng. CSDE 2020.* doi: 10.1109/CSDE50874.2020.9411601.

Iwendi, C., Srivastava, G., Khan, S. and Maddikunta, P.K.R. (2020). Cyberbullying detection solutions based on deep learning architectures. *Multimed. Syst.* doi: 10.1007/s00530-020-00701-5.

Jones, E. (2021). *Search Results for: ISO 27001 Certification Standards and Audit Controls.* https://www.easemybrain.com/?s=ISO+27001+Certification+Standards+And+Audit+Controls+ [Accessed 10 Dec., 2021].

Kastrenakes, J. (2018). Instagram will now warn users close to having their account banned. https://www.theverge.com/2019/7/18/20699393/instagram-account-ban-warning-message-moderation-update [Accessed 18 Nov., 2021].

Kay, G. (2021). Mark Zuckerberg said policing bullying is hard when the content is 'not clearly illegal' —in 44 states, cyberbullying can bring criminal sanctions. https://www.businessinsider.com/mark-zuckerberg-said-its-hard-to-police-cyberbullying-2021-3?r=US&IR=T [Accessed 26 Nov., 2021].

Kietzmann Jan, Hermkens Kristopher, McCarthy Ian and Silvestre Bruno. (2011). Social media? Get serious! Understanding the functional building blocks of social media. *Business Horizons*, 54: 241–251. 10.1016/j.bushor.2011.01.005.

Koetsier, J. (2020). *Report: Facebook Makes 300,000 Content Moderation Mistakes Every Day.* https://www.forbes.com/sites/johnkoetsier/2020/06/09/300000-Facebook-content-moderation-mistakes-daily-report-says/?sh=18a32a1d54d0 [Accessed 20 Oct., 2021].

Kvalnes, O. (2020). *Ethical Dilemmas of Social Media and How to Navigate Them.* https://www.bi.edu/research/business-review/articles/2020/07/ethical-dilemmas-of-social-media--and-how-to-navigate-them/.

Lepper, J. (2019). *Instagram Recruits Influencers to Tackle 'Banter' for Anti-Bullying Week.* https://charitydigital.org.uk/topics/topics/instagram-recruits-influencers-to-tackle-banter-for-anti-bullying-week-6857 [Accessed 18 Oct., 2021].

Leskin, P. (2021). Facebook content moderator who quit reportedly wrote a blistering letter citing stress-induced insomnia among other trauma. https://www.businessinsider.com/Facebook-content- moderator-quit-with-blistering-letter-citing-trauma-2021-4?r=US&IR=T [Accessed 10 Nov., 2021].

Linvill, D.L., Boatwright, B.C., Grant, W.J. and Warren, P.L. (2019). The Russians are Hacking my Brain! Investigating Russia's internet research agency twitter tactics during the 2016 United States presidential campaign. *Comput. Human Behav.*, 99(May): 292–300. doi: 10.1016/j.chb.2019.05.027.

Local Solicitors. (2021). *The Law on Cyberbullying*. https://www.localsolicitors.com/criminal- guides/ the-law-on-cyberbullying [Accessed 20 Dec., 2021].

Meijer, C.R.W.D. (2018). *Blockchain versus GDPR and who should adjust most*. https://www.finextra. com/blogposting/16102/blockchain-versus-gdpr-and-who-should-adjust-most [Accessed 27 Nov., 2021].

PHYS.ORG. (2018). *Facebook Adds New Tools to Stem Online Bullying*. https://phys.org/news/2018-10-Facebook-tools-stem-online-bullying.html [accessed 28 Oct., 2021].

Praveena, A. and Smys, S. (2017). Ensuring data security in cloud-based social networks. *Proc. Int. Conf. Electron. Commun. Aerosp. Technol. ICECA 2017*, 2017(January): 289–295. doi: 10.1109/ ICECA.2017.8212819.

Ramasubbu, S. (2021). *Is Sexting Illegal?* https://www.mobicip.com/blog/sexting-laws [Accessed 20 Dec., 2021].

Rewaria, S. (2021). Data privacy in social media platform: Issues and challenges. *SSRN Electron. J.*, pp. 1–27. doi: 10.2139/ssrn.3793386.

Roca, L. and Christie, R. (2018). *Blockchain: What is it and can I protect it via patents?* https://www. lewisroca.com/assets/htmldocuments/blockchain.pdf [Accessed 20 Dec., 2021].

Sri, T. (2021). *How can Data Analytics Help us Prevent Crimes?* https://seleritysas.com/blog/2021/05/18/ how-can-data-analytics-help-us-prevent-crimes/ [Accessed 5 Dec., 2021].

Statista. (2021). Percentage of social media users in the United States who have a private social media account as of September 2018. https://www.statista.com/statistics/934874/users-have-private-social-media-account-usa/ [Accessed Oct. 20, 2021].

Strickland, P. and Dent, J. (2017). Online harassment and cyberbullying. *House of Commons*, No. 07967, pp. 1–30. [Online]. Available: https://researchbriefings.files.parliament.uk/documents/CBP-7967/ CBP-7967.pdf.

Supreme Assignments. (2020). *Ethical Issues in Cyberbullying*. https://www.supremeassignments. com/2020/01/23/ethical-issues-in-cyber-bullying/ [Accessed 4 Dec., 2021].

VerSprite. (2020). *Top 3 Motives Why Cybercriminals Attack Social Media According to 2020 Threat Trends*. https://versprite.com/blog/top-motives-hackers-attack-social-media-2020/ [Accessed 13 Dec., 2021].

Vincent, J. (2020). *YouTube brings Back More Human Moderators after AI Systems Over-censor*. https:// www.theverge.com/2020/9/21/21448916/youtube-automated-moderation-ai-machine-learning-increased-errors-takedowns [Accessed 8 Nov., 2021].

Vivekanandarajah, A. (2019). *Can Data Analytics and Machine Learning Prevent Cyberbullying?* https:// seleritysas.com/blog/2021/06/11/can-data-analytics-and-machine-learning-prevent-cyberbullying/ [Accessed 15 Dec., 2021].

Walker, T., Mckinley, M., Lee, M. and Kee, F. (2018). Ethical Issues in Social Media Research for Public Health, 108(3): 343–348. doi: 10.2105/AJPH.2017.304249.

White, S.K. (2019). *What is COBIT? A Framework for Alignment and Governance*. https://www.cio.com/ article/228151/what-is-cobit-a-framework-for-alignment-and-governance.html [Accessed 30 Nov., 2021].

Worrall, W. (2021). *The Psychological Cost of Hacking*. https://hacked.com/the-psychological-cost-of-hacking/ [Accessed 28 Oct., 2021].

Zivkovic, L. (2021). *Artificial Intelligence is now being used to Detect Cyberbullying in School Children*. https://www.unite.ai/artificial-intelligence-is-now-being-used-to-detect-cyberbullying-in-school-children/ [Accessed 6 Dec., 2021].

# Index

**A**

ACPO 42–44
algorithm 106, 108–114, 120, 125, 127
Ambient assisted living 49, 50, 52, 54, 56, 58, 69
anonymity 51, 59, 88, 140, 192–194, 197, 232
Article 7 of Regulation (EU) No. 596/2014 76
Artificial intelligence (AI) 203, 204, 206, 209–212, 214, 216–224, 235, 240
Artificial neural network 106, 112, 114
Asian countries 153, 155, 159, 160, 166, 168, 169
authenticity 203, 207, 208, 212, 221

**B**

blockchain 1, 2, 7–9, 12–14, 16, 18–21, 24–27, 74

**C**

Code of conduct 234
Communication act 2003 237
Communication decency act 2–4
Computer misuse act 1990, 237
COVID-19 102, 109, 112, 118–120
crime 43, 45, 75, 76, 81, 130, 133–135, 137–139, 142, 145, 146, 148, 149, 165, 172–188, 192–199, 235–237, 239
cyber abuse 229, 233–237, 239, 241, 242, 244
cyber attacks 196
cyber propaganda 34
cyber security 15
cyber stalking 242
cybercrime 194–197, 199
cyberspace 199

**D**

data mining 102, 105–108, 110, 111, 113, 114, 120, 126, 127
data protection 209

deepfake 6, 36, 81, 82, 98, 203–205, 207–211, 221
digital coercive control 130, 133, 138, 139, 147, 149
digital investigation 197
digital policing 192
digital rights 203, 205, 207, 212
digital rights management 203, 205, 207, 212
disaster 172, 173, 175–187
disinformation 31–39, 41, 45, 74–76, 79, 81, 82, 87, 88, 90, 98, 233, 240
domestic abuse 130, 131, 134–143, 145, 148, 149, 174

**E**

economic theory of crime 181
ethical concern 110, 140, 198, 232

**F**

fact checking 44, 45
fake news 1–3, 5–9, 26, 27, 31–39, 44, 45, 73–75, 77–80, 82, 88, 90, 98, 152–159, 162–166, 168–170, 209, 229, 240, 243
forensics investigation 43

**G**

General Data Protection Regulation (EU) 2016/679 13, 19, 24, 98, 204, 208, 209, 223, 234, 238, 239
governance 239, 244

**H**

Hannah clarke case study 148
honeycomb model 229, 244

**I**

impacts 157, 160–162, 165
information governance 1, 12, 13, 15, 19, 20, 23, 26

Internet law and fake news  5, 33
Internet of Things (IoT)  49–51, 53, 56, 130–133, 137, 139–142, 144, 148–150

**J**

jurisdiction  25, 177, 195–197

**K**

Kruskal-Wallis test  57

**L**

legislative and regulatory controls  97

**M**

Machine learning (ML)  73, 77–80, 82, 87–90, 92, 98, 109–113, 203, 204, 206, 207, 209–212, 216–224, 235, 240–244
malware threats  102
Mann-Whitney-Wilcoxon test  57
misinformation  2, 3, 5, 6, 8, 12, 15, 19, 20, 22–24, 26, 31–36, 38–46, 73–80, 82, 85–91, 93, 96–99
multimedia privacy  203, 206, 207
multimedia security  204

**N**

Naïve Bayes  106, 109, 112, 113

**O**

open-refine tool  118
OSINT  106, 107, 109, 110

**P**

pandemic  5, 6, 102, 109, 120, 172–188
prediction  105–115, 117, 120, 121, 126, 127
privacy  49–53, 55, 56, 60–64, 69, 229–232, 238
profiling and predicting  102

**R**

regulatory framework for social media  42

**S**

security  50–54, 56, 69, 203–209, 213, 216, 217, 220–222, 224
smart home  49, 50, 52, 53, 57
social media  1–5, 8–10, 12–16, 18–23, 25, 26, 152–169, 172, 173, 229–236, 238–244
social media regulations  4
stock exchange  73–75, 77, 79–82, 84–87, 89–94, 96, 98, 99

**T**

technology facilitated abuse  131, 133
The dark web  192–199
The internet  192, 193, 199